Mobilizing nature

Manchester University Press

Cultural History of Modern War

Series editors Ana Carden-Coyne, Peter Gatrell, Max Jones,
Penny Summerfield and Bertrand Taithe

Centre for the
Cultural History
of War

Mobilizing nature

The environmental history of war and militarization in Modern France

~

CHRIS PEARSON

Manchester University Press

Manchester and New York

Distributed in the United States exclusively by Palgrave Macmillan

Published by Manchester University Press
Oxford Road, Manchester M13 9NR, UK
and Room 400, 175 Fifth Avenue, New York, NY 10010, USA
www.manchesteruniversitypress.co.uk

Distributed in the United States exclusively by
Palgrave Macmillan, 175 Fifth Avenue, New York,
NY 10010, USA

Distributed in Canada exclusively by
UBC Press, University of British Columbia, 2029 West Mall,
Vancouver, BC, Canada V6T 1Z2

British Library Cataloguing-in-Publication Data
A catalogue record for this book is available from the British Library

Library of Congress Cataloging-in-Publication Data applied for

ISBN   978 0 7190 8439 3 *hardback*

First published 2012

The publisher has no responsibility for the persistence or accuracy of URLs for any external or third-party internet websites referred to in this book, and does not guarantee that any content on such websites is, or will remain, accurate or appropriate.

Typeset in Minion
by Servis Filmsetting Ltd, Stockport, Cheshire
Printed in Great Britain
by the MPG Books Group Ltd

Contents

Illustrations

Illustrations

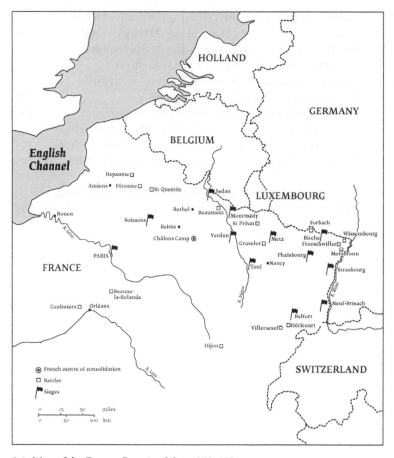

0.1 Map of the Franco-Prussian War, 1870–1971

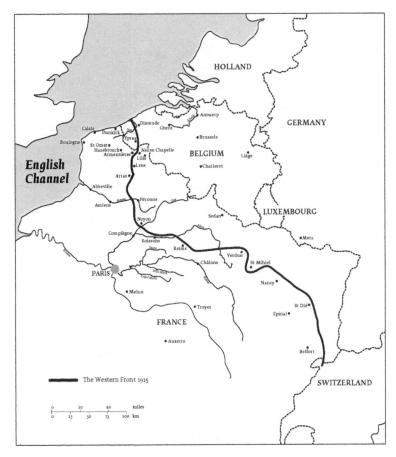

0.2 Map of the Western Front, 1915

0.3 Map of France during the Second World War

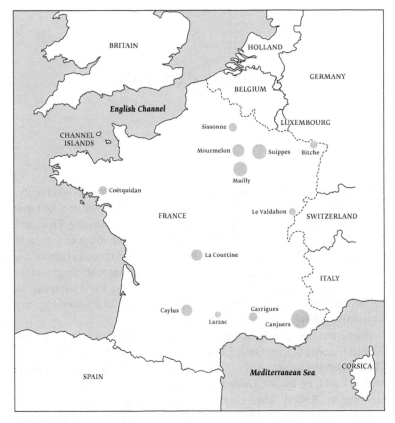

0.4 Map of major French army bases

Acknowledgements

I would like to thank everyone who has contributed to this book. Firstly, thanks to the University of Bristol 'Militarized Landscapes' project team – Peter Coates, Tim Cole, and Marianna Dudley – for sharing ideas and making the serious study of militarized landscapes more fun than it probably should be. The project was funded by the Arts and Humanities Research Council under its 'Landscape and Environment' programme. Further financial support for this book came from the University of Bristol and the University of Warwick and I also wish to acknowledge my supportive colleagues at both institutions.

Numerous people helped me with my research in France, in particular Patrick Facon, Philippe Guth, Christophe Kintz, and Philippe Pierrejean. Thanks also to Graham August, Jean-Pierre Cuq, Claude d'Abzac-Epezy, Michel Gaudeau-Pacini, Gilles Granereau, Jean-Jacques Gleize, Laurent Henninger, Robert Lindeckert, Gérald Montagut, Jean-Christophe Romer, Pascal Tonton, Claire Vignon, Ariane Wilson, Sybille Wilson, and the staff of the archives and libraries I visited throughout France.

Hugh Clout, William Doyle, Josie McLellan, Geoff Pearson, and Karine Varley were kind enough to read and comment on various chapters. Readers' reports for Manchester University Press helped me to clarify further my ideas and remove errors. For comments, suggestions, support and questions I thank Jean-Paul Amat, Victoria Basham, Philippe Boulanger, William Cronon, Martine Deweer, Martin Evans, Mathieu Galliot-Bismuth, Martin Hurcombe, Julian Jackson, Peter Jones, Rod Kedward, Eugene Palka, John Peaty, Edward Rose, William Storey, Rachel Woodward, and various conference and seminar audiences, especially the participants of the Militarized Landscapes conference held at the University of Bristol in September 2008. A special thank you is offered to Bertrand Taithe for his invaluable support of this book during its various stages and to Emma Brennan at Manchester University

Acknowledgements

Press for commissioning it. Thanks also to Jane Imlah at Warwick Design for producing the maps.

And last, but certainly not least, I thank my wife Dulcie for her love, encouragement and support as this book took shape amidst broken noses and wrists, and long distance commuting. I dedicate it to her.

Archival abbreviations

ADA	Archives départementales de l'Aveyron
ADAM	Archives départementales des Alpes-Maritimes
ADBDR	Archives départementales des Bouches-du-Rhône
ADC	Archives départementales du Calvados
ADGA	Archives départementales du Gard
ADGI	Archives départementales de la Gironde
ADI	Archives départementales de l'Isère
ADL	Archives départementales des Landes
ADMA	Archives départementales de la Marne
ADME	Archives départementales de la Meuse
ADMO	Archives départementales de la Moselle
ADS	Archives départementales de la Somme
ADV	Archives départementales du Var
AMC	Archives municipales de Comps-sur-Artuby
AMMJ	Archives municipales de Martignas-sur-Jalle
CACAN	Centre des archives contemporaines des Archives nationales (Fontainebleau)
CHAN	Centre historique des Archives nationales (Paris)
IHEDN	Institut des hautes études de défense nationale (Paris)
NA	National Archives (London)
SHD-DAA	Service historique de la Défense-Département de l'armée de l'Air
SHD-DAT	Service historique de la Défense-Département de l'armée de Terre

Introduction

Siegfried Sassoon, Royal Welch Fusilier officer and celebrated British war poet, recalls the intensity and inescapability of the First World War trench environment in his memoirs: 'trench life was an existence saturated by the external senses . . . Freedom from its oppressiveness was what I longed for'.[1] Like millions of other soldiers Sassoon lived and fought in the trenches of the Western Front that stretched across France and Belgium, a deadly environment that at times could feel all encompassing. Marked by death, mud, shells, rats, craters, dead bodies, and barbed wire, the militarized environment of the Western Front was amongst the most extreme that has ever existed, scarring soldiers' minds and bodies, societies and cultures, and the land itself.[2]

But despite their extreme character, the trenches were part of a far longer and geographically dispersed environmental history of militarized environments in modern French history. In this book I trace the creation, maintenance, and contestation of these militarized environments from the establishment of France's first large-scale and permanent army camp on the Champagne plains in 1857, to military environmentalism in the first decade of the twenty-first century. In doing so, I aim to shed light on the evolving and profoundly historical relationship between war, militarization, and the environment.

Defining militarized environments

I treat militarized environments as simultaneously material and cultural sites that have been partially or fully mobilized to achieve military aims.[3] Using a broad definition and thinking globally, militarized environments might encompass military food supply chains, wartime manufacturing sites, military roads, military recruitment centres on town high streets, and checkpoints in areas such as the West Bank, as well as military bases, battlefields, air bases, navy bases, and fortifications.[4] But whilst recognizing the flexible definitions of militarized environments, I adopt a narrower approach in this book to make it manageable and coherent. My focus is on the environmental history of sites in rural and metropolitan France that the French and other militaries have directly mobilized to prepare for, and to wage, war.[5] They include such sites as army camps, weapons testing facilities, and air bases, as well as battlefields and other combat zones, but not maritime militarized environments, which arguably deserve their own book.

The militarized environments under study are striking in their multiplicity. They are variously sites of combat, experimentation, internment, death, protest, biodiversity, modernization, and memorialization. They are also international places. At various points, North American, British, colonial, German, and Italian troops have mobilized, occupied, fought, and trained in the French environment. First World War cemeteries and the memorial landscapes of the D-Day beaches remain places of international importance and serve as reminders of the transnational character of many French militarized environments.[6] And although this book focuses on the environmental history of militaraization within metropolitan France, moving between national, regional, and local scales, it speaks to issues that mark militarized environments across the globe, such as civilian displacement, anti-base protests, and military environmentalism.[7] This is certainly not a history of French exceptionalism. As subsequent chapters show, the British army militarized supposedly empty and marginal lands in the 1850s and 1890s for army training grounds like its French counterpart.

The histories of war preparation sites, such as army camps and training grounds, are far more hidden than those of battlefields. How many tourists driving along the southern *corniche sublime* of the spectacular Verdon Gorges in Provence realize that they are following the northern edge of Canjuers Camp, France's largest militarized environment at 35,000 ha?[8] The relative concealment of Canjuers Camp within the surrounding countryside is hardly surprising since the French military has repeatedly tried to hide its installations from view (using, for instance, trees as screens). When concealment has not been possible, the military has made it very clear to civilians that they are barred from militarized environments through the use of barbed wire, fences, checkpoints and 'keep out' signs. In democratic societies it is vital to examine critically the often secretive military control and ownership of land that might otherwise be returned to civilian use. As Rachel Woodward argues, this is 'a critical issue almost *because* of it relative invisibility'.[9] By focusing on the French case, I aim to encourage reflection and discussion on the global issue of military control and use of the environment.

Due to geographical concealment and archival restrictions, many militarized environments remain 'blank spots' in our understandings of French history, even though they have shaped, and, in turn, been shaped by, wider historical developments.[10] For instance, Châlons Camp became a showcase for Napoleon III's imperial ambitions during the Second Empire and part and parcel of his regime's attempt to modernize the French countryside. One hundred years later during the Cold War, air bases, weapons testing facilities, and other installations became sites within which the wider tensions of the Franco-American relationship were expressed and negotiated, as well as key components of French defence and foreign policies. This book therefore attempts to show how militarized environments need to be integrated into our understandings of French history, as they have been in other national contexts, and seeks to demonstrate that militarization is an important, if overlooked, factor in the environmental history of France.[11]

Bringing a more sustained focus to the long-term environmental history of military bases and other sites of war preparation is necessary because they have acted as a more consistent form of environmental militarization than battlefields. Despite the sometimes drastic modification of the French environment during wartime, the French military has controlled swathes of national territory over a longer period of time to prepare for war, particularly since the establishment of Châlons Camp in 1857. By 2008 the Ministry of Defence owned 258,824 ha (or approximately 0.5 per cent) of national territory, making it the largest user of state-owned land, with the Var and Marne *départements* the most heavily militarized.[12]

Despite their relative obscurity, French military bases and training grounds have sometimes become the focus of media and public attention. This was the case when Wilbur Wright drew huge crowds to Auvours Camp in 1908 as he pioneered modern aviation techniques. The decade-long struggle against army camp extension on Larzac plateau during the 1970s then attracted national and international support and has since been named by *Le Nouvel Observateur* magazine as one of the '100 places that made France'.[13] More sinisterly, Mourmelon Camp (as

Châlons Camp was renamed in 1935) became infamous as the site of mysterious disappearances of young soldiers in the 1980s.[14] In addition, army camps have appeared incognito on TV and cinema screens. Canjuers Camp has provided the backdrop for car adverts and televised car rallies (the latter immortalized by Jean Graton in his Michel Vaillant comic book *L'inconnu des 1000 pistes*), whilst *Amélie* director Jean-Pierre Jeunet recreated the trenches of the Western Front at Montmorillon Camp for his 2004 film *A Very Long Engagement*.[15]

It would be misleading, however, to place the environmental histories of military bases and battlefields in opposite to each other, since they are intimately linked. Military bases and other installations co-existed with combat zones during the Franco-Prussian and world wars, acting as training and supply sites. Meanwhile, some battlefields have remained militarized after the signing of peace treaties; the French army established Tahure Camp (later renamed Suippes Camp) and Moronvilliers Camp on land damaged by four years of warfare between 1914 and 1918. The interlocking histories of these militarized environments demonstrate that the relationship between the environment, war and militarization transcends the overly neat division of the past into 'wartime' and 'peacetime'.[16]

Rethinking militarization as a 'more-than-human' process

As well as transcending the war/peace binary, militarization underscores the artificiality and arbitrariness of the 'nature' and 'culture' divide. Scholars have conceptualized militarization as a political, economic, social, cultural, and spatial process, treating it as a fundamentally human phenomenon.[17] This book recognizes that these are important facets of militarization and covers many of them. But it also argues that to understand militarization more fully we also need to take into account its 'more-than-human' character.[18] For militarization takes place in, through and, at times, against, the environment. It entails multiple and intimate military engagements with the environment and is only made possible through an active mobilization of environmental features, including topography, climate, vegetation, and animals. Furthermore, it is within the militarized environment that military ideas, strategies, bodies, and technologies emerge, interact with, and co-shape, nature.[19] Throughout the period under study in this book, army commanders have kept faith with the belief that the soldier is moulded through a combination of military culture, discipline, and training that takes place within the environment, despite the possibilities now offered by computer-simulated training.[20]

Militarization entails the active mobilization of nature, understood as thoroughly domesticated and hybrid.[21] But, as the events of 1870–71 and 1939–40 show, the French mobilization of nature to prepare for war was no guarantee of military success. When war broke out in 1870, 1914, and 1939, the French military, along with its allies and enemies, mobilized nature to wage war. The environment offered shelter, camouflage, and military advantages. But much relied on the ability of different national military organizations to exploit these possibilities. As I discuss in chapter 2, Prussia and its allies made far better use of topography than the French army during the Franco-Prussian War.

As well as combat terrain, the environment was a site of natural resource extraction. During warfare, the French and other militaries took timber, firewood, and other resources from the French environment to sustain combat. They have also mobilized thousands of horses, dogs, carrier pigeons, and other animals for transportation, communication, and other duties whilst fighting on French soil. Militarized environments, then, are 'contact zones' between military personnel and a range of nonhuman entities, such as animals, vegetation, weather conditions, and so on.[22]

But this engagement with, and mobilization of, nature has not been a smooth process. Nature's unpredictability, dynamism, and indifference to human suffering have raised repeated problems for the military. From mud, rats, and lice in the trenches, to the Allies' difficulty in overcoming Normandy's *bocage* landscape after the D-Day landings, environmental conditions have raised a series of problems and obstacles to be tolerated, overcome, or bypassed. Outcomes therefore arose as products of the emerging relationship between human design and the unintentional vibrancy of nature. Allied military tactics during the battle of Normandy developed in relationship to the challenges posed by *bocage* and in the latter decades of the twentieth century the French army reinvented the problematic vegetation of its training grounds into an environmental success story. The military has had to take nature into account. As political scientist Timothy Mitchell argues, 'human agency appears less as a calculating intelligence directing social outcomes and more as a product of a series of alliances in which the human agent is never wholly in control'.[23]

Militarized environments, then, are contact zones between different actors – human and nonhuman – with a diverse range of capabilities and influence. So although human agency plays a vital role in the period under study in this book – the military is a powerful organization and its purposeful mobilization of nature has had profound social and environmental consequences for which it needs to be held accountable – I try to capture a sense of the liveliness and unpredictability of the nonhuman world in which it operates. Animals, climate, vegetation, and topography play an integral, but non-deterministic, part in the story.

My aim is emphatically not to replace human agency with nonhuman agency. Instead it is to show how different forms of agency have interacted and challenged each other in often unequal and unpredictable ways within the militarized environment.[24] The unevenness of power relations needs highlighting. For as well as being 'more-than-human', militarization is a profoundly political process in which there have been winners and losers, to put it somewhat crudely. The military mobilization of nature to wage war has resulted in environmental and social consequences. To varying degrees, the Franco-Prussian and World Wars modified the environments in which they were fought. Shells, bullets, bombs, vehicles, and other weapons and technologies churned up land, felled trees, killed animals, and ruined crops. The military's control over nature was not complete, but it clearly exerted considerable power over the environment. As part of the environments in which war takes places, humans have suffered due to the militarization of the environment; despite some resistance, many farmers and other civilians have lost their land, livelihoods, and lives. Power and agency were (and are) intimately bound up in the military mobilization of nature. This is also evident in how the military has viewed and represented the environment.

The military environmental perspective

The military's environmental perspective is complex.[25] Class and other social factors, as well as the diversity of militarized environments, mean that there is no single military environmental perspective. The planners and engineers of the *génie militaire*, overseers of the infrastructure of French militarized environments, represent a particular viewpoint within the military as a whole: educated, technically minded, and composed of officers.[26] Their environmental perspective presumably differs to those of the recruits who trained in the camps. The soldiers' experience of training within militarized environments is frustratingly hard to capture, although the postcards of Mailly Camp from the beginning of the twentieth century (discussed in chapter 3) offer some insight. In contrast, soldiers' relationship with battlefield environments is easier to uncover; memoirs and other sources shed some light on how weather, wildlife, geology, and vegetation shaped combat experience in diverse ways.

Nonetheless, some generalizations about the military's environmental perspective are possible. Military personnel have frequently viewed the environment in a reductive and instrumental way, focusing on the best means to extract maximum military advantage from it. From a 'terrain and tactics' point of view, the realm of traditional military geography, the environment appears as an 'ally' or 'enemy', an advantage or obstacle during combat.[27] From a peacetime training perspective, military planners identified supposedly depopulated and economically backward 'wastelands' as ideal locations for camps, training grounds, and firing ranges. They sought to simplify the coveted region, using maps and reports to assess the cost of acquiring the land and the most efficient ways to militarize it. In assessing the land to fit their reductionist military perspective, they overlooked the complexity of local communities and the environments in which they lived and worked. James C. Scott has argued that 'state simplifications, the basic givens of modern statecraft . . . did not successfully represent the actual activity of the society they depicted, nor were they intended to; they represented only that slice of it that interested the official observer'. Moreover, 'when allied with state power' they enabled 'much of the reality they depicted to be remade'.[28] Scott's analysis holds true in the case of French militarized environments as military planners simplified the environment and moulded it to fit their objectives with a high level of success; most of the large-scale militarized environments they envisaged saw the light of day, from Châlons Camp in the 1850s to Canjuers Camp in the 1960s and 1970s, thereby displacing civilians from their homes and land.

To legitimate its appetite for land, the military has sought to tie its geographical expansion to wider civilian concerns. From at least the creation of Châlons Camp in 1857 to the peak of Cold War military expansion in the 1960s and 1970s, it has repeatedly claimed that replacing dilapidated farms and economically marginal land with military installations will bring progress and prosperity to backward regions and imbue them with national purpose. The militarization-as-progress narrative has evolved over time. In the 1850s, militarization was equated with imperial grandeur and the reclamation of so-called wastelands. Between 1871 and 1914 the military and its supporters portrayed militarized environments as sites of national renewal and security against the threat of German aggression. And during the Cold War, military planners sought to tie their territorial ambitions with wider state-led plans to modernize and 'balance' the French countryside.

But despite such changes, the military's desire for space and cheap land and its simplification of local economies and environments remained remarkably constant until the Larzac protest of the 1970s. Since Larzac, the military has abandoned territorial expansion and sought to legitimize its control of national territory by portraying its lands as reservoirs of biodiversity. This form of military environmentalism aims, problematically, to link militarization with wider civilian environmental objectives at a time when environmentalism has thoroughly infiltrated French society. Overlooking its own role in displacing local populations to create sites emptied of civilians, the military now claims that its lands' human emptiness and ecological fullness play an essential role in helping France meet its nature protection and sustainability goals.[29]

The military's *soi-disant* environmentalist turn is partly explained by changes in the background and education of its recruits and its desire to be seen as more open and inclusive in the post-Cold War and post-Larzac era.[30] But there is some ecological basis to its claims. As in other countries, long-term military ownership of certain training grounds and other installations has unintentionally kept urbanization, intensive agriculture, and tourism at bay. Certain sections of some militarized environments therefore support areas of grasslands, marshland, woodlands and other habitats which have disappeared or are threatened elsewhere. This development is particularly striking in Champagne, where the grasslands and woodlands of army training grounds contrast with neighbouring fields of monoculture crops. Although military environmentalism requires critical scrutiny, has its limits (operational readiness takes precedent over environmental considerations), and it is essential to bear in mind the wider environmental impact of military activities, such as pollution and extensive resource consumption, its emergence points to how militarization has, in places, created different environments to civilian ones and how the military environmental perspective has partially changed.[31]

Furthermore, military environmentalism provides the vehicle through which the military has embraced the term 'environment'. French geographers first used *'environnement'* in 1942[32] but the military only adopted it in the latter decades of the twentieth century. Before then, military documents referred to specific aspects of what we would now call the environment: *landes* (heathlands); *plaine* (plains); *terrain* (ground); *sol* (ground or soil); and *plateau* (plateau).[33] Although military (and civilian) usage of the term 'environment' is relatively recent, I use it throughout this book, in a similar way to historians who apply the concepts of 'gender' and 'race' to periods in which these words did not exist or had significantly different meanings. This approach is not without problems. But it does have some advantages, particularly as 'environment' suggests the deep interrelationship and interconnectedness between humans and their surroundings.[34]

Civilian–military boundaries

The military's adoption of the term 'environment' and the language of environmentalism attests to the exchanges between civilian and military spheres as France became a 'light-green society'.[35] If environmentalism now provides the basis for some military–civilian cooperation, militarized environments have mostly been places of friction and tense negotiations between civilians and the military. For most of the period under study in this book, military representations of empty and worthless land fit only for militarization have rubbed up against local populations' emotional and physical attachments to their environment. What may seem like an ideal training ground to a military engineer is invariably someone's home, farmland, pastureland, or forest.

Unequal power relations have marked military–civilian interactions. Like its counterparts in other countries, the French military has continually attempted to displace and dispossess economically marginal and politically isolated communities.[36] Yet despite their position of relative weakness vis-à-vis the military, local politicians, farmers, foresters, and nature protection societies have repeatedly tried to limit the impact of training grounds and other militarized environments on their lives, livelihoods, and land. Similarly, they and other civilians have tried to prevent, or at least limit, the environmental ramifications of militarization during wartime.

In a direct challenge to the military's narrative that militarization equals progress and modernization, civilians have equated militarization with the sterilization of land. The civilian 'militarization-as-sterilization' counter-narrative emerged during the creation of Châlons Camp in the 1850s, became more prominent and emotive during the First World War, and perhaps reached its peak during the establishment of Canjuers Camp when anti-base campaigners equated militarization with the death of nature.

However, it was not until the Larzac struggle that civilian protesters succeeded in thwarting a large-scale military project. As discussed in chapter 8, many factors explain the success of the Larzac campaign. But a vital one was the protesters' successful mobilization of nature *against* militarization. Throughout the campaign, they mobilized emotive and effective images of the wild and domestic environments that would be lost to militarization, thereby bringing an overlooked, windswept, and rugged plateau in south-western France into the national consciousness. In particular, protesters reinvented the plateau's sheep as symbols of peaceful farming standing in direct opposition to the destruction wrought by militarization. Larzac is the most famous anti-base campaign. But the frequent episodes of civilian opposition to militarized environments form an important, if overlooked, aspect of French anti-militarism and are part of the global constellation of civilian campaigns against militarized environments.[37]

Sparks have tended to fly when civilian and military environments rub up against each other. Yet amidst the frictions, connections have been forged between civilians and neighbouring militarized environments. Military sites have been places of employment for local populations; witness the concerns about unemployment following North Atlantic Treaty Organisation's (NATO) withdrawal from France in 1967, and when the French government announced its plans to close bases as part of its plan to modernize and restructure the armed forces in 2008. Numerous military bases have also provided pastureland for sheep, a practice which continues into the present day. As these examples suggest, the history of militarized environments is more complex than suggested by the image of military domination over helpless civilians. Throughout this book, I therefore aim to show how militarized and civilian environments overlap, as well as oppose, each other. The fluid military–civilian boundary illustrates once again the complexity of the history of French militarized environments and the military mobilization of nature.

Notes

1 Siegfried Sassoon, *Memoirs of an Infantry Officer* (London: Faber and Faber, 1931), 49.
2 On the enduring traces of the First World War on the French environment, see Stéphane Audoin-Rouzeau, Gerd Krumeich, and Jean Richardot, *Cicatrices: La Grande Guerre aujourd'hui* (Paris: Editions Tallandier, 2008).
3 On the 'socio-material' character of sites of war preparation, see Doug Mercer, 'Future-histories of Hanford: The material and semiotic production of a landscape', *Cultural Geographies*, 9:1 (2002), 42.

4 Edmund P. Russell, 'Afterword: Militarized landscapes', in Chris Pearson, Peter Coates, and Tim Cole (eds), *Militarized Landscapes: From Gettysburg to Salisbury Plain* (London: Continuum, 2010), 233–7. There is evidently much overlap between 'militarized landscapes' and 'militarized environments'. In this book, I use the latter term because environment suggests a greater level of human immersion within, and interaction with, the nonhuman world. On the distinction between landscape and environment within the context of the First World War, see Dorothee Brantz, 'Environments of death: Trench warfare on the Western Front, 1914–1918', in Charles E. Closmann (ed.), *War and the Environment: Military Destruction in the Modern Age* (College Station: Texas A&M University Press, 2009), 68–91.

5 Despite the growing interest in environmental histories of war, environmental historians have so far tended to focus on the environmental dimensions of militarization during wartime itself. See, for instance, Judith A. Bennett, *Natives and Exotics: World War II and Environment in the Southern Pacific* (Honolulu: University of Hawai'i Press, 2009); Closmann, *War and the Environment*; Chris Pearson, *Scarred Landscapes: War and Nature in Vichy France* (Basingstoke: Palgrave Macmillan, 2008); Edmund P. Russell and Richard P. Tucker (eds), *Natural Enemy, Natural Ally: Toward an Environmental History of Warfare* (Corvallis: Oregon State University Press, 2004).

6 On the D-Day beaches as international memorial sites, see Tristram Hunt, 'One last time they gather, the greatest generation', *The Observer*, 6 June 2004, 1.

7 Kent E. Calder, *Embattled Garrisons: Comparative Base Politics and American Globalism* (Princeton: Princeton University Press, 2007); Jeffrey Sasha Davis, 'Military natures: Militarism and the environment', *Geojournal*, 69 (2007), 131–4; Catherine Lutz (ed.), *The Bases of Empire: The Global Struggle against U.S. Military Posts* (New York: New York University Press, 2009); Pearson, Coates, and Cole, *Militarized Landscapes*; Rachel Woodward, *Military Geographies* (Oxford: Blackwell, 2004).

8 In 2000, I travelled along the *corniche sublime* (or D19, to give the road its official name) completely unaware of Canjuers Camp. At least one guidebook, however, identifies military installations as a threat to southern France's environment. Dana Facaros and Michael Pauls write that 'the army . . . has commandeered enormous sections of the wilderness . . . and regularly blows them to smithereens in manoeuvres and target practice'. *South of France* (London: Cadogan Guides, 2002 [1992]), 95.

9 Woodward, *Military Geographies*, 12, emphasis in original.

10 On military sites as 'blank spots', see Trevor Paglen, *Blank Spots on the Map: The Dark Geography of the Pentagon's Secret World* (New York: Dutton, 2009). There is scant scholarly work on the relationship between French sites of war preparation and the environment. For exceptions, see chapters

in Jacques Aben and Jacques Rouzier (eds), *Défense et aménagement du territoire* (Montpellier: ESID, 2001); Jean-François Chanet, *Vers l'armée nouvelle: République conservatrice et réforme militaire, 1871–1879* (Rennes: Presses Universitaires de Rennes, 2006); Christophe Kintz, 'L'évolution du domaine militaire attribué à l'Armée de terre en France métropolitaine depuis 1945 et ses implications sur l'aménagement de l'espace, l'urbanisme et l'environnement' (PhD dissertation, Université de Paris IV-Paris-Sorbonne, 2000); Olivier Pottier, *Les bases américaines en France (1950–1967)* (Paris: L'Harmattan, 2003); Philippe Boulanger, *Géographie militaire* (Paris: Ellipses, 2006).

11 On militarized environments in other countries, see Marianna Dudley, 'Greening the MOD: An environmental history of the UK defence estate, 1945–present' (PhD dissertation, University of Bristol, 2011); John Childs, *The Military Use of the Land: A History of the Defence Estate* (Berne: Peter Lang, 1998); Stephen Dycus, *National Defense and the Environment* (Hanover, NH, and London: University Press of New England, 1996); David Havlick, 'Logics of change for military-to-wildlife conversions in the United States', *Geojournal*, 69 (2007), 151–64; Woodward, *Military Geographies*. On French environmental history, see Michael Bess, *The Light-Green Society: Ecology and Technological Modernity in France, 1960–2000* (Chicago: University of Chicago Press, 2003); Caroline Ford, 'Nature, culture, and conservation in France and her colonies, 1840–1940', *Past and Present*, 183 (2004), 173–98; Nicholas Green, *The Spectacle of Nature: Landscape and Bourgeois Culture in Nineteenth-century France* (Manchester: Manchester University Press, 1990); Tamara L. Whited, *Forests and Peasant Politics in Modern France* (New Haven: Yale University Press, 2000).

12 Linda Verhaeghe 'Conservation faune sauvage: Convention avec le Ministère de la Défense', Ministère de la Défense website, www.defense.gouv.fr/breves/ conservation_faune_sauvage_convention_avec_le_ministere_de_la_defense, accessed 2 June 2010; 'Les premières rencontres défense biodiversité', Défense et environnement website, 2 June 2010, http://defenseetenvironnement. blogspot.com/2010/06/les-premieres-rencontres-defense.html?utm_source =feedburner&utm_medium=email&utm_.campaign=Feed%3A+DefenseEt Environnement+%28DEFENSE+ET+ENVIRONNEMENT%29, accessed 2 June 2010; Raymond Regrain, 'Les territoires de l'armée en France métro-politaine', *Mappe Monde*, 88:1 (1988), www.mgm.fr/PUB/Montpelier/ M188/p.38–41.pdf, 40, accessed 4 May 2010. By way of comparison, the UK Ministry of Defence owns 241,000 ha or approximately 1 per cent of national territory, whilst the US Department of Defense owns 10.1 million ha. Woodward, *Military Geographies*, 13.

13 '100 lieux qui ont fait la France', *Le Nouvel Observateur*, 26 July–1 August 2007, 39. British Quaker Roger Rawlinson described the Larzac struggle as 'without doubt the first large sustained Gandhian type struggle in Europe in

our times'. *The Battle of Larzac* (New Malden: Fellowship of Reconciliation, 1976), 1.

14 Jean-Noël Kapferer, 'Les disparitions de Mourmelon: Origine et interprétation des rumeurs', *Revue française de sociologie*, 30:1 (1989), 81–9.

15 *Autres images de Canjuers*, film directed by Guy Touraine (1984); Jean Graton, *Michel Vaillant: L'inconnu des 1000 pistes* (Paris: Editions Fleurus, 1980); Thierry Lemaire, 'Tournage . . . Un long dimanche de fiançailles', *L'Echo du Village en ligne*, 5 November 2003, http://echo.levillage.org/imprimer.cbb?idarticle=5215, accessed 12 October 2007.

16 On the links between the environmental histories of wartime and peacetime, see Edmund P. Russell, *War and Nature: Fighting Humans and Insects with Chemicals from World War 1 to Silent Spring* (New York: Cambridge University Press, 2001).

17 John Gillis (ed.), *The Militarization of the Western World* (New Brunswick and London: Rutgers University Press, 1989); Catherine Lutz, *Homefront: A Military City and the American Twentieth Century* (Boston: Beacon Press, 2001); Ann Markusen, Peter Hall, Scott Campbell, and Sabina Deitrick, *The Rise of the Gunbelt: The Military Remapping of Industrial America* (New York: Oxford University Press, 1991); Eyal Weizman, *Hollow Land: Israel's Architecture of Occupation* (London: Verso, 2007).

18 I borrow the phrase 'more-than-human' from Sarah Whatmore, 'Materialist returns: Practising cultural geography in and for a more-than-human world', *Cultural Geographies*, 13 (2006), 600–9.

19 On human–nonhuman co-shaping, see Donna Haraway, *When Species Meet* (Minneapolis: University of Minnesota Press, 2008), 134.

20 This view is not restricted to the French military. See Richard W. Dixon, 'Training the force: Bioclimatological considerations for military training', in Eugene J. Palka and Francis A. Galgano (eds), *Military Geography from Peace to War* (Boston: McGraw-Hill Custom Publishing, 2005), 367. See also Rachel Woodward, 'Locating military masculinities: Space, place, and the formation of gender identity in the British army', in Paul R. Higate (ed.), *Military Masculinities: Identity and the State* (Westport and London: Praeger, 2003), 43–55.

21 On human–nature hybridity, see Donna Haraway, *Simians, Cyborgs, and Women: The Reinvention of Nature* (New York: Routledge, 1991); Sarah Whatmore, *Hybrid Geographies: Natures, Cultures, Spaces* (London: Sage, 2002); and Richard White, *The Organic Machine: The Remaking of the Columbia River* (New York: Hill and Wang, 1996). Sverker Sörlin and Paul Warde argue that once nature comes into contact with humans it ceases to be 'nature' and becomes the 'environment'. 'Making the environment historical: An introduction', in Sverker Sörlin and Paul Warde (eds), *Nature's End: History and the Environment* (Basingstoke: Palgrave Macmillan, 2009), 2–3. Whilst I have some sympathy with their argument, I believe that the concept

of 'nature' still has analytical value, as long as we recognize the deep and multiple interconnections between it and humanity.

22 On human–nonhuman 'contact zones', see Haraway, *When Species Meet*, 204–46.

23 Timothy Mitchell, *Rule of Experts: Egypt, Techno-Politics, Modernity* (Berkeley: University of California Press, 2002), 10. On the need to take into account the vibrancy of the material world, see Karen Barad, 'Posthumanist performativity: Toward an understanding of how matter comes to matter', *Signs: Journal of Women in Culture and Society*, 28:3 (2003), 801–31.

24 My approach is influenced by Actor Network Theory (ANT) as advanced by Bruno Latour (amongst others). But I recognize that ANT has a tendency to downplay human agency and level out power relations. For thoughtful critiques of ANT that argue for power and inequality to be given greater prominence, see Noel Castree, 'False antitheses? Marxism, nature, and actor-networks', *Antipode*, 34:1 (2002), 111–46; Don Mitchell and Scott Kirsch, 'The nature of things: Dead labor, nonhuman actors, and the persistence of Marxism', *Antipode*, 36:4 (2004), 687–705.

25 Due to time and space constraints, this book does not pay significant attention to the militarization of science (broadly defined). Readers interested in this area might wish to consult Matthew Farish, *The Contours of America's Cold War* (Minneapolis: University of Minnesota Press, 2010); Russell, *War and Nature*; and the special issue of *Social Studies of Science*, 33:5 (2003) on 'Earth Sciences in the Cold War'.

26 On the composition and evolution of the *génie militaire* in postwar France, see Kintz, 'Evolution du domaine de l'Etat', 53–65; *Revue historique de l'armée*, 22:1 (1966), *numéro spécial: le génie*.

27 I explore this approach in chapter 2.

28 James C. Scott, *Seeing Like a State: How Certain Schemes to Improve the Human Condition Have Failed* (New Haven and London: Yale University Press, 1998), 3.

29 For reflections on emptiness and presence within militarized environments, see Tim Cole, 'Military presences, civilian absences: Battling nature at the Sennybridge Training Area, 1940–2008', *Journal of War and Culture Studies*, 3:2 (2010), 215–35.

30 Oliver Pottier, *Armée-nation: Divorce ou réconciliation: De la loi Debré à la réforme du service national, 1970–2004* (Paris: L'Harmattan, 2005), 76–7.

31 For a critique of military environmentalism, see Rachel Woodward, 'Khaki conservation: An examination of military environmentalist discourses in the British army', *Journal of Rural Studies*, 17 (2001), 201–17. For a defence of the military's environmental record, see Kent Hughes Butts, 'Why the military is good for the environment', in Jyrki Käkönen (ed.), *Green Security or Militarized Environment* (Aldershot: Dartmouth, 1994), 83–109. According to John McNeill and David S. Painter, the US military has had the largest

impact on global ecosystems. 'The global environmental footprint of the U.S. military, 1789-2003', in Closmann, *War and the Environment*, 10-31.

32 Jean-Louis Tissier, 'Du milieu à l'environnement: L'émergence d'un concept dans le discours des géographes français', in René Neboit-Guilhot and Lucette Davy (eds), *Les français dans leur environnement* (Paris: Editions Nathan, 1996), 19.

33 These examples are taken from ADGI 2 R 74 Daussy, 'Établissement d'un polygone d'artillerie dans le canton de La Teste', 18 June 1872; Charles-Alexandre Morin, *Le Camp de Châlons en 1858 au point de vue hygiénique et médical: Hygiène des camps en général* (Paris: Jules Masson, 1858).

34 More reflection is needed on what environmental historians mean by 'environment', although there is not the space to do the topic justice here. Not least, the history of the term 'environment' has yet to be fully fleshed out. A useful starting point is Paul Warde, 'The environment: The "out there" idea', paper presented at 'Environmental histories: Local places, global processes', AHRC network workshop, University of Cambridge, 5 November 2010. Furthermore, there is no single societal understanding of the 'environment'. A French survey conducted in the 1990s found that the word held different meanings for respondents. Philippe Collomb, France Guérin Pace, Nacima Baron-Yellès, and Jacques Brun, *Les Français et l'environnement* (Paris: Editions de l'Institut National d'Etudes Démographiques, 1998), 22-3.

35 Bess, *Light-Green Society*.

36 Ryan Edgington, 'Fragmented histories: Science, environment and monument building at the Trinity Site, 1945-1995', in Pearson, Coates, and Cole, *Militarized Landscapes*, 189-207; Carole Gallagher, *American Ground Zero: The Secret Nuclear War* (Cambridge, MA: MIT Press, 1993); Gregory Hooks and Chad L. Smith, 'The treadmill of destruction: National sacrifice areas and Native Americans', *American Sociological Review*, 69:4 (2004), 558-75; Valerie L. Kuletz, *The Tainted Desert: Environmental and Social Ruin in the American West* (New York: Routledge, 1998).

37 On French anti-militarism, see Jolyon Howorth and Patricia Chilton (eds), *Defence and Dissent in Contemporary France* (London: Croom Helm, 1984); Nicolas Faucier, *Pacifisme et antimilitarisme dans l'entre-deux-guerres (1919-1939)* (Paris: Spartacus, 1983); Paul B. Miller, *From Revolutionaries to Citizens: Antimilitarism in France, 1870-1914* (Durham, NC: Duke University Press, 2002); Pottier, *Armée-nation*, 23-36; Jean Rabaut, *L'antimilitarisme en France 1810-1975: Faits et documents* (Paris: Hachette, 1975). On campaigns against militarized environments across the globe, see Dudley, 'Greening the MOD'; Pearson, Coates, and Cole, *Militarized Landscapes*; Lutz, *Bases of Empire*; Woodward, *Military Geographies*, 126-51; Patrick Wright, *The Village That Died for England: The Strange Story of Tyneham* (London: Jonathan Cape, 1995).

1

The Emperor's new camp (1857–70)

In 1857 Emperor Napoleon III invited celebrated photographer Gustave Le Gray to visit the newly established Châlons Camp to record its imperial glory. Sprawling over 12,000 ha of the Champagne countryside, the camp took its name from the town of Châlons-sur-Marne, although it was actually much closer to the villages of Mourmelon-le-Grand and Mourmelon-le-Petit.[1] Le Gray's photographs, which were collated in albums and presented by Napoleon to his officers, capture the camp's grandiose Imperial Quarter and its 'exotic' North African Zouaves soldiers, as well as the military manoeuvres conducted on the dusty flat plains of Champagne.[2] It was not just Le Gray who documented the scenes of army life; between August and October 1857 *L'Illustration*, *Le Monde illustré*, and *Le Moniteur* all sent reporters and illustrators to the camp. The Emperor and Empress spent several weeks each summer in its imperial quarter, and Parisian society and foreign dignitaries descended on the camp, as did peasants apparently eager to catch a glimpse of the Empress.[3] Châlons Camp enjoyed, according to one military encyclopaedia, a 'real celebrity'.[4]

Châlons Camp marked a fresh stage in the militarization of the French environment; its surface area and permanence heralded a new form of military camp. Henceforth, the French army would mobilize nature more systematically to train its soldiers and test its weaponry, overseeing the militarization of ever increasing swathes of national territory. But in one important sense, Châlons Camp stands out from the secretive militarized environments of the early twenty-first century. From its inception, it was conceived as a public space and an imperial showcase.

Napoleon and his followers heralded the camp as a symbol of France's military and imperial splendour that would create better soldiers. Their bodies and minds were to be formed within the environment through a combination of military training and exposure to terrain and climate. But this mobilization of nature was not without risks. At a time when environmental disease aetiologies held sway, army doctors continually monitored the influence of the camp's topography, climate, and other potentially noxious nonhuman agents on soldiers' minds and bodies. The camp's anxiety-provoking medical geographies are overlooked within nineteenth-century French medical history and global environmental histories of health.[5] This chapter aims to shed light on them.

Despite worries over the camp's potentially harmful environment, the creation of Châlons Camp heralded the beginning of the military narrative that identified supposedly empty and worthless land as ideal for militarization. Tapping into the dominant expert views that this part of Champagne was economically insignificant, Napoleon and his supporters heralded the camp as a vector of modernization and improvement, linking it with the Second Empire's wider plans to develop France's territory. It stood between tradition and modernity; the Second Empire portrayed it simultaneously as a link to France's imperial past and a means to its modernization. But local farmers and critical observers challenged the designation of the Champagne plains as wastelands and opposed the creation of the militarized environment. Far from being an unproblematic showcase of France's imperial glory, Châlons Camp was a highly ambiguous site.

Early militarized environments

Long before the creation of Châlons Camp, military forts were some of the most prominent signs of the militarization of the French environment. When constructing forts, military engineers deployed their geographical knowledge to strengthen France's natural defences. Famously, Marshal de Vauban (1633–1707), France's most illustrious military engineer, devised an extensive system of land and sea fortifications. In places, these forts harnessed and modified the environment. Vauban's fortification of Marsal in Lorraine used stagnant water from surrounding marshland to boost the site's defences.[6] Hundreds of years later, observers still praise how Vauban's fortifications maximized surrounding topography and hail him as one of the best geographers of his time.[7]

Small-scale or impermanent camps and training grounds also dotted the environment. In preparation for an attack on the English coastline,

Napoleon I established six camps on the French side of the Channel in 1803 (each with an artillery range) and, between 1804 and 1805, 70,000 soldiers held reviews, manoeuvres, and celebrations at Boulogne Camp. On 31 July 1805 he also ordered the creation of a firing range in Fontainebleau forest where trainees from the nearby military school would each get to fire cannonballs and bombs at least thirty times a year.[8]

Once Napoleon's nephew, Louis-Napoleon Bonaparte, established the Second Empire through his coup d'état of December 1851, the limitations of such training grounds became all too apparent. For although the Second Empire would prevail in the Crimean War (1853–56) the victory could not hide its military weaknesses. Furthermore, the more extensive deployment of increasingly powerful infantry rifles and artillery cannons militated in favour of larger camps. Existing ones, such as Lannemezan (Hautes-Pyrénées), Saint-Maur (Val-de-Marne), Satory (Yvelines), and Sathonay (Rhône) were simply too small.[9] In addition, the cost and inconvenience of conducting military manoeuvres on private land was prohibitive. Manoeuvres of 31,000 men over 147 ha at Boulogne Camp in 1854 had destroyed vegetation and cost 170,000 francs in rent and compensation to landowners.[10] Local populations resented their land's temporary militarization. In the Marne, peasants may have welcomed the manure deposited by cavalry horses to fertilize their fields, but, on the whole, manoeuvring troops threatened their livelihoods.[11]

Châlons Camp marked a pronounced shift in the militarization of the French environment. Its size and permanence were intended to overcome the deficiencies of existing camps and create an army better equipped for modern warfare. Napoleon III's entourage dubbed it a serious military establishment, in marked contrast to previous camps. Philippe Le Bas, scholar at the Ecole normale supérieure and Napoleon III's strict but devoted former tutor, scorned the frivolity of Compiègne Camp (established by Louis XIV in the Oise in 1696), whose function had been largely ceremonial. The luxury and decadence of Compiègne, where troops had paraded purely to satisfy Madame de Maintenon's desire for war simulacra, had outweighed its military purpose, much to Le Bas's evident dismay.[12]

Frivolity was hardly absent at Châlons. The camp boasted a hippodrome, falconry, and numerous hunting opportunities for officers, while regular troops amused themselves by playing games, decorating their tents with branches and garlands, keeping pets, and dressing up the camp's dogs in the style of Zouaves.[13] But war preparation seems to have been accorded higher priority than before; Napoleon III reminded his soldiers in September 1858 that the camp was a 'serious [military] school'.[14]

It is impossible to say whether soldiers welcomed the arrival of this 'serious school'. But it is clear that Châlons Camp was part of Napoleon III's efforts to consolidate the French army and strengthen his relationship with it. Having backed him during his *coup d'état* of 2 December 1851, Napoleon III felt well-disposed towards the army and introduced a range of reforms in its favour, including faster promotion, a new military code, and the re-forming of the Imperial Guard.[15] The Second Empire's militarism was then expressed through, and partly formed within, the Emperor's new camp.

Its size and permanence made Châlons the first modern military base in France. It also represented a turning point in the militarization of the French environment. Before and during its establishment, the military narrative that labels its coveted land as empty and desolate, and therefore ideally suited for militarization, began to crystallize.

A land ripe for militarization?

Across the English Channel, and partly in reaction to the perceived threat of the Second Empire's militarism, the British army identified what one observer described as 'dreary and repellent' heath and common land around Aldershot (Hampshire) as ideal for militarization. It snapped up between 2,800 and 3,200 ha of land and established permanent barracks in 1858 and firing ranges in the 1860s, whilst bars, brothels, and dance halls opened up to cater for the soldiers.[16] The Second Empire followed a similar formula as it sought to mobilize supposedly worthless land for its new camp.

Napoleon III and his military planners chose an area known derogatorily as *la Champagne pouilleuse* as the site of their new military camp. *La Champagne pouilleuse* (or more politely, *la Champagne crayeuse* [clayey]) stretched over 900,000 ha from Rethel in the north to Troyes in the south. Although the region's light soils had encouraged its early and extensive cultivation, new farming techniques made the cultivation of heavier soils elsewhere a more attractive proposition. As a consequence, by the beginning of the eighteenth century the area was characterized by depopulation. Cultivation was limited to the land around the settlements that nestled in valleys, while grasslands (or *savarts*) stretched over the higher ground. The region's reputation as a fertile agricultural centre, dating back to Roman times, had faded into distant memory as the designation 'pouilleuse' emerged.

It is difficult to translate accurately the meaning of 'pouilleuse'. The best translations are perhaps 'lousy' or 'squalid'. The precise origins of the term remain obscure but it is probable that it came into use at the beginning of the eighteenth century and was then employed in the Grande Encyclopaedia of 1753. The encyclopaedists' use of the term points to its circulation within Enlightenment 'expert' circles. At a time when unproductive land was considered ripe for scientifically informed improvement and management, numerous elite outsiders, including Goethe, Arthur Young (a leading British agricultural writer), and the renowned French historian Jules Michelet, viewed the region as desolate, empty, and backward.[17]

Given the elite background of many military officials at this time, it is not surprising that they parroted this elite interpretation of the region's environment. The emergence of institutionalized geographical knowledge (the Geographical Society of Paris was founded in 1821) gave a veneer of scientific certainty to their appraisals of the area's climate, topography and vegetation. For Dr Riolacci, army doctor and member of the Paris Anthropology Society, it was comprised of 'infertile fields' and was the sole preserve of sheep, offering only the 'most unhappy and desolate view' to the traveller.[18] Similarly, Army medical officer Dr Charles-Alexandre Morin labelled it a 'sad and monotonous land' with 'poor vegetation'.[19] It is hard to know whether or not Riolacci and Morin consciously tapped into the damning elite views of the region to underscore its suitability for military training. Either way, supposedly empty and unproductive land meant cheaper land and the easier displacement of local populations.

The French army's recent experience of colonial conquest in Algeria, when, amongst the violence of French military operations, certain army officers believed that farming would 'pacify' and 'improve' the local population,[20] is likely to have predisposed its officers to treat the supposedly backward *Champagne pouilleuse* as another region in need of conquest and improvement. Colonel Susane depicted an immense and empty land. Echoing colonial and military narratives of the Algerian desert, and overlooking the existence of villages and farms, he claimed that only 'meagre' trees broke up the monotony 'like palm trees in the Sahara'.[21]

The site seemed ripe for military-led internal colonization and military officials hailed the land's suitability for military training. Morin argued that the mainly flat, extensive, and sparsely covered plains suited large-scale troop manoeuvres.[22] Charles Bousquet, a member of Napoleon III's Imperial Guard, even claimed that it would have been 'impossible' to have found a better location for the camp, as its streams, porous soil, and varied terrain allowed the army to conduct different styles of manoeuvres. The vineyard-covered hills beyond the camp even formed a 'rampart' from northerly winds. In his narrative of military-led development, the 'dismal and silent plains' would now be 'populated by the elite of French soldiers'.[23] Having deemed the Champagne plains land ripe for militarization, the Second Empire transformed 12,000 ha of it into an army camp and imperial showcase.

The imperial militarized environment

Creating the imperial militarized environment required considerable effort and money. On 15 November 1856 Napoleon III decreed that the acquisition of the land was in the public interest (*d'utilité publique*) and that the departments for war and finances should secure the land and compensate its owners in accordance with the law of 3 May 1841. Army engineer Captain Weynand was charged with establishing the camp whilst the Marne's prefect communicated which parcels of land were to be expropriated and set the rates of compensation. In Louverey, for instance, 1,764 francs were offered to six landowners for land totalling just over six hectares. Expropriation juries, established in each affected commune, oversaw the compensation of landowners from 17 August 1857 to 24 December 1858.[24] Settling the camp's boundaries, however, was a relatively drawn out process; Weynand had yet to finalize the perimeter in 1860.[25]

But Napoleon III was impatient and ordered the camp's inauguration before the expropriation process was complete. Weynand worked under considerable pressure to fulfil his wishes, constructing imperial pavilions and rudimentary barracks for the camp's headquarters (the vast majority of troops would be accommodated in tents). Napoleon III therefore inaugurated the camp on 30 August 1857, after an outlay of 490,000 francs. Amid choirs and much fanfare, he told members of his elite imperial guard, 22,000 of whom would shortly conduct the first manoeuvres in the camp, that he had brought them here so that they could 'draw from the communal camp life a united spirit, discipline, and instruction'.[26]

Sympathetic observers lost little time in heralding Châlons as a new kind of military camp that would guarantee the Second Empire's imperial ambitions. Given the military background of the authors, and restrictions on freedom of speech during the Second Empire, these accounts present the camp in glowing terms. Riolacci's hyperbolic statement that Châlons Camp was 'one of the most important institutions that the Second Empire had given France' set the tone.[27]

Napoleon III certainly had grand ambitions for the camp. The public displays of military and imperial grandeur held there formed part of the series of rituals and ceremonies, such as the inaugurations of statues, boulevards, and railway lines, designed to highlight his regime's achievements.[28] With its imperial pavilions, railway station, barracks, imperial farms, theatre, stables, library, and tents, described in lavish and admiring detail by writers such as Adolphe Guerard, Châlons Camp was a material manifestation of the Second Empire's imperial ambitions.[29]

During its inauguration, Napoleon III stated that his soldiers would learn the art of war in camps, just as the Romans had done.[30] The mention of Roman soldiers was no accident as Napoleon III sought to promote the Roman Empire as a model for his own.[31] According to this imperial narrative, the camp was a visible and tangible link between the Second Empire and France's Roman heritage, a site of Roman-esque splendour and military might standing proud on the plains of Champagne. The mobilization of Châlons Camp's demanding physical environment was to reconnect physically the Second Empire's soldiers to Rome's all-conquering legionaries. Morin drew direct comparisons between Châlons Camp and the military camps of the Roman Empire, the 'true school of the soldier'.[32] Riolacci similarly pointed to the success of Roman training camps from which sprung the 'qualities that had made the army invincible'. It was in the camp where the Imperial army fortified itself and instilled military skills and discipline into its soldiers. The Second Empire, it hardly needed stating, was drawing on this formidable legacy.[33]

Presenting it as a clash between civilization and barbarity, writers during the Second Empire stressed the stark contrasts between Roman legionaries and the forces of Attila the Hun who had fought near the site of Châlons Camp. The first hundred or so pages of Riolacci's exposition of Châlons Camp recounted how the Gauls and Romans had repelled waves of barbarians from the East, including the ferocious Huns. Riolacci's distaste for the Huns (who apparently had 'no notion of morals or religion') was seemingly a thinly veiled attack on the Russian enemy with which France had grappled during the Crimean War and was perhaps a calculated move to ingratiate himself with Napoleon III (who loathed Russia).[34]

But it was historian and geographer Adolphe Guerard who stressed most vividly the startling contrast between the Huns and the Second Empire. Accompanied by sketches of a scowling Attila and a dignified Napoleon, Guerard labelled the Huns' culture as 'barbarism' and the Second Empire as 'civilisation'. Attila represented 'evil' and Napoleon 'good'. It was by a 'strange destiny' that Châlons Camp had been established so close to Attila's former camp, located between the villages of La Cheppe and Cuperly. Napoleon III would now send the 'fine and valiant children of France' to train at Châlons Camp separated by only a few leagues (and fourteen centuries) from the site of the 'hideous and terrible offspring of the destructive Hun'.[35] But in geopolitical terms, Châlons' location was more than a quirk of fate. Alongside the training possibilities offered by Champagne's plains, the mistrust of France's powerful eastern neighbour influenced the decision to locate the camp between Paris and the Prussian border.[36]

The spectre of Napoleon I's First Empire also hovered over the camp. Bousquet outlined how the Napoleonic camps had resisted all 'softness and excess'. In his view, it was no coincidence that the soldiers who had trained at Boulogne Camp eventually triumphed against Austro-Russian forces at the battle of Austerlitz in 1805 (he made no mention, however, of the First Empire's defeat at Waterloo).[37] As during the Roman and first Napoleonic empires, the soldier of the Second Empire would emerge through demanding physical contact with the elements. This military mobilization of nature continues today, in France and beyond. As Rachel Woodward argues, the training ground environment becomes 'a challenging location against which the soldier-recruit is pitted, and in response to which skills and identities of the soldier are to be constructed'.[38]

On a more representational level, military symbols and ceremonies, such as the camp's inauguration, highlighted the links between Napoleon III and Napoleon I.[39] For even if Napoleon III lacked the military sensibilities of his uncle, France's soldiers were reportedly 'proud to be once more under the command of an Emperor, and one who, unlike his Bourbon and Orléans predecessors, knew how to sit on a horse'.[40]

But beyond the imperialistic froth, what was life like in the camp? It is impossible to generalize as thousands of troops manoeuvred there.[41] Manoeuvres also varied according to infantry, artillery, and cavalry units, even if they are always began early in the morning.[42] But training failed to match the imperial narrative of the camp as a tough military school. In 1857 Napoleon III led eleven carefully planned large-scale manoeuvres which, according to Bousquet, were designed to resemble war as much as possible. In reality, a desire for imperial spectacle sat alongside military imperatives. Echoing Madame de Maintenon's love of battle recreations and the more recent public spectacle of Camp de Fontainebleau in 1839, the Empress herself rewarded the best shots with prizes and 'a large number of curious people' came to watch the manoeuvres.[43]

Bousquet presented a somewhat romanticized vision of life in the camp. During the manoeuvres of 1857, he recorded how the reveille disturbed the 'profound silence' and 'absolute tranquillity' of the 'vast plains' and how the morning dew on the soldiers' tents glistened like 'diamonds'.[44] The reality was more mundane. Manoeuvres in the camp's early years set the rhythm for subsequent ones. In 1864, cannon shots still woke up troops at 5am (4am on days of the large-scale manoeuvres) for a day of exercises and manoeuvres punctuated with pauses for food and relaxation. At 10pm, a cannon shot heralded lights out.[45] The repetitive and regimented character of the manoeuvres was not to everyone's taste. One anecdote has it that certain cavalry officers became so fed up with charging in the same direction at the same tree that they chopped it down. But innovation was not totally absent; the army tested the Chassepot rifle there and conducted research on tent materials, military cuisine, and the effect of draft work on horses.[46]

At times, weather disrupted the military routine. South-westerly winds on 1 September 1857 brought a 'real deluge' during manoeuvres and the troops had to retreat to their tents. Heavy rain and strong winds reappeared eight days later, flattening the recently constructed barracks and disrupting manoeuvres. By the beginning of October, rain had turned the camp into a 'real swamp' rendering manoeuvres impossible.[47] Conversely, dust and reflections from the clayey soil during hot weather reportedly resulted in conjunctivitis, ulcers, and night-blindness. High temperatures during manoeuvres also resulted in sunstroke for many soldiers, some of whom had to retire.[48] It is unclear whether some soldiers might have feigned sunstroke to avoid training. Nonetheless, the army could not ignore unpredictable and adverse weather conditions. Along with its topography and vegetation, the camp's climate continued to cause deep unease amongst army doctors.

Problematic medical geographies

The nineteenth century saw the medicalization of France. Not only did the medical profession expand and become more organized, but 'medical discourse infused all areas of French society'.[49] Châlons Camp was no exception.

From the mid-nineteenth-century medical perspective, careful assessments of topography, climate, and other environmental features made perfect sense. Before the 'bacteriological revolution' of the late nineteenth century, doctors believed that dirt and unhealthy environments could cause disease. The French public hygienists of the early nineteenth century, led by such figures as Jean-Baptiste Parent-Duchâtelet and Louis-René Villermé (many of whom had military backgrounds[50]), believed that detailed, empirical knowledge was needed to help guard against the potentially harmful impact of dirt, miasmas, and overcrowding on human health. Although they directed much of their attention towards supposedly squalid and overcrowded urban areas, the countryside received some attention. Indeed, before Louis Pasteur's discoveries, 'no self-respecting physician or hygienist would presume to say anything authoritative about public health without first specifying the geographical region under discussion'.[51]

By the mid-nineteenth century, military doctors were part of the increased specialization of French medicine, training in their own hospitals with their own curriculum.[52] But like their civilian counterparts, they too fixated on topography, climate, dirt, and other potentially harmful geographical features. And like civilian doctors, military ones saw themselves as leading a crusade to make France physically and morally cleaner. As Morin stated, military hygiene is 'a science that surveys [and] modifies the moral and material conditions of soldiers'.[53] For physical and moral reasons, therefore, mobilizing nature for military training in the mid-nineteenth century required careful consideration of climate, vegetation, and topography.

In military discourse, *la Champagne pouilleuse* was hygienic enough for military training. Ironically, military commentators welcomed the health-preserving properties of a land they elsewhere described as 'lousy'. The official camp journal of 1857 even claimed that the 'vigour of local populations is the proof of the area's salubrity'.[54] As doctors trained in the principles of military hygiene, Riolacci and Morin placed great importance on the area's health-giving geographies. Riolacci welcomed the clumps of trees that exerted a beneficial influence on the climate (as well as offering training possibilities). The grass that covered the plains also prevented the white clay soil from blinding soldiers, and its quick-drying qualities gave it resilience against the impact of horses' hooves and soldiers' boots.[55] Morin similarly praised the porous soil that prevented the formation of pools and mud-baths, as well as the plateau's 'fresh air'. He reserved particular praise for the water supplies drawn from the Cheneu River. For despite its 'milky colour' that might 'inspire some repugnance', the water was a pleasure to drink and he speculated that it may even help prevent diarrhoea.[56] The irony that Morin and Riolacci portrayed the region as empty, yet paid careful attention to the minutiae of its topography and climate, seems to have been lost on them.

Despite agreeing that the area was healthy, medical officers continued to fret about the camp's environment; it might be potentially harmful. In the mid-nineteenth century, medical opinion held that climatic and seasonal variations caused disease. In this vein, Morin identified medical problems caused by Châlons Camp's climate. He reported how nocturnal humidity and low temperatures, combined with stifling daytime temperatures led to 'illnesses of the digestive tube, and rheumatic ailments'.[57] More seriously, Goffres admitted that the development of lung infections was particularly rapid in the camp due to the 'influence of the atmospheric variations to which [it] is exposed'.[58]

At a time when miasma theory also dominated popular and expert explanations of disease causation, the air that soldiers breathed posed a potentially greater threat than extremes of temperature. According to miasma theory, air transmitted harmful diseases into humans from decaying biological matter.[59] Morin therefore heralded the precautions taken against miasmas at Châlons Camp by Baron Félix Hippolyte Larrey, Napoleon III's surgeon and member of the Academy of Sciences and other learned societies. In line with public hygienist theories, Morin feared marshland and celebrated how Larrey had regulated and diverted the course of the Cheneu River to remove the dangers posed by its 'marshy edges'. These areas of stagnant water might have emitted malaria, and their removal prompted Morin to celebrate the camp's absence of 'sources of miasma'.[60]

The involvement of Larrey is telling. As the son of Baron Dominique-Jean Larrey, Napoleon I's Chief Surgeon and Surgeon General of the First Empire's army, Larrey *fils* was the epitome of French military and imperial medicine. The fact that he personally oversaw the diversion of the Cheneu River underscores military hygienists' fear of miasmas. His reporting to Napoleon III on matters concerning the camp's 'sanitary organization' similarly highlights how seriously the army treated the camp's potentially dangerous environment.[61]

Despite Larrey's intervention, concerns about the Cheneu River persisted, especially as the main troop encampment lay alongside the river. Writing in 1865, Goffres proposed that the abundant vegetation growing on the river bank and considerable quantities of 'vegetative detritus' should be removed to lessen their potential harm on the health of troops. Alongside vegetation, animals posed a problem. Goffres expressed concern that cavalrymen kept their horses' harnesses in their tents, thereby exposing themselves to the 'noxious odour' of saddles 'impregnated with horses' sweat'. 'Nothing is less hygienic', he concluded.[62] Like other hygienists, he firmly believed in the importance of separating animal and human bodies.

These anxieties about the influence of the camp's geographies on soldiers' health sat uneasily with the confident imperial rhetoric that greeted Châlons Camp. The mobilization of nature for military goals carried environmentally rooted risks that required careful monitoring. Practitioners of medical military science in the Second Empire, who claimed Roman roots for their discipline, treated air, water, and soil as potentially harmful agents that could undermine military training. As Linda Nash has argued, 'when viewed from the perspective of health, the nineteenth-century environment was neither passive nor necessarily benign in its natural state'.[63] Military hygienists viewed climate, vegetation, and other geographical features as active and potentially harmful agents, due, in part, to the porous boundaries between the soldiers' bodies and the nonhuman world. And whilst they claimed to be in control of the camp's geographies through detailed empirical assessments, the amount of ink spilled on the camp's medical geographies demonstrates that a strong sense of unease lingered on.

As well as paying careful attention to the Châlons Camp's medical geographies, Napoleon III and his supporters intended it to act as a vector of modernization. For them, the camp simultaneously recreated imperial traditions and glories whilst pointing a way forward to a more productive and rational future.

Militarization as environmental modernization

Guerard admiringly noted how Roman soldiers 'easily put down roots where they camped', leading to the establishment of new cities.[64] Napoleon III's plans for Châlons Camp were slightly different. He intended it to bring material progress to *la Champagne pouilleuse* and further his regime's agricultural policies. His instructions to Weynand during the camp's creation laid bare the camp's multiple functions as a site of military training, imperial spectacle, and territorial 'improvement'. They included the order to 'drain the swampy parts and to sow the entire manoeuvring ground to create either a beautiful lawn or artificial fodder'.[65]

Châlons Camp therefore became integrated into the Second Empire's attempt to reclaim supposedly unproductive land. Napoleon III publicly stated that land reclamation reinforced the foundations of his regime and strengthened his imperial ambitions: 'agricultural progress should be an object of our constant solicitude because its improvement or decline leads to the prosperity or decadence of empires'.[66] The Second Empire's policy of 'interior colonization' aimed to boost agricultural production to ward off food shortages and keep pace with neighbouring countries. Interior colonization targeted 130,000 ha of 'wasteland', including the reclaiming of 13,000 ha from lakes in the Sologne and the planting of extensive pine forests in the Landes region of south-west France.[67]

Napoleon III's desire to improve *la Champagne pouilleuse* built on previous schemes. In 1705 Jean-Baptiste de Pinteville established a plantation of Scots pine at Cernon; between 1755 and 1760 Antoine de Pinteville followed suit with more extensive plantations. Forty-six years later, Bourgeois de Jessaint wished to 'cover these vast uncultivated plains with useful vegetation'.[68] In the mid-nineteenth century, afforestation remained the order of the day. Napoleon III ordered Weynand to plant trees along the camp's perimeter (a project that never saw the light of day), around the imperial quarter, along the Cheneu valley, and along roads.[69] In all, the army reportedly planted 12,000–15,000 trees annually in the camp. But the trees struggled to grow in the thin soils and many needed replacement. Initially, the tree nursery at Trianon provided the majority of the trees, but in order to maintain supplies, military authorities created their own nursery in the camp between Mourmelon-le-Petit and Mourmelon-le-Grand.[70]

The regime also pursued agricultural development. Napoleon III ordered the creation of eight imperial farms around the camp's periphery, including Bouy and Suippes farms. Constructing farm buildings, laying roads, hiring personnel, and securing livestock – 1,000 Swiss cows and 500 ewes arrived in 1858 alone – was not cheap; by 1861 the investment had reached just over a million francs. Napoleon III reportedly took a keen interest in the farms, whose objectives were to feed troops, showcase modern farming techniques, and cultivate the land around the camp.[71] Expressing his belief that the army's modernization schemes would radiate beyond the camp, Riolacci declared, in the moralizing tones of the hygienist movement, that the camp would ensure the 'moral and material regeneration of *la Champagne pouilleuse*'.[72]

Riolacci's bold claim was not entirely divorced from reality as the army oversaw an increase in agricultural production. Some 2,000 ha were cleared to sow wheat, oats, potatoes, barley and other crops, and in 1862 the farms produced 16 tonnes of wool, 75 tonnes of meat, and 121,000 litres of milk. Horse and human manure from the camp also helped fertilize local fields, while the camp's size stimulated agricultural production in the area. At the same time, military authorities allowed civilians to pasture their sheep on the camp (outside of the summer manoeuvring season), even if the sheep were reportedly allowed to overgraze, thereby threatening the precarious survival of the camp's vegetation.[73] The use of the camp for civilian pasturing laid bare the intermingling and overlapping of military and civilian land use within the camp.

In addition, military authorities encouraged soldiers to tend gardens, which constituted a more informal and diffuse way of cultivating sections of the camp's environment. Army doctors praised such efforts, believing them to improve soldiers' morale and the camp's physical aspects. Goffres celebrated how the 'green and flowery borders' created amongst the tents gave the camp 'the most picturesque appearance'. Morin, meanwhile, celebrated how the gardens broke up the 'monotony' of the view across the plains. He also applauded how they exerted a purifying effect on the region's climate, as well as offering soldiers food, distraction, and reminders of their pre-army agricultural life.[74] For these hygienists, the gardens were healthy, aesthetically pleasing, and morally improving.

Overlooking the centuries-long existence of agriculture in the area before the army's arrival, a 1872 account went further, contrasting the soldiers' gardens with the 'uncultivated nature' of Champagne and claiming that they demonstrated how the land was cultivatable with care and effort.[75] The evocation of these 'soldier-gardeners' added a new dimension to myth of the 'soldier-peasant' and acted as forerunners to twentieth-century soldiers' efforts to create gardens to humanize and domesticate militarized environments.[76]

Gardening, farming, and afforestation underscore how Châlons Camp was a key component of the Second Empire's attempts to reclaim, rationalize, and cultivate unproductive tracts of the French countryside. Second Empire officials saw militarization as a means of territorial modernization elsewhere. In 1860 Joseph Ferrand argued that the army should construct canals and roads, plant trees and dig drains to bring 'progress' to the Landes, drawing on the 'close affinity between the soldier and everything that concerns the land'.[77] But Châlons Camp was the most prominent militarized vector of 'internal colonization' and its inclusion within the Second Empire's land reclamation project further cemented the conflation of militarization and progress.

But certain peasants and local officials challenged the military narrative that coupled militarization with the improvement of the countryside. As in the Landes region, where local inhabitants opposed the regime's afforestation scheme, the Champagne plains were emphatically not an empty wilderness.[78] In fact, only 27.6 per cent of the camp's surface area was *uncultivated* at the time of its creation; its establishment therefore entailed the expropriation of land from 237 farmers. Local politicians had urged Napoleon III to take agricultural interests into account. The mayor of Cuperly protested to the Minister for War in 1856 that 'on our territory all the farms are today destroyed . . . the farmers are alarmed and in desperate straits'.[79] A member of the Marne's general council summed up the concerns of local landowners, complaining how they had lost crops and been forced from their homes; 'across our region there reigns an atmosphere of unease and anxiety'.[80] As well as adding weight to the view that the countryside was far from compliant during the Second Empire and that rural communities engaged with national politics in the mid-nineteenth century,[81] the civilian equation of militarization with the sterilization of land would prove to be a recurrent feature in the subsequent history of French militarized environments.

A discrepancy between state and local land valuations lay at the heart of the matter. Part of the appeal of the Champagne plain from the point of view of military planners was the relative cheapness of the land. Yet landowners from Jonchery-sur-Suippe claimed that the state's experts had failed to fully appreciate and value the productivity of their land which 'produced everything that it was asked to'. They argued that state experts had further 'slandered' the region by overlooking the products derived from sheep. In short, the land was profitable and the deployment of more advanced agricultural techniques could have led to its further cultivation.[82] From their perspective, state officials had misread the environment.[83]

Opinion also diverged amongst agricultural experts. Writing in 1866, Eugène Bablot-Maître, a farmer at Jonchery-sur-Suippe and member of the National Academy of Paris, claimed that the state's property agents had thoughtlessly bought into the unfair myth of *la Champagne pouilleuse* that portrayed the region as sterile and worthless. As a consequence, they had underestimated the land's value. Pointing out that the expropriated land's value differed according to its proximity to water sources,

Bablot-Maître argued that with more fertilizer the region's agriculture could match any other's. Most significantly, Bablot-Maître directly challenged the idea that Châlons Camp had developed the region's agriculture. On the contrary, he argued that war and militarization had repeatedly undermined Champagne's agricultural development.[84]

Bablot-Maître had a point, even if his view may have been coloured by bitterness over the perceived low rates of compensation. For although military farms and forest plantations cultivated some land (as outlined above), the camp's presence undermined local agriculture. Despite the state making some concessions to farmers, such as only taking possession of sown land after harvest-time and paying some compensation, the camp's creation contributed to a more general rural exodus. In Mourmelon-le-Grand alone seventy inhabitants left to find work elsewhere.[85] Châlons Camp was therefore a problematic vector of agricultural development because it displaced local farmers and disrupted agriculture.

Conclusion

Militarization through Châlons Camp transformed this area of Champagne. For Guerard the contrast between 1856 and 1858 was striking. In 1856, the site had been 'gloomy and silent'. In 1858 it played host to the enthusiasm and bustle of 'our brave soldiers'.[86] Displaced farmers held a different view, and unsuccessfully opposed the militarization of their land. Either way, Châlons was a new kind of camp and the first modern French militarized environment. It heralded the emergence of the military narrative that identified so-called wastelands as ideal sites for militarization, even if the concerns of army doctors about the camp's medical geographies exposed how this military mobilization of nature was far from straightforward.

The camp's military record was also mixed. In terms of its size and the resources and attention lavished on it, Châlons Camp represented a break from previous camps. Yet it offered no guarantee of military success. Throughout the 1860s French commanders and officers were either unwilling or unable to break from an out-dated style of training founded on regimented, formal manoeuvres ill-suited to modern warfare. Their lack of tactical awareness became evident once Napoleon III summoned leading officers to Châlons Camp for a *Kriegspiel* (war game) after the Prussian victory against Austria in 1866. The results were disappointing; leadership and initiative were notable by their absence.[87]

The following year, General Trochu attacked the army's out-dated training manuals (which were based on eighteenth-century texts) and the overly complicated style of manoeuvring that was impossible to recreate on the battlefield.[88]

Realism was in short supply. During manoeuvres the 'French' side always won. The inadequacy of French military training compounded the Second Empire's failure to implement successfully other much-needed military reforms, such as expanding conscription, establishing a peacetime military organization easily adaptable to wartime and creating effective reserve units, despite the efforts of Marshal Niel.[89] These failings became all too apparent once war broke out with Prussia in 1870.

Notes

1 Reims and Suippes had lobbied to have the camp named after them, but Châlons had prevailed. Just Berland, *Le Camp de Châlons sous l'empire* (Paris: Service historique de l'Armée, 1955), 12–13.

2 *Une visite au camp de Châlons sous le Second Empire* (Paris: Musée de l'Armée, 1996).

3 Nadine Chossat, *Mourmelon-le-Grand: Cité champenoise et militaire* (Mourmelon-le-Grand: Ville de Mourmelon-le-Grand, 1999), 44; Charles Bousquet, *La Garde impériale au Camp de Châlons* (Paris: Blot, 1858), 148; Gérard Bieuville, 'Le camp de Châlons sous le Second Empire', in *Camp de Châlons sous le Second Empire*, 20.

4 Comte de Chesnel, *Dictionnaire des armées de terre et de mer, Encyclopédie militaire et maritime, première partie A–F* (Paris: Armand le Chevalier, 1863), 213.

5 For recent work on the medical history of nineteenth-century France, see David S. Barnes, *The Great Stink of Paris and the Nineteenth-Century Struggle against Filth and Germs* (Baltimore: Johns Hopkins University Press, 2006); Catherine J. Kudlick, *Cholera in Post-Revolutionary France: A Cultural History* (Berkeley: University of California Press, 1996). On the environmental history of health, see Gregg Mitman, *Breathing Space: How Allergies Shape our Lives and Landscapes* (New Haven: Yale University Press, 2007); Linda Nash, *Inescapable Ecologies: A History of Environment, Disease, and Knowledge* (Berkeley: University of California Press, 2006).

6 Jean-Pierre Husson and Etienne Martin, 'Etude de géohistoire de la place forte de Marsal: Analyse de l'hydrosystème de défense', in *Vauban, militaire et économiste sous Louis XIV*, vol. 1., Jean-Pierre Salzman (ed.), *Vauban et Marsal à l'époque de Louis XIV: Le sel, la fiscalité, la guerre* (Nancy: Editions annales de l'est, 2009), 118.

7 François Dallemagne and Jean Mouly, *Patrimoine militaire* (Paris: Editions

Scala, 2002), 92–5; Yves Lacoste, *La géographie, ça sert, d'abord, à faire la guerre* (Paris: François Maspero, 1976), 16.

8 Chesnel, *Dictionnaire des armées de terre et de mer*, 212; *Correspondance militaire de Napoléon 1er: Extraite de la correspondance générale et publiée par ordre du ministre de la guerre*, vol. 2 (Paris: Plon, 1876), 494; *Correspondance militaire de Napoléon 1er: Extraite de la correspondance générale et publiée par ordre du ministre de la guerre*, vol. 3 (Paris: Plon, 1876), 135–6.

9 Richard Holmes, *The Road to Sedan: The French Army, 1866–70* (London: Royal Historical Society, 1984), 199–200.

10 *Journal du Camp de Châlons-sur-Marne en 1857* (Paris: Imprimerie impériale, 1858), 1; D. Riolacci, *Le Camp de Châlons* (Paris: Dumaine, 1865), 174.

11 Georges Clause, 'L'environnement civil du camp de Châlons', in *Camp de Châlons sous le Second Empire*, 28; Dominique Bilogli, 'Contraints et facteurs logistiques d'ancien régime: Le déplacement des troupes dans le royaume de France (XVIe–XVIIIe siècle)', in Jacques Aben and Jacques Rouzier (eds), *Défense et aménagement du territoire* (Montpellier: ESID, 2001), 49–57.

12 Philippe Le Bas, *L'Univers: Histoire et description de tous les peuples. France: Dictionnaire encyclopédique*, vol. 4 (Paris: Firmin-Didot Frères, 1860), 63.

13 Berland, *Camp de Châlons*, 80, 289–99.

14 Quoted in Bousquet, *Garde impériale*, 144–5.

15 James F. McMillan, *Napoleon III* (London: Longman, 1991), 58; David B. Ralston, *The Army of the Republic: The Place of the Military in the Political Evolution of France, 1871–1914* (Cambridge, MA: MIT Press, 1967), 17.

16 Jacqueline Tivers, 'The home of the British army: The iconic construction of military defence landscapes', *Landscape Research*, 24:3 (1999), 305–6.

17 Roger Brunet, *Atlas et géographie de Champagne, pays de Meuse, et Basse Bourgogne* (Paris: Flammarion, 1918), 161–3; Joseph Garnotel, *L'ascension d'une grande agriculture: Champagne pouilleuse-Champagne crayeuse* (Paris: Economica, 1985), 3; Clause, 'Environnement civil', 25; Xavier de Planhol and Paul Claval, *An Historical Geography of France*, trans. Janet Lloyd (Cambridge: Cambridge University Press, 1994 [1988]), 364; Roger Dion, *Le Paysage et la vigne: Essais de géographie historique* (Paris: Payot, 1990), 175–87. Experts continued to disparage *la Champagne pouilleuse* well into the twentieth century, including geographer Jean-François Gravier in his influential *Paris et le désert français: Décentralisation, équipement, population* (Paris: Le Portulan, 1947), 361–2. For an overview of Enlightenment views of nature, see Peter Coates, *Nature: Western Attitudes since Ancient Times* (Cambridge: Polity Press, 1998), 68–81; Max Oelschlaeger, *The Idea of Wilderness: From Prehistory to the Age of Ecology* (New Haven: Yale University Press, 1991), 68–96.

18 Riolacci, *Camp de Châlons*, 170. Although the army of the Second Empire was more egalitarian than that of the Restoration, only 32 per cent of students

attending the Ecole polytechnique received a grant and many of them came from military and civil service families. William Serman, *Les officiers français dans la nation, 1848–1914* (Paris: Aubier Montaigne, 1982), 9.

19 Charles-Alexandre Morin, *Le Camp de Châlons en 1858 au point de vue hygié-nique et médical: Hygiène des camps en général* (Paris: Jules Masson, 1858), 20.

20 Diana K. Davis, *Resurrecting the Granary of Rome: Environmental History and French Colonial Expansion in North Africa* (Athens, OH: Ohio University Press, 2007), 52–3. On the violence of the French army's campaign in Algeria, see Benjamin Claude Brower, *A Desert Named Peace: The Violence of France's Empire in the Algerian Sahara, 1844–1902* (New York: Columbia University Press, 2009).

21 M. Susane, *La Champagne pouilleuse* (Metz: F. Blanc, Imprimeur de l'Acadé-mie Impériale, 1857), 7–8. Riolacci also compared the trees of *la Champagne pouilleuse* to oases in the Sahara desert. *Camp de Châlons*, 180. On nineteenth-century representations of sterility and oases in the Sahara, see Brower, *Desert Named Peace*, 207–13.

22 Morin, *Le Camp de Châlons*, 19.

23 Bousquet, *Garde impériale*, 82–3.

24 ADMA 2 Q 406 Préfecture du département de la Marne, 'Camp de Châlons', 12 June 1857.

25 ADMA 2 Q 405 Génie, Camp de Châlons, 'Procès-verbal de bornage de ligne de circonscription du camp de Châlons', 3 August 1860.

26 Berland, *Camp de Châlons*, 13–20, 28. Quote on page 20.

27 Riolacci, *Camp de Châlons*, 163.

28 David Baguley, *Napoleon III and His Regime: An Extravaganza* (Baton Rouge: Louisiana State University Press, 2000), 158–66, 193.

29 Adolphe Guerard, *Camp de Châlons* (Châlons-sur-Marne: Eugène Laurent, 1858), 84–7.

30 Berland, *Camp de Châlons*, 20–1.

31 Napoleon III was fascinated by Caesar and, assisted by a team of scholars, produced a two-volume history of the Roman emperor. Baguley, *Napoleon III*, 79–89.

32 Morin, *Camp de Châlons*, 17.

33 Riolacci, *Camp de Châlons*, 116, 135. See also Guerard, *Camp de Châlons*, 81–2.

34 Riolacci, *Camp de Châlons*, quote on page 46. In a similar vein, Morin was delighted that Châlons Camp was close to the site of the Catalauniques battle where Aetius had defeated Attila's forces in 451 BCE. Morin, *Camp de Châlons*, 18–19. On Napoleon III's anti-Russian sentiments, see J.M. Thompson, *Louis Napoleon and the Second Empire* (Oxford: Blackwell, 1954), 145.

35 Guerard, *Camp de Châlons*, 7–73. Quote on page 68. On French perceptions

of Russia in the nineteenth century, see Robert Gildea, *Children of the Revolution: The French 1799–1914* (London: Penguin, 2009), 214–19.

36 Chesnel, *Dictionnaire des armées*, 213.
37 Bousquet, *Garde impériale*, 13–20.
38 Rachel Woodward, 'Locating military masculinities: Space, place, and the formation of gender identity in the British army', in Paul R. Higate (ed.), *Military Masculinities: Identity and the State* (Westport and London: Praeger, 2003), 44–7.
39 Baguley, *Napoleon III and His Regime*, 163.
40 Thompson, *Louis Napoleon*, 228. On the relationship between Napoleon III and the army, see McMillan, *Napoleon III*, 58; Ralston, *Army of the Republic*, 17.
41 Between 1859 and 1863, numbers peaked at 35,000 in 1859. Docteur Goffres, *Considérations historiques, hygiéniques et médicales sur le Camp de Châlons* (Paris: Victor Rozier, 1865), 4.
42 Morin, *Camp de Châlons*, 25.
43 Bousquet, *Garde impériale*, 146, 152; Nicholas Green, *The Spectacle of Nature: Landscape and Bourgeois Culture in Nineteenth-Century France* (Manchester: Manchester University Press, 1990), 174.
44 Bousquet, *Garde impériale*, 204–5.
45 Goffres, *Considérations historiques, hygiéniques et médicales*, 42.
46 Bieuville, 'Camp de Châlons', 19.
47 Bousquet, *Garde impériale*, 146–55, 164, 264.
48 Morin, *Camp de Châlons*, 109, 114.
49 Ann La Berge and Mordechai Feingold, 'Introduction', in Ann La Berge and Mordechai Feingold (eds), *French Medical Culture in the Nineteenth Century* (Amsterdam: Rodopi, 1994), 3.
50 Erwin H. Ackerknecht, 'Hygiene in France, 1815–1848', *Bulletin of the History of Medicine* 22 (1948), 119.
51 Barnes, *Great Stink of Paris*, 64–78, 116. On the French hygienist movement, see Ann La Berge, *Mission and Method: The Early 19th-Century French Public Health Movement* (Cambridge: Cambridge University Press, 1991).
52 George Weisz, 'The development of medical specialization in nineteenth-century Paris', in La Berge and Feingold, *French Medical Culture*, 156–6.
53 Morin, *Camp de Châlons*, 1.
54 *Journal du Camp*, 2.
55 Riolacci, *Camp de Châlons*, 188–91.
56 Morin, *Camp de Châlons*, 6–11, 53–5. In fact, securing sufficient supplies of potable water proved to be an arduous and time-consuming task; by 1865 water was drawn from 204 wells. Berland, *Camp de Châlons*, 36–46; Goffres, *Considérations historiques, hygiéniques et médicales*, 20.
57 Morin, *Camp de Châlons*, 56–7.
58 Goffres, *Considérations historiques, hygiéniques et médicales*, 5–6, 12–14. Quote on 14.

59 Caroline Hannaway, 'Environment and miasmata', in W.F. Bynum and Roy Porter (eds), *Companion Encyclopaedia of the History of Medicine*, vol.1 (London: Routledge, 1993), 292–308.

60 Morin, *Camp de Châlons*, 12, 29. On the perceived links between marshland and disease in nineteenth-century France, see Barnes, *Great Stink of Paris*, 110–13; William Coleman, *Death Is a Social Disease: Public Health and Political Economy in Early Industrial France* (Madison: University of Wisconsin Press, 1982).

61 L.-J.-B. Bérenger Féraud, *Le Baron Hippolyte Larrey* (Paris: Libraire Fayard Frères, 1899), 56.

62 Goffres, *Considérations historiques, hygiéniques et médicales*, 18, 26.

63 Nash, *Inescapable Ecologies*, 27.

64 Guerard, *Camp de Châlons*, 82.

65 Quoted in Berland, *Camp de Châlons*, 216.

66 Quoted in Roger Sargos, *Contribution à l'histoire du boisement des Landes de Gascogne* (Bordeaux: Delmas, 1949), 41.

67 Hugh Clout, *The Land of France 1815–1914* (London: Allen & Unwin, 1983), 48, 52–5; Samuel Temple, 'The natures of nation: Negotiating modernity in the *Landes de Gascogne*', *French Historical Studies*, 32:3 (2009), 419–46 According to Alain Plessis, the Second Empire increased cultivated land by 1,500,000 ha bringing the total to a level 'unparalleled in all of French history' (26,500,000 ha). *The Rise and Fall of the Second Empire 1852–1871*, trans. Jonathan Mandelbaum (Cambridge: Cambridge University Press, 1985), 105.

68 Quoted in Brunet, *Atlas et géographie de Champagne*, 163. See also Octave Beuve, *La Question du Boisement de la Champagne pouilleuse au XIIIe siècle* (Troyes: Imprimerie et Lithographie Paul Nouel, 1911); R. Leroux, 'Reboisement et défrichement de la Champagne crayeuse', *Revue forestière française*, 10 (1961), 607.

69 On afforestation during the Second Empire, see Tamara L. Whited, *Forests and Peasant Politics in Modern France* (New Haven: Yale University Press, 2000), 61–3.

70 Berland, *Camp de Châlons*, 216–17.

71 Ibid. 195–6, 201.

72 Riolacci, *Camp de Châlons*, 172.

73 Berland, *Camp de Châlons*, 203, 224; Clause, 'Environnement civil', 27.

74 Goffres, *Considérations historiques, hygiéniques et médicales*, 28; Morin, *Camp de Châlons*, 124–6. Quote on 126.

75 Camille Husson, *Étude sur le camp de Châlons: L'homme préhistorique et le cultivateur actuel* (Toul: Imprimerie de T. Lemaire, 1872), 56.

76 Gérard de Puymège, *Chauvin, le soldat-labourer: Contribution à l'étude des nationalismes* (Paris: Editions Gallimard, 1993); David M. Hopkin, *Soldier and Peasant in French Popular Culture, 1766–1870* (Woodbridge: Royal Historical Society/Boydell Press, 2003); Kenneth I. Helphand, *Defiant*

Gardens: *Making Gardens in Wartime* (San Antonio: Trinity University Press, 2006).

77 Joseph Ferrand, *Les landes de Gascogne: Etude sur leur état actuel et sur les mesures à prendre pour hâter leur régénération* (Paris: Panckoucke, 1860), 52.

78 On protests in the Landes, see Louis Girard, *La politique des travaux publics du Second Empire* (Paris: Armand Colin, 1952), 233; Samuel Temple, 'Forestation and its discontents: The invention of an uncertain landscape in Southwestern France, 1850-present', *Environment and History*, 17 (2011), 19–22.

79 Chossat, *Mourmelon-le-Grand*, 41–2.

80 Quoted in Berland, *Camp de Châlons*, 19.

81 Edward Berenson, 'Politics and the French peasantry: The debate continues', *Social History*, 12:2 (1987), 213–29.

82 *Considérations et notes sur le rapport général des terres de la commune de Jonchery encloses dans le périmètre du Camp de Châlons* (Châlons-sur-Marne: T. Martin, 1858).

83 On state simplifications and mis-readings of the environment, see James C. Scott, *Seeing Like a State: How Certain Schemes to Improve the Human Condition Have Failed* (New Haven: Yale University Press, 1998).

84 Eugène Bablot-Maître, *Etude sur la Champagne agricole et sur l'amélioration du sol champenois* (Châlons-sur-Marne: T. Martin, 1866), 10–13.

85 Chossat, *Mourmelon-le-Grand*, 43. On the rural exodus in nineteenth-century France, see Evelyn B. Ackerman, 'Alternative to rural exodus: The development of the commune of Bonnières-sur-Seine in the nineteenth century', *French Historical Studies*, 10:1 (1977), 126–48.

86 Guerard, *Camp de Châlons*, 84.

87 Ralston, *Army of the Republic*, 21. On outdated French military manoeuvres, see Raoul Girardet, *La société militaire dans la France contemporaine 1815-1939* (Paris: Plon, 1953), 112–14.

88 General Trochu, *L'armée française en 1867* (Paris: Amyot, 1867), 205–28. The effectiveness of training courses on the Chassepot was similarly undermined by their overly theoretical nature. Holmes, *Road to Sedan*, 57–8, 192–8, 203–4.

89 Holmes, *Road to Sedan*, 22–3; McMillan, *Napoleon III*, 123–4.

2

Militarized environments during the 'terrible year' (1870–71)

In 1871, G. T. Robinson, the *Manchester Guardian*'s special correspondent, published a book on his experiences of the Franco-Prussian War. He contrasted the beauty of nature with the destruction of war, describing how the wind had tickled the vineyards near St-Quentin and how 'soon, too soon, this is all to be reduced to an arid, brown and barren waste'. For Robinson, war disrupted the peaceful and productive French countryside. Yet reminders of more serene times remained during the conflict. Travelling from the battlefield of Gravelotte back to Metz, he heard a 'lark singing high up in the air there to greet the coming sun. Not all the noise and din and carnage of yesterday has driven him away, and he sings gaily as ever, although his natal field is strewn with dead and dying men. What a lot of odd contrasts one finds in life'.[1] Robinson's reflections highlight how the conflict created new militarized environments that infringed on civilian ones. This was a source of wonder and sadness for observers. He also reminds us how the war took place in and through the environment.

The war started within the context of French anxieties about Prussia's ascendancy after its victory over Austria in 1866, which was compounded by months of bellicose diplomacy between France and Prussia over Bismarck's efforts to install a Hohenzollern prince on the Spanish throne. On 15 July 1870 the Second Empire mobilized its troops. The day after, Prussia and its German allies followed suit. On 19 July 1870 France declared war on Prussian, amidst much public enthusiasm. The Franco-Prussian War had begun. The Second Empire's inadequate military reforms and the French high command's failure to seize the initiative meant that the conflict mainly militarized the fields, forests, villages, and vineyards on the western side of the Rhine. After a series of disastrous battles and political crises, Napoleon III surrendered at Sedan on 2 September 1870. Sedan marked the end of the Second Empire but not the war; the refusal of the leaders of the newly formed republican Government of National Defence to cede any French territory meant that the conflict continued. The war therefore militarized urban centres and their hinterlands, including Paris, which held out against Prussia and its allies until the conclusion of the war in January 1871.

The French experience of the war was painful, traumatic, and humiliating. Along with the subsequent establishment and bloody repression of the Paris Commune, it became part of France's 'terrible year' which has stimulated a vast historiography that emerged in the immediate postwar years.[2] Yet the environment rarely takes centre stage in accounts of the war. In contrast, this chapter brings the environmental dimensions of the conflict to the fore. This matters because the war is part of the *longue durée* environmental history of war and militarization in modern French history; during its relatively short duration the environment became a tactical concern, battlefield site, and 'victim' in the sense that the combat transformed fields, forests, and other features of the countryside. 'Victim' is usually used to refer to humans. I use the term here to draw attention to how the war prompted contemporaries to apply these notions to nonhumans; animal protection organizations, as well as some soldiers, treated injured and slaughtered military horses as victims of the war. In such a way the humanitarian impulse that emerged during the war was extended to nonhumans, attesting to the porous boundaries between social, cultural and environmental history during this time.[3]

The heavy involvement of animals in the conflict is an overlooked aspect of its totalizing tendencies. So far, historians have mainly focused on the mobilization of human resources and the deployment of new military technologies when considering the Franco-Prussian War as a forerunner to total war in the twentieth century.[4] But we also need to consider its 'more-than-human' dimensions, which are apparent in a variety of ways. The war was only made possible through the active mobilization of nature. Both sides sought to mobilize terrain and animals to secure victory. Opponents in skirmishes and full-scale battles sought to exploit the lie of the land to their advantage and soldiers pillaged food and other supplies from the countryside. After French defeat at Sedan, militarized environments spread across the country as *francs-tireurs* partisans took to hills and forests, regular soldiers trained in hastily improvised rural camps, and the countryside around Paris became heavily militarized. But the war's environmental history did not end after the signing of the armistice as local authorities sought to control its potentially harmful biological traces by cleaning up former battlefield sites to mitigate the pollution from poorly buried human and animal corpses. I turn first to the ways in which the opposing armies sought to exploit environmental features.

Terrain and tactics

The term 'battlefield' is misleading as it can conjure up images of a flat, tightly defined, featureless space. The Franco-Prussian War amply underlines the term's inadequacy; battles took place in varied locales. As volunteer nurse Emile Delmas pointed out, large troop numbers and powerful modern weaponry meant that combat zones rarely had a 'confined range'. Instead, they sprawled across 'villages or hamlets, woods, ravines, watercourses, and undulations'. The Froeschwiller battlefield, for instance, included villages, tobacco fields, hop fields, orchards, vineyards, and woods near the summits.[5] The war did not take place on an environmental blank canvas.

The war's geographical aspects and the relationship between terrain and tactics fascinated non-combatant military observers. British Royal Artillery officer Henry Knollys travelled over 150 miles on horseback in the autumn of 1870 to analyse the influence of terrain on the outcome of battles. Interestingly, his perception of battlefields was mediated by his previous experiences of the militarized environments of British training grounds; the plain between Forbach and Spicheren was 'not unlike . . . Aldershot heath minus the heather and dust'.[6] British military historians have continued this fascination with terrain and tactics, often beginning their accounts of battles with a detailed description of the environment. George Hooper paid close attention to battlefield terrains in his 1897 history of the war, such as the 'irregularly undulating and wooded region' of Vionville.[7] Michael Howard's 1961 narrative similarly pays careful attention to topography, vegetation, and climate.[8]

But for combatants, geography could be a matter of life or death, victory or defeat. They fought within, through, and against environmental conditions, principally topography, vegetation, and weather. Both sides tried to turn these elements to their advantage, with Prussia and its allies enjoying greater success. At the battle of Gravelotte (18 August 1870), Prussian troops used forest cover in the Gorze valley to advance unseen up to French positions.[9] They also concealed themselves so well in the forests around Metz that, according to one observer, besieged

French army chiefs considered 'every wood . . . an enemy'.[10] Prussia and its allies succeeded in turning forests and other features of the militarized environment into natural allies.

Where existing terrain did not suit its purpose, the Prussian army adapted it. During the siege of Paris Prussian troops fortified their positions by breaching canals to flood fields to the north of the city, constructing communication trenches, and modifying gardens, woods, and fields.[11] Charles Winn, an English baron following Prussian forces, expressed his admiration of how Prussian army engineers 'did not fail to turn to account, by every species of artificial means, the natural strength of the ground' during the siege of Metz through the construction of rifle pits created at 'cunning angles along the edges of [the] valleys'.[12] Although Winn did not see it in such terms, his linking of 'artificial means' and 'natural strength' underscores the hybrid character of militarized environments. Of course, armies have long since modified the environments in which they have fought and famous military thinkers, such as Sun Tzu and Carl von Clausewitz, have provided the theoretical underpinnings.[13] But new technologies and Prussian geographical knowledge turned the militarized environments of the Franco-Prussian War into 'organic machines', to use Richard White's term, designed to facilitate the destruction of enemy forces.[14]

Like the Prussian army, French forces modified the environment. General Trochu tried to boost Paris's defences by destroying villages, roads, and railways within a fifty-mile radius of the city and ordering the razing of the Bois de Boulogne and St Cloud and Versailles forests.[15] Enemy observers even praised some of the positions French soldiers held before battles. Prussian commander Count Helmuth von Moltke described the advantages of the French position at Rote Berg on the Spicheren heights (Moselle) from which it was possible to survey the surrounding valleys, whilst drawing protection from ravines and woods. Rote Berg offered the French an 'exceptional advantage' with its 'precipitous and almost inaccessible cliff'.[16] Similarly, Major-General Albert Pfiste of the First Württemberg Landwehr Battalion underlined the benefits of the French position at Froeschwiller (Bas-Rhin): 'the vegetation and the conformation of the ground everywhere supply covered and hidden positions for reserves, giving opportunities for breaking out suddenly'.[17]

But favourable topography and vegetation cover was no guarantee of military success. At Rote Berg and Froeschwiller the French failed to convert their geographical advantage into victory. German troops experienced difficulties during their assault on Rote Berg's steep slopes, but they eventually prevailed; the French may have had a good position but they lacked sufficient artillery to stop them.[18] And during the battle of Froeschwiller on 6 August 1870, German forces overcame geographical obstacles to claim victory as the influence of decision-making, blunders, luck, weapon capabilities, and troop endurance came into play. During the battle, French cavalry units had failed to appreciate how features of the agricultural environment, such as trees, hedges, fields, and vineyards, would undermine their cavalry charges. In the event, cavalrymen and their horses became ensnared in hop poles and wire, making them easy targets for Prussian artillerymen.[19] In such a way, terrain and weather presented certain possibilities or 'affordances' but were not deterministic in influencing the outcome of battles.[20]

Froeschwiller points to the French army's failure to mobilize geography effectively. French observers lost no time in bemoaning this deficiency after the war. As he details in his 1871 account of the war, Delmas was shocked to arrive in the Vosges and find that the French government had actually prevented local communities from fortifying the area. Roads were still intact, no trenches had been dug, and trees were still standing. He felt that a few hours work (which local communities were apparently willing to undertake) would have made the terrain hostile for enemy soldiers.[21] Delmas's concerns were echoed in numerous other publications. In 1880, Alfred Duquet deplored the French army's geographical fecklessness, despairing at how French forces had failed to take up strategic positions on the hills above Beaumont-en-Argonne.[22]

Delmas's and Duquet's interventions contributed to a thorough and ongoing critique of military geographical knowledge in late nineteenth-century France, which at times became heavily politicized. A particularly scathing attack came from Pierre Defourby, the priest of Beaumont-en-Argonne and witness to the battle that took place there. He lamented how their poor reconnaissance and knowledge of terrain meant that French officers had failed to take up valuable positions on the hills. Instead, the French troops had camped in the valley and so German forces had easily surprised and over-run them. The lowpoint of this catalogue of errors was the French general who allegedly arrived at Sedan and mistook the Meuse River for the Moselle. In contrast to poor French military cartography, Defourby praised the extremely detailed maps used by the German army, which showed even 'the tiniest paths and smallest farms, complete with hedges and bushes'.[23] Defourby blamed the 1789 revolution for the farcical state of French geographical knowledge, illustrating how the state of military geographical knowledge became a pawn in the political struggle over secularization and education fought by Catholics and Republicans throughout nineteenth-century France.[24]

The army responded to such criticism by introducing courses in military geography at Saint-Cyr and the Ecole supérieure de la guerre, whilst the governments of the Third Republic promoted geography in schools. The discipline of geography in France therefore became increasingly militarized and was treated as integral to the nation's survival.[25]

Although she does not refer directly to the Franco-Prussian War, geographer Rachel Woodward offers a compelling critique of the militarization of geographical knowledge and education as 'the spatial expression of militarism and military activity'.[26] But the Franco-Prussian War shows how civilian observers also voiced militarized conceptions of terrain. For instance, Lewis Appleton, a passionate advocate of peace, made frequent mention of military vantage points, such as the 'good panoramic view' of the battlefield from Froeschwiller heights.[27] Attention to terrain and tactics served military purposes but it also held a wider appeal and seeped into civilian accounts.

In addition, Woodward overlooks militarized descriptions of the environment that do not fit neatly into the terrain and tactics framework. Some military officers were not immune to the aesthetic charms of the countryside. Describing the countryside around Saarbrücken and Spicheren, General Hans von Kretschman noted 'a strikingly beautiful view of the surrounding landscape. A zone of luxuriant woodland enframe[d] a region of hills of gentle ascent'.[28] In a similar vein, positioned at the Frénois heights before the Sedan battle, Prussian officer and political advisor Verdy du Vernois poetically recalled 'a beautiful and fresh morning, the layers of morning mist rose from the forest. Mixing with the bivouac fires, they form a sea of impenetrable clouds'.[29] Experiencing victory or defeat coloured memories. On the morning of the battle of Sedan, and in stark contrast to du Vernois's experience, George Bibescu, an officer attached to the French seventh army corps, recorded how the morning was 'sad and cloudy; it seemed as if the day was sorry to appear'.[30] These somewhat whimsical and romantic depictions of the environment illustrate how militarized geographical perspectives are more complex that Woodward allows.

Weathering the war

On the whole, experiences of the war's militarized environments were far less poetic than du Vernois remembered. Living, fighting, and working outdoors entailed often unpleasant exposure to the elements. Robinson recalled spending a wet night in the French trenches at Augny (near Metz): 'knee-deep in water, nowhere to sit down, unable to keep even a pipe alight, the very memory of it is miserable'.[31] Two months later French soldiers at Le Bourget, near Paris, were soaked 'to the bone' by 'torrential rain' and sunk into the sodden ground.[32] Heavy rain in the days leading up to Sedan further sapped French spirits. Cavalry captain Aragonnès d'Orcet wrote how repeated rain at Raucourt (Ardennes) 'contributed greatly to our suffering' as he and his unit had no option but to sleep in the mud.[33] Exposure to rain and mud drained the morale of French troops. But good weather could also raise their spirits. Officers remember how sunshine at Remilly on 30 August 1870 brought to life the 'beautiful nature' of the surrounding countryside, lifting spirits and imbuing troops with a sense of confidence and serenity.[34]

The weather also shaped the combat experience of Prussia and its allies. During the battle of Beaumont-eu-Argonne the mild weather and pleasant scenery apparently made the fighting more enjoyable for Bavarian soldiers.[35] The glow of victory seems to have imbued some accounts, which border on the pastoral. Prussian troops apparently slipped into the rhythms of country life during the siege of Paris, according to infantry general Albert von Holleben. They reportedly enjoyed the countryside around Paris, particularly towards the end of September when the weather was 'splendid' and the 'gardens were still full of flowers'. In glowing tones, von Holleben describes how soldiers tended sheep, repaired threshing machines, and gathered fruits and potatoes; 'we were both peasants and warriors'.[36] Here was the Prussian counterpart to the French myth of the soldier-peasant.

But nothing could disguise the fact that harsh weather brought misery to both sides. The environmental hardships of the trenches during the First World War are well known (see chapter 4). The winter of 1870–71 provided a partial taste of what was to come. Baron von der Goltz documents how during the siege of Metz 'the skies opened wide their sluices' turning the army camps into 'extensive swamps'. The poor weather created health problems; the rain washed away the thin layers of earth covering human and horse remains and a 'penetrating odour of decaying corpses of men and horses empoisoned the air'.[37] It was equally hard, if not impossible, to escape the exceptionally cold winter weather, when temperatures reportedly dropped to '15 below freezing point'.[38] Whilst preparing for an attack at Le Bourget, General Trochu's troops suffered in bitterly cold conditions that made it impossible to dig trenches and erect tents. The lack of firewood fully exposed the already demoralized soldiers to the biting north wind and almost a thousand troops suffered from frostbite.[39]

As well as making conditions miserable for combatants, cold weather even threatened to undermine physical aspects of the militarized environment. During the siege of Paris, Prussian troops feared that freezing weather would render useless their flooding of the countryside. They repeatedly tested the solidity of the ice covering the areas they had flooded to see if French forces would be able to cross them in the event of an attack.[40] Snow storms also hindered accurate firing during the siege.[41] Yet the cold did not put ingenuity on hold. On 8 and 9 December 1870, sculptors serving in the Nineteenth Battalion of the National Guard in Paris's thirteenth arrondissement crafted statues out of snow. Jean-Alexandre-Joseph Falguière's *La Résistance*, a masculinized female figure defiantly crossing her arms, became the most celebrated snow statue, and drew press and public attention.[42] Prussian and French troops experienced the same cold weather, but they imbued it with different meanings. For the former, it threatened their siege installations. For the latter, it provided the material for a defiant sculpture and became part of artistic production during the war (even if, like the ice, French hopes ultimately melted).

As had been the case during the American Civil War half a decade earlier, weather conditions were an important aspect of the human–nonhuman history of the Franco-Prussian War.[43] Another was the relationship between humans and animals within the militarized environment.

Animals at war

Animals inhabited the war as symbols. On the eve of war, journalist Jules Clarétie imagined two black crows flying through the grey skies over the Rhine delighting over the forthcoming carnage when war would 'bloody the green waters of the Rhine [and] redden the hills'. As they flew, the elder crow explained to his young companion how 'the time of huge meals has come' and how they would feast on the corpses. Consciously or unconsciously, Clarétie tapped into long-standing cultural assumptions that crows delight in feeding on dead bodies on battlefields. He used the crows' glee to underscore the horrors of war.[44] But animals were more than symbols. They became physically embroiled in the war as unintentional auxiliaries to combat.

Horses played a particularly prominent role. Both sides mobilized thousands of horses, even if haemorrhoids and other ailments had prevented Napoleon III from riding his horse during the ceremonial parade as his troops left Paris. Armies mobilized horse extensively on the battlefield, despite the fact that traditional cavalry charges were becoming increasingly obsolete. Like its deployment of topography, French military incompetence meant that the army failed to make the best use of its equine auxiliaries. Certain French cavalry officers struggled to recognize the difference between training grounds and battlefields. Aragonnès d'Orcet delighted in the regimented French cavalry charges at Reichshoffen/Froeschwiller and took pride from the fact that Marshal Patrice MacMahon judged that they exhibited the same high standards displayed during manoeuvres.[45] But such charges entailed a huge loss of life on the battlefield. Hundreds of men and horses were killed or injured as they charged over vineyards, fences, and hop-plantations under heavy fire. Aragonnès d'Orcet's preference for form over function illustrates how the French army had failed to modernize its cavalry units.

The greater use of artillery and the limitations of horses over rugged and steep terrain rendered traditional cavalry charges largely obsolete as an effective military tactic. Lieutenant-Colonel Bonie, trying to draw some lessons from the war, lamented that French cavalry charges started at an 'absurd distances' and how, after galloping for 2,000 yards, the horses were 'completely blown on arriving at the wished for point'.[46] Sedan further brought the disadvantages of traditional cavalry charge into sharp focus. Here, repeated French cavalry charges failed to make any difference to the battle, with many men and horses falling down declivities and quarries under heavy fire in and around Garenne forest.[47] Aragonnès d'Orcet himself narrowly avoided falling down a precipice due to the actions of his 'brave' horse which jumped over a high hedgerow to safety.[48] Although many would hesitate to attribute bravery, a supposedly human quality, to animals, Aragonnès d'Orcet had no such qualms.[49]

Military culture and experience shaped how the different armies mobilized the same animal species. Prussian forces had built on their experience of their 1866 war with Austria to improve their deployment of cavalry units. They successfully used horse-borne reconnaissance teams to gather intelligence and prepare the terrain for infantry and artillery units.[50]

Before Sedan, horses, like human soldiers, lived in poor conditions both on and off the battlefield. Bonie remembers how during the poor weather of August 1870 horses were as 'miserable' as the soldiers: 'the wind blew away a portion of their rations, and, pressing together, with their heads out, they endeavoured to protect themselves against the weather'.[51] The specificity of place played a role in how the horses fared. At Verdun, Knollys observed how the horses had become 'surprisingly sleek and fat' from feeding on the area's abundant foliage.[52]

The fate of France's militarized horses was bound to that of the army. As the Sedan battle became increasingly hopeless for the French, Napoleon III surrendered along with 83,000 men and 6,000 horses.[53] But, unwilling to let their horses fall into German hands, French soldiers released many of them. As the horses galloped off, horrific scenes ensued. Bonie remembers how the horses, 'deprived of their usual food . . . commenced to fight, and tore each other to pieces'. As such, 'defeat did not spare them any more than ourselves'.[54] For the *Daily News*' correspondent, the horses' fate symbolized the futility of the battle; wounded horses 'stood dismally here and there, wondering, perhaps, what it could all mean'.[55] Like the French themselves, the army's horses seemed defeated and distraught.

The nascent French animal protection movement was powerless to prevent harm to animals during the war (the French Société protectrice des animaux had been founded in 1845 and the 1850 Grammont Law prohibited the abuse of animals in public).[56] Contemporaries were shocked at the wartime treatment of horses. Winn, who otherwise revelled in the excitement of war, was disturbed by an image of a wounded horse, bearing the marks of at least five bullet holes, which wandered around the muddy ground trying to find food after the battle of Gravelotte. This was 'one wretched animal I have not been able to forget amongst the many sights of human suffering I witnessed'.[57] The British Royal Society for the Prevention of Cruelty to Animals (RSPCA) was so concerned about the suffering of horses 'which have rendered perhaps the most valuable service to the soldier' that it wrote to the French and German ambassadors, urging that wounded horses should be shot to put an end to their suffering.[58] This intervention on behalf of the horses mirrored the concerns for human health expressed by the Red Cross and other organizations.[59] But unlike the attention devoted to wounded soldiers and civilians, little, if anything, was provided for equine casualties of the war.

French observers portrayed the Prussian slaughter of horses as further proof of that nation's barbarity, atrocities to be filed alongside the killing of innocent French men, women, and children. At Morsbronn, Delmas watched Prussian troops, whom he labelled 'executioners', slaughter only lightly wounded horses. The operation did not run smoothly. Bullets frequently missed the horses' vital organs and the animals ran off with 'jets of blood' squirting from them. On being shot again, the horses stumbled forward, let out a 'last and loud sigh', and died. Delmas claimed the Prussians were not slaughtering for humanitarian reasons. Rather, they were unwilling to take the horses with them or leave them with the local population. The 'barbarous spectacle' supposedly provided evidence of the Prussians' 'merciless and logical dispositions' that they followed 'without emotion' and 'responsibility'.[60] For Delmas, the Prussian treatment of horses reflected their wider inhumanity and indifference to suffering. Bertrand Taithe argues that 'in putting so much emphasis on the sentimental representation of civilians suffering at the hand of their German tormentors, the French turned the war into a conflict of values and civilization'.[61] Bringing to light the alleged mistreatment of horses was part of this struggle.

But Prussian combatants were not indifferent to the horses' suffering. Von der Goltz noted how many were left 'motionless awaiting death by hunger; half broken down, some sat on their haunches, others licked the slime at their feet . . . Scarcely to be distinguished from the universal grey of the soil, carcases of horses lay in the morass'.[62] Furthermore, French army horses lived and died in appalling conditions. Besieged horses at Metz, like their human counterparts, were on restricted rations. French troops conducted sorties out of the city in search of leaves and branches but this was not enough to sustain the horses which slowly began to starve. Some resorted to stripping bark off trees and eating each other.[63]

Dead horses at Metz posed a problem for French troops. In the absence of disinfectant, and to guard against the 'pernicious action of miasmas', they dug deep trenches in which to bury the dead horses.[64] Early nineteenth-century public hygienists, such as Alexandre Parent-Duchâtelet, who abhorred the health threat posed by rotting animal carcasses, would no doubt have applauded the digging of horse-graves.[65] But the soldiers' efforts at Metz could not hide the vast quantities of rotting equine corpses. After the siege, Quaker relief worker John Bellows recorded how a stench comparable to a 'slaughterhouse' hung over the site of General Achille Bazaine's former camp (where between 30,000–40,000 horses had been reportedly slaughtered during the siege) despite the frost and subsequent Prussian attempts to clean up the site.[66]

Dead horses provided visual and olfactory evidence of the war's destructive character and traced its geography. Alongside human corpses buried in hastily improvised cemeteries, decaying horse carcasses and graves became a common sight. Travelling along the road from Givonne to Daigny (near Sedan), Appleton saw a land 'thick with graves of men, of noble steeds, who knew no malice, and perpetrated no wrong'.[67] Dead horses represented the horror of the war in fictional accounts, such as Marie-Louise Gagneur's novel *Chair à canon* with its descriptions of the 'hideous' sight of dead horses with their 'bloated stomachs' and 'legs sticking up in the air'.[68] Their perceived innocence added to the tragedy.

Armies mobilized horses to fight in cavalry units and to transport men and *matériel*. But hungry soldiers and civilians also used them to supplement their diets. For one French soldier trapped in Metz, eating horse meat was bearable with salt and lentils, even if officers kept the best cuts for themselves. Infantrymen would sneak over to cavalry encampments, capture and kill a horse, and sell the meat. But it was apparently best not to think too carefully about the meat's provenance when taking it to the wine merchant at Porte de Thionville who would grill the horse-flesh.[69] Parisians similarly consumed horseflesh during the siege of their city; up to 650 were slaughtered each day for the table.[70] Horses were devoured by weapons on the battlefield and literally by hungry soldiers and civilians.

As well as horses, wartime conditions pushed besieged Parisians to turn to other, rarely consumed animals. Some of these culinary adventures have become part of the city's mythology. One notable episode was when a select group of wealthy inhabitants of the famously food-obsessed city infamously feasted on the zoo's elephants, yaks, and zebras. In this case, commercialism (the meat was purchased from exclusive butchers) and a desire to demonstrate character, explain the devouring of these exotic meats, rather than the exigencies of hunger.[71]

For those who could not secure elephant or yak meat, domestic animals were the only alternative. Nathan Sheppard, an American who kept a journal throughout the Paris siege, attended a dinner consisting of such delicacies as 'Jugged cat with mushroom', 'Roast donkey and potatoes', 'Rats, peas, and celery', and 'Mice on toast'; 'it would be difficult to take a restaurant meal now in Paris, without being served one of the animals', he concluded.[72] Like the zoo animals, dogs, rats, and cats were only available to the rich; a rat cost almost three francs in January 1871 (or the daily pay of two soldiers).[73] If dog, cat, donkey, or rat meat was too expensive, eating the odd blackbird was another way of easing hunger pains.[74] The eating of these animals highlights how the war altered human–animal relations and bestowed new roles on animals: pets and pests became food.

Besieged Parisians mobilized animals in other ways. Along with hot air balloons, carrier pigeons became a vital means of communication. After the Prussians had severed the normal communication routes that linked Paris to the outside world, besieged citizens sent out hot air balloons with pigeons on board. The pigeons then flew back to the capital carrying official despatches and private messages on microscopic photographs.[75] L'Espérance, the pigeon-fanciers' club of Paris, oversaw the recruitment of the birds, their training, and their release from the balloons. The figures given for the number of birds and messages vary, from 354 to 407 birds and from 95,000 to 250,000 messages.[76] One estimate has it that just over 25 per cent of the birds reached home,[77] another, that 50 birds managed the return journey home on 59 occasions.[78] Harsh winter weather, the birds' limited training, and the attention of avian predators and human hunters contributed to this relatively low success rate.

Nonetheless, the pigeons provided an invaluable service and Parisians so respected them that they were spared from the dinner table. They also achieved fame overseas. Sydney Hodge wrote a poem celebrating how the pigeons carried messages 'day by day' through 'storm and shine'. The RSPCA's newspaper celebrated the pigeons' 'military skill' and hoped that their actions would lead to greater justice and kindness being shown towards the 'poor despised pigeon'.[79] These animal rights campaigners argued that the contribution and 'skill' of pigeons meant that they had earned the right to respect and recognition from society in peacetime. They aimed to use the war to change attitudes towards animals. The role of animals in war therefore became part of the wider nineteenth-century campaign for animal rights.[80]

A final way in which war modified human–animal relationships was that the siege brought rural animals into the quasi-militarized environment of Paris. Refugees from surrounding villages transported their animals with them as they fled to the relative safety of Paris, much to the consternation and amusement of urbanites. At this time of severe food shortages, sheep and cattle grazed in Luxembourg Gardens and the Bois de Boulogne. Soldiers in the military camp established in the city centre, meanwhile, stabled their horses on the banks of the Seine.[81] As these episodes suggest, the siege blurred the lines between the countryside and the city as elements of rural life became features of the urban environment. At the same time, the war militarized the French countryside in a variety of ways.

The militarized countryside

As well as creating battlefield militarized environments amongst the fields, forests, vineyards, and villages of eastern France, soldiers sought provisions and other supplies from the land. France's chaotic mobilization, during which supply routes were severely disrupted, placed a burden on the countryside's resources as ill-disciplined and hungry French troops pillaged food from peasants.[82] French soldiers were not the only pillagers; during the siege of Metz, 10,000 of their Prussian counterparts fanned out into surrounding villages in search of provisions.[83] Such sights were depressing for Clarétie who was apparently moved to tears when he saw Prussian soldiers taking potatoes from fields at Givonne (it is unclear whether he felt the same emotion when French soldiers pillaged from farmers).[84]

Rural communities resented the militarization of their land. Their disgruntlement was justified as wartime manpower shortages in the fields led to a contraction of cultivated land.[85] But their plight did not go unnoticed. Fundraising events helped humanitarian and financial aid to reach them from as far afield as Northumberland, Scandinavia, and Quebec.[86] As part of the postwar reconstruction process, Quakers oversaw the importing of seeds and animals into the French countryside. In August 1871 James Long brought a 400-head herd from Spain to the Loire region. A group of Spanish farmers helped the cows settle into their new home following reports that they were 'restive' during milking being unaccustomed to the French language.[87]

Military camps and training grounds further militarized the countryside. Due to poor French planning during the mobilization, the Second Empire based its operational troops in hastily improvised camps.[88] Chaos similarly ruled at Châlons Camp. On arriving at the camp after defeat at Froeschwiller, MacMahon's defeated and demoralized troops laid waste to the camp in a frenzy of looting and drinking. Even so MacMahon managed to form an army of 130,000 men between 13 and 17 August. But on hearing that Prussian forces were reportedly twenty-five miles from the camp, MacMahon ordered its destruction. In the end, Prussian troops entered the camp, seized *matériel*, and remained there until November 1872.[89] The camp's role as an imperial spectacle and military school ended in this ignominious way.

After French defeat at Sedan, the government of National Defence established new military camps, thereby intensifying the militarization of the countryside and its geographical extent. The training of

Gardes nationaux mobiles in these camps was a major component of Gambetta's 'mass militarisation' of French society.[90] Overall, the camps housed 635,838 men, 250,000 of whom were still stationed in them at the armistice. The camps were hastily improvised and often situated in poorly chosen sites; autumn rains submerged some of them.[91] So while camp regulations stressed that 'well-observed' discipline was 'the principal force of the army', poor training and living conditions led to troop revolts.[92]

'Mass militarisation' took nongovernmental forms with the creation of *francs-tireurs* partisan groups who exploited mountainous and/or wooded terrain to launch attacks and ambushes on German troops and supply lines. They effectively harassed the Prussian forces besieging Paris, who reportedly felt 'like cowboys in Indian country'.[93] Regular soldiers loathed and feared *francs-tireurs*. Despite being an observer, British officer Knollys nervously scanned hedgerows with his field-glasses for any sign of them.[94] But like regular soldiers, *francs-tireurs* suffered from rain and cold temperatures and modified the terrain in which they operated. For instance, Pierre Bliard and his men set fire to woods near Paris in January 1871.[95]

To a greater degree than their regular counterparts, *francs-tireurs* celebrated the aesthetic qualities of the environments in which they fought. In language that Second World War resistance fighters would later echo (see chapter 6), they contrasted the freedom they felt in the hills with the stifling atmosphere of the occupied plains. Comte de Belleval records how in the Haute-Saône's wooded hills 'one breathe[d] freely in this ever so pure atmosphere'. Even his two companions, who were 'more positivists that poets', were awestruck by the 'splendid panorama' that they observed in the hills beyond Giromagny. Descriptions of the romantic splendour of forests and mountains, with their fir trees 'majestic like the pillars of a giant cathedral', served to invest the *francs-tireurs*' resistance with a sense of poetic heroism, creating a semi-militarized sense of the sublime.[96]

Despite the spread of militarized environments throughout the countryside, it was possible to find pockets of tranquillity. Even at Bazeilles, where an 'odious, deathly smell' hung in the air after the Sedan battle, roses and blue flowers 'blossomed peacefully' in the ruined gardens.[97] The militarized environment was not all encompassing; remnants of civilian environments remained. At a wood near St Privat, Bellows compared the war-torn French environment with the peaceful English one he had recently left:

Here all was repose. The dew hung bright on the branches and sparkled on the carpet of mosses and lichens on either hand, and the air was too still even to rustle the few dead leaves that still clung to the trees. It was just such a wood as I was walking through a few weeks since on the banks of the Canal at Cirencester.[98]

But as a pacifist and aid-worker, Bellows was not blind to war's material scars. On closer inspection he found that the apparently 'ploughed land' at St Privat was actually terrain 'trampled by thousands of footmarks, and furrowed deep by wheels of cannon'. Elsewhere, a 'lovely ravine' was juxtaposed with the 'débris of battle', including broken tent poles and helmets.[99] Traces of human and animal deaths haunted the apparently peaceful nature of former battlefields.

Other observers echoed this narrative of a disrupted countryside, creating a sense of opposition between peacetime and wartime environments. Appleton saw scenes of 'blank desertion' near Metz, where shells had 'furrowed fields' and reduced poplar trees to an environment that was 'desolate and bare'. The land was equally devastated at Froeschwiller: 'those once smiling plains and vine-clad slopes are torn ruthlessly asunder, only to receive the mangled remains of ten thousand victims, and to be deluged with precious lifeblood'.[100] Death had saturated and transformed the earth. Robinson feared that 'it will be some years before this country [around Metz] is fruitful once again. When I last saw those hill sides there was not a vegetable vestige left on them'.[101]

Appleton, as a pacifist, may have intended his horrific descriptions of the war-torn environment to underscore the conflict's barbarity. And Robinson, as a journalist, may have highlighted the war's devastation to add colour to his account. But military observers were also struck by the countryside's rapid transformation. Von der Goltz noted the combat's environmental impact: 'What a country there was round Metz! All around were villages and farms burnt down, fields devastated, gardens trampled under foot, and to crown all, far and wide, fields of corpses'.[102] Knollys also recorded ample evidence of how war had altered the countryside at Sedan and beyond. At La Moncelle the 'clover-crop was trampled and the ploughed land beaten hard by the thread of the throng; the hedge was broken down and the trees scarred with bullet-marks'. At Mouzon, meanwhile, the countryside had been stripped bare as if 'a flight of locusts had passed over the land, and had thrown the inhabitants many degrees backwards in the scale of prosperity'.[103] The speed of this transformation struck Knollys and others. Delmas observed how Froeschwiller was peaceful and happy at 6am on 6 August 1870. By midday, buildings were burnt, trees felled, houses trampled, and guns and soldiers were everywhere.[104]

War therefore appeared as an agent of destruction to civilians and officers alike. The impact of militarized environments on the countryside, particularly in northern and eastern France, laid bare the social and environmental ramifications of this 'more-than-human' conflict. But these did not end with the signing of an armistice at the end of January 1871.

Neutralizing the battlefields

By the end of January 1871 the French army was demoralized and depleted after a series of military defeats in the provinces. The final straw was the disintegration of General Bourbaki's forces near the Swiss border on 26 January 1871. With hunger stalking besieged Parisians, the French government called a ceasefire and negotiated an armistice with the Germans. But France's troubles continued. Disgruntled with the National Assembly's decision to base itself at Versailles and the other so-called 'measures against Paris', radical National Guardsman and politicians resisted the French army's attempts to reclaim the artillery cannon at Montmartre in mid-March and declared the Paris Commune. The Commune's radical political programme and its bloody repression by the French army in May 1871 have understandably held the attention of public and scholarly interest.[105] But as events unfurled in Paris, efforts were made elsewhere to neutralize the war's militarized environments.

The most pressing task was burying the dead. Burials began during the conflict itself, usually the day after the battle. Heavy casualty rates and high temperatures in August 1870 meant that prompt burials were of the essence. Consequently, fresh mounds of earth were invariably evidence that a battle had taken place in the vicinity. The emphasis on speed sacrificed the dignity of the dead and caused other problems. Not least, the shallow depth of burial sites meant that corpses broke through the topsoil. To remedy the situation, local communities had erected makeshift wooden crosses and German occupation authorities exhumed and burnt bodies at certain sites, such as Sedan, to prevent the spreading of disease. But these were only temporary measures.

Given public hygienists' oft-expressed fear that inadequately buried bodies caused disease, Belgian authorities were deeply alarmed by the makeshift graves on the French side of the border. On hearing reports that dogs were digging up limbs, birds of prey feasted on horse corpses, and freezing temperatures had opened up 'large cracks' in the ground, they sent a team in March 1871 to investigate ways of preventing 'noxious miasmas' spreading beyond the former Sedan battlefield. The team of doctors, chemists, and engineers, headed by Dr Lante, found numerous instances of poorly buried human and animal bodies that produced reportedly insufferable smells. Clarétie had proved prophetic; crows were indeed feeding on corpses. Through exhuming and burning dead horses then burying their ashes under a layer of lime and earth planted with hemp and oats, the Belgians claimed to have neutralized thousands of graves. Monsieur Créteur alone disinfected 3,213 graves, of which 1,986 were human and 1,227 animal.[106] The sense of relief that the Belgians had neutralized the threat to public health was palpable. Albert Brun, under-prefect of Sedan, praised their work and promised that the relevant French authorities would monitor and protect the tumuli and make sure that inquisitive dogs left them alone.[107]

As the years passed, French authorities established more permanent and solemn cemeteries. The law of 4 April 1873 issued detailed instructions, fixing the price of land on which the tombs lay to allow the state to expropriate the land. In addition, soldiers buried in isolated spots were to be exhumed and reburied in larger cemeteries.[108] Such measures were intended to meet France's obligations under the postwar Treaty of Frankfurt (1871), but they did not please farmers, on whose land the graves lay. Many began to demand compensation for lost revenue due to the disruption caused to crop planting and some neglected to maintain the graves. Meanwhile, one landowner near Belfort sued the government because decomposing corpses had polluted his water supply.[109] In such a way, the rotting corporal remnants of combat continued to exert an influence on local ecologies long after the cessation of hostilities. Nonetheless, the government succeeded in burying 87,396 soldiers at a cost of 2,887,896.21 francs. But it could not stamp out vandalism to German graves and monuments; the eagle on the German monument at Mars-la-Tour was removed so many times that local authorities eventually decided not to replace it.[110]

Alongside erecting memorials, visiting the former battlefields was another way for the French to honour the memory of their dead and seek meaning in the war.[111] Publishers produced guidebooks to cater to the demand. But battlefield visitors expecting vistas of devastation were likely to feel disappointed. In his guidebook to Froeschwiller battlefield,

Alfred Touchemolin began with a description of the 'green valley' where the battle had taken place, complete with its 'joyful panorama' of forests and wheat and tobacco fields. The illustrations accompanying the text reinforced the impression of an area returned to peaceful productivity. One entitled 'Vineyards and orchards where the charge of the 8th and 9th Cuirassiers passed' depicted a tranquil bucolic scene that bore no evidence of the charge of 1,200 armoured cavalrymen and their horses at Morsbronn. Another, of the 'General view of Prussian positions from Morsbronn plateau', showed two travellers absorbing a serene panorama of trees, hills, and churches as birds flew overhead.[112] The countryside, briefly but often brutally disrupted by the war, had regained its peaceful atmosphere, at least according to this guidebook.

Memorialization often entails the attempt to freeze or maintain environments in a particular state to encourage the construction and perpetuation of memory. Yet the fact that memorial sites exist in dynamic environments complicates immeasurably any attempt to 'embalm' them.[113] This was apparent after the Franco-Prussian War. As Touchemolin reported, vegetation growth was rapidly effacing the traces of conflict. Aquatic plants 'half covered' two crosses by a stream in the village of Reichshoffen. In a nearby forest clearing, where a couple of streams provided a 'peaceful murmur', two unmarked graves were 'already hidden under the grass'.[114] In this case, the environment's vibrancy posed a potential obstacle to the war's memorialization.

But nature could also be harnessed to remember. Both France and Germany mobilized trees as symbols of resistance and remembrance. Trees on Elasshausen plateau that were too riddled with bullets to be sold for wood became emblems of resistance for French commentators, whilst German authorities demanded that trees at Wissembourg be replanted to return the site to its 1870 state so that it would act as a more faithful reminder of their victory.[115]

Although former battlefields were liable to change, they remained impregnated with meaning. Georges Ducrocq's 1911 account of his travels in Alsace and Lorraine (which were then part of Germany) related how forty years after the conflict the 'vast plains' around Metz were now 'covered with wheat, clover, and oats'. Nonetheless, the land was still 'soaked with the blood of our fathers' and 'tiny wooden crosses dotted the landscape'.[116] Borders had changed, but the site's significance as a place of French sacrifice and loss remained. The evocation of soil seeped in French blood served to maintain a vivid connection between the French nation and the lost provinces.

Commentators declared that these former militarized environments held lessons for the French. According to Ducrocq, the French population at Wissembourg still brought their children to the 'summit of the hill' to teach them about the heroic resistance of French forces, a patriotic education that he believed would eventually 'bear fruit'.[117] Likewise, right-wing nationalist writer Maurice Barrès, whose home town of Charmes had been occupied by the Prussians during the war, claimed that the land filled with French war dead near Metz would inspire 'discipline' within the French. Individuals, he asserted, needed to root themselves collectively 'in the land of our dead'.[118]

As well as imbuing them with political and nationalist meaning, French commentators sought to re-militarize the former battlefields. In 1905 Henri Bonnal, former Professor of Military History, Strategy, and Tactics at the École Supérieure de Guerre (who had also seen combat during the 1870–71 war), asserted that battlefield environments held an educational value for soldiers. He believed that with 'a bit of imagination' French soldiers could use photographs of battlefield sites to reconstruct the military history and draw lessons.[119] The militarized character of these environments lingered on.

Conclusion

Well over a century after the end of the war, the French are still encouraged to visit former battlefield sites of the Franco-Prussian War. The Parc naturel régional de Lorraine has developed a tour of the war's memorial sites to boost tourism and enhance their educational value. But the sites have now lost their nationalistic meanings and the emphasis is now on reconciliation.[120] But the Parc's re-interpretation of the sites underlines how war is still remembered and understood within the (changed) environment in which it was once fought. It reminds us too that the war was fought within, through, and, at times, against, the environment. It was only made possible through the active mobilization of nature. In this 'more-than-human' history, militarized environments became contact zones between soldiers and the environment and between military and civilian spheres. As the next chapter shows, the war had further environmental ramifications. After 1871, successive governments of the newly installed Third Republic sought to remake France's military geographies to strengthen and rejuvenate the army and, by extension, the nation. In doing so, they oversaw the creation of new militarized environments.

Notes

1 G. T. Robinson, *The Fall of Metz: An Account of the Seventy Days' Siege and the Battle Which Preceded It* (London: Bradbury, Evans & Co, 1871), 67, 83.
2 For an excellent introduction to the conflict's historiography, see Bertrand Taithe, *Citizenship and Wars: France in Turmoil, 1870–1871* (London: Routledge, 2001), 5–16.
3 Rachel Chrastil, 'The French Red Cross, war readiness and civil society, 1866–1914', *French Historical Studies* 31:3 (2008), 445–76; Bertrand Taithe, *Defeated Flesh: Welfare, Warfare, and the Making of Modern France* (Manchester: Manchester University Press, 1999).
4 Taithe, *Citizenship and Wars*, 22–30.
5 Emile Delmas, *De Froeschwiller à Paris: Notes prises sur les champs de bataille* (Paris: Alponse Lemerre, 1871), 36–8.
6 Henry Knollys, *From Sedan to Saarbruck, via Verdun, Gravelotte, and Metz: By an Officer of the Royal Artillery* (London: Tinsley Brothers, 1870), 37, 45, 195, 243.
7 George Hooper, *The Campaign of Sedan: The Downfall of the Second Empire August–September 1870* (London: George Bell and Sons, 1897), 168–9.
8 Howard's description of Froeschwiller ridge, in which he highlights the French troops' *'position magnifique'* with its 'pattern of alternating spurs and re-entrants three to four miles in extent, comparable to a system of bastions and curtains; a natural fortress-system making possible a devastating cross-fire', is typical. *The Franco-Prussian War: The German Invasion of France, 1870–1871* (London: Hart-Davis, 1961), 105.
9 François Roth, *La guerre de 1870* (Paris: Fayard, 1990), 77; Howard, *The Franco-Prussian War*, 203.
10 Robinson, *Fall of Metz*, 198.
11 Roth, *Guerre de 1870*, 207; Howard, *Franco-Prussian War*; 329, Helmuth von Moltke, *The Franco-German War of 1870–71*, trans. Archibald Forbes (London: James R. Osgood, McIlvaine & Co., 1893), 140.
12 Charles Winn, *What I Saw of the War at the Battles of Speichern, Gorze, and Gravelotte: A Narrative of Two Months Campaigning with the Prussian Army of the Moselle* (Edinburgh: William Blackwood, 1870), 140.
13 Arthur Westing, *Warfare in a Fragile World: Military Impact on the Human Environment* (London: Taylor & Francis, 1980), 14; Sun Tzu, *The Art of War*, trans. Thomas Cleary (Boston: Shambhola Publications, 1988), 17, 44, 143; Carl von Clausewitz, *On War*, ed. and trans. Michael Howard and Peter Paret (Princeton: Princeton University Press, 1984), 417–52.
14 Richard White, *The Organic Machine: The Remaking of the Columbia River* (New York: Hill and Wang, 1995). On hybridity, see 'A Cyborg Manifesto' in Donna Haraway, *Simians, Cyborgs, and Women: The Reinvention of Nature* (New York: Routledge, 1991), 149–81. On the use of new technologies to

wage war, see Daniel Pick, *War Machine: The Rationalization of Slaughter in the Modern Age* (New Haven: Yale University Press, 1996), 177.

15 Geoffrey Wawro, *The Franco-Prussian War: The German Conquest of France in 1870–1871* (Cambridge: Cambridge University Press, 2003), 237.

16 Von Moltke, *Franco-German War*, 21.

17 Albert Pfister, 'The Battle of Wörth', in J. F. Maurice (ed. and trans.), *The Franco-German War 1870–71 by Generals and Other Officers Who Took Part in the Campaign* (London: Swan Sonnenshein, 1900), 84.

18 Winn, *What I Saw of the War*, 16.

19 Roth, *Guerre de 1870*, 48.

20 The confrontation at Froeschwiller was part of a battle that also took place around Reichshoffen and Woerth and is variously referred to by any of these place names. Throughout this chapter I refer to the place closest to the particular events that I discuss. On affordances, or the possibilities that an object (or environment) suggests to the human brain, see Carl Knappett, *Thinking Through Material Culture: An Interdisciplinary Perspective* (Philadelphia: University of Pennsylvania Press, 2005), 45–50.

21 Delmas, *Froeschwiller à Paris*, 140.

22 Alfred Duquet, *Froeschwiller, Châlons, Sedan* (Paris: G. Charpentier, 1880), 306.

23 Pierre Defourny, *L'armée de Mac-Mahon et la bataille de Beaumont (en Argonne): Lettres à Madame Urquhart sur la guerre et la situation présente* (Brussels: Devaux et Cie, 1871), 42–4, 56–60.

24 Ralph Gibson, 'Why Republicans and Catholics couldn't stand each other in the nineteenth century', in Frank Tallett and Nicholas Atkin (eds), *Religion, Society and Politics in France since 1789* (London: Hambledon, 1991), 107–20; Robert Gildea, *Education in Provincial France, 1800–1914: A Study of Three Departments* (Oxford: Clarendon, 1983); Theodore Zeldin (ed.), *Conflicts in French Society: Anticlericalism, Education, and Morals in the Nineteenth Century* (London: Allen & Unwin, 1970).

25 Pierre Boulanger, *La géographie militaire française, 1871–1939* (Paris: Economica, 2002); Pierre Boulanger, *Géographie militaire* (Paris: Ellipses, 2006), 14–17; Paul Claval, *Histoire de la géographie française de 1870 à nos jours* (Paris: Editions Nathan, 1998), 19, 34. Geography, however, had not been totally absent from military education during the Second Empire. See Félix Oger, *Géographie physique, militaire, historique, politique, administrative et statistique de la France* (Paris: Mallet-Bachelier, 1860). On the militarization of geography in Britain, see D. R. Stobbart, 'Geography and war: The "new geography" and the "new army" in England, 1899–1914', *Political Geography*, 11:1 (1992), 87–99.

26 Rachel Woodward, 'From military geography to militarism's geographies: Disciplinary engagements with the geographies of militarism and military activities', *Progress in Human Geography*, 29:6 (2005), 724.

27 Lewis Appleton, *Reminiscences of a Visit to the Battlefields of Sedan, Gravelotte, Spicheren, and Wörth and the Bombarded Towns of Thionville, Metz, Strasbourg, Bitche* (London: Simpkin, Marshall & Co., 1872), 76, 91.

28 Hans von Kretschman, 'The Battle of Vionville-Mars-la-Tour', in Maurice, *Franco-German War*, 106.

29 Quoted in Roth, *Guerre de 1870*, 121.

30 Georges Pierre Bibesco, *Campagne de 1870: Belfort, Reims, Sedan* (Paris: Henri Plon, 1872), 137.

31 Robinson, *Fall of Metz*, 159.

32 Henri Dichard, *Une page de l'histoire du siège de Paris par les Prussiens: La Première affaire du Bourget par un garde mobile* (Paris: Chez Mauger, Capart et Cie, 1871), 28.

33 Gaspard-Marie-Stanislas-Xavier Aragonnès d'Orcet, *Froeschwiller, Sedan et la Commune, racontés par un témoin*, ed. L. le Peletier d'Aunay (Paris: Perrin, 1910), 105.

34 Commandant Corbin and Colonel d'Andigné quoted in Auguste Alexandre Ducrot, *La Journée de Sedan* (Paris: E. Dentu, 1871), 94.

35 Roth, *Guerre de 1870*, 77; Howard, *Franco-Prussian War*, 203.

36 Albert von Holleben, 'The investment of Paris', in Maurice, *Franco-German War*, 274–5.

37 Baron von der Goltz, 'St Privat-la-Montagne and Metz', in Maurice, *Franco-German War*, 192–3.

38 John Bellows, *The Track of the War around Metz and the Fund for the Non-combatant Sufferers* (London: Trübner and Co., 1871), 49.

39 Howard, *Franco-Prussian War*, 359.

40 Von Holleben, 'Investment of Paris', 306.

41 Von Moltke, *Franco-German War*, 264.

42 Hollis Clayson, *Paris in Despair: Art and Everyday Life under Siege, 1870–71* (Chicago: University of Chicago Press, 2002), 273–83; Taithe, *Citizenship and Wars*, 30.

43 Kathryn Shively Meier, 'Fighting in "Dante's Inferno": Changing perceptions of Civil War combat in the Spotsylvania Wilderness from 1863 to 1864', in Chris Pearson, Peter Coates, and Tim Cole (eds), *Militarized Landscapes: From Gettysburg to Salisbury Plain* (London: Continuum, 2010), 50; Ted Steinberg, *Down to Earth: Nature's Role in American History* (New York: Oxford University Press, 2002), 98.

44 *Rappel* had turned down the piece because of its sinister nature. It was eventually published in Jules Clarétie, *La France envahie, juillet à septembre 1870: Forbach et Sedan, impressions et souvenirs de guerre* (Paris: Georges Barba, 1871), ix–xvi. On images of crows feasting on the corpses of slain warriors, see Boria Sax, *Crow* (London: Reaktion, 2003), 34, 46–7, 64.

45 Aragonnès d'Orcet, *Froeschwiller, Sedan et la Commune*, 47–8.

46 Lieutenant-Colonel Bonie, 'The French cavalry in 1870', in Arthur L.

Wagner (ed.), *International Series No. 2: Cavalry Studies from Two Great Wars* (Kansas City: Hudson-Kimberly Publishing Company, 1896), 61.

47 Von Moltke, *Franco-German War*, 96.
48 Aragonnès d'Orcet, *Froeschwiller, Sedan et la Commune*, 117.
49 On anthropomorphism, see Lorraine Daston and Gregg Mitman (eds), *Thinking with Animals: New Perspectives on Anthropomorphism* (New York: Colombia University Press, 2005).
50 Wawro, *Franco-Prussian War*, 60–3.
51 Bonie, 'French cavalry', 37.
52 Knollys, *Sedan to Saarbruck*, 105.
53 The figures come from Karine Varley, *Under the Shadow of Defeat: The War of 1870–71 in French Memory* (Basingstoke: Palgrave Macmillan, 2008), 2.
54 Bonie, 'The French Cavalry', 97–8.
55 Quoted in G. Fitz-George, *Plan of the Battle of Sedan accompanied by a Short Memoir* (London: Edward Stanford, 1871), 81.
56 Kathleen Kete, *The Beast in the Boudoir: Petkeeping in Nineteenth-Century Paris* (Berkeley: University of California Press, 1994), 5.
57 Winn, *What I Saw of the War*, 90.
58 'The wounded in battle', *The Animal World*, 1:2, 1 September 1870, 216.
59 Chrastil, 'French Red Cross'; Taithe, *Defeated Flesh*.
60 Delmas, *Froeschwiller à Paris*, 65–6.
61 Taithe, *Citizenship and Wars*, 37.
62 Von der Goltz, 'St Privat-la-Montagne and Metz', 199.
63 Quesnoy, *Campagne de 1870*, 144, 156.
64 Ibid. 156.
65 Kete, *Beast in the Boudoir*, 6.
66 Bellows, *Track of the War*, 29.
67 Appleton, *Reminiscences*, 34.
68 Marie-Louise Gagneur, *Chair à Canon* (Paris: E. Dentu, 1872), 142.
69 A. Lambert, *Souvenirs du siege de Metz* (Chartes: Imprimerie Durand, 1908), 20–1.
70 Roth, *Guerre de 1870*, 364.
71 Rebecca L. Spang, '"And they ate the zoo": Relating gastronomic exoticism in the siege of Paris', *Modern Language Notes*, 107 (September 1992), 752–73; Clayson, *Paris in Despair*, 173–7.
72 Nathan Sheppard, *Shut Up in Paris* (London: Richard Bentley & Son, 1871), 152. See also Adolphe Michel, *Le siège de Paris, 1870–71* (Paris: Librairie A. Courcier, 1871), 262–4.
73 Taithe, *Defeated Flesh*, 112.
74 Colin Jones, *Paris: Biography of a City* (London: Allen Lane, 2004), 373.
75 J. D. Hayhurst, 'The pigeon post into Paris 1870–1871', www.cix.co.uk/~mhayhurst/jdhayhurst/pigeon/pigeon.html, 3, accessed 16 April 2010.

76 See Jilly Cooper, *Animals in War* (London: Heineman, 1983), 97; Michèle Martin and Christopher Bodnar, 'The illustrated press under siege: Technological imagination in the Paris siege, 1870–1871', *Urban History*, 36:1 (2009), 79; Gregory Kipper, *Investigator's Guide to Steganography* (Boco Raton: CRC Press, 2004); Roth, *Guerre de 1870*, 238.

77 Alfred Henry Osman, *Pigeons in the Great War: A Complete History of the Carrier Pigeon Service during the Great War, 1914 to 1918* (London: Racing Pigeon Publishing Co., 1929), 16.

78 Hayhurst, 'Pigeon post', 8.

79 'News from Paris, 1870', *The Animal World*, 2:15, 1 December 1870, 35–6. Hodge's poem is on page 35.

80 On animal protection in nineteenth-century France, see Kete, *Beast in the Boudoir*, 5–21.

81 Clayson, *Paris in Despair*, 173; Roth, *Guerre de 1870*, 203, 207. Howard estimates that 40,000 oxen and 250,000 sheep grazed in the Bois de Boulogne, *Franco-Prussian War*, 320.

82 Howard, *Franco-Prussian War*, 71; Richard Holmes, *The Road to Sedan: The French Army, 1866–70* (London: Royal Historical Society, 1984), 85.

83 Roth, *Guerre de 1870*, 87.

84 Jules Clarétie, *Le champ de bataille de Sedan* (Paris: Alphonse Lemerre, 1871), 39.

85 Howard, *Franco-Prussian War*, 289–91, 377; Roth, *Guerre de 1870*, 224–5; Annie Moulin, *Peasantry and Society in France since 1789*, trans. M.C. Cleary and M.F. Cleary (Cambridge: Cambridge University Press, 1991), 123–4; Eugen Weber, *Peasants into Frenchmen: The Modernisation of Rural France 1870–1914* (London: Chatto and Windus, 1979), 293.

86 CHAN F^{10}1602 Ministre des Affaires étrangères to Ministre de l'Agriculture, 4 September 1871; CHAN F^{10}1602 Ministre des Affaires étrangères to Ministre de l'Agriculture, 30 October 1871; Frank Puaux, *Souvenirs de la campagne de Sedan: Conférences données à Stockholm, Copenhague, Upsala et Gothembourg au profit des français victimes de la guerre* (Stockholm: P.A. Norstedt, 1871).

87 William K. Sessions, *They Chose the Star: Quaker Work in France 1870–1875* (London: Friends Relief Service, 1944), 34–5.

88 Roth, *Guerre de 1870*, 24.

89 Nadine Chossat, *Mourmelon-le-Grand: Cité champenoise et militaire* (Mourmelon-le-Grand: Ville de Mourmelon-le-Grand, 1999), 68.

90 Taithe uses the phrase 'mass militarisation' in *Citizenship and Wars*, 24.

91 Ibid. 10, 23–5; Roth, *Guerre de 1870*, 239.

92 SHD-DAT L N 15 Léonce Détroyat, Général de division commandant le camp de la Rochelle, 'Ordre général no. 1', [n.d.]; SHD-DAT L N 15 Commandant le camp de Sathonay [n.d.].

93 Quoted in Wawro, *Franco-Prussian War*, 289.

94 Knollys, *Sedan to Saarbruck*, 89.
95 Alphonse Turlin, *Historique sommaire du bataillon des francs-tireurs bour-bonnais: Son origine et ses opérations* (Moulins: Imprimerie C. Desrosiers, 1871), 12; Pierre Bliard, *Au Mont-Valérien en 1870: Impressions et notes d'un capitaine de francs-tireurs* (Paris: Etudes [n.d.]), 3.
96 Comte de Belleval, *Journal d'un capitaine de francs-tireurs* (Paris: E. Lachaud, 1872), 13–14, 25.
97 Puaux, *Souvenirs de la campagne de Sedan*, 47–8.
98 Bellows, *Track of the War*, 77.
99 Ibid. 31, 53–4.
100 Appleton, *Reminiscences*, 54–7, 92.
101 Robinson, *Fall of Metz*, 102.
102 Von der Goltz-Pasha, 'St Privat-la-Montagne and Metz', 183.
103 Knollys, *Sedan to Saarbruck*, 13, 77.
104 Delmas, *Froeschwiller à Paris*, 72.
105 Gay L. Gullickson, *Unruly Women of Paris: Images of the Commune* (Ithaca: Cornell University Press, 1996); Martin P. Johnson, *The Paradise of Association: Political Culture and Popular Organizations in the Paris Commune of 1871* (Ann Arbor: University of Michigan Press, 1996); Robert Tombs, *The War against Paris, 1871* (Cambridge: Cambridge University Press, 1981).
106 Hippolyte Guillery, *Compte rendu raisonné de l'assainissement du champ de bataille de Sedan et de la partie de la Meuse qui le traverse* (Brussels: Imprimerie de E. Guyot, 1871), 16, 22–4, 38, 44.
107 Ibid. 63–5.
108 ADS KZ 2777 E. de Goulard, Ministère de l'Intérieur to Préfets, 'Tombes militaires', 6 May 1873.
109 Varley, *Under the Shadow of Defeat*, 58–60.
110 Rachel Chrastil, *Organizing for War: France 1870–1914* (Baton Rouge: Louisiana State University Press, 2010), 75.
111 David G. Troyansky, 'Memorializing Saint-Quentin: Monuments, inau-gurations and history in the Third Republic', *French History*, 13:1 (1999), 48–76; Varley, *Under the Shadow of Defeat*.
112 Alfred Touchemolin, *Guide du touriste sur le champ de bataille de Froeschwiller* (Strasbourg: Edouard Fietta, [n.d.]), 5–6, drawings 18 and 19.
113 Brian Black, 'Addressing the nature of Gettysburg: "Addition and detrac-tion" in preserving an American shrine', *Reconstruction*, 7:2 (2007), http://reconstruction.eserver.org/072/black.shtml, accessed 5 September 2008; Andrew Charlesworth and Michael Addis, 'Memorialisation and the eco-logical landscapes of Holocaust sites: The cases of Auschwitz and Plaszow', *Landscape Research*, 27:3 (2002), 229–51; Chris Pearson, *Scarred Landscapes: War and Nature in Vichy France* (Basingstoke: Palgrave Macmillan, 2008), 168–74.

114 Touchemolin, *Guide du touriste*, 12, 15.
115 Varley, *Under the Shadow of Defeat*, 115.
116 Georges Ducrocq, *La blessure mal fermée: Notes d'un voyageur en Alsace-Lorraine* (Paris: Plon, 1911), 53–4.
117 Ibid. 103.
118 Maurice Barrès, *L'oeuvre de Maurice Barrès*, vol. 5, annotated by Philippe Barrès (Paris: Club de l'honnête homme, 1966 [1925]), 92.
119 Henri Bonnal, 'Préface', in Henri Famelart, *Vues des champs de bataille de Wissembourg et de Froeschwiller, 4 et 6 août 1870* (Paris: Librairie militaire, R. Chapelot, 1905). Famelart's panoramic and close-up images used legends and arrows to indicate key strategic positions and events in the now peaceful landscapes.
120 Pascal Jacquemin, 'Préface', in Stéphane Przybylski and Paul Filippi, *Les champs de bataille de 1870: Sentiers découvertes* (Metz: Editions Serpenoise, 2007), 3.

3

Remaking militarized environments in the wake of defeat (1871–1914)

Following the terrible year of 1870–71, the French struggled to come to terms with the sense of humiliation following their defeat to Germany and the pain of what one writer described as the 'open wound' of the 'lost' provinces of Alsace and Lorraine.[1] Historians have debated the extent to which France sought *revanche* against Germany, but it seems clear that France lacked the will to launch a war against Germany to reclaim Alsace and Lorraine.[2] Rather than revenge, the French state and civil society sought to recover from the upheavals and wounds of 1870–71 and prepare themselves to meet the perceived military threat of Germany, in part through the emulation of German military and social policies.[3] The prospects for renewal seemed bleak. An influential choir of voices, including doctors, social scientists, and writers, advanced the idea that *fin-de-siècle* France was entering a period of national degeneration marked by depopulation, rising levels of crime and madness, and the feminization of men.[4] The defeat of 1871 seemed to offer concrete evidence of decline. Perhaps most worryingly, doctors claimed that France lost one army corps a year to preventable infant diseases.[5]

Despite its leading role in the military defeat of 1870–71 the army was portrayed as a means of securing the nation's security against future German aggression and a way of combating national decline. Alongside sporting and shooting clubs, rural military camps and urban garrisons became sites of national defence and masculine renewal in which a 'culture of force' could, in theory, take root.[6] Successive Third Republic governments therefore sought to rebuild and strengthen the French army and rebuild its links with the nation. The embrace shared by Marshal MacMahon and Adolphe Thiers, the president of the republic, during the well-attended parade of 120,000 soldiers at Longchamp in June 1871, set the tone.[7]

The Third Republic's attempt to rejuvenate France and rebuild its army reverberated environmentally through the creation of new militarized environments. Although most scholarly attention has focused on the creation of urban militarized environments, this chapter argues that rural sites were integral to the efforts to remake army and nation.[8] It explores the army's mobilization of forests to strengthen France's eastern border and the harnessing of ever-larger expanses of the French countryside for its training purposes. Writing in 1873, military cartographer Armand Jusselain hoped that all French people would soon learn to use guns to counter the German military threat and that the whole country would be 'covered in targets, like an enormous firing school'.[9] The complete militarization of France remained a chimera, but military reforms did intensify the profusion and extent of militarized environments.

Environmental militarization during this time was a fluid process. Between 1871 and 1873, the army favoured rural camps. From 1873 it coveted urban caserns (or barracks) with easily accessible training grounds in the surrounding countryside, whilst from 1897 it oversaw the creation of larger-scale rural camps. As had been the case during the establishment of Châlons Camp, the army continued to target supposedly marginal and economically worthless wastelands. But after 1871 it coupled its expansionary objectives with the imperatives of national defence and renewal rather than imperial pretensions and territorial improvement. As this chapter explores, militarized environments once again became contact zones between the army and disgruntled civilians and between soldiers and the environment. But once again the mobilization of nature was no guarantee of success. On the available evidence, it seems that many of the soldiers based in the new camps experienced boredom rather than a sense of masculine rejuvenation. Similarly, larger training areas did not mean that the army succeeded in fulfilling their potential for training and weapons testing. The remaking of France's militarized environments and the mobilization of nature between 1871 and 1914 were complicated affairs during which the reality often failed to match the rhetoric.

Fortifying the frontier

In the wake of defeat, military authorities invested the terrain of eastern France with heightened strategic purpose. Losing Alsace and Lorraine left the defences of France's eastern borders in tatters. Working on the assumption that the most likely route of German invasion would come through these regions, the Third Republic attempted to fortify the redrawn border. General Raymond Adolphe Séré de Rivière, France's chief military engineer from January 1874, aimed to build a string of forts stretching from the Moselle to the Meuse to form a flexible and coordinated barrier to future German offensives. Despite some opposition within military circles, Séré de Rivière succeeded in building a series of 166 forts and 166 batteries, focused on Verdun, Toul, Epinal, and Belfort. Yet rapid developments in artillery meant that the forts quickly became obsolete and by the 1880s military engineers began reinforcing existing forts and constructing new ones. While they succeeded in building more modern forts, such as Douaumont near Verdun, many had still not been reinforced with steel and concrete by the outbreak of the First World War.[10]

The expense and difficulty of fort construction partially explains why military planners incorporated forests within their defensive system. They mobilized Argonne, Haut de Meuse, and Woëvre forests to fill in the gaps between forts.[11] The post-1871 incorporation of forests into France's national defences was the latest chapter in their militarization. In the eighteenth and nineteenth centuries, the army and navy had consumed wood for fortifications and ships, from forests as far apart as the Landes and Franche-Comté. Defensive considerations also partly motivated Napoleon I's law of 1803 which stipulated that landowners must consult forestry conservators before carrying out felling.[12] The Second Empire's decree of 16 August 1853 further stated that requests to fell in public and private forests within the Frontier Zone required approval from the Mixed Commission of Public Works. However, Napoleon III's keenness for rural development and economic liberalism diluted these strategic considerations.

The more active mobilization of forests after 1871 entailed increased military control over them. In the wake of defeat, military engineers prosecuted those who had felled illegally during the 1870–71 war. On 3 March 1874 they enlarged the Frontier Zone to incorporate Paris, thereby extending felling restrictions and preventing clearances in forests surrounding the capital. Conducted under the auspices of a mixed military–civilian commission, military control was incomplete. Yet the military prevented numerous communes from felling, despite opposition. Unsurprisingly, restrictions were most severe along the Franco-German frontier.[13] The forest's militarization was further reinforced in 1875 with the creation of a military forestry corps, which numbered 6,000 in 1900. To combat the disastrous experience of 1870–71, the army hoped that these units would bring their knowledge of forested terrain to military operations in the event of war.[14]

Their role in forest conservation has prompted François Reitel to argue that army personnel unintentionally became ecologists '*avant la lettre*'.[15] Can we treat army forest policies as a forerunner of twentieth-century nature protection or even a militarized version of nineteenth-century civilian efforts to protect valued natural sites and reforest Alpine and Pyrenean mountain slopes? Similarities are evident with nineteenth-century civilian foresters and landscape preservationists. Most notably, neither sought to protect nature for nature's sake. For the army, defence considerations were paramount. For civilians, a range of diverse factors, such as flood prevention, tourism, and bourgeois aesthetic ideals, motivated their actions.[16] Civilian and military forms of nature protection therefore shared a highly anthropocentric conception of, and engagement with, the nonhuman world. However, the important difference in aims, approaches, and understandings of nature make comparisons between military foresters and twentieth-century nature protectionists tenuous at best.

From the countryside to the casern?

Alongside mobilizing forests to defend France's eastern border, army chiefs set about rethinking and expanding France's army camps. In the years following defeat, varying opinions concerning the correct geographical place of the army jostled for dominance. Some doctors treated the countryside as an unhealthy place. They feared the harmful climates and atmosphere of boredom that supposedly inflicted rural army camps. But others saw the countryside as a healthy site of national regeneration.[17] For his part, Thiers wanted to keep troops away from what he regarded as the dangerous and revolutionary atmosphere of cities. Therefore, in addition to taking over and, in some cases expanding, Gambatta's Franco-Prussian War-era army camps, Thiers oversaw the creation of new ones.[18]

Military commentators hailed them as modern camps from which a better army would emerge. An article in *Avenir militaire* stressed that the soon-to-be constructed 1,200 ha camp of Valbonne (Rhône) would be a 'model [camp] in every way'. It would stand in stark contrast to poor conditions of the 'so-called' camp of Sathonay, which had only limited barrack space and lacked proper training and firing grounds. The article paid particular attention to water supplies. At Sathonay Camp, soldiers had been forced to collect water from a small stream. At Valbonne Camp the water would gush freely from taps. This marked 'real progress'.[19] As in the civilian sphere, the provision of running water was equated with modernization and civilization.[20]

Like the Second Empire, the newly installed republic favoured supposedly empty, relatively cheap land for its military camps and firing ranges. General Chanzy oversaw the construction of a 1,500 ha camp on 'heathland (*landes*)' at Ruchard near Chinon forest (Indre-et-Loire). Echoing descriptions of Châlons Camp, *Avenir militaire* enthused how the 'immense plain . . . seemed purpose built for the establishment of a camp'.[21] Cheap and deserted land was also prioritized for artillery ranges. A 16 May 1872 circular from Minister of War General de Cissey to prefects required them to find suitable sites (8 to 10 km in length with a width of 1 km) for training grounds near to the towns where new artillery garrisons would shortly be based. He stressed that land was only to be rented or bought if it was mainly flat, unpopulated, and situated away from busy communication routes. Yet de Cissey's suggestion that prefects emphasis the economic benefits of militarization to counter possible civilian opposition suggests that the army realized that local communities would not necessarily greet its installations with open arms.[22]

In response to de Cissey's request, officials in the Gironde département proposed a number of sites. Among them was a 'vast, almost deserted plain of minimal value' near Cazaux lagoon in the commune of La Teste, 50 km south-west of Bordeaux. A map accompanying the report showed how the firing ranges (represented as pink and yellow rectangles) would overlay the civilian geography of roads, canals, and pastureland. The narrative of military-induced rural development developed during the Second Empire re-emerged; the report suggested that army horse manure could fertilize and cultivate the area.[23]

Hygiene concerns continued to play a role. In language that recalled the anxieties that accompanied the creation of Châlons Camp, the report on Cazaux highlighted how the land was 'dry, healthy, airy, and sandy'. Furthermore, it stressed that the nearby Atlantic ocean and the pure waters of Cazaux lagoon would benefit the 'health of the men and horses and help guard against a large number of diseases commonly found in camps and garrisons'. Soldiers and horses would thrive in the 'hygienic and therapeutic conditions' and military rations could be supplemented by the abundance of seafood. Significantly, the report presented an image of this area of the Landes region as a healthy place, in contrast to earlier portrayals of the region as a dank, dirty, unhealthy wasteland.[24]

Yet there was military opposition to placing soldiers in rural camps. A forthright article in *Avenir militaire* lambasted the poor conditions in the camps where wet winters created 'inevitable' health problems as soldiers and their animals were reduced to 'wading through mud night and day'. Alongside paving roads in the fight against mud, the soldiers' other main occupation was chasing away the huge rats which ate everything in sight. This was good sport, 'but not an essentially military activity'. Soldiers, the article concluded, would be better housed in urban garrisons.[25] Mud, rats, and rain provided inappropriate conditions in which to rebuild the army. The article's author got his wish. The Government of Moral Order (brought to power in 1873) decreed that soldiers, whose numbers had increased since the conscription law of 1872, should be grouped in permanent garrisons in urban barracks. Henceforth, the army was to serve as a model of discipline, hygiene, and vigour for urban dwellers, as well as assuring social order.[26]

Environmental factors still mattered in the city. Those town councils who lobbied for barracks and the accompanying commercial opportunities and prestige, played to concerns over military hygiene, stressing the favourable topography, impeccable cleanliness, and healthy climate of their town and surrounding countryside. H. de Lacombe, for instance, argued that Orléans's state forest would be perfect for an artillery range.[27] Military authorities and town councils also worked together to secure clean water supplies for the urban garrisons, further cementing the link between army and nation.[28] But geography could sometimes count against a particular location. In 1874, General Montaudon opposed the installation of a barrack on the right bank of the Somme River at Amiens because of nearby marshy ground.[29] Poor water supplies could also lead to public outcry and civilian criticisms of the army.[30] As in the countryside, the army took environmental conditions into account during its militarization of urban areas.

But despite the army's migration towards towns and cities, it maintained a strong rural presence. Not least, horses and troops in urban barracks required food sourced from local farms. Therefore, town councils militating for a barrack highlighted their hinterland's agricultural abundance. Local agriculture might, in turn, benefit from urban barracks. If circumstances permitted, the Ministry for War allowed soldiers (many of whom had agricultural backgrounds) to help farmers with their harvest. From the farmers' perspective, soldiers provided a relatively cheap form of labour at a time of human resource shortages in the fields. Some army officials, however, complained that less scrupulous farmers abused the privilege by overworking and under-feeding their 'soldier-peasants'.[31] A further sign of tension was that some farmers sought to claim compensation for damage to their land caused by manoeuvring troops.[32] Eugen Weber has argued that the army was one of the main institutions that transformed 'peasants into Frenchmen' between 1870 and 1914. Whilst there is undoubtedly some truth in this, the localized, reciprocal, and at times fraught relationships between the army and farmers nuances Weber's centralized, 'top-down' approach.[33] The army may have been an agency of change, but it was also an agency of disruption and resentment in the countryside.

Large-scale military manoeuvres created temporary, but geographically expansive, militarized environments and brought the army once again into the countryside. The need for better tactical military *savoir-faire* had been brutally exposed during the 1870–71 war. The Germany military acted as both model and threat. One commentator lambasted Second Empire-era manoeuvres as nothing more than a 'parody of war'. Unlike Prussian manoeuvres, they had prevented officers and soldiers from understanding and deploying terrain according to the principles of 'military science'.[34] But some progress was made towards nurturing German-style tactical and geographical awareness. A *New York Times* journalist, who observed French army manoeuvres whilst on vacation near Saint Omer in September 1874, reported how French army manoeuvres had become more realistic and that officers showed more aptitude in reconnaissance, 'choosing ground', and directing attacks.[35]

In the years that followed, sympathetic journalists, painters, and foreign observers glorified the army's annual autumn manoeuvres. Although Major Hoff recognized that they brought disruption to the countryside during harvest time, he believed that the manoeuvres were a 'spectacle and a godsend' for locals (who could claim compensation for damage to their land).[36] The manoeuvres were rendered as evidence of France's resurgent army. As one journalist asserted, the manoeuvres demonstrated that 'the country can place its confidence' in its soldiers. Their discipline, energy and '*sang-froid*' meant that France's security was 'absolute'.[37] Paintings by Edouard Detaille and other artists jostled with postcard images to represent the splendour of the manoeuvres. They similarly tried to show how the French army was powerful, effective, disciplined and that its officers and soldiers had now learnt how to read and deploy terrain.[38] Although it is hard to measure how soldiers experienced these manoeuvres it is clear that tactics and discipline were not always on their mind. Instead, ad hoc poaching of wildlife provided amusement and a supplement to army rations.[39]

Although the army established urban garrisons and continued with temporary, large-scale manoeuvres, it still sought permanent camps and training grounds in remote and sparsely populated rural areas. We should therefore not overestimate its migration to urban areas. In 1873 it created a temporary camp in the southern part of the Brocéliande forest in Brittany. Coëtquidan Camp, as it became known, was made permanent in 1878 through the expropriation of over 1,000 ha for an artillery range.[40] Soldiers and officers continued to bemoan country life in new rural camps country. A decree of 4 December 1874 established the infantry camp of Avord on an 'arid plain' near Bourges (Cher). Recruits stationed there found secluded rural life, with its limited distractions, tedious, especially in winter. All there was to do on days off, wrote one disgruntled trainee, was to 'walk along the Angy road' which was as 'flat as your hand' or go into Bourges to 'note that the grass on rue Moyenne had grown by several centimetres'.[41] Army chiefs were perhaps glad that their men were isolated from the temptations of the emerging consumer and mass entertainment culture in the cities, but it seems that the latter tolerated, rather than embraced, rural life. Yet it was something that officers and soldiers would have to become increasingly used to as the military mobilization of supposedly empty and unproductive land intensified in the 1880s and 1890s.

Expanding militarized environments

Technological and political factors pushed the army to search for ever larger camps and firing ranges. New artillery cannons, pioneered by artillery officer Charles Ragon de Bange in the 1870s and 1880s, boasted greatly increased ranges and the conscription law of 1889 strengthened the principle of universal service laid out in the law of 1872, through tightening exemptions regulations. Its reduction of service from five to three years and the increase in the time spent in reserve and territorial units raised total manpower by a third and were designed to cement the links between army and nation.[42] Furthermore, by the 1880s many French citizens were prepared to play a more active role in the defence of their country. Training societies sprung up to prepare young men for military service through physical exertion and military-style discipline, numbering 900 by 1891.[43] The atmosphere was ripe for further environmental militarization.

It should now come as no surprise that military authorities in the 1880s and 1890s prioritized supposedly uncultivated, empty, and marginal sites for their installations. This was the case with Auvours camp near Le Mans in 1881, established on 'flat, sandy, sterile, and marshy' land.[44] Their search for new militarized environments also took them to places as far apart as the Mediterranean coast and northern France. In 1892 the state bought nearly all of Ile du Levant, an island lying off the Provençal coastline. Having hosted Napoleonic-era forts, a penal colony, and failed vineyards, the island would henceforth become a naval firing zone. Three years later, the state expropriated 885 ha of vines, fields, and pine forests between the Saint-Cyr hills and the Mediterranean coastline to create Carpiagne Camp.[45] In the Aisne département of northern France, cheap and sparsely populated land prompted the creation of Sissonne Camp in 1895, where repeated extensions saw its size rise to 6,000 ha by 1914.[46]

To all intents and purposes, the democratic Third Republic was less militaristic than the imperialist Second Empire. By the 1880s and 1890s, the army received flack from many quarters: members of the bourgeoisie resented universal conscription, socialists and anarchists denounced militarism, popular satirical novels mocked military conventions, and officers' prestige declined continuously. [47] Furthermore, the dubious conviction and imprisonment of Captain Alfred Dreyfus for allegedly passing on military secrets to the German military attaché in Paris led to intense Republican scrutiny and criticism of the army. Nonetheless, the army, supported by Third Republic governments, intensified the proliferation of militarized environments.

The year 1897 was a major turning point in militarization of the French countryside as the army cemented and extended its policy of mobilizing the remoter swathes of the French countryside to base and train its troops. It launched an expansion programme with a budget of 50 million francs and announced the creation of new camps at Larzac, Mailly, and La Courtine.[48] In doing so, it mirrored developments across the Channel: in the 1890s the British army established a permanent camp on Dartmoor and in 1902 purchased over 16,000 ha of Salisbury Plain and established permanent camps there at Tidworth and Bulford.[49]

For some of the effected French rural communities, the arrival of a military camp offered a potential influx of jobs, money, and prestige. Consequently, the communes of Millau, La Cavalerie and L'Hospitalet-du-Larzac ceded 3,000 ha of communal land on the rocky, windswept

Larzac plateau for the establishment of the camp in 1899.[50] The militarization of Larzac ushered in changes to the plateau, even if the continuation of pasturing on camp maintained a civilian presence within the militarized environment. Henceforth, the plateau would be exposed to sirens, warning signs, road closures, and a cacophony of gun and shell fire during manoeuvres. The new camp brought changes to the patterns of daily life on the plateau. Each firing day, the mayor of La Cavalerie was charged with ringing the church bell to warn those locals who had secured the authorization to pasture their sheep on the range to remove themselves and their animals from danger.[51]

The army's foray into southern France for new camps and training grounds was a departure from its habitual concentration in the north and east. Its establishment of Mailly Camp on 2 July 1902, however, brought it back to its training heartland of Champagne. In his 1906 guide to the camp, Captain Menu noted the geographical continuities, stating that 'the nature of the terrain [at Sissonne, Châlons, and Mailly camps] . . . is practically identical'.[52]

While the physical similarities of the camps struck Menu, what is now most striking are the similarities in the pro-military discourses surrounding the establishment of Mailly and Châlons camps. Arthur Robert's guide to Mailly Camp highlighted how Champagne's plains had witnessed the defeat of Attila and how the camp would not only serve as an 'establishment of first class military instruction' but would form 'an important school of patriotism that will make the heart of all of France beat in unison with its soldiers'. Mailly Camp represented an 'incontestable and primordial utility for France'.[53]

Alongside parroting the militarized discourse of the Second Empire, such language bound Mailly Camp to French national identity at a time when nationalist sentiments were riding high after the Moroccan Crisis.[54] It also emphasized the role the army played in securing France's safety vis-à-vis its German neighbour and sought to reconnect French society with its armed forces after the upheavals of the Dreyfus Affair. In a similar vein, patriotism infused Menu's insistence that the outline of Mailly Camp resembled the shape of France. This added an explicitly militarized dimension to the patriotically inspired re-imaginings of France's geography in the early twentieth century (through such means as the Tour de France cycling race and the publications of geographer Paul Vidal de la Blache).[55]

In a further echo of Châlons Camp's creation, Robert and Menu emphasized the suitability of the Mailly area for militarization. Robert suggested that there was nowhere better in France for military training, praising the 'healthy climate . . . impregnated by the most pure air'.[56] But as with Châlons Camp, there was the sense that the land was potentially harmful for soldiers' well-being. Therefore, army engineers laid turf over the white clayey soil within the built camp to prevent sun glare and imported soil to plant maple, plane, and other trees for shade. They also installed wells, water towers, and a sewerage system. The lengthy description accorded to the water and waste system in Robert's guide undoubtedly attests to pride in these feats of engineering. He lauded Mailly as not just a patriotic camp but a healthy and modern one, thereby incorporating it into the wider project of cleansing, modernizing, and 'civilizing' the Republic through public health measures.[57]

Once again echoing the rhetorical fanfare that greeted Châlons Camp, Robert portrayed Mailly as a vector of agricultural progress. Although claiming that he held no wish to insult *la Champagne pouilleuse* (as 'cereals grow marvellously' in the region), Robert described the camp as a 'green oasis' in a 'monotonous and sad' land which would boost local agriculture; military manure would now fertilize farmer's fields.[58]

If Robert portrayed the camp as a site of modernization and improvement, certain postcards of the camp portrayed it as fitting seamlessly into local rural traditions. They presented the surrounding countryside as peaceful and untroubled by the military camp. One shows women and children tending a gaggle of geese with the church of Mailly-le-Camp serving as a backdrop. Another features a rundown farmhouse nestling among trees alongside a suitably rustic family and dog.[59] The nineteenth century visual idiom of a peaceful, eternal, and rooted countryside infused these postcards. As with landscape paintings of civilian places, they show the French countryside as a 'natural environment that was itself a motif of lyricism and meditation, a school of truth and modesty, and a source of refreshment on which national continuity could draw'.[60]

But other postcards of the camp disrupted this rural visual trope by representing militarization as a force of destruction and transformation. One shows the slowly crumbling former church of Dègue now 'occupied' by sappers and infantrymen, and others show expropriated farms now located in the 'dangerous zone'. These images must have been painful for the former inhabitants; the farm at La Custonne has a disintegrating thatched roof and blown out windows.[61]

To be fair to Robert, his account of the camp gave some space to its disruptive character. He recognized, to an extent, the social impacts of militarization, admitting that the camp had dispossessed 2,345 landowners and that ill-feeling existed towards the army, despite compensation payments.[62] Local town halls did indeed demand compensation for the loss of their roads and hunting rights, which the Ministry for War did its best to resist.[63] These local protests provided a counter-narrative to the language of modernity and patriotism that greeted the camp and laid bare the hollowness of the army's claims that the land had been empty and worthless.

The military–civilian tensions at Mailly Camp were part of a wider questioning of the military ownership of land as it expanded in the early twentieth century. Military–civilian relations also soured at Souge Camp (created in 1897). This followed initial cooperation; Martignas town hall had ceded the army land for an access road, allowed it to open a quarry in a forest, and, on at least two occasions, locals and soldiers united to fight forest fires on the range.[64] But at a meeting held on 5 April 1902 to discuss the creation of a temporary artillery firing ground, the mayor of Martignas voiced his concerns over the lack of fire-prevention measures. In response, Captain Verguin pointed out that the Ministry for War had ordered bush clearance near batteries, targets, and access roads.[65] Although they had lost their land to military training, civilians near Souge Camp maintained a watchful eye on management of militarized environments. The balance of power may have been weighted in the army's favour, but it did not enjoy *carte blanche*. The examples of Mailly and Souge camps provided localized and less-ideologically driven critiques of militarization than that of socialist and anarchist anti-militarism, which was becoming more organized during this time, buoyed, in part, by the Dreyfus Affair.[66] But they were important counterarguments to those seeking to conflate military and national renewal.

Picturing life in the camps

As the army mobilized new sites for war preparation, thousands of new recruits came to live and work in the camps under universal conscription laws. Evidence on how they experienced these militarized environments is scant. But postcards offer some clues.

Nowadays, images of soldiers training are largely restricted to recruitment posters and films or to rare artistic portrayals of everyday life on military bases.[67] But at the beginning of the twentieth century, publishers mass-produced postcards of soldiers' life in French army camps that soldiers sent to their families and friends. As well as acting as channels of communication between military and civilian spheres, the postcards' images and the messages scrawled on the back of them provide some insight, however partial and incomplete, into how soldiers experienced camp life. And although the army remained hierarchical and its upper ranks remained the preserve of the elites, the postcards presented more democratic images of camp life than those produced of Châlons Camp by Gustave Le Gray (see chapter 1) and were part of the attempt to 'republicanize' the army.[68] In such a way, militarized environments became embedded within the visual culture of the Third Republic as sites of war preparation and masculine renewal.

The postcards of Mailly Camp represent it as a place of militarized, masculine renewal. Manoeuvres and military training mobilized environmental features in a variety of ways. Recruits of the Saint-Cyr school used gradients to practise scaling, while flat grasslands were deployed for artillery and infantry fire (see figure 3.1).[69]

These images suggest that training within the environment turned the recruit into a soldier and seem designed to show how the camps and their environments enabled the rejuvenation of French masculinity.[70] Strengthened physically through military training in the camp, soldiers would be able to defend their loved ones and the nation against potential threats.

But different sentiments could be found on the back of the postcards. Manoeuvres were tiring rather than rejuvenating. One recruit called Raymond described to his uncle and aunt the rigours of rising at 4.00 a.m. to 'make a little war in the camp' and the tiring marching and hunger that followed.[71] The postcards' images also glossed over the growing boredom and dissatisfaction with army life. On the back of one postcard, the sender regretted being 'in this blasted camp'.[72] Such feelings were probably typical as military morale declined, undermined as it was by soldiers' own anti-military activities in camps and garrisons, falling numbers of candidates entering Saint-Cyr, and a sense that 'more battles were fought against the working class than against foreign invaders' (in June 1907, for instance, cavalrymen cracked down on demonstrators in Narbonne, killing civilians).[73]

Ironically, the postcards' images undermined the narrative that Mailly was an exemplary hygienic camp. Instead, they show it as contact zone between soldiers, animals, and their waste. Contradicting medical beliefs that human and animal bodies should be kept separate, postcards represent the camp's dogs as companions, posing with their masters in front of army tents, and as workers, training to be first aid dogs (see figure 3.2).[74]

3.1 'Ecoles à feu – Pièce de 120 court – Attendant le commandement: Feu!'

Horses also worked within the militarized environment and unintentionally took part in manoeuvres by dragging artillery cannons over ditches.[75] As if to make up for the horrors inflicted on horses during the Franco-Prussian War, other postcards pictured them at rest, drinking from water troughs, and having their feet inspected.[76] Whether working or resting, horses produced manure. Any local farmer deprived of fertilizer would have coveted the sloppy, copious piles of horse dung stagnating in the foreground of one of the postcards, although many doctors would have been horrified.[77]

As well as a site of war preparation, the postcards represent Mailly Camp as a place of leisure. The one sent by the aforementioned Raymond shows a relaxed group of soldiers fishing for crayfish in a tree-lined stream. There was also time for even less energetic activities. A postcard entitled 'walk in the woods' features soldiers lying and standing around in shady woodland, smoking, drinking, and nibbling snacks (see figure 3.3).[78]

The atmosphere of relaxed male camaraderie is also evident in a postcard entitled 'the work of stable guards' on which the men are shown reclining under a row of trees.[79] These bucolic images helped deflect attention away from less respectable military leisure activities, such as drinking, gambling, and prostitution, and, with public and familial

263 — CAMP DE MAILLY. — *Les Chiens ambulanciers.*   ND. Phot.

3.2 'Camp de Mailly – Les chiens ambulanciers'

MAILLY LE CAMP — Promenade sous les Bois

3.3 'Mailly le Camp – Promenade sous les bois'

audiences in mind, they represented the camps as wholesome sites of work and leisure.[80] They also seem designed to reassure relatives that their militarized loved ones were comfortable and well. 'Decoration of Tents' shows soldiers embellishing the exterior of their tents with carpets of flowers and ivy draped around the porches, thereby making the camp more homely, pastoral, and individualized.[81] According to these images, the army of the Third Republic looked after its citizen-soldiers.

The postcards show army camps as sites of work and leisure, and of spaces of war preparation and masculine renewal. But the comments on the back suggest that the army's aims struggled to be met. The same is true regarding the final aspect of militarized environments in *fin-de-siècle* France that this chapter explores: the testing and development of new military technologies and weapons.

Testing new technologies

At a time when Austria, Germany, Italy, and Britain mobilized their army training camps to refine infantry and artillery firing techniques, French fears of falling behind militarily were never far from the surface. As a consequence, on the expanses of grass and scrubland of France's new camps, officers taught soldiers how to manipulate and deploy cannons and other weapons.[82] Although the army's deployment of new weaponry should not be overestimated – Paul Miller argues that military authorities fell into a 'kind of technological torpor' and failed to fully realize the importance of heavy artillery and machine guns[83] – some military bases became sites of technological experimentation. From the 1890s onwards, military engineers developed the use of observation balloons. One nicknamed 'La Saucisse' (the Sausage) was used to observe manoeuvres at Souge Camp.[84] The army also conducted experiments involving firing machine guns at balloons at Châlons Camp in 1912.[85] Testing these new technologies became part of the visual spectacle of *fin-de-siècle* France; 'the Sausage' featured on postcards of Souge Camp.

But it was feats of endurance and daring in aeroplanes that proved the most popular. In summer 1908, aviator Wilbur Wright arrived in France to conduct aerial trials. Unable to find a suitable site among the cultivated fields around Paris, Wright identified the artillery range at Auvours Camp as an ideal spot. After overcoming its initial reluctance, the army granted him use of the range over a four-month period. Every evening, between 2,000 and 3,000 spectators would gather at the site whilst on 21 September 1908 a crowd of 10,000 watched him complete a flight of 1 hour 31 minutes. In freezing conditions on 31 December 1908, Wright went further and scooped the 20,000-franc Michelin prize for the longest flight in France for that year (2 hours and 20 minutes).[86] Wright's time at Auvours Camp not only blurred civilian and military boundaries within the militarized environment, but brought the emerging public consumption of the spectacular into the countryside.[87]

Not to be outdone, pioneering French army officers begun to promote military aviation, leading to the search for geographically suitable training sites. Ferdinand Marzac identified lagoons as ideal impact zones for aerial bombing ranges because they were uninhabited and their flat surfaces of water allowed for the installation of moving targets and accurate recordings of the location of projectiles. However, Marzac deemed some lagoons unsuitable. These included Vaccarès and Berre lagoons in Provence (too many tourists), Bourget and Annecy lakes (located in mountainous regions), and Hourtin and Grand-Lieu lagoons (too marshy). His Bordeaux childhood, meanwhile, focused his mind on the 5,608 ha lagoon at Cazaux, which officials had already proposed as a possible military site (see above). In December 1913 Marzac assessed Cazaux's potential *in situ*, but the outbreak of war the following year put the project on hold.[88] Nonetheless, the militarization of aviation was well underway.[89]

Aviation schools promised prestige and investment for local towns. Bordeaux's mayor therefore enthusiastically welcomed the possibility of establishing a national military aviation school in the region, proposing that its communication routes and 'immense heathlands' made it ideal for aerial training. In December 1910 he put forward a motion to create an aviation school near Saint-Médard-en-Jalles. Bordeaux's town councillors shared his enthusiasm and unanimously adopted the motion.[90] Aviation heralded a new kind of militarized environment that made use of land *and* the sky above.

But although the army oversaw some technical innovations and investment in military training sites camps rose from 2,995,000 francs in 1908 to 4,600,000 in 1911, France still lagged behind Germany, where the equivalent of 14,346,000 francs was spent on training camps in 1911 alone. The promise of new technology could also not overcome the continuation of poor training techniques and conscription laws which would fail to provide a sufficient number of soldiers in the event of war with Germany.[91] Indeed, some soldiers experienced the training they received as dull and ineffective. Major Simon wrote that 'on the range, what mattered was not to hit the target frequently, but to adopt the precise posture called for by regulations, even if the marksman's physique made this uncomfortable for him'.[92]

New technologies also stoked civilian–military tensions. The increased range of modern weaponry caused unease amongst the army's civilian neighbours; the mayor of Saillans (Gironde) signalled that bullets were landing in farms and vineyards neighbouring the Saillans firing range and disrupting agriculture. The chief army engineer provided the far from reassuring response that thus far no human or animal had been hit.[93] A similar problem occurred near the impact zone of Châlons Camp where military authorities admitted that it was 'well-known' that projectiles fell near, and even within, Suippes and Piémont farms.[94] In such a way, errant shells contributed to anti-military feelings in the countryside.[95] The troubled deployment of new technologies underscores once again how reality failed to match military rhetoric. As such, the expansion of militarized environments in *fin-de-siècle* France was no guarantee of future military success.

Conclusion

In the wake of defeat and under the shadow of German military might, the Third Republic remade France's militarized environments. Ideas about whether the army should be based in the city or the countryside played a role in the location of the new militarized environments, especially in the 1870s. But by the turn of the twentieth century, the army's training centre of gravity was firmly located in rural areas. These militarized environments, such as Mailly and Larzac camps, have proved enduring, thereby removing land from civilian use throughout the twentieth century and into the twenty-first. Despite civilian opposition, the Third Republic oversaw the militarization of ever larger and dispersed swathes of the French countryside to prepare its armed forces for war and to renew French masculinity. Although the mobilization of nature was problematic and far from successful, it intensified still further with the outbreak of the First World War in the summer of 1914.

Notes

1 Georges Ducrocq, *La blessure mal fermée: Notes d'un voyageur en Alsace-Lorraine* (Paris: Plon, 1911).
2 Robert Gildea, 'Eternal France: Crisis and national self-perception in France 1870–2005', in Susana Carvalho and François Gemenne (eds), *Nations and Their Histories: Constructions and Representations* (Basingstoke: Palgrave Macmillan, 2009), 140; Bertrand Joly, 'La France et la Revanche (1981–1914)', *Revue d'Histoire Moderne et Contemporaine*, 46:2 (1999), 325–47.

3 Rachel Chrastil, *Organizing for War: France 1870-1914* (Baton Rouge: Louisiana State University Press, 2010); Allan Mitchell, *Victors and Vanquished: The German Influence on Army and Church in France after 1870* (Chapel Hill: University of North Carolina Press, 1984); David B. Ralston, *The Army of the Republic: The Place of the Military in the Political Evolution of France, 1871-1914* (Cambridge, MA: MIT Press, 1967), 350.

4 Christopher E. Forth and Elinor A. Accampo (eds), *Confronting Modernity in Fin-de-Siècle France: Bodies, Minds, and Gender* (Basingstoke: Palgrave Macmillan, 2009); Ruth Harris, *Murders and Madness: Medicine, Law and Society in the Fin-de-Siècle* (Oxford: Clarendon, 1989); Robert Nye, *Masculinity and Male Codes of Honour in Modern France* (Oxford: Oxford University Press, 1993); Karen Offen, 'Depopulation, nationalism and feminism in fin-de-siècle France', *American Historical Review*, 89:3 (1984), 648-76; Koenraad W. Swart, *The Sense of Decadence in Nineteenth-Century France* (The Hague: Martinus Nijhoff, 1964).

5 Mary Lynn McDougall, 'Protecting infants: The French campaign for maternity leaves, 1890s-1913', *French Historical Studies*, 13:1 (1983), 92.

6 Christopher E. Forth uses the term 'culture of force' in *The Dreyfus Affair and the Crisis of French Manhood* (Baltimore: Johns Hopkins University Press, 2004), 205-17. On sporting and shooting clubs, see Chrastil, *Organizing for War*, 112-26. On the army as a means of national renewal, see Odile Roynette, '*Bon pour le service': L'expérience de la caserne en France à la fin du XIXe siècle* (Paris: Belin, 2000).

7 Robert Gildea, *Children of the Revolution: The French 1799-1914* (London: Penguin, 2009), 410-11.

8 Jean-François Chanet, *Vers l'armée nouvelle: République conservatrice et réforme militaire, 1871-1879* (Rennes: Presses Universitaires de Rennes, 2006); Roynette, '*Bon pour le service*'.

9 Armand Jusselain, *De la reproduction des cartes topographiques pendant la guerre en province, 1870-71* (Paris: Librairie Militaire de J. Dumaine, 1873), 38-9. Shooting clubs expanded rapidly in the years following defeat, numbering 900 by 1885. Benoît Lecoq, 'Les sociétés de gymnastique et de tir dans la France républicaine (1870-1914)', *Revue historique*, 559 (1986), 157-66.

10 Chanet, *Vers l'armée nouvelle*, 78-9; Jean-Pierre Husson, 'Les empilements géostratégiques et leurs héritages: Etude appliquée à l'espace lorrain', *Stratégique*, 82:3 (2001), 59-80; Mitchell, *Victors and Vanquished*, 53-60, 112-14; François Dallemagne and Jean Mouly, *Patrimoine militaire* (Paris: Editions Scala, 2002), 68-79.

11 Jean-Paul Amat, 'Le rôle stratégique de la forêt, 1871-1914: Exemples dans les forêts lorraines', *Revue historique des armées*, 1 (1993), 63.

12 Paul Walden Bamford, *Forests and French Sea Power, 1660-1789* (Toronto: University of Toronto Press, 1956); Hamish Graham, 'For the needs of the

royal navy: State interventions in the communal woodlands of the Landes during the eighteenth century', *Proceedings of the Western Society for French History*, 35 (2007), 135–48, http://quod.lib.umich.edu/cgi/t/text/text-idx?c =wsfh;view=text;rgn=main;idno=0642292.0035.009, accessed 11 November 2011; François Vion-Delphin, 'La consommation militaire en bois Franc-comtois', in Andrée Corvol and Jean-Paul Amat (eds), *Forêt et guerre* (Paris: L'Harmattan, 1994), 117–25.

13 Chanet, *Vers l'armée nouvelle*, 79.

14 'Utilité des forêts au point de vue militaire', *Avenir Militaire*, 389, 11 November 1877, 3; Jean-Paul Amat, 'Forêt et défense du territoire: France du nord-est, 1871–1914', *Stratégique*, 56 (1992), 316.

15 François Reitel, 'Le rôle de l'armée dans la conservation des forêts', in Corvol and Amat, *Forêt et guerre*, 49. The situation was very different in Algeria where botanists and foresters identified the army as the main cause of defor-estation. Diana K. Davis, *Resurrecting the Granary of Rome: Environmental History and French Colonial Expansion in North Africa* (Athens, OH: Ohio University Press, 2007), 125.

16 Caroline Ford, 'Nature, culture, and conservation in France and her colo-nies, 1840–1940', *Past and Present*, 183 (2004), 173–98; Nicholas Green, *The Spectacle of Nature: Landscape and Bourgeois Culture in Nineteenth-Century France* (Manchester: Manchester University Press, 1990); Tamara L. Whited, *Forests and Peasant Politics in Modern France* (New Haven: Yale University Press, 2000).

17 Roynette, *'Bon pour le service'*.

18 Chanet, *Vers l'armée nouvelle*, 80; Guy Pedroncini (ed.), *Histoire militaire de la France de 1871 à 1940*. Vol. 3 of André Corvisier (ed.), *Histoire militaire de la France* (Paris: Presses Universitaires de France, 1992), 38.

19 'Camp de la Valbonne', *Avenir militaire*, 86, 27 August 1872.

20 David S. Barnes, *The Great Stink of Paris and the Nineteenth-Century Struggle against Filth and Germs* (Baltimore: Johns Hopkins University Press, 2006), 194–228.

21 'Camp de Ruchard', *Avenir militaire*, 92, 27 September 1872.

22 ADGI 2 R 74 Ministère de la Guerre, 'Création de nouvelles garnisons d'artillerie', 16 May 1872. Despite financial restraints and a lack of suit-ably trained officers, Thiers was determined that France should expand and improve its artillery. Mitchell, *Victors and Vanquished*, 64.

23 ADGI 2 R 74 Daussy, 'Établissement d'un polygone d'artillerie dans le canton de La Teste', 18 June 1872.

24 Ibid.

25 'Les camps', *L'Avenir militaire*, 102, 16 November 1872, 2.

26 Chanet, *Vers l'armée nouvelle*; Roynette, *'Bon pour le service'*. On the archi-tecture of French garrisons, see François Dallemagne, *Les casernes françaises* (Paris: Editions Picard, 1990).

27 H. de Lacombe, *Note sur le projet d'une école d'artillerie à Orléans* (Orléans: Imprimerie D'Emile Puget, 1872), 12.

28 Odile Roynette, 'L'armée et la conquête de l'eau dans les villes du Nord de la France à la fin du XIXe siècle', in Philippe Bragard, Jean-François Chanet, Catherine Denys, and Philippe Guignet (eds), *L'armée et la ville dans l'Europe du Nord et du Nord-Ouest: Du XVe siècle à nos jours* (Louvain: Bruylant-Academia), 47–57.

29 Chanet, *Vers l'armée nouvelle*, 204–27.

30 Roynette, 'Armée et la conquête de l'eau', 56–7.

31 Chanet, *Vers l'armée nouvelle*, 252–7.

32 Ibid., 257–8. See also Roynette, *'Bon pour le service'*, 286.

33 Eugen Weber, *Peasants into Frenchmen: The Modernisation of Rural France 1870–1914* (London: Chatto and Windus, 1979), 293–9. Weber's account has proved influential yet controversial. For a recent appraisal, see 'Dossier: Revisiting Eugen Weber's peasants into Frenchmen', *French Politics, Culture, and Society*, 27:2 (2009), 84–141.

34 'Les manoeuvres militaires', *Avenir militaire*, 91, 22 September 1872. See also, Mitchell, *Victors and Vanquished*, 74.

35 'The French Army', *The New York Times*, 29 September 1874.

36 Major Hoff, *Les grandes manoeuvres*, illustrations par Edouard Detaille (Paris: Boussod, Valdon et Cie, 1884), 17.

37 H. M. *Les grandes manoeuvres d'armée en 1894: Notes et impressions* (Saint-Nazaire: Grande Imprimerie, 1894), 16.

38 François Robichon, *L'armée française vue par les peintres, 1870–1914* (Paris: Editions Herscher/Ministère de la Défense, 1998); Didier Dubant, *Les grandes manoeuvres en France de 1901 à 1913* (Saint-Cyr-sur-Loire: Alan Sutton 2007); Hoff, *Grandes manoeuvres*.

39 H. M., *Grandes manœuvres*, 6.

40 Pierre Bridier, *Le camp de Coëtquidan va-t-il dévorer Brocéliande?* (Beignon: P. Bridier, 1984), 15; Edouard Maret, *Saint-Cyr Coëtquidan* (Rennes: Ouest-France, 1984), 3; Communauté de Communes de Ploërmel, *Campeneac-Gouhel: Vélo Promenades*, no. 6, www.ploermel/com/ploermel.com/pdf/decouvrir/se-detendre/voie-verte-velopromenades/vp6_2088.pdf, accessed 3 March 2009. At Coëtquidan Camp the army re-invented civilian displacement as a military training opportunity. A 1937 publication noted the 'tactically useful' ruined hamlets. *Notice relative aux camps de Coëtquidan et Gaël* (Rennes: Imprimerie de l'Ouest-Eclair, 1937), 5–6.

41 'L'école des sous-officiers au camp d'Avord', *L'Avenir militaire*, 400, 6 January 1877, 1.

42 Jean Doise and Maurice Vaïse, *Diplomatie et outil militaire, 1871–1991: Politique étrangère de la France* (Paris: Editions du Seuil, 1992 [1987]), 34–5, 55–6, 94; Douglas Porch, *The March to the Marne: The French Army, 1871–1914* (Cambridge: Cambridge University Press, 1981), 23–44; and

Ralston, *Army of the Republic*, 34–48, 96–115; Roynette, *'Bon pour le service'*. In addition, as France sought to keep pace with its European neighbours, the number of its army units increased significantly. The number of infantry regiments increased from 144 in 1875 to 173 in 1914 and the number of artillery regiments from 30 in 1872 to 62 in 1914. Jules Maurin, 'Les constructions militaires en France sous la IIIe République avant la Première guerre mondiale', in Jacques Aben and Jacques Rouzier (eds), *Défense et aménagement du territoire* (Montpellier: ESID, 2001), 225.

43 Chrastil, *Organizing for War*, 113.

44 Chef de bataillon Gerrée, 'L'assainissement du camp d'Auvours', *Revue du Génie militaire* (May–June 1952), 157.

45 Émile Jahandiez, *Les îles d'Hyères: Histoire, description, géologie, flore, faune* (Toulon: Etablissements Rébufa et Rouard, 1929), 159–61; Jean-Marie Guillon, 'Les îles d'Hyères aux XIXe et XXe siècles', in Jean-Pierre Brun (ed.), *Les îles d'Hyères: Fragments d'histoire* (Arles: Actes Sud, 1997), 110; Capitaine Delsart, 'Construction du Centre d'instruction de l'arme blindée et cavalerie (C.I.A.B.C.) au Camp de Carpiagne (Bouches-du-Rhône)', *Bulletin technique du génie militaire*, (1971), 194.

46 *Le Camp de Sissonne: Plans et historique du camp, organisation militaire* (Reims: Matot-Braine, 1914), 4.

47 Paul B. Miller, *From Revolutionaries to Citizens: Antimilitarism in France, 1870–1914* (Durham, NC: Duke University Press, 2002), 33–6; William Serman, *Les officiers français dans la nation, 1848–1914* (Paris: Aubier Montaigne, 1982), 15–16.

48 Bernard Lecocq, 'Partie A: 1901–1914', in Luc Dias (ed.), *Camp militaire national de La Courtine: 1901–2001, cent ans d'histoire* (La Courtine: Groupement de camp, 2001), 24–5.

49 Marianna Dudley, 'Greening the MOD: An environmental history of the UK defence estate, 1945-present' (PhD dissertation, University of Bristol, 2011), 83. John Childs, *The Military Use of the Land: A History of the Defence Estate* (Berne: Peter Lang, 1998), 119.

50 ADA 31 R 2 Général Faure Biguet to Préfet de l'Aveyron, 'Au sujet du Camp projeté sur le plateau de Larzac', 26 September 1899.

51 ADA 31 R 2 'Procès-verbal de conférence portant établissement du régime du champ de tir temporaire du Larzac', 20 September 1901.

52 Capitaine Menu, *Notice sur l'installation du camp d'instruction de Mailly* (Paris and Nancy: Berger-Levrault, 1906), 3.

53 G. Bonnet, 'Avant-propos', in Arthur Robert and Arsène Thévenot, *Guide du camp de Mailly De la ville d'Arcis-sur-Aube et des communes limitrophes du camp* (Arcis-sur-Aube: G. Bonnet, 1908), 3. In this edition of the guide, Robert wrote the section on the camp itself and Thévenot the section on the surrounding region.

54 Ralston, *Army of the Republic*; Eugen Weber, *The Nationalist Revival in*

France, 1905–1914 (Berkeley and Los Angeles: University of California Press, 1968).

55 Menu, *Notice sur l'installation du camp*, 4; Georges Vigarello, 'The Tour de France' and Jean-Yves Guimar, 'Vidal de la Blache's Geography of France', in Pierre Nora (ed.), *Realms of Memory: Rethinking the French Past, Vol. 2: Traditions*, trans Arthur Goldhammer (New York: Columbia University Press, 1997), 186–209, 468–500.

56 Robert and Thévenot, *Guide du camp de Mailly*, 9–10.

57 Menu, *Notice sur l'installation du camp*, 6–7, 15, 18, 34–6; Robert and Thévenot, *Guide du camp de Mailly*, 14–21; Barnes, *Great Stink of Paris*, 3, 194–228.

58 Robert and Thévenot, *Guide du camp de Mailly*, 8, 11, 22. An infantry regiment's guide to the camp similarly celebrated how its greenery broke up *la Champagne pouilleuse's* 'monotonous and sad aspect'. *Guide-Itinéraire du 79e régiment d'infanterie. Camp de Mailly-Nancy: 16 juillet–4 août 1910* (Nancy: Imprimerie Berger-Levrault, 1910), 12.

59 'Mailly-le-Camp – Paysage champenois, undated postcard', sent 12 June 1908; 'Environs de Mailly', undated postcard, sent 17 May 1909. This postcard, and all subsequent ones of Mailly Camp, is from the private collection of Philippe Pierrejean. See also his book *Mailly-le-Camp* (Saint-Cyr-sur-Loire: Editions Alan Sutton, 2007).

60 François Cachin, 'The painter's landscape', in Pierre Nora (ed.), *Rethinking France: Les lieux de mémoire, vol. 2: Space* (Chicago: University of Chicago Press, 2006), 299.

61 'Camp de Mailly – Vieille église de la Dègue occupée par les sapeurs et les tirailleurs', undated postcard; 'Camp de Mailly – Pimbraux – Ferme expropriée située dans la zone dangereuse des tirs', undated postcard produced by Librairie militaire Guérin, sent 8 September 1907; 'Camp de Mailly – La Custonne – Ferme expropriée située dans la zone dangereuse des tirs', undated postcard.

62 Robert and Thévenot, *Guide du camp de Mailly*, 9, 23.

63 ADM 2 Q 416 Ministre de la Guerre to Préfet de la Marne, 'Organisation d'un camp d'instruction près de Mailly (Aube)', 8 July 1902.

64 ADGI 2 R 65 Convention entre l'état et la commune de Martignas relative à la cession gratuite de terrains dans les bois de cette commune', 20 March 1898; ADGI 2 R 65 Garde Général des Eaux et Forêts, 'Rapport: Exploitation d'une carrière de gravier pour le service de la guerre', 6 July 1898; ADGI 2 R 66 Général Varaigne to Préfet de la Gironde, 'Incendie au champ de tir de Souge', 28 May 1899; ADGI 2 R 66 Général Varaigne to Préfet de la Gironde, 'Incendie au champ de tir de Souge', 6 May 1899.

65 ADGI 2 R 68 'Procès-verbal de conférence concernant l'utilisation du champ de tir de Souge comme champ de tir de circonstance pour l'artillerie', 5 April 1902.

66 Miller, *Revolutionaries to Citizens*, 36–64.
67 Rachel Woodward, *Military Geographies* (Oxford: Blackwell, 2004), 119; Rachel Woodward, 'Military landscapes/militære landskap: The military landscape photography of Ingrid Book and Carina Hedén', in Chris Pearson, Peter Coates, and Tim Cole (eds), *Militarized Landscapes: From Gettysburg to Salisbury Plain* (London: Continuum, 2010), 21–38.
68 Serman, *Officiers français*, 17; Judith Surkis, *Sexing the Citizen: Morality and Masculinity in France, 1870–1920* (Ithaca: Cornell University Press, 2006), 218. The postcards' democratic nature was underscored by the way in which they allowed the expression of multiple perspectives and how their circulation was only made possible through rising literacy rates and developments in print technologies. Martin Lyons, 'What did the peasants read? Written and printed culture in rural France, 1815–1914', *European History Quarterly*, 27:2 (1997), 190.
69 'L'Ecole de Saint-Cyr au camp de Mailly – Exercices en campagne, une escalade', undated postcard; 'Ecoles à feu – Piece de 120 court – Attendant le commandement: Feu!' undated postcard, sent 6 May 1908.
70 On the anxieties about French masculinity at this time, see Nye, *Masculinity and Male Codes of Honour; Forth, Dreyfus Affair*. On the military as means of rejuvenating masculinity, see Roynette, *'Bon pour le service'*, 406. The form of masculinity represented in these postcards is far less martial than that depicted in Napoleonic France. Michael J. Hughes, 'Making Frenchmen into warrior: Martial masculinity in Napoleonic France', in Christopher E. Forth and Bertrand Taithe (eds), *French Masculinities: History, Culture and Politics* (Basingstoke: Palgrave Macmillan, 2007), 51–66.
71 'Camp de Mailly – La pêche aux écrevisses', undated postcard produced by Bazar militaire A. Nieps.
72 'Camp de Mailly – Les travaux de propreté', undated postcard produced by Bazar militaire A. Nieps, sent 26 January 1919[?].
73 Miller, *Revolutionaries to Citizens*, 117–19, 123.
74 Untitled and undated postcard, sent 22 July 1906; 'Camp de Mailly – Les chiens ambulanciers', undated postcard.
75 'Camp de Mailly – Artillerie de campagne, passage d'un fossé', undated postcard produced by ND Phot.
76 'Au camp de Mailly – L'abreuvoir', undated postcard produced by Liégeois; 'Au camp de Mailly – La visite des chevaux', undated postcard produced by Liégeois, sent 29 June 1909.
77 'Camp de Mailly – Le pansage', undated postcard produced by Verry-Morillon; Barnes, *Great Stink of Paris*, 196–202.
78 'Mailly-le-Camp – Promenade sous les bois', undated postcard, sent 22 September 1910. In a similar vein, a postcard of Souge Camp entitled 'Rest after manoeuvres' has a group of soldiers lying and standing on the edge of woodland, their rifles resting in pyramid shapes. 'Camp de Souge

(Gironde) – Repos après la manoeuvre', undated postcard, AMMJ Fonds P. Neveu.

79 'Camp de Mailly – Le travail des gardes d'écurie', undated postcard, sent 13 April 1910.

80 Roynette, *'Bon pour le service'*, 386–92. On military attempts to regulate the 'sexual hygiene' of soldiers, see Surkis, *Sexing the Citizen*, 214–19, 230–41.

81 'Camp de Mailly – Décorations des tentes', undated postcard produced by Neurdein Frères.

82 Marie-Armand Laithiez, *Deux manoeuvres avec tir réel à Sissonne en 1908: Contribution à l'étude des principales questions soulevées par la conduite des feux et l'instruction du groupe* (Paris: R. Chapelot, 1909). By 1910, approximately 700 120 mm and 155 mm cannons were in use. Porch, *March to the Marne*, 233–4.

83 Miller, *Revolutionaries to Citizens*, 120.

84 'Camp militaire de Souge (Gironde) – La Saucisse d'observations de manoeuvres', undated postcard, AMMJ Fonds P. Neveu. See also Doise and Vaïse, *Diplomatie et outil militaire*, 134–7.

85 S. Renard, *Note sur le tir de l'infanterie contre les objectifs aériens* (Paris: Libraire militaire Chapelot, 1912), 19.

86 Fred Howard, *Wilbur and Orville: A Biography of the Wright Brothers* (Mineola, NY: Dover Publications, 1988), 249, 282–9. On Michelin's encouragement of aviation, see Stephen L. Harp, *Marketing Michelin: Advertising and Cultural Identity in Twentieth-Century France* (Baltimore: Johns Hopkins University Press, 2001), 167–71. Military bases elsewhere made for suitable flying sites. On the other side of the Atlantic, Wilbur's brother Orville flew planes at Fort Myer, Virginia.

87 Vanessa R. Schwartz, *Spectacular Realities: Early Mass Culture in Fin-de-Siècle Paris* (Berkeley: University of California Press, 1998).

88 ADGI 2 R 74 Ingénieur ordinaire, Bordeaux, 'Établissement de champs de tir', 8 July 1872; Corinne Micelli, 'L'homme de Cazaux: Ferdinand Marzac', *Air Actualités*, 595, October 2006, 58–60; Eliane Keller and Patrick Boyer, *Cazaux: De l'Ecole de tir aérien, ETA, à la base aérienne 120, 1913–1962* (Arcachon: Société historique et archéologique d'Arcachon et du pays de Buch, 2002), 9. On the origins of aviation in the Landes département, see *Au dessus des pins et des vagues: Les débuts de l'aviation dans les Landes jusqu'en 1940* (Mont-de-Marson: Archives départementales des Landes, 1994).

89 John H. Morrow, 'Knights of the sky: The rise of military aviation', in Frans Coetzee and Marilyn Shevin Coetzee (eds), *Authority, Identity and the Social History of the Great War* (Oxford: Berghahn Books, 1995), 310.

90 ADGI 2 R 76 'Extrait du registre des délibérations du conseil municipal de la ville de Bordeaux', 6 December 1910.

91 Porch, *March to the Marne*, 193–4, 200–2, 232–45; Alistair Horne, *The French Army and Politics, 1870–1970* (London: Macmillan, 1984), 21–9; Gerd

Krumeich, *Armaments and Politics in France on the Eve of the First World War: The Introduction of Three Years Conscription 1913–1914*, trans. Stephen Conn (Leamington Spa: Berg, 1984).

92 Quoted in Miller, *Revolutionaries to Citizens*, 119.

93 ADGI 2 R 69 'Procès-verbal de conférence relatif à la détermination du régime du champ de tir de Saillans pour la garnison de Libourne', 11 May 1904.

94 SHD-DAT 3 V 30 Médecin Inspecteur Général Vaillard and Général Goetschy, 'Avis commun au sujet de la possibilité d'installer au camp de Châlons un second camp pour les troupes soit vers Suippes, soit dans l'angle sud-est du champ de manoeuvres vers Cuperly, 7 October 1911.

95 Miller, *Revolutionaries to Citizens*, 105–9.

4

The 'mangled earth' of the trenches[1]
(1914–18)

Four years of trench warfare between 1914 and 1918 transformed farmland and forests in northern and eastern France into muddy, cratered,
and toxic places. The scale and extent of the militarized environment of
the Western Front was unprecedented, and the changes that it brought
to the environment fascinated and appalled observers. Mark Plowman,
a British infantry officer who later resigned his commission on grounds
of conscience, presented an apocalyptic view of the Somme trench environment, which had 'lost its nature, for, pitted everywhere with shell-
holes, it crumbles and cracks as though it has indeed been subject to an
earthquake'.[2] French artilleryman Henry Malherbe similarly stressed the
unnatural character of 'modern' battlefields 'covered with innumerable
scars, swollen by artificial mounds and heaps . . . [giving] one the curious
impression of being used up, of artificiality, of the abstract'. Nature and
technological modernity had seemingly merged: 'the broken trees lying
on the blackened and shell-pitted earth are impregnated with the smell
of chemicals'.[3]

Disfigured, transformed, artificial. These are words commonly used
to describe the trench environment in both contemporary and scholarly
accounts. Paul Fussell, amongst others, has argued that the unnatural
and artificial character of the trenches and the response to it of war poets,
writers, and painters marked the end of romantic appreciations of nature
and the beginning of representations of nature as ironic and unnatural.
This was in line with the modernist forms of cultural expression that
emerged from the brutal experience of war.[4] The trenches did indeed
constitute a thoroughly hybrid environment created through a combination of weapons, terrain, soldiers, and climate. But, as this chapter

argues, overstressing their artificiality obscures soldiers' embodied and visceral experience of dwelling in the militarized environment and their un-ironic observation and appreciation of nature. Furthermore, it was only through the mobilization of natural resources, such as timber, that armies were able to supply themselves and fight the war. By outlining the Western Front's environmental history, this chapter aims to show how the First World War was fought in, through, and against nature.[5]

In the unprecedented militarized trench environment millions of soldiers lived, fought, and died. In this chapter I attend to how they experienced and responded to the trench environment and how they mobilized nature to fight, survive, and seek solace. Although the militarized environment often seemed all-encompassing and overwhelming, nature could, at times, provide some comfort and sustenance. For combatants, nature was both ally and enemy and something to be mobilized or endured.[6] Soldiers were not the only inhabitants of the 'more-than-human' environment of the trenches. They brought with them horses, donkeys, dogs, and pigeons and unwillingly shared their living space with less welcome creatures, such as rats and lice. These creatures helped or hindered soldiers, becoming allies or enemies.

The war was fought and sustained through the creation of militarized environments in the trenches and beyond. Behind front lines, soldiers sought to harness the soil's productivity through gardening and farming, whilst the trenches sucked in natural resources, such as timber, from the rest of France and beyond.[7] Armies also mobilized fields and forests to train their soldiers and pilots, leading to protests from displaced and inconvenienced locals. So whilst France as a whole mobilized politically, culturally, and economically for war, pockets of opposition to militarization emerged in rural France.

In terms of wartime environmental annihilation, the Western Front has been perhaps only matched globally by the bombing of Japanese cities during the Second World War and the Agent Orange-led defoliation of jungle during the Vietnam War.[8] It was certainly the most intensive and destructive instance of environmental militarization in French history. For although the battles of the Franco-Prussian War had transformed the countryside in which they were fought (see chapter 2), these changes were minor in comparison with the environmental repercussions of the First World War. The technological might of the 'war machine' seemed poised to completely obliterate human and nonhuman life along the Western Front and observers were shocked and dismayed by the war's sterilization of the countryside.[9] Between 1914 and 1918, therefore, the civilian narrative of 'militarization-as-sterilization' gained more prominence and became imbued with an even greater sense of loss, transformation, and destruction.

The sterilization of the countryside

The first stages of the war were ones of movement. But after a French offensive into Alsace and Lorraine achieved nothing and the German Schlieffen Plan to attack north-eastern France through Belgium definitively collapsed during the battle of the Marne (6–9 September), the front lines stabilized over 700 km from the North Sea to the Swiss border during the autumn of 1914. On what became known as the Western Front, soldiers literally dug themselves into the earth. As one observer commented, 'the shovel and the pickaxe [are] true combat weapons in this war'.[10]

As is well-known, both sides constructed lines of trenches connected by communication trenches and protected by barbed wire and look-out posts, which were relatively easy to defend but much harder to take in an attack. Between the trenches lay 'no man's land', which artillery shells, rain, and a relatively high water table turned into an environment of mud, craters, and stagnant pools strewn with human and animal corpses, barbed wire, and ordnance. The scale and kinds of weaponry deployed during the war, from shells to poisonous gas, obliterated all forms of life, human and nonhuman.[11] The militarized environment of the Western Front therefore became, in the words of T.E. Hulme, a place full 'of dead things, dead animals here & there, dead unburied animals, skeletons of horses destroyed by shell fire'.[12]

If sterility implies the absence of life and infertility, it seemed that the war had sterilized vast swathes of northern and eastern France. The violent language of novelist William Arthur Dunkerley conveys the deep emotional response that he felt when confronted by the replacement of 'smiling countrysides' with 'stark, black, bristling wastes' where trees had been reduced to 'blasted trunks' complete with 'dud shells protruding from their carcasses'.[13]

Even allowing for the restrictions imposed by wartime censorship and the difficulties of travelling within the war zone,[14] the thoroughness of sterilization penetrated the accounts of war journalists. *The Times* correspondent Gerald Fitzgerald Campbell described how in Apremont forest (Meuse) it was possible to walk through the trench-ridden environment and 'never see a leaf. Nothing is left of the trees but scattered stumps cut clean off by the shells close to the ground'.[15] Given the scale of destruction and the impossibility of gaining a comprehensive overview of the war, journalists felt disorientated and powerless within the militarized environment.[16] The same was true for certain combatants. Of Mametz Wood (Somme) in August 1916, Plowman wrote that it is 'nothing more than a small collection of thin tree-trunks standing as if a forest fire had just swept over them'.[17] The rapidity of the change was startling.

Nationalistic concerns informed representations of the sterilized environment as portrayals of the blighted countryside justified war against Germany. William Dyson, an Australian cartoonist who volunteered for military service, depicted 'a landscape the like of which man has never gazed upon since early chaos brooded over all'. But overlooking his own country's role in creating the militarized environment, Dyson asserted that the devastated regions were the 'finished product . . . towards which that vast Teutonized industry of war is working'.[18] In a similar vein, British novelist Arnold Bennett identified the German 'war machine' as the agent of destruction and sterilization. He revelled in bucolic French countryside near the front lines that exuded 'peace, majesty, grandeur' and of which the heavily cultivated character testified to 'the mild, splendid richness of the soil of France'. Yet, as Bennett reminded his readers, the front lines were only five miles away; other equally pretty and productive French rural locales lay beyond German lines waiting to be liberated. Bennett's portrayal of the desolated area at Notre-Dame-de-Lorette (Somme) where shells had 'sterilized the earth' similarly underscored the tragedy that had befallen the 'incomparable soil of France'. Bennett's determination to provide compelling evidence of the tragic consequences of German militarism seems intended to inspire opposition to it.[19]

Bennett and others mobilized images of nature as an imaginative resource, creating the sense that war entailed sterilization and that the German army bore the main responsibility. However, combatants on both sides of no man's land mobilized nature to wage war, with all the environmental disruption that entailed.

Mobilizing nature in the trenches

The mobilization of terrain and topography had begun before the establishment of trench warfare during the initial war of movement. For instance, French forces had held the 'Grand Couronné' hill near Nancy, whose steep, wooded slopes helped repel repeated German attacks between 5 and 9 September 1914.[20] But German troops made effective use of terrain elsewhere. Field-Marshal Sir John French noted how they occupied a 'very strong position' on a high plateau in the Aisne valley in September 1914 where tree cover made it 'impossible' for the British to evaluate their strength.[21] Contributing to the notion that geography mattered, British geographers enthusiastically joined the war effort. Douglas William Freshfield, president of the Royal Geographical Society (RGS), stated that 'war and geography are closely connected. A grasp of the features of the country, the right maps and intelligence to use them, are among the first requirements of a soldier'. The RGS sought to inform the military's campaign with geographical knowledge and launched a project to create a 1:1 million map of Europe in anticipation of an Allied breakthrough.[22]

The stabilization of lines on the Western Front undermined the need for such a map. But geography continued to matter, even if military commanders could no longer get an overall sense of the battle from a single vantage point (unlike German high command at Sedan in 1870) and were slow to adapt their strategic thinking to the conditions of trench warfare.[23] From Mont Kemmel (near Ypres in Belgium) to the forts of Verdun, both sides coveted high ground and bitterly fought for it because it offered vital observation posts and artillery positions. In addition, soldiers sought out ravines, disused quarries, and folds in the land because they offered valuable concealment.[24]

Forests too offered cover, provided of course that they had not been destroyed by shells. Unsurprisingly, foresters highlighted forests' importance, portraying them as a key military resource. Charles Guyot, former professor and director of the French national forestry school at Nancy, argued that French soldiers had overcome the fear of the forest that they had displayed in the 1870–71 war and now 'considered it as the best element for safety and support'.[25] Guyot's intervention was undoubtedly intended to highlight the national importance of forests and so raise the status of foresters and pave the way for forests' eventual postwar reconstruction. But there was some truth in it. Forests did provide cover from planes and artillery positions and had slowed the advance of German troops at Viel-Armand and Argonne. At least one French officer appreciated the role played by forests. With their 'gaping wounds', they therefore deserved nation recognition.[26]

In the absence of forest cover and where terrain offered few possibilities for concealment, soldiers adapted the environment to seek shelter. In this sense, the trench system was a way of creating protection in the absence of natural cover.[27] Camouflage was another means of concealment. Unlike other European armies, the French had failed to introduce uniforms that blended into the surrounding environment. For although, after years of resistance from traditionalists, the French government passed a law in July 1914 introducing the blue-grey '*bleu-horizon*' army uniforms, there was no time to implement this change by the outbreak of war. Therefore, French soldiers went to the front wearing the bright red trousers they had worn since the July Monarchy.[28]

The French army took camouflage more seriously as the war progressed. A 1916 training manual suggested camouflaging machine gun positions with branches and grass to make them 'disappear into the land'. A gunner could likewise camouflage himself by adding leaves and grass to his kepi.[29] The attempt to mimic nature and blend into the environment was taken to new levels as both sides used fake trees as artillery observation posts. But camouflage had its limits. One British soldier recalled how he had come across a German machine gunner hidden up a tree on 'the neatest little platform you ever saw, painted so that it was invisible'. But the platform did not provide total concealment and safety. Upon being discovered, the German gunner was shot.[30]

Military use of camouflage in the First World War was, in part, informed by naturalists' observations of patterns and mimicry amongst animals.[31] Animals also entered the trench militarized environment in far more concrete ways.

Animals in the trenches

The military mobilization of animals during the war was, at times, symbolic. As well as featuring on propaganda posters, animal imagery appeared on actual war machines. In 1916, Captain Félix Antonin Gabriel Brocard adopted the stork as the insignia for his aerial combat group. The stork not only represented aerial prowess but was intended to remind French fighter pilots of need to reclaim the lost provinces of Alsace and Lorraine (storks were known to nest in the regions' chimneys).[32] But physical animal labour was more important than symbolism as belligerent nations mobilized thousands of horses, mules, donkeys, dogs, and pigeons to fulfil varied but essential roles. So although the conflict's technological and industrial aspects are well-known, its animal history deserves far more attention.[33]

Equid transport was essential to the daily functioning of the trenches. Cavalry charges became obsolete in the militarized environment of the trenches. Bar the odd horse-mounted patrol, the vast majority of horses, mules, and donkeys on the Western Front pulled machine guns and artillery canons and carried supplies through the mud. The militarization of horses has a long history, but in terms of numbers and organization, it reached a climax in the First World War. In the first twelve days of the war, Britain mobilized 165,000 horses. Numbers reached a peak in August 1917 when the British Expeditionary Force (BEF) deployed 368,000 horses and 82,000 mules on the Western Front.[34] It was not just the BEF that relied on horses; the German cavalry mobilized 715,000 horses, while the French army requisitioned 700,000 equids in 1914 alone.[35]

A gloating tone sometimes infiltrated publications on the importance of four-legged transport. One British commentator declared that 'the motor-mad mechanic may think that his chance has come, but generals who have to lead an army over water-logged plains . . . will demand horses'.[36] Captain Sidney Galtrey similarly stressed the vital role played by horses, donkeys, and mules, arguing that the army would have been 'immobile and impotent' without them.[37] As a member of the army's remount service and a racing journalist, Galtrey was overly keen to emphasis their importance. But his claims were not without foundation. For despite developments in mechanized transport during the war (the French army boasted 90,000 motor vehicles by 1918), equids still pulled 80 per cent of artillery pieces in the French army at the time of the armistice.[38]

The heavy demand for horses reached out from the Western Front to the stud farms of North America from which the British army imported thousands of Percheron horses. Like its human recruits, the British army trained and physically shaped the horses to turn 'civilian' bodies into military ones.[39] Galtrey outlined, with much pride, how the army transformed this 'raw material' of 'shoeless, long-haired, tousled-maned, ragged-hipped' horses into the 'well-fed, clean and healthy horse' that was 'ready for France'. His description came complete with 'before and after' paintings.[40] Once fashioned and trained to meet the army's needs, the physical agency of the horses and mules unwittingly supported and sustained the conflict. That is not to say that the abilities of horses and mules were equal. In places, mules could get through areas of mud that horses found impassable.[41]

Galtrey portrayed the disciplined equid as stoic and compliant. He praised the 'silent, plodding, uncomplaining' qualities of the horses, donkeys, and mules that 'gallantly' served the British Empire. 'Good' mules were adaptable and docile whilst 'bad' ones were stubborn and unwieldy.[42] It is hard not to read celebrations of the mules' stoicism and obedience as qualities that human soldiers should aspire to.

The unforgiving militarized environment of the Western Front took its toll on these militarized animals. But compared to the Franco-Prussian War, greater efforts were made to care for them. According to Galtrey, the British Army Veterinary Service's care of horses developed as the war progressed, meaning that horses were better protected from the 'unnatural rigours of hardship and exposure and those other menaces imposed by modern warfare'.[43] The BEF's treatment of horses impressed civilian observers. As if to prove the civilized and humane character of the British army, in stark opposition to industrial, barbaric German militarism (see above), Bennett reported approvingly on a 'horse-hospital' near Boulogne where thousands of wounded horses recuperated in meadows. On seeing the level of care given to a horse as it emerged from an operation, Bennett felt that it was 'impossible . . . to think of him as a mere horse!'[44] The BEF's attention to the horses' well-being was not entirely self-motivated, and followed pressure from animal welfare groups about the treatment of animals in war.[45] But despite better care, the Western Front was still a place of hardship. The rigours of the front lines meant that it could still take hours to remove mud from a horse's coat and harness after a day's work.[46] Equids' suffering was a source of distress for the animals and their human companions; the sight and sounds of animal suffering engraved themselves in soldiers' minds and memories.[47]

Like horses and mules, dogs provided transportation on the battlefield, carrying food and supplies between trenches and, in the Belgian army, pulling guns. Their physicality and trainability meant that dogs were perhaps the most versatile animal on the battlefield. They were mobilized as guard dogs, messenger dogs, laid telegraph wires, and located injured soldiers in no man's land (a 1916 German publication estimated that 600 dogs had saved over 3,000 lives in this way).[48]

As with horses, and with Germany leading the way, armies increasingly institutionalized the use of dogs as the war continued. In 1916, the British War Office authorized Lieutenant Colonel Richardson to establish a military dog-training school at Shoeburyness, which was then transferred to Natley Ridge in the New Forest as the number of canine recruits increased. France followed suit in 1917, when Captain Malric took charge of the Military Canine Service based at Satory to train liaison, guard, and medical dogs. And once it entered the war, the United States army used bloodhounds to locate corpses and land mines. In all, armies mobilized tens of thousands of dogs. In 1917 and 1918 France alone enlisted 15,000 dogs, of which 5,321 died.[49]

Dogs' agility, size, and speed meant that they could carry messages across the militarized environment better than humans. But sometimes distance and terrain defeated even them. Carrier pigeons stepped, or rather flew, into the breach. Like horses, mules, and dogs they too became the object of military planning, training, and organization. The British and French armies had approximately 22,000 pigeons each in service on the Western Front by the end of the war.[50]

Armies mobilized and militarized dogs, horses, and pigeons through institutional channels. But at the same time, soldiers and animals came together in more intimate and informal ways in the 'more-than-human' trench environment. Pet-keeping offered company, amusement, and an emotional outlet. As novelist and veteran Pierre Dumarchey recalled, even the 'hardest [soldiers] softened in front' of their animals.[51] Second Lieutenant Hector MacQuarrie of the Royal Field Artillery, who was hugely attached to his Brussels Griffin cross, advised American soldiers to keep a pet because they 'humanize the front' and 'keep you from being too lonely at night'.[52] Pet dogs were also common in the German trenches; most famously, Adolf Hitler kept a fox-terrier named Fuchs as a pet.[53] Cats, attracted to the trenches' abundant rat populations, were also particularly welcome.[54] In contrast, some soldiers made pets and mascots out of non-domesticated animals. G.P. Roberts of the Royal Marine Artillery Howitzer Brigade and his men looked after a wounded jackdaw, feeding and making 'a fuss of' it, while French soldiers in Argonne forest captured squirrels for mascots.[55]

Whether wild or domestic in origin, pets were part of the trenches' atmosphere of 'surrogate domesticity'.[56] Alongside gardening and adding 'homely touches', such as mirrors and family portraits, to the trenches, it was became a way of coping emotionally with trench life and alleviating its dispiriting mixture of physical hardship, fear, and boredom.[57] So too was observing the fragments of nonhuman life that survived in the trenches.

Seeking solace in nature

An enduring myth of the war is that soldiers' experience of pastoral, sunny environments during the summer of 1914 ended with the onset of muddy, mechanical, and brutal trench warfare. Furthermore, Dennis Showalter has described the military operation zones along the Western

Front as 'urbanized environments', characterized by 'noise, confusion, and filth', best suited to those used to city life.[58] Whilst there is some truth in both these notions, soldiers in the trenches continued to observe and rejoice in those remnants of the countryside not yet obliterated by the war.[59]

Fond recollections of birdsong pepper veterans' accounts of trench life as symbols of hope and solace. Against the odds, birds had adapted to the militarized environment of the Western Front, feeding on the insects that thrived in the trenches and nesting in remains of trees. Waterfowl also gathered on water-logged shell holes and starlings mimicked the whistle blasts used to warn of enemy planes.[60] Birdsong provided reassurance for soldiers of different nationalities. In the words of one Scottish soldier: 'if it weren't for the birds, what a hell it would be! I watch them singing, and something comes into my throat that it makes me almost greet'.[61] Birdsong was a reminder that life survived within the brutal environment of the trenches. Herbert Sulzbach of the 63rd (Frankfurt) Field Artillery Regiment wrote that even though the 'whole landscape had turned to war' the cuckoos and turtle-doves 'don't mind' and keep on singing 'as though the war were none of their damned business'.[62] Birdsong was significant for soldiers, hence the anger of privates in the Devonshire Regiment when their corporal shot dead a small bird that sung in a tree near their trench.[63]

Despite their militarization, forests offered a sense of repose and connection with nature. Guyot claimed that soldiers serving in the forest experienced 'an intimate life with nature' and learned to admire the forest's changing seasons.[64] His romanticized view of forest life was shared by some soldiers. French artilleryman Gaston Pastre enjoyed walking in the 'magnificent' forests of Lorraine and snoozing in hammocks in Argonne forest.[65] Stationed for eight days in a forest that was a 'paradise for wild birds' and wild flowers, Sulzbach felt 'enchanted' to be alone with his thoughts ('I don't suppose I'll ever be sitting like this again, out in the midst of nature for several days').[66]

Unsurprisingly, the countryside behind front lines provided more opportunities for pastoral contemplations than front lines. Army Chaplin William Drury awoke one morning at Piquigny near Amiens in 'unspoilt countryside, beautiful with autumn colouring' and walking up to a hilltop château from which he could see 'how fair the Somme must have been before it was blasted by shells'.[67] Streams, rivers, and fields offered some possibility of rest and rejuvenation before or after a stint on front lines. Paul Delaunay found calm among streams and lush fields when resting at Salmagne (Meuse): 'it was finally calm and like a return to life'.[68] Swimming in rivers, ponds and canals was infinitely preferable to wallowing in the mud of the trenches. Edmund Blunden, poet and second lieutenant in the Royal Sussex regiment, enjoyed the 'unexpected luxury' of swimming in the La Bassée Canal (Somme).[69] German soldiers shared similar experiences. On resting in sunny fields and as birds sang near his billet at Les Petites-Armoises (Ardennes), Sulzbach remarked that 'you suddenly notice once again that you are alive; actually it's more like feeling that you've risen from the dead'.[70]

Based on these accounts, the attention soldiers paid to nature suggests that a distinctly non-ironic form of nature appreciation flourished on the Western Front, alongside the depictions of a warped, modernist, and artificial nature that Fussell emphasises.[71] Falling within the Romantic tradition of nature as a source of spiritual nourishment and mental renewal,[72] it represents an alternative militarized environmental perspective to the terrain and tactics approach.

Even those poets and artists associated with the modernist artistic response to the trenches found repose and solace in surviving pockets of woodlands, orchards, and farmland. War poet Siegfried Sassoon remembered the 'luxury' of a moment alone by a stream before going into battle, noting how the 'water-haunting birds whistled and piped, swinging on the bulrushes and tufted reeds, and a tribe of little green and gold frogs hopped about in the grass'.[73] Similarly, artist Paul Nash, writing to his wife in March 1917, noted that 'flowers bloom everywhere'. Even in war-torn wood, shoots sprouted on 'broken trees' and a nightingale sung from its 'bruised heart'. The combination of nature's aesthetic beauty and its resilience made Nash constantly 'alive to [its] significance'.[74] The survival, however tiny, of birds, flowers, and other forms of life, is significant because it demonstrates that militarization was never complete. Or, to use a term commonly associated with war in the twentieth century, it was not 'total'.[75]

Fighting against nature

The survival of nature offered combatants some emotional solace and a fragile sense of hope. But it is important not to overemphasize nature's serenity. For despite enjoying the 'splendid natural surroundings', Sulzbach was aware that death was never far away.[76] Sulzbach's account points to how nature appreciation mingled with thoughts and images of death and destruction. Georges Lafond remembers how on the ground around the parapet of his trench, 'daisies, buttercups, wild poppies, and cornflowers have sprung up and blossomed, opening out to nature, the sun, and life'. Observing the flowers prompted Lafond to reflect how they would be caught in crossfire and mingle with the bodies of the dead. Lafond's emotional reaction to the flowers ('nature has never seemed so moving') moved him to tears and thoughts of his wife and family.[77] Furthermore, the harshness of the trench environment overshadowed nature's beauty. Six months after revelling in the beauty of flowers blooming in trenches, Nash experienced a brutal post-battlefield environment of 'stinking mud', 'black, dying trees', and annihilated horses and mules. The country was 'one huge grave . . . unspeakable, godless, hopeless'.[78] And at times it was impossible to pay attention to nature. For instance, many soldiers were too tired to 'comment' on the 'dramatic and captivating' scenery they passed through on their march to Thievres (Somme).[79]

The trenches were extreme environments. For combatants, they were oppressive and seemingly inescapable.[80] Shells, gas, and other forms of weaponry all 'altered the environment in such a way as to make it uninhabitable'.[81] Environmental conditions also contributed, in no small way, to the misery. John Buchan, author of *The Thirty-Nine Steps* and a 24-volume military history of the 'Great War', even claimed that 'it was the hostile elements and the unkindly nature of Mother Earth' that 'vexed' soldiers more than 'casual bombardments'.[82] Buchan perhaps goes too far, but for many soldiers it seemed like they were fighting against nature.

Mud was one of the most demoralizing aspects of the trench environment. Rain, shells, soldiers' boots, and underlying geological conditions combined to make it a 'natural enemy' for combatants. Mud dragged the soldier down, physically and emotionally.[83] The French trench newspaper *Le Bochofage* outlined how 'men die of mud, as they die of bullets, but more horribly. Mud is where men sink – and what is worse – where their souls sink'.[84] The 'slimy greenish water' stagnating in shell-holes could suck men down too. 'Get into one and you would probably never get out', warned Dunkerley who was haunted by mud after visiting the Flanders battlefields. Its 'ubiquitous' quality was captured in his poem 'Mud': 'Mud on the ground, and mud in the air/And mud in your grub, and mud everywhere'.[85]

Mud's sinking qualities turned simple actions into frustratingly difficult procedures. It made moving between trenches at night-time even more unpleasant for philosopher and poet T.E. Hulme:

It's bad enough walking over uneven ground in the dark at any time when you don't know whether your foot is landing on earth or nothing the next step. Every now & then you fell over & got up to your knees in the mud . . . you got bullets flying over your head from the German trenches in all directions. Nobody worries about these however, all you can think of is the mud.[86]

The widespread use of duckboards (wooden pre-fabricated walkways) offered some relief. But even these wobbled, sunk into the mud, or floated away.[87] In places the mud got so bad that it became almost liquid; Delaunay memorably described the slime in the trenches at Woëvre as 'liquid mud'.[88]

Sunshine transformed the trench environment. It could dry out even the most tenacious mud. Drury recorded how sun 'hardened' the once 'waist-deep' mud 'into an extra-ordinary, hard-baked maze of shell holes and old trenches'.[89] On the whole, fine weather made the militarized environments more bearable. Spring buds after a tough winter raised morale; Hulme wrote in March 1915 that 'I don't suppose any of us ever waited for Spring with so much interest. One does notice physical things here tremendously'.[90] But the heat could also cause discomfort; Lieutenant John Stainforth complained in August 1916 that 'it's all just heat, flies, and monotony. I'd give worlds for green fields and blue water, instead of stony white chalk, blinding in the sun-dazzle and scorching to touch'.[91]

Despite such complaints, warm weather was generally preferable to cold weather. According to writer Francis Marre, the cold was as 'fearsome' as German soldiers. But, Marre reassured his readers, both adversaries could be defeated, whilst French soldiers' heroism made them 'oblivious' to everything.[92] Such patriotic sentiments, however, could not disguise the discomfort that cold weather caused and the ensuing struggle to keep warm. In temperatures that apparently reached as low as minus 29 degrees at night-time, Pastre was reduced to sending his men out to hunt boars and foxes to keep warm, defying the army ban on hunting.[93] Cold weather paid no heed to nationality. Due to fierce winds, poet John McCrae and his fellow combatants had 'not had our clothes off since last Saturday, and there is no near prospect of getting them off', whilst Sulzbach recalled how the mud and cold in December 1914 sapped German morale.[94]

Alongside mud, rain, and freezing temperatures, vermin added to soldiers' misery as the ecological conditions of trenches favoured lice, mice, flies, mosquitoes, cockroaches and, perhaps most infamously, rats.[95] Accounts of the rats' size and ferociousness have undoubtedly been exaggerated; one British private claimed that 'if they were put in a harness they could have done a milk round, they were that big, yes, honest'.[96] Whatever their size, rats were a source of extreme discomfort. As MacQuarrie advised American soldiers, 'you will find that you are not the only kind of animal that occupies the trenches, although you are possibly the only uncomfortable one'. MacQuarrie shuddered to think how the rats (who were 'as big as cats') survived and he was not alone in feeling discomfort from the fact that they feasted on the corpses of dead soldiers.[97]

Rats' physical presence in the trenches raised anxieties about soldiers' health. In response, zoologists at the faculty of sciences at Rennes wrote a guide outlining the best ways to get rid of rats in the trenches, including dogs, traps, and poison. Precautions should also include burning or burying deeply all waste.[98] Others took a more direct approach. The war against the rats, according to Plowman, was 'prosecuted with the fiercest determination' with guns and bayonets.[99] Furthermore, some soldiers reportedly doused them in petrol and set them alight.[100] Yet there was little chance of escape from the ubiquitous rat.

Lice enjoyed even greater proximity with soldiers and constituted an even greater source of discomfort.[101] Lice infection rates in the trenches stood at nearly 90 per cent; one soldier remembers how 'our shirts always housed little crawly insect families'.[102] To combat lice, BEF entomologists recommended that soldiers wore silk undergarments, kept hair short, and changed their clothing as often as possible. In the trench environment, however, these instructions were impossible to follow. The BEF, along with other armies, therefore ended up deploying more effective delousing procedures, such as disinfectants, to prevent the spread of trench fevers and other illnesses.[103] Lice were itchy and unwelcome reminders that the trenches were a 'more-than-human' militarized environment. As well as fighting human opponents, soldiers waged their own war against lice, rats, mud, and the weather. But the wider environment also provided food, shelter, and other material necessities.

Mobilizing nature beyond the trenches

The trenches were the most concentrated and severe militarized environment on the Western Front. But vast military supply and support networks maintained them, meaning that militarized environments radiated out from the front lines into the countryside of northern and eastern France and beyond.[104]

The land behind front lines offered the chance to obtain food, even though hunting was strictly prohibited in army zones. French military commanders, for instance, encouraged their troops to create vegetable gardens behind front lines. In the Seventh Army zone all camps were to possess a vegetable garden (if the terrain allowed it) overseen by a head gardener and tended by troops.[105] But the number of gardens was always limited. So whilst they provided a small supplement to military rations, the search for food became a more substantial operation involving larger-scale military farming, especially once governments and armies began to realize that resources were not limitless.[106]

Individual units and commanders spearheaded the first British efforts at military farming. As well as helping to fill empty stomachs, officers hoped that farming would boost morale.[107] British military farming operations saw two thousand British soldiers harvesting hay on land captured during the 1916 Somme offensive and the planting of approximately 200 ha of vegetable gardens with the aid of German prisoners of war.[108] By 1917, and with supply chains under increasing strain due to the submarine blockade, the Quartermaster-General of the British Zone introduced military farming on a wider and more formal scale. The flag ship was an 18,210 ha Central Farm on abandoned land at Roye (Somme). Despite difficulties in securing sufficient manpower, the first 2,023 ha of the Central Farm had been ploughed by March 1918 with the help of tractors and convalescing horses (many of whom were only capable of light agricultural work having been blinded by gas). The German offensive of 21 March 1918 brought an end to this attempt to exploit the rich agricultural land of northern France and the farm was evacuated.[109] The British army, like its French and German counterparts, therefore remained heavily dependent on external food and other supplies. Rural French soldiers, for instance, benefited from the frequent food parcels sent to them by their worried families.[110]

But as well as being agents of agricultural disruption (see below), soldiers provided some aid to farmers. Military horse manure provided invaluable fertilizer for fields, and military manpower was an important boost for farmers at a time when both were in short supply. Overall, 300,000 soldiers worked in French fields (as of 22 June 1917).[111] Of course, these figures need to be set against the estimated three million French farmers who, by the end of the war, had exchanged their fields for the trenches as part of the war effort.[112]

Despite the mass mobilization of farmers into the army, the French government tried to wring the maximum productivity from the land. Jules Méline, French agricultural minister, declared his wish to 'cultivate all of France's soil and extract from it all that can be produced'.[113] The government treated boosting agricultural production as essential to overcoming Germany and ensuring 'total victory'.[114] A 1917 government report speculated that winning the war would be a case of who could resist 'hunger and cold' longest. The war had entered a new phase, passing from the 'period of steel' to one of 'wheat'. To intensify agricultural production, the report recommended clamping down on price speculation, providing more credit and manpower to farmers, and bringing a military discipline to the fields. In addition, natural resources overlooked in peacetime were to be mobilized to support agriculture. The report proposed harvesting seaweed and other marine fertilizers from the French coastline. Tree leaves and twigs could serve as animal feed and reeds and heather as litter. At the same time, an 'unrelenting war' must be led against animals that damaged crops, with poison as the main weapon.[115] Mass, totalizing warfare entailed enlisting such marginal economic resources as twigs and heather, at least in theory. But the multiple problems afflicting French agriculture kept agricultural production low. Not least the mobilization of agricultural labourers into the army contributed to huge declines in crop harvests (the wheat harvests of 1915 and 1916 were 80 per cent less than that of 1914).[116] France, like Britain, was forced to rely on massive imports of North American wheat and other products, comprising a serious blow to the country's faith and pride in its ability to feed itself.[117]

As well as food, armies on the Western Front required huge amounts of *matériel*. Bennett reported seeing 'hills of coils of the most formidable barbed wire' and 'stacks of timber', as well as sacks to be filled with earth for 'improvised entrenching'. All were gathered in 'unimagined quantities'.[118] Along with coal and steel, wood was an essential raw material. Bennett visited a front-line trench which was 'like a long wooden gallery. Its sides were of wood, its ceiling was of wood, its floor was of wood'.[119] As Bennett's observations suggest, trench warfare consumed timber on an enormous scale.[120] Once the USA entered the war in April 1917, the American Expeditionary Force similarly sought wood and timber for stakes, dugout shelters, trench entrance ways, signposts, roads, bridges, railway sleepers, and fuel.[121] Wood physically propped up the trenches. Without this mobilization of France's natural resources, trench combat would have been impossible.

As a consequence, the war militarized forestry production. The scale of military felling alarmed observers. French foresters, trained to believe that their own forest management policies balanced timber exploitation with forests' long-term future, were alarmed by what they saw as the military abuse of the forest. Contributors to *Revue des Eaux et Forêts* voiced their concerns. One lamented how 'vicious [military forest] exploitations' left stumps cut too low and felled plantations before they reached maturity.[122] Another deplored how soldiers cut down trees for shelter without considering how such 'barbarous treatment' of the forest would lead to its degradation. Forests were therefore 'more than paying their war tribute'.[123] French foresters expected forests to play their part in the national war effort but they did not want them sacrificed in the process.[124]

Voicing such concerns sought to justify foresters' claims that they should exercise greater control over the felling. One forester, who signed his articles in *Revue des Eaux et Forêts* 'L.P.', contrasted correct military felling that had been overseen by foresters in Roumare forest (near Rouen) with the reportedly chaotic, unsupervised felling in the nearby Verte forest. Whilst recognizing that the military could not fully follow civilian peacetime forest regulations, L.P. argued that if properly managed (by, of course, the forest administration) French forests could provide vital resources *and* be saved for the future.[125] L.P.'s line of argument evolved slightly once he had been mobilized and charged with producing timber for railway sleepers. Whilst he still claimed that soldiers felled without thought for the future, he placed more stress on patriotic military–civilian cooperation.[126] Another (unnamed) mobilized forester advanced the need for civilian–military collaboration more stridently; at a time when 'Mars has called Velléda', foresters needed to forget some of their treasured management principles. He also attacked L.P.'s criticism of military felling, stressing that it was generally conducted 'with the most extreme prudence'.[127]

Despite their disagreements, these militarized foresters were cogs in a wider system of military–civilian wartime felling. July 1915 saw the creation of the French Army Forestry Service (AFS), whose difficult remit was the reconciliation of military felling and forest conservation within the army zone. Its role was one of coordination and control; it alone was permitted to designate and oversee felling in forests within the army zone. Regular military units, who were forbidden from exploiting forestry resources themselves, passed their requests to the AFS. It also policed forest conservation through such measures as banning soldiers from tying their horses to trees and bivouacking in the forest without permission. A 'serious punishment' was promised to those who infringed its rules.[128] Foresters also mobilized forests for defensive reasons, helping the army fortify Sénart forest near Paris, by felling trees to create better sight lines.[129] The relationship between the army and foresters was therefore complex, characterized as it was by competition, criticism, and cooperation.

As the war progressed and civilian and military demands for wood saw no signs of relenting, forests were exploited further and further away from the front lines and army zones. These included state forests in the south-east that had remained relatively unscathed until spring 1917. However, the operation was hardly an overwhelming success as poor forest roads meant that felled trees often lay rotting in the forest.[130] In a bid to control felling outside of the army zone, the French Minister for Agriculture created the General Committee for Forests in May 1917 (later renamed General Committee for Woods), which also liaised with British and American forces.[131]

But the arrival of the American Expeditionary Force (AEF) further intensified the military exploitation of French forests. Although USA domestic forestry production rose to meet escalating wartime military and civilian needs, the difficulties of transporting timber across the submarine-ridden Atlantic meant that the AEF strove to meet its timber needs in French forests. With the agreement and cooperation of the French government, and overseen by an Allied commission, two American regiments – the 10th Engineers (Forestry) and the 20th Engineers (Forestry) – arrived in France with the unenviable task of supplying 12,000 board feet per month of sawn lumber along with 15,000 telephone and telegraph poles and 35,000 cubic metres of firewood.[132]

France and the USA may have been allies, but the latter's mobilization of French forest resources sparked tensions. Although the French government granted the use of its forests to the USA, it strove to maintain its sovereignty: French state foresters had the power to approve all American requests, negotiate prices, and inspect felling operations. The diary of Lieutenant Colonel William B. Greeley, Chief of the Forestry Section (20th Engineers), lays bare his frustrations with his French counterparts. He felt that they only offered him a 'more or less begrudging cooperation' and were determined to get the best prices, hold back supplies for their own troops, and exploit the most accessible and productive forests themselves.[133] But despite the tensions between French and American foresters and equipment shortages, the 20,000 American foresters based in France produced almost 220 million board feet of lumber, 3,051,137 standard-gauge railway sleepers, 1,926,693 miscellaneous round products (including entanglement poles), and 534,000 cords of firewood by the end of the war.[134]

The Western Front also sucked in forestry resources from Britain. Like other armies, the BEF required almost endless quantities of wood and, with submarine warfare drastically curtailing timber imports, the country was forced to fall back on its own meagre forests to supply its army and munitions factories. Between 1916 and 1918 timber felling was twenty times pre-war levels and approximately 182,000 ha (or almost half the surface area of productive forests) were razed.[135] This intense mobilization of British forests alarmed US forest journalist Percival Ridsdale, who foresaw 'the utter destruction of most' British forests.[136] In fact, forester Edward Percy Stebbing admitted that Britain was 'was now engaged in cutting down, in sacrificing, such woods as we have in this country'.[137]

But forests were more than a military resource. They also became a political tool as their destruction was mobilized to highlight German barbarity. For French commentators, any evidence of their own army's misuse of the forest paled into insignificance in comparison with the German army's over-exploitation of forests in its occupied French territories. Guyot asserted that after the war the French would find their forests 'wrecked by the invader's axe'.[138] It was not just French forests that were perceived to have suffered under German occupation. Ridsdale speculated that German forces had also stripped forests bare in Belgium and had done a 'great deal of cutting' in the territory they controlled in Poland and western Russia.[139] Materially and imaginatively, therefore, the First World War was a key moment in the relationship between wood and warfare.[140]

The military extraction of natural resources was one way in which the war created new militarized environments beyond the front lines. The creation of numerous new military bases and training grounds was another sign of the Western Front's fluid boundaries.

Preparing for war during war

Bases and training grounds served a variety of purposes during the war. Among them were training troops in trench warfare, testing weapons, and providing places of repose for soldiers recovering from life in the trenches.[141] It is hard to determine the exact number of these installations. But to give some indication, there were eighty-five summer instruction camps for the 1917 contingent of French troops in metropolitan France.[142] Although some French training centres made use of existing facilities, such as Souge, Châlons, and Garrigues camps, others were hastily improvised, raising concerns about hygiene and health. A report by two *députés* on rest camps in the Fifth Army region, for instance, found dirty kitchens, poor facilities, and unfortunate locations. One was built on a slope so that one wall of the barrack was buried in earth with 'disadvantages' for troop hygiene and the building would be at the 'mercy of flooding after a storm or heavy rain'. The barracks themselves were built with unseasoned wood and were already starting to fall apart. Some soldiers in the Verdun army, meanwhile, slept in barges on the Meuse canal, raising fears of how they would cope with a 'truly harsh winter climate'.[143]

Despite the far from ideal living conditions in many training camps, the army invested these sites with patriotic meaning. Guidelines for infantry training prepared in 1915 presented them as places in which soldiers developed physical and moral discipline and where they would learn to understand 'the glory of receiving wounds when fighting for the country [and] the beauty of death on the battlefield'. Life in the camps was intended to fill troops with an 'ardent desire to leave for the front'.[144] But we need to question seriously whether these aims were met. The reasons why French soldiers continued to fight in the face of demoralizing conditions and risk of death were far more complex than the belief in nineteenth-century ideals of battlefield glory and sacrifice. The defence of their families, loyalty to the Republic, shifting perceptions of the utility of offensive action, and their evolving identities as 'citizen-soldiers' provide far more convincing explanations of why they fought, particularly as the war dragged on.[145]

Although no match for the rigours of life in the trenches, training could be tough. Plowman recalls being put through a gruelling day of training at the 'Bull Ring', an infamous British training camp at Etaples (Pas-de-Calais): 'it is hot work, and there is a fierce, vindictive atmosphere about this place which makes its name of "Bull Ring" intelligible'.[146] But even within the centre of the demanding militarized environment of the Bull Ring, vestiges and reminders of peaceful civilian environments remained. After completing marching drills, firing practices, and obstacle courses, Plowman was still able to imagine that the sand dunes 'must make a place of delightful holiday. Even today one's eyes wandered instinctively toward the blue estuary that lay below us, where the tiny white sail of a yacht moved slowly up-stream'.[147]

Sassoon also found moments of calm within the militarized environment of the Fourth Army's school at Flixecourt (Somme). The training may have been largely ineffectual ('parades and lectures . . . failed to convince me of their affinity with our long days and nights in the Front Line'), but Sassoon, along with his fellow officers, enjoyed the relative calm and peace of the camp, even treating it as a 'holiday'. At the camp Sassoon revelled in the calm atmosphere, complete with chirping birds and blossom-laden trees:

> Loosening my belt, I looked at a chestnut tree in full leaf and listened to the perfect performance of a nightingale. Such things seemed miraculous after the desolation of the trenches. Never before had I been so intensely aware of what it meant to be young and healthy in fine weather at the onset of summer. The untroubled notes of the nightingale made the Army School seem like some fortunate colony which was, for the sake of appearances, pretending to assist the struggle from afar. It feels as if it's a place where I might get a chance to call my soul my own.[148]

The feelings of youth, renewal, and appreciation for nature that Sassoon felt are a far cry from the intended use of army schools as preparatory spaces for combat.

Many of these training camps were created on once-civilian land. Even during wartime, militarizing a civilian environment could prove to be a torturous process. British instructions indicate that consideration was given to local feelings, at least on paper. The Royal Flying Corps (RFC) insisted that 'once a piece of ground has been taken, care must be exercised to prevent encroachments on the neighbouring plots' as it 'causes direct hardship' to civilian populations. The RFC also encouraged its French interpreters to impress on local populations that the British were 'very aware of the sacrifice that they ask of [them] and are very keen to avoid causing them any unnecessary annoyance or loss'. They should also inform locals that that the RFC chooses training grounds in a 'thoughtful and serious way'.[149]

But in practice, such principles lost out to military imperatives, resulting in civilian–military tensions. The case of Bailleul Camp (Nord) provides ample illustration. In 1914 and 1915 individual BEF units liaised directly with local French authorities to rent land for training.[150] The position of the latter was the most delicate as they tried to find a way of satisfying the training needs of their ally while allaying the concerns of local populations disgruntled at losing their land. The Mission militaire française (MMF), a French army body created to liaise with the BEF, encouraged the British to use abandoned or fallow land for training rather than fields. It also requested that British officers consult with local mayors to 'reconcile the diverse interests'.[151]

But military imperatives overrode civilian interests. A MMF order of 6 July 1916 allowed the British to conduct manoeuvres at Bailleul, barring civilians from accessing their land and paving the way for eventual compensation.[152] In January 1917 the British Second Army requested the camp's extension from 140 to 240 ha to allow brigade-size manoeuvres and trench digging.[153] The request was too much for local farmers and Bailleul's mayor, who argued that the extension would swallow up intensively cultivated land at a time when the French government was trying to boost agricultural production. They also pointed out that the British presence had already ruined existing crops.[154] Eugène Contyl, president of the local agricultural society, similarly opposed the camp on patriotic grounds, claiming that the 'national interest' was agricultural production which 'our allies should understand'. Although self-interest undoubtedly infused his intervention, Squadron chief Maleissye-Melun, French liaison officer with the Second Army, supported his viewpoint.[155] In the end the protests succeeded and the Second Army abandoned the camp's extension. But there was a sting in the tail as it simultaneously requested an extension to their camps in the neighbouring communes of Berthen and Boeschepe.[156] Nonetheless, the episode shows how civilians could challenge the creation of militarized environments, even in wartime, and that there was some room for manoeuvre with British military authorities.[157]

The strains at Bailleul occurred elsewhere as military activity hindered civilian farming behind the front lines. Soldiers' occupation of, and incessant movement through, fields made it extremely difficult, if not impossible, for some farmers in the Somme to cultivate their land.[158] In places, their presence directly damaged existing crops. Cavalry units at Bussy-les-Daours, for instance, destroyed crops as they rode across farmers' fields.[159] French farmers were also upset – and not without reason – by incorrect requisitioning of their livestock and the damage caused to their property by military hunting, billeting, and installations at a time of severe scarcity and material hardship.[160] Many would have agreed with Senator Gomot, President of the National Society for the encouragement of Agriculture, who stated that wherever the cannon sounds 'arable soil is struck by infertility'.[161] Civilians once again equated militarization with sterility. Furthermore, the rural opposition to militarization, however limited, nuances the argument that 'the consent of the rural population remained a decisive stabilizing element in the French nation accepting the prolongation of war'.[162]

The tensions over agriculture exposed competing civilian and military environmental perspectives. For military planners, land was assessed for its suitability to train troops and test weapons and the ease and cost of its requisition. Time, for them, was of the essence.[163] For farmers, the land, which may have been farmed by their family for generations, was their home and livelihood. In particular, at a time of food shortages, crops were a valuable resource, in both a nutritional and monetary sense. This explains why Charles Courtier, a farmer from Lizy-sur-Ourcq (Seine-et-Marne), was so desperate to save some of his wheat once aviators had left his land for the front in April 1918.[164] The militarization of farmland alarmed civilian authorities in the higher echelons of government. The Minister for Agriculture complained to the Somme's Prefect that 'his attention was constantly being called to the damage' training camps 'caused to sown or ploughed areas in the army zone', leading to an expansion of uncultivated land.[165]

The mobilization of nature for military training and weapons testing militarized sites beyond northern and eastern France. As planes became increasingly important to the war effort and airmen became feted as heroes of the sky engaged in life-and-death aerial combats, the dunes, forests, lagoons, and coastline of south-western France caught the eye of military officials. At Cazaux (see chapter 3) Ferdinand Marzac lobbied for the establishment of an aviation school and firing ground, which was officially opened in May 1915. By January 1916, the school boasted 767 officers and trainees. In 1918, Marzac opened a second site at nearby Biscarosse to accommodate more powerful airplanes, such as the Caudron G.4. At a site bordered by forests and the Atlantic Ocean, pilots fired at targets positioned on dunes. In all, the school trained 13,000 students who fired 26 million cartridges between 1915 and 1918.[166]

Aviation schools radiated a sense of glamour. John Morrow has argued that 'the exhilaration of flight, the conquest of space and speed, the sense of mastery over others and the environment that was absent in land warfare, composed the attraction of military aviation'.[167] But the reality of training was less heroic and glamorous. At Biscarosse continual take-offs and landings created ruts in the sandy ground leading to up to ten planes a day overturning. As with infantry and artillery training grounds, there was a discrepancy between the rhetoric and reality of these wartime militarized environments.

Conclusion

Away from the relative calm of south-west France, events on the Western Front in 1918 brought the war to a close. In an attempt to capitalize on the defeat of Russia, Germany launched an offensive on 21 March 1918. It pushed the British Fifth Army back by forty miles, placing Paris within range of 'Big Bertha' artillery pieces. By May 1918 French forces were pegged back south of the Marne River and the German army had taken the most ground on the Western Front since 1914. But the Allied series of counter-offensives from 15 July 1918, under Marshal Ferdinand Foch's command, exploited weak points in the new German positions. Aided by their numerical advantage in tanks and planes and superiority in manpower and resources, the Allies succeeded in putting pressure on German lines.

Success on the Western Front combined with food shortages in Germany and Allied breakthroughs in Bulgaria, Hungary, and Italy, leading to the signing of an armistice in Foch's railway carriage stationed in a clearing in Compiègne Forest on 11 November 1918. These final months of the war were the most bloody since the stabilization of the Western Front in autumn 1914; Germany lost 1.76 million men through death, injury, or capture between March and November 1918 and French losses mounted to 306,000 in the same period.[168]

As well as ending the slaughter, the armistice brought an end to the militarized environment of the trenches and the wartime mobilization of nature. The war had transformed swathes of northern and eastern France into denuded, cratered environments and militarized more distant sites through military farming, felling, and training. The militarized environment of the trenches is the most extreme featured in this book. But despite the environmental sterilization occasioned by mechanized warfare, combatants sought out and celebrated the surviving remnants of vegetation and animal life. This was one way in which they mobilized nature in the trenches.

Militarized environments between 1914 and 1918 were thoroughly hybrid spaces, acting as contact zones between civilians and the military and between humans and nonhumans. Writing in March 1917, it had seemed to Paul Nash that soldiers had been in the grip of both 'War and Nature; the former has become a habit so confirmed, inevitable, it has its grip on the world just as surely as spring or summer'.[169] With the cessation of hostilities war loosened its grip on the French environment. But there was no escaping its environmental aftermath. French

society faced the daunting prospect of trying to find meaning in environments of slaughter whilst demilitarizing and reconstructing the wartorn
countryside.

Notes

1 Henry Malherbe described the Western Front's environment as one of
'mangled earth'. *The Flaming Sword of France: Sketches from an Observation
Post of the French Artillery near Verdun,* trans. Lucy Menzies (London and
Toronto: J. M. Dent, 1918), 3.

2 Mark Plowman [Mark VII, pseud.], *A Subaltern on the Somme in 1916*
(London: J. M. Dent, 1927), 43.

3 Malherbe, *Flaming Sword of France,* 4.

4 Paul Fussell, *The Great War and Modern Memory* (Oxford: Oxford
University Press, 1977); Modris Eksteins, *Rites of Spring: The Great War
and the Birth of the Modern Age* (Boston: Houghton Mifflin, 1989); Martin
Hurcombe, *Novelists in Conflict: Ideology and the Absurd in the French
Combat Novel of the Great War* (Amsterdam: Rodopi, 2004), 51–78; Samuel
Hynes, *A War Imagined: The First World War and English Culture* (London:
Bodley Head, 1990), chapter 9. For an account that places more emphasis
on the continuation of traditional cultural practices, see Jay Winter, *Sites
of Memory, Sites of Mourning: The Great War in European Cultural History*
(Cambridge: Cambridge University Press, 1995).

5 Military, political, social, and cultural histories have been the main focus of
scholarly accounts of the war. An important exception is Dorothee Brantz,
'Environments of death: Trench warfare on the Western Front', in Charles
E. Closmann (ed.), *War and the Environment: Military Destruction in the
Modern Age* (College Station: Texas A&M University Press, 2009), 68–91.
Geographers have also tackled aspects of the war's geography. Michel
Cabouret, 'De l'influence des facteurs géographiques dans les opérations de
la grande guerre (1914–18) en Lorraine: Le rôle des cuestas', in Jean-Pierre
Husson (ed.), *Territoires, paysages et héritages* (Nancy: Université de Nancy
2, 2001), 107–11, and various chapters in Andrée Corvol and Jean-Paul
Amat, (eds), *Forêt et guerre* (Paris: L'Harmattan, 1994) The war has sparked
a vast historiography and there is not the space to do it justice here. For
a succinct overview, see Antoine Prost and Jay Winter, *Penser la Grande
Guerre: Un essai d'historiographie* (Paris: Editions du Seuil, 2004).

6 For the concept of natural allies and enemies, see Edmund P. Russell
and Richard P. Tucker (eds), *Natural Enemy, Natural Ally: Toward an
Environmental History of Warfare* (Corvallis: Oregon State University Press,
2004).

7 On the war's environmental dimensions beyond France, see Tait Keller, 'The
Mountains Roar: The Alps during the Great War', *Environmental History,*

14:2 (2009), 253–74; William Kelleher Storey, *The First World War: A Concise Global History* (Lanham: Rowman and Littlefield, 2009).

8 Carola Hein, Jeffry M. Diefendorf and Ishida Yorifusa (eds), *Rebuilding Urban Japan after 1945* (Basingstoke: Palgrave Macmillan, 2003); Arthur Westing, *Ecological Consequences of the Second Indochina War* (Stockholm: SIRPI, 1976).

9 On the image of war as an unstoppable machine, see Daniel Pick, *War Machine: The Rationalization of Slaughter in the Modern Age* (New Haven: Yale University Press, 1996).

10 Jules Claudin Gervais-Courtellemont, *Les champs de bataille de Verdun: Photographies directes en couleur* (Paris: L'Edition française illustré, 1917), 40.

11 Brantz, 'Environments of death', 81–2.

12 T. E. Hulme, *Further Speculation*, ed. Sam Hynes (Minneapolis: University of Minnesota Press, 1955), 157.

13 William Arthur Dunkerley [John Oxenham, pseud.], *High Altars: The Battlefields of France and Flanders as I Saw Them* (London: Methuen, 1918), 18. Similarly, Plowman described the country near Fricourt as 'stricken waste', *Subaltern on the Somme*, 41.

14 Matthew Farish, 'Modern witnesses: Foreign correspondents, geopolitical vision, and the First World War', *Transactions of the Institute of British Geographers*, 26 (2001), 273–87.

15 Gerald Fitzgerald Campbell, *Verdun to the Vosges: Impressions of the War on the Fortress Frontier of France* (London: Edward Arnold, 1916), 136–7, 276.

16 Farish, 'Modern witnesses'.

17 Plowman, *Subaltern on the Somme*, 42.

18 William Dyson, *Australia at War: A Winter Record made by Will Dyson on the Somme and at Ypres during the Campaigns of 1916 and 1917* (London: Cecil Palmer and Hayward, 1918), 46–7.

19 Arnold Bennett, *Over There: War Scenes on the Western Front* (London: Methuen, 1915), 42–3, 122–3.

20 Cabouret, 'De l'influence des facteurs géographiques', 108.

21 Quoted in Henry William Carless Davis, *The Battle of the Marne and Aisne* (Oxford: Oxford University Press, 1914), 23. See also Hilaire Belloc, 'The geography of war', *Geographical Journal*, 45:1 (1915), 1–13.

22 Michael Heffernan, 'Geography, cartography and military intelligence: The Royal Geographical Society and the First World War', *Transactions of the Institute of British Geographers*, 21:3 (1996), 507. French geographers similarly mobilized themselves. Michael Heffernan, 'The spoils of war: The Société de Géographie de Paris and the French Empire', in Morag Bell, Robin Alan Butlin, and Michael J. Heffernan (eds), *Geography and Imperialism, 1820–1940* (Manchester: Manchester University Press, 1995), 228–9.

23 Eksteins, *Rites of Spring*, 100–2; Stephan Kern, *The Culture of Time and Space, 1880–1918* (Harvard University Press, 2003 [1983]), 300; Wencke Meteling, 'German and French regiments on the Western Front, 1914–1918', in Heather Jones, Jennifer O'Brien, and Christoph Schmidt-Supprian (eds), *Untold War: New Perspectives in First World War Studies* (Leiden: Brill, 2008), 33.

24 Harold. A. Winters, Gerald E. Galloway Jr., William J. Reynolds, and David W. Ryne, *Battling the Elements: Weather and Terrain in the Conduct of War* (Baltimore and London: Johns Hopkins University Press, 1998), 43; Alexander von Kluck, *The March on Paris and the Battle of the Marne, 1914* (London: Arnold, 1923), 71–2; and Gervais-Courtellemont, *Champs de bataille de Verdun*, 38.

25 Charles Guyot, *La forêt et la guerre* (Nancy: Imprimerie Berger-Levrault, 1917), 5–7. See also J. Demorlaine, 'L'importance stratégique des forêts et la guerre', *Revue des Eaux et Forêts*, 17:31 (February 1919), 27.

26 Quoted in 'Le rôle militaire des forêts', *Le Chêne*, 14 (1918), 839.

27 For a useful description of the geography and organization of the trenches, see Tony Ashworth, *Trench Warfare, 1914–1918: The Live and Let Live System* (London: Macmillan, 1980), 2–7.

28 David G. Herrmann, *The Arming of Europe and the Making of the First World War* (Princeton: Princeton University Press, 1997), 73, 204.

29 Centre d'instruction de mitrailleuses de Coëtquidan, *Aide-mémoire du chef de section de mitrailleuses* (Rennes: Oberthür, 1916), 110.

30 *The Great Advance: Tales from the Somme Battlefield Told by Wounded Officers and Men on the Arrival in Southampton from the Front* (London: Cassell, 1916), 34.

31 Roy R. Behrens, 'Revisiting Abbott Thayer: Non-scientific reflections about camouflage in art, war and zoology', *Philosophical Transactions of the Royal Society B*, 364 (2009), 497–501.

32 *Le diable, la cigogne et le petit lapin: 1914–1918 les aviateurs inventent une héraldique nouvelle* (Paris: Service historique de l'armée de l'air, 2004), 40–1; Jon Guttman, *Groupe de Combat 12 'Les Cigognes': France's Ace Fighter Group in World War I* (Oxford: Osprey Publishing, 2004), 8. On animal imagery during the war see, Steve Baker, *Picturing the Beast: Animals, Identity and Representation* (Urbana and Chicago: University of Illinois Press, 2001), 37–45.

33 On technology during the war, see Edmund P. Russell, *War and Nature: Fighting Humans and Insects with Chemicals from World War I to Silent Spring* (New York: Cambridge University Press, 2001), 37–52; Dennis Showalter, 'Mass warfare and the impact of technology', in Roger Chickering and Stig Förster (eds), *Great War, Total War: Combat and Mobilization on the Western Front, 1914–1918* (Cambridge: Cambridge University Press, 2000), 83; Storey, *First World War*, 161–3. On industry in France, see Gerd

Hardach, 'Industrial mobilization in 1914–1918: Production, planning, and ideology', in Patrick Fridenson (ed.), *The French Home Front 1914–1918* (Oxford: Berg, 1992), 57–88.

34 Sidney Galtrey, *The Horse and the War* (London: Country Life and George Newnes, 1918), 16; John Singleton, 'Britain's military use of horses, 1914–1918', *Past and Present*, 139:1 (1993), 190.

35 Brantz, 'Environments of death', 85; Damien Baldin, 'Les animaux en guerre: Animaux soldats et bestiaire de guerre (1914–1918)', in Damien Baldin (ed.), *La guerre des animaux, 1914–1918* (Peronne: Historial de la Grande Guerre, 2007), 17.

36 Albert J. Frost, *The Shire Horse in Peace and War* (London: Vinton & Company, 1915), 121–2.

37 Galtrey, *Horse and the War*, 13.

38 Showalter, 'Mass warfare'; Baldin, 'Animaux en guerre', 18.

39 On the military disciplining of military bodies, see Joanna Bourke, *Dismembering the Male: Men's Bodies, Britain and the Great War* (London: Reaktion, 1996).

40 Galtrey, *Horse and the War*, 25. North America eventually supplied 429,000 horses and 275,000 mules. See Singleton, 'Britain's military use of horses', 183–9, for these figures and further information on the procurement of horses.

41 Plowman, *Subaltern on the Somme*, 147.

42 Galtrey, *Horse and the War*, 79, 86.

43 Ibid., 76. For instance, the army discontinued the excessive clipping of horses after the experience of 1916–17 had shown that they needed a thick coat for warmth (88).

44 Bennett, *Over There*, 158–9.

45 Hilda Kean, *Animal Rights: Political and Social Change in Britain* (London: Reaktion, 1998), 166–7.

46 Singleton, 'Britain's military use of horses', 191.

47 Leo van Bergen, *Before my Helpless Sight: Suffering, Dying, and Military Medicine on the Western Front, 1914–1918* (Aldershot: Ashgate, 2009), 25–6.

48 Martin Monestier, *Les animaux-soldats: Histoire militaire des animaux des origines à nos jours* (Paris: Le Cherche Midi, 1996), 49–53.

49 Susan McHugh, *Dog* (London: Reaktion, 2004), 115; G.R. Durrant, 'A brief history of the Royal Army Veterinary Corps', *Veterinary History*, 11 (summer 1978), 3–5; Monestier, *Animaux-soldats*, 57; Arnold Arluke and Robert Bogdan, *Beauty and the Beast: Human-Animal Relations as Revealed in Real Photo Postcards* (Syracuse: Syracuse University Press, 2010), 79. See also Paul Mégnin, *Les Chiens de France: Soldats de la Grande Guerre* (Paris: Albin Michel, [n.d.]).

50 Alfred Henry Osman, *Pigeons in the Great War: A Complete History of the*

Carrier Pigeon Service during the Great War, 1914 to 1918 (London: Racing Pigeon Publishing Co., 1929), 6, 29; Jonathan Wajerowski, 'La Grande Guerre des pigeons voyageurs', in Baldin, *Guerre des animaux*, 61; Raymond Zaepffel, *Le pigeon voyageur: Historique, élevage, concours, maladies* (Paris: Librairie agricole de la maison rustique, 1926), 25.

51 Pierre Dumarchey [Pierre Mac Orlan, pseud.], *Verdun* (Paris: Editions Latines, 1935), 142.

52 Hector MacQuarrie, *How to Live at the Front: Tips for American Soldiers* (Philadelphia and London: J. B. Lippincott, 1917), 215–21. On pets and mascots in the US navy during the war, see Arluke and Bogdan, *Beauty and the Beast*, 38–48.

53 Nigel Jones, *The War Walk: A Journey Along the Western Front* (London: Cassell, 2004), 38.

54 William Drury, *Camp Follower: A Padre's Recollection of Nile, Somme, and Tigris during the First World War* (Dublin: Exchequer Printers, 1968), 120.

55 Quoted in Alexander McKee, *Vimy Ridge* (London: Souvenir Press, 1966), 63; Gaston Pastre, *Trois ans de front: Belgique, Aisne et Champagne, Verdun, Argonne, Lorraine. Notes et impressions d'un artilleur* (Paris: Berger-Levrault, 1918), 170.

56 Showalter, 'Mass warfare', 81.

57 Kenneth I. Helphand, *Defiant Gardens: Making Gardens in Wartime* (San Antonio: Trinity University Press, 2006), 21–59; Michael Roper, *The Secret Battle: Emotional Survival in the Great War* (Manchester: Manchester University Press, 2009), 124. The psychological benefits of pet-keeping are now becoming better understood. Deborah L. Wells, 'The effects of animals on human health and well-being', *Journal of Social Issues*, 65:3 (2009), 523–43.

58 Showalter, 'Mass warfare', 88.

59 Brantz, 'Environments of death', 71.

60 Hugh Gladstone, *Birds and the War* (London: Skeffington & Son, 1919), 125, 145, 154–6.

61 Quoted in ibid. 134. See also Colin Campbell Sanborn, 'List of birds made during eighteen months' service in France and Germany', *The Wilson Bulletin: A Quarterly Journal of Ornithology*, 32:2 (1920), 41–7.

62 Herbert Sulzbach, *With the German Guns: Four Years on the Western Front 1914–1918*, trans. Richard Thonger (London: Frederick Warne, 1981 [1973]), 60. See also John McCrae, *In Flanders Fields and Other Poems* (London: Hodder and Stoughton, 1919), 106.

63 Giles Eyre, *Somme Harvest: Memories of a P.B.I. in the Summer of 1916* (London: Jarrolds, 1938), 124. See also Peter Hart, *The Somme* (London: Weidenfeld and Nicolson, 2005), 63.

64 Guyot, *Forêt et la guerre*, 8. Maurice Biollay's poems also romanticized

forests' wartime contribution. *La forêt en armes: Heures de guerre* (Paris: E. Figuière & Cie, 1920).
65 Pastre, *Trois ans de front*, 161, 184.
66 Sulzbach, *With the German Guns*, 80.
67 Drury, *Camp Follower*, 109.
68 Paul Delaunay, *Paysage de guerre et choses du vieux temps: Carnets d'un aide-major* (Paris: Amédée Legrand, 1921), 44.
69 Edmund Blunden, *Undertones of War* (London: Richard Cobden-Saunderson, 1928), 74.
70 Sulzbach, *With the German Guns*, 54.
71 Fussell, *Great War and Modern Memory*.
72 Peter Coates, *Nature: Western Attitudes since Ancient Times* (Cambridge: Polity, 1998), 125–39; Max Oelschlaeger, *The Idea of Wilderness: From Prehistory to the Age of Ecology* (New Haven: Yale University Press, 1991), 97–132.
73 Siegfried Sassoon, *Memoirs of an Infantry Officer* (London: Faber and Faber, 1931), 64.
74 Paul Nash, *An Autobiography and Other Writings* (London: Faber and Faber, 1949), 187–9.
75 On applying the concept of 'total war' to the First World War, see Chickering and Förster, *Great War, Total War*.
76 Sulzbach, *With the German Guns*, 80. Death was never far away. One group of German soldiers swimming way behind the lines were killed by a wayward shell. Van Bergen, *Before My Helpless Sight*, 32.
77 Georges Lafond, *Covered with Mud and Glory: A Machine Gun Company in Action*, trans. Edwin Gile Rich (Boston: Small, Maynard, and Company, 1918), 223.
78 Nash, *Autobiography*, 211.
79 Blunden, *Undertones of War*, 86–7.
80 Eric J. Leed, *No Man's Land: Combat and Identity in World War I* (Cambridge: Cambridge University Press, 1979), 79–80.
81 Brantz, 'Environments of death', 81.
82 John Buchan, *A History of the Great War, Vol. 2, From the Battle of Verdun to the Third Battle of Ypres* (London: Thomas Nelson and Sons, 1922), 201.
83 Delaunay, *Paysage de guerre*, 37; Stéphane Audoin-Rouzeau, *Men at War 1914–1918: National Sentiment and Trench Journalism in France during the First World War*, trans. Helen McPhail (Oxford: Berg, 1992), 36–9.
84 Quoted in Audoin-Rouzeau, *Men at War*, 38. See also Pastre, *Trois ans de front*, 49, 161. On the underlying geological conditions that contributed so much to the widespread mud, see Peter Doyle, *Geology of the Western Front, 1914–1918* (London: Geologists' Association, 1998).
85 Dunkerley, *High Altars*, 24, 54–5.

The 'mangled earth' of the trenches (1914–18)

86 Hulme, *Further Speculation*, 154.

87 Sassoon, *Memoirs of an Infantry Officer*, 45; Frank N. Schubert, 'All wooden on the Western Front', *Journal of Forest History*, 22:4 (1978), 180.

88 Delaunay, *Paysage de guerre*, 37.

89 Drury, *Camp Follower*, 145.

90 Hulme, *Further Speculation*, 165. See also Pastre, *Trois ans de front*, 202.

91 Quoted in Malcolm Brown, *The Imperial War Museum Book of the Western Front* (London: Sidgwick & Jackson, 1993), 55.

92 Francis Marre, *Dans les tranchées du Front* (Paris: Bloud et Gay, 1915), 57–61.

93 Pastre, *Trois ans de front*, 194.

94 McCrae, *In Flanders Fields*, 104; Sulzbach, *With the German Guns*, 45. See also Eksteins, *Rites of Spring*, 103.

95 Van Bergen, *Before My Helpless Sight*, 126.

96 Private Thomas McIndoe, quoted in Max Arthur, *Forgotten Voices of the Great War: A New History of the WWI in the Words of the Men and Women Who Were There* (London: Ebury Press, 2002), 97.

97 MacQuarrie, *How to Live at the Front*, 214. See also Jonathan Burt, *Rat* (London: Reaktion, 2006), 83–4; Marc Ferro, *La grande guerre 1914–1918* (Paris: Editions Gallimard, 1969), 163.

98 Laboratoire de Zoologie, Station Entomologique, Faculté des Sciences de Rennes, *Renseignements gratuits sur les animaux nuisibles: Animaux nuisibles aux soldats en campagne* (Rennes: Imprimerie Oberthur, 1915), 7–8. On the links between lice and disease in the trenches, see van Bergen, *Before My Helpless Sight*, 142.

99 Plowman, *Subaltern on the Somme*, 77–8.

100 Dumarchey, *Verdun*, 146. Pierre Chaine fictionalized rats' close proximity with the soldiers in his popular book *Les mémoires d'un rat* (Paris: A l'oeuvre, 1917).

101 Laboratoire de Zoologie, *Renseignements gratuits*, 1.

102 Quoted in McKee, *Vimy Ridge*, 63. For the infection rate, see Jeffrey A. Lockwood, *Six-Legged Soldiers: Using Insects as Weapons of War* (Oxford: Oxford University Press, 2009), 80.

103 Lockwood, *Six-Legged Soldiers*, 82–3.

104 On military supply chains, see Showalter, 'Mass warfare', 81–3.

105 SHD-DAT 16 N 822 Ve Armée, Etat-major, 1e bureau, 'Consigne générale pour les camps et cantonnements de la Ve Armée', 6 July 1917; SHD-DAT 16 N 822 VIIe Armée, Etat-major, 1e Bureau, 'Règlement provisoire sur le service des camps et cantonnements', 10 January 1918. On soldiers' gardening during the war, see Helphand, *Defiant Gardens*, 21–59.

106 Showalter, 'Mass warfare', 83.

107 J.H. Forrester Addie and A.T.A. Dobson, 'Agriculture behind the lines in France', *Journal of the Ministry of Agriculture*, 27:8–9 (1921), 682.

Mobilizing nature

108 Craig Gibson, 'The British army, French farmers, and the war on the Western Front, 1914–1918', *Past and Present*, 180 (2003), 215.

109 Addie and Dobson, 'Agriculture behind the lines', 682–8. Gibson, 'British army', 229–32.

110 Jean Doise and Maurice Vaïse, *Diplomatie et outil militaire, 1871–1991: Politique étrangère de la France* (Paris: Editions du Seuil, 1992 [1987]), 290; Martha Hanna, 'Spaces of war: Rural France, fears of famine, and the Great War', in Patricia M.E. Lorcin and Daniel Brewer (eds), *France and its Spaces of War: Experience, Memory, Image* (New York: Palgrave Macmillan, 2009), 47.

111 SHD-DAT 7 N 549 Commission de la reprise agricole française, 'Résumé de la séance du 22 juin 1917'.

112 Michel Gervais, Marcel Jollivet, and Yves Tavernier, *Histoire de la France rurale. Tome 4: La fin de la France paysanne de 1914 à nos jours* (Paris: Seuil, 1976), 39.

113 ADS 99 R 3254 Jules Méline to Président [of France?], 24 March 1916. On wartime agriculture in other countries, see Peter E. Dewey, *British Agriculture in the First World War* (London: Routledge, 1989); Joe Lee, 'Administrators and agriculture: Aspects of German agricultural policy in the First World War', in Jay Winter (ed.), *War and Economic Development* (Cambridge: Cambridge University Press, 1975), 229–38; and Avner Offer, *The First World War: An Agrarian Interpretation* (Oxford: Clarendon Press, 1989).

114 John F.V. Keiger, 'Poincaré, Clemenceau, and the quest for total victory', in Chickering and Förster, *Great War, Total War*, 247–63.

115 CHAN F¹⁰2185 'Note sur les mesures à prendre d'urgence pour intensifier la production agricole en France', 15 May 1917. On the potential for social unrest due to food shortages, see Tyler Stovall, 'The consumer's war: Paris, 1914–1918', *French Historical Studies*, 31:2 (2008), 293–325.

116 Hanna, 'Spaces of war', 46. See also Pierre Barral, 'La paysannerie française à l'arrière', in Jean-Jacques Becker and Stéphane Audoin-Rouzeau (eds), *Les sociétés Européennes et la guerre de 1914–1918* (Nanterre: Publications de l'Université de Nanterre, 1988), 237–43.

117 Gervais, Jollivet, and Tavernier, *Histoire de la France rurale*, 44; André Kaspi, *Le temps des américains, 1917–1918: Le concours américain à la France en 1917–1918* (Paris: Publications de la Sorbonne, 1976), 58–69; Hanna, 'Spaces of war', 47.

118 Bennett, *Over There*, 42–3.

119 Ibid. 59.

120 Tamara Whited estimates that approximately four million steres (or cubic metres) of timber, the annual production of construction-grade timber in France, were used to construct the trenches. *Forests and Peasant Politics in Modern France* (New Haven and London: Yale University Press, 2000), 162. See also *Les Eaux et Forêts du 12e au 20e siècle* (Paris: CNRS, 1987), 626.

121 Schubert, 'All wooden', 180–1.

122 Hébard de Villeneuve, 'Constatation et évaluation des dommages matériels résultant des faits de guerre et concernant les forêts, annexe au rapport général présenté au nom de la commission supérieure', *Revue des Eaux et Forêts*, 8:44 (1 August 1915), 673. On French forest management, see Whited, *Forests and Peasant Politics*.

123 C. de Lesseux, 'Les forêts de France et la guerre', *Revue des Eaux et Forêts*, 14:7 (1 April 1916), 110–14.

124 Their apprehension points to the differences between military and civilian attitudes towards timber felling that would arise once again during the Second World War. Chris Pearson, *Scarred Landscapes: War and Nature in Vichy France* (Basingstoke: Palgrave Macmillan, 2008), 52–6.

125 L.P., 'Exploitations forestiers pour l'armée', *Revue des Eaux et Forêts*, 13:46 (1 October 1915), 710–12.

126 L.P., 'Exploitations forestières pour les besoins de l'armée', *Revue des Eaux et Forêts*, 14:3 (1 February 1916), 54–5.

127 Un forestier aux armes, 'Simples réflexions sur le service forestier aux armées', *Revue des Eaux et Forêts*, 14:3 (1 February 1916), 56–8; Un forestier aux armées, 'Le service forestier aux armées: Nouvelles réflexions', *Revue des Eaux et Forêts*, 14:11 (1 June 1916), 172–4.

128 SHD-DAT 16 N 910 'Instruction relative à l'exploitation des ressources en bois, sur le territoire de la Vᵉ armée', 17 July 1917.

129 Yoann Gauvry (ed.), *Sénart, forêt retranchée: Mémoires et traces de la Grande Guerre* (Paris: Office national des forêts, 2008), 38.

130 *Eaux et Forêts du 12e au 20e siècle*, 626; Andrée Corvol, 'La réquisition des bois du sud-est: Une chance ratée (1914–1918)', in Corvol and Amat, *Forêt et guerre*, 133–6.

131 Whited, *Forests and Peasant Politics*, 163.

132 Joshua West, 'Forests and national security: British and American forest policy in the wake of World War I', *Environmental History*, 8:2 (2003), 279–81; David A. Clary, 'The biggest regiment in the army', *Journal of Forest History*, 22:4 (1978), 182–3; James E. Fickle, 'Defense mobilization in the southern pine industry: The experience of World War I', *Journal of Forest History*, 22:4 (1978), 206–33.

133 George T. Morgan, 'A forester at war: Excerpts from the diaries of Colonel William B. Greeley, 1917–1919', *Forest History*, 4:3–4 (1961), 4–5.

134 Clary, 'Biggest regiment in the army', 184.

135 West, 'Forests and national security', 4–5.

136 Percival Sheldon Ridsdale, 'Shot, shell and soldiers devastate forests', *American Forests*, 22 (1916), 338.

137 Quoted in Ibid., 338.

138 Guyot, *Forêt et la guerre*, 12. One forester, however, recognized that the situation was more complicated, and that the Germans were felling according to

their own forest management style. J. Reynaud, 'Nos forêts et les allemands', *Revue des Eaux et Forêts*, 14:19 (1 October 1916), 292–3.

139 Ridsdale, 'Shot, shell and soldiers', 334, 337.

140 John R. McNeill, 'Woods and warfare in world history', *Environmental History*, 9:3, (2004), 388–410; Richard P. Tucker, 'The world wars and the globalization of timber cutting', in Russell and Tucker, *Natural Enemy, Natural Ally*, 110–41.

141 As it adapted to the conditions of trench warfare, the French army encouraged practical exercises, including storming trenches and moving through communication lines in recreated battlefield landscapes. Similarly, British training camps in France featured reproductions of German trenches in preparation for future operations. 'Instruction de l'infanterie dans les dépôts'; SHD-DAT 17 N 387 Lieutenant-Colonel de Bellaigue de Bughas to Général Commandant en Chef, July 1916; Wencke Meteling, 'German and French Regiments', 24. British soldiers also trained in trench warfare back home on Salisbury Plain and other sites. John Schofield, 'Aftermath: Materiality on the Home Front, 1914–2001', in Nicholas J. Saunders (ed.), *Matters of Conflict: Material Culture and the First World War* (Abington: Routledge, 2004), 199–200.

142 SHD-DAT 7 N 548 'Contingent de 1917: Centres d'instruction d'été (à partir du 15 Avril)' [n.d.].

143 SHD-DAT 16 N 822 Sous-secrétaire d'Etat du Service de santé militaire to Général Commandant en Chef, Direction Arrière, Santé, G.Q.G, 31 December 1917.

144 SHD-DAT 7 N 549 Grand quartier général des armées de l'est, 'Instruction de l'infanterie dans les dépôts', 19 August 1915.

145 Audoin-Rouzeau, *Men at War*, 155–88; Leonard V Smith, *Between Mutiny and Obedience: The Case of the French Fifth Infantry Division during World War I* (Princeton: Princeton University Press, 1994).

146 Plowman, *Subaltern on the Somme*, 13.

147 Ibid., 13. The Bull Ring was a large camp; more than a million men passed through it between June 1915 and September 1917. Douglas Gill and Gloden Dallas, 'Mutiny at Etaples base in 1917', *Past and Present*, 69 (1975), 88–112.

148 Sassoon, *Memoirs of an Infantry Officer*, 14. On the effectiveness of BEF training schools, see Paddy Griffith, *Battle Tactics of the Western Front: The British Army's Art of Attack, 1916–18* (New Haven and London: Yale University Press, 1994), 188–90.

149 SHD-DAT 17 N 387 G.O.C., Royal Flying Corps in the Field, C.R.F.C. 1938/1.C., 7 October 1917; SHD-DAT 17 N 387 Officier interprete [sic] attache [sic] a [sic] l'Etat-Major du Royal Flying Corps to Interpretes [sic] attaches [sic] au Corps, [n.d.]. See also SHD-DAT 17 N 387 General, Commanding Second Army, to Quartermaster General, 2 December 1917.

150 From January 1916 the British army was also authorized to requisition land. Gibson, 'British army', 197–8.

151 SHD-DAT 17 N 387 Lieutenant-colonel de Bellaigue de Bughas, Directeur des services de la Mission militaire française to Lieutenant-Général Quartermaster Général des armées britanniques en France, November 1916. See also Gibson, 'British army', 198–9.

152 SHD-DAT 17 N 387 Colonel Directeur des services de la Mission militaire française attachée à l'armée britannique, 'Arrêté concernant l'établissement d'un camp d'instruction', 6 July 1916.

153 SHD-DAT 17 N 387 Chef d'Escadrons de Maleissye-Melun, Agent de liaison attaché à la 2ᵉ armée britannique to Lieutenant-colonel, Directeur des services, Mission militaire française, 19 January 1917.

154 SHD-DAT 17 N 387 Maire de Bailleul to Préfet du Nord par l'intermédiaire de le Sous-préfet d'Hazebrouck, 11 January 1917.

155 SHD-DAT 17 N 387 Eugène Cortyl to an unnamed Lieutenant, 9 January 1917; Maleissye-Melun, to Directeur des Services, Mission militaire française.

156 SHD-DAT 17 N 387 Chef d'Escadrons de Maleissye-Melun, Agent de liaison attaché à la 2ᵉ armée britannique to Lieutenant-colonel, Directeur des services, Mission militaire française, 25 January 1917.

157 On Franco-British relations behind the lines, see Gibson, 'The British army'.

158 ADS KZ 2759 Maire de Proyat to Préfet de la Somme, 28 December 1916.

159 ADS 99 R 3254 Directeur des Services agricoles to Préfet de la Somme, August 1916.

160 ADS 6 M 2036 Préfet de la Somme to Maires du département, 12 November 1914; Gibson, 'British army', 187–9.

161 Quoted in *Revue des Eaux et Forêts*, 8:36 (1 March 1915), 574.

162 Leonard V. Smith, Stéphane Audoin-Rouzeau and Anette Becker, *France and the Great War, 1914–1918* (Cambridge: Cambridge University Press, 2003), 66.

163 SHD-DAT 17 N 387 The Quarter Master General, British Armies in France, to Chief of the French Mission, 27 June 1916.

164 ADSM 2 R 37 Charles Courtier to Commissaire à l'agriculture, 10 April 1918; ADSM 2 R 37 Préfet de Seine-et-Marne to Commissaire à l'agriculture, 20 April 1918.

165 SHD-DAT 17 N 387 Ministre de l'Agriculture et du Ravitaillement to Préfet de la Somme, 13 February 1918.

166 Corinne Micelli, 'L'homme de Cazaux: Ferdinand Marzac', *Air Actualités*, 595, October 2006, 61; Eliane Keller and Patrick Boyer, *Cazaux: De l'école de tir aérien ETA à la base aérienne 120, 1913–1962* (Arcachon: Société historique et archéologique d'Arcachon et du pays de Buch, 2002), 18; A. Lagunerand, 'Biscarrosse: Avec les pionniers de l'aviation . . . ' *Cercle Cartophile de l'Adour*, 12, April 1990, 23.

167 John H. Morrow, 'Knights of the sky: The rise of military aviation', in Frans
     Coetzee and Marilyn Shevin Coetzee (eds), *Authority, Identity and the Social
     History of the Great War* (Oxford: Berghahn Books, 1995), 317.
168 Smith, Audoin-Rouzeau and Becker, *France and the Great War*, 147–54.
169 Nash, *Autobiography*, 187.

5

Demilitarization and militarization
(1918–40)

The Western Front's environmental history continued after the signing
of the Armistice in 1918. Four years of trench warfare had created new
environments that contemporary witnesses treated as wastelands and
wildernesses. Engineer and photographer Sir Alexander Kennedy, who
visited the war zones in October 1918, September 1919, and spring 1920,
observed how the road at Chemin des Dames 'practically disappears in
the wilderness' and how the view from Mort Homme ridge 'in all directions seems to cover nothing but shell-pocked wastes'.[1] In certain places,
mud, corpses, unexploded ordnance, trench remains, blackened tree
stumps, ruined villages, barbed wire and craters had all but replaced the
countryside of 1914. The scale of the transformation was unprecedented.
But the wartorn environment was not static. Make-shift cemeteries,
the recommencement of farming, and spontaneous vegetation growth
had already begun to alter locales within the war zones by the time of
Kennedy's later visits.

Militarization during the war had been an active and hybrid process.
So too was post-armistice demilitarization. After the war, the French
state and society faced a series of difficult political, cultural, economic, and environmental choices on tackling the wartorn environment.
Economic considerations were central. By the time Kennedy and others
had begun documenting the sterilized environment, reconstruction
work had already begun; the agricultural land and industries of northern
and eastern France were too valuable to leave in their obliterated state.[2]
But in the remaining areas of 'red zone' (those areas so mutilated that
the French state deemed them too costly to restore), a 1923 law outlined
three options; forestation, militarization, and memorialization. Whether

the land was to be demilitarized or remain militarized, all of these projects required active, and at times difficult, mobilizations of nature. Memorial and cemetery designers exploited topography and vegetation to commemorate the dead; foresters planted trees to literally green the red zone; and the army mobilized terrain and climate to train its troops. Demilitarization and militarization, then, continued to unfold as 'more-then-human' processes.

As France tried to recover from one war, its army planned for future ones, resulting in the modernization and expansion of its camps and training grounds. Familiar patterns re-emerged. Military planners targeted supposedly empty and uncultivated land, remained concerned about the dangers of the training environment, and faced the displeasure of dispossessed farmers and other landowners. Despite such problems, and as anxieties over international security heightened during the 1930s, the state and military oversaw the fortification of the Franco-German border, adding new layers of militarized environments to eastern France. This remilitarization of the environment culminated in the conflicts of 1940.

As this chapter explores, the history of militarized environments between 1918 and 1940 was characterized by the lingering physical and cultural legacies of one war and the ever-heightening fears, and then arrival, of another. We begin the story with the devastation wreaked by the First World War.

Visualizing the battlefields

The physical transformation ushered in by four years of trench warfare was profound. It seemed that war had turned the once-productive farmland and forests of northern and eastern France into wildernesses and wastelands. In 1920, Sorbonne university geographer Albert Demangeon outlined the war's impact on France's countryside in apocalyptical language. The 'cataclysm' had 'overturned everything' and the 'zone of death' stretched for 500 km. The once carefully cultivated land on which the conflict had unfolded had become 'a desert, a wild steppe'.[3] Agricultural experts agreed that the conflict had turned once fertile fields into desolate wastelands. 350,000 ha of the Somme and Pas-de-Calais had been devastated and the former battlefields of the former *département* were 'of the most lamentable desolation'. It seemed that this land would forever remain an 'uncultivated and uninhabitable desert'.[4]

Images of these sterilized wastelands entered the cultural sphere, in

part, through guidebooks.[5] Having promoted military aviation in the
years before the war (see chapter 3), the Michelin company produced
a series of twenty-nine battlefield guidebooks between 1917 and 1921.
At their launch in 1917, the historian Ernest Lavisse celebrated how
the guidebooks would allow visitors to inspect the battlefields, providing an important lesson in 'present history'.[6] Historians have studied
Michelin and other guidebooks in some detail.[7] Here, I focus on their
representation of wartorn environments.

As battlefield tourism increased after the cessation of hostilities, the
guidebooks portrayed a war-ravaged land. The land near Nauroy (Marne),
for instance, was 'pounded' by shells, 'ravaged' by mines, and 'furrowed'
with trenches.[8] The Ailette river valley at Chemin des Dames, with its
ruined villages and 'ravaged' forests, offered a comparably bleak view to
the tourist, scenes repeated at the Somme and Verdun battlefields.[9]

Intentionally or not, Michelin's guidebooks echoed key narrative
tropes that commentators had advanced during and after the Franco-
Prussian War (see chapter 2). The first was that the war had destroyed
a once bucolic countryside. The English language version of the Somme
guidebook portrayed a peaceful, pre-war, rural land of 'undulating hills
and broad table-lands' covered in crops and interspersed with villages,
small woods, roads, and orchards. Four years of war had 'robbed the
district of its former aspect. The ground, in a state of complete upheaval,
is almost levelled in places, while the huge mine-craters give it an appearance of a lunar landscape'.[10] The transformation of the countryside to an
unearthly, lunar environment underscored the enormity of the destruction: the Western Front, like the moon, was incapable of supporting life.

The scale of war's destructive powers had increased dramatically
since 1871, making the disruption to rural lives and environments ever
more startling. But echoing accounts of the 1870–71 war, Michelin's
guidebooks described topography, vegetation, and other environmental
features to set the scene for the battles. In other words, the guidebooks'
maps, photographs, and text mobilized the wartorn countryside to
document the war's military history. One guidebook mapped out the
geography of the Chemin des Dames in militarized terms: its 'steep
slopes, swampy ditches, underground galleries, and maze of steep
sided valleys' had made it a 'natural fortress'.[11] And like histories of the
1870–71 war, the guidebooks stressed the advantage of reaching high
ground to understand how the battles had unfolded, such as Côte 200
near Perthes-les-Hurles (Marne), the scene of heavy fighting on 15 July
1918.[12]

Michelin claimed objectivity for its guidebooks. But their images were far from neutral. Alongside the accompanying text, Michelin packaged them as evidence of German aggression, arguing that France had fought a defensive war with tenacity and honour.[13] The depictions of ruined environments reinforced the company's belief that Germany had wantonly destroyed the French countryside (and treasured aspects of the built environment, such as Reims). This devastation reportedly exposed the barbarity of German *Kultur*. The guidebooks' anti-German tone had in fact been forged during the war, when André Michelin had launched the series in response to rumours that the German firm Baedeker was about to begin publishing battlefield guides.[14] Like depictions of obliterated environments during the early war years (see chapter 4), Michelin mobilized images of the sterilized countryside to advance its politics. In such a way, the meanings of militarized environments were malleable and manipulated according to political objectives.

Demilitarizing the Western Front

Despite its supposedly educational value, local state officials and communities refused to accept that the Western Front would remain in its desolate state, given that the land was once valuable and productive. Before the war, 2,125,087 ha of the devastated regions had been ploughed land; 426,609 ha pasture; 596,072 ha forests; 46,790 ha marshes and lagoons; and 111,792 ha buildings, roads, and railways.[15] In fact, agricultural officials had already begun planning for reconstruction during the war: the Office de Reconstitution Agricole was founded on 6 August 1917. They had also begun assessing damage and re-starting agriculture in certain areas, such as those of the Somme liberated from German troops.[16]

These efforts were the forerunners of official postwar war damage assessments and reconstruction programmes. The French government initially classified 3,300,000 ha as devastated regions, spreading over 4,726 communes across ten *départements*. Barbed wire lay over a surface area of 375,000,000 m^2, and 333,000,000 m^3 of trenches required filling in. The war damage, however, was not uniform. In 1919, Génie Rural officials divided the land into three categories and mapped them in different colours. The 'blue zone' covered 1,694,500 ha (51 per cent of the total area) and required only limited attention, whilst the yellow zone spread across 1,495,000 ha (45 per cent of the total area) and required more work. Meanwhile, officials deemed that the 116,800 ha (4 per cent of the total area) of the 'red zone' were so damaged that the cost of restoring the land would be higher than it could ever be worth.[17] Demangeon put the overall cost of the war damage at a staggering 120 billion francs. For him, the country's economic life would only be restored when houses had been rebuilt and fertility restored to the soil.[18] France would be economically weakened until the land was successfully demilitarized, making environmental restoration part and parcel of the wider postwar reconstruction of France.

Demilitarizing wartorn environments was, and is, costly and labour-intensive.[19] Restoring the Western Front was no exception. Before restoration proper could take place, the land needed to be cleared of military detritus and then levelled. The Service des travaux de premi-ère urgence (succeeded by the Service des travaux de l'Etat) continued the wartime work of army munitions disposal services and undertook the early postwar emergency clearance and restoration work. It relied heavily on prisoner-of-war labour, until its disbandment in spring 1920. Despite labour shortages, frustrations, and disagreements between state officials and *sinistrés* (the local populations whose houses and land had been damaged or destroyed during the war), the combined efforts of the various state agencies, private firms, and local communities made good progress in clearing munitions and levelling out farmland; 75 per cent of this work was completed by January 1921.[20]

Once land had been demilitarized by the early 1920s, plans for its future use began to coalesce. Despite some nostalgia for the pre-war countryside, evident in the Michelin guidebooks, the decision was taken not to return the land to its exact former state. Instead, reconstruction paved the way for the modernisation of the built environment and agri-cultural plot consolidation, conducted under the framework of the plan-ning and compensation laws of March and April 1919.[21] Militarization, demilitarization and reconstruction were therefore important factors in environmental change in interwar France.

By 1930, the reconstruction of the towns, villages, and farmland of the devastated regions was essentially finished. This transformation was plain to see. Major General Sir Ernest Swinton's exposition of the battle-fields twenty years after the end of hostilities contrasted 'before' photos of muddy, cratered land, with 'after' ones of restored farmland, trees, and other signs of the re-emergent civilian life. 'Man and nature have wrought a miraculous transformation', he wrote.[22] Swinton's observa-tion is apt. It was the combination of human effort and planning and the ability of grasses and crops to grow in the reconstituted soil that allowed the countryside to be made productive once more.

If the former militarized environments had been left to regenerate spontaneously, different kinds of vegetation would have thrived. This was evident on those sites that the reconstruction process overlooked, where broom, bracken, heather, and so-called weeds prospered on the combat-disturbed terrain, covering over the traces of war. Travelling through the war zones in October 1918, Kennedy saw 'roads, fields, orchards . . . already covered with rank herbage altogether disguising their original nature'. Thiepval plateau was 'a wilderness of weedy vegetation, and the weeds seem to have swallowed up the redoubts altogether'. At Delville Wood the ground and the few remaining tree stumps were 'thickly covered with rank weeds'.[23] Designating a plant a 'weed' is highly subjective, dependent on time, place, cultural norms, scientific understandings, and individual perspectives.[24] Kennedy's obvious dislike for these types of vegetation suggests that he considered them out-of-place and unwelcome. The weeds symbolized war's melancholy, uncontrollable, and nefarious aspects. Unlike poppies, they served no commemorative function and were agriculturally unproductive, thereby serving as reminders of the war's sterilization of the French countryside.

Reconstructing France's forests

Like weeds, trees spontaneously regenerated within former militarized environments. In less damaged forests, isolated clumps of vigorous oak trees prospered; the opening up of forest cover during the war had aided their successful seeding in 1917. Other types of trees also began to absorb and cover up the traces of conflict.[25] For foresters trained to favour productive and planned forests, this spontaneous vegetative growth was unacceptable. In 1926 and 1928, they employed labourers to clear 700 ha of undergrowth and shrubs that had thrived in the Saint-Mihiel region on sites where supposedly 'abusive' military felling had taken place. This unwelcome vegetation threatened to crowd out foresters' preferred species of oak, beech, and ash.[26] The oft-repeated phrase of nature repairing itself under human guidance summed up foresters' preferred alternative to natural regeneration. According to J. Demorlaine, head of the French forestry battalion and Professor at the Institut national agronomique, it was only through the patient combination of nature and the intelligent work of the forester that the forests would regenerate.[27]

The restoration of forests to something resembling their former state was a longer-term process than reconstructing agricultural land. Echoing wartime anti-German rhetoric, chief US forester Henry S. Graves linked the destruction of forests with that of the built environment: 'the cathedrals of nature like the cathedrals built by man became the object of the destructive genius of the Hun'. For Graves, ravaged forests must now be 'cleared and a new forest started, like the rebuilding of a demolished village'.[28] Similarly, the French Minster for Agriculture declared, 'several years will suffice to restore Reims cathedral if we commit the necessary resources. But however much we spend, it will take at least a century before the forest of Viel-Armand will recover its former splendour'.[29] In this vein, assistant Director of the Service de l'inspection du credit foncier de France, Edmond Michel, estimated that it would take sixty years for the forests to produce construction grade timber once again, and only then could they be 'considered reconstituted'.[30]

It is no surprise that French foresters, informed by economic considerations and long-standing anxieties concerning deforestation, elevated reforestation to a task of national importance. Although numerically depleted by the war, they had begun planning forest reconstruction during the war itself, debating such issues as war damage compensation and the most appropriate species with which to replant.[31] Drawing on the notions of patriotic duty and sacrifice circulating in postwar France,[32] and seeking to link reforestation with national identity, foresters portrayed trees as arboreal counterparts to the celebrated figure of the *poilu*, the tenacious infantryman that had saved France at Verdun and other battles. They argued that forests had earned the right to regenerate. Demorlaine asserted that forests should be saved from the 'devastating axe' after their wartime suffering and in recognition of the services they had rendered to France.[33]

As with agricultural land, reconstructing forests along the former Western Front required damage assessment. The uneven sylvan impact of trench warfare complicated the picture. While some trees had been obliterated, others were still standing, even if the bullets in their trunks made their exploitation arduous, if not impossible. The Meuse *département* had suffered the most damage to communal forests (66,000 ha) and the Ardennes had the highest levels of destruction to private forests (79,715 ha).[34] Overall figures for forest damage vary, but it now seems clear that 200,000 ha required clearance and restoration work after the war.[35] After damage assessment, land clearance, and the filling in of trenches had been completed, replanting could begin. Alongside paying war reparations, Germany provided France with trees and seeds to replant its forests, including 153,000 resinous plants, 118 kilos of resinous seeds, and 1,400 kilos of acorns in 1921 and 1922.[36] Despite such assistance, a lack of manpower, unwanted vegetation growth, forest fires, and hungry rabbits feeding on shoots hampered reforestation.[37]

Nonetheless, by December 1927 most of the land clearance, soil preparation, and planting were completed. Foresters did not hold back in congratulating themselves. Jules Forget, the Meuse's former forestry conservator, praised the endurance, energy, professionalism, and intelligence of foresters who had completed a task that once seemed 'beyond human ability'.[38] The restoration of some forests, however, did not begin until the 1930s. For instance, the replanting of Barisis wood only got underway in 1930, as did the tendering for the initial ground clearance and levelling work in Apremont forest.[39]

Agricultural and forest reconstruction demilitarized swathes of the former Western Front, restoring it to civilian use and productivity. Demilitarization and reconstruction were achieved through the intermingling of human and nonhuman processes and national and local interests.

But the future of the 'red zone' – land that would not be reconstructed – remained politically contentious during the 1920s. The law of 17 April 1919 had enabled the state to take control of the red zone but many local communities fought to have their land excluded from it to enable re-cultivation. Farmers in the Somme were especially successful at persuading the state to reclassify their land; in spring 1920 the Somme's prefect reduced the *département*'s red zone from 28,000 ha to 8,000 ha and by 1928 only 441 ha of land on the Thiepval plateau remained within it.[40] Red zone discontents in the Meuse were far less successful than their counterparts in the Somme.[41] Under the law of 24 April 1923 the state expropriated eleven communes in the Meuse in their entirety. Local discontent continued. Out of the 6,953 landowners who still found themselves in the red zone, 267 refused to accept the compulsory purchase of their land.[42] Under the framework of the 1923 law the red zone was not to be reconstructed; forestation, memorialization, and continued militarized were its fates. All involved mobilizations of nature. This chapter will now explore each of these in turn.

Transforming the red zone (I): Foresting Verdun

In Britain the government encouraged the planting of forests as a strategic national reserve after the extensive felling undertaken during the First World War.[43] In France, meanwhile, the state and its foresters mobilized trees as agents of demilitarization on areas of the red zone, especially in

the Meuse *département*. Forests planned in accordance with the supposedly rational principles of forest management were intended to replace
chaotic wartorn environments pockmarked with trenches, shell holes,
unexploded ordnance, and barbed wire.

The state deemed afforestation a cheap and viable way of demilitarizing the battlefields and restoring a degree of productivity to the land, a
view enthusiastically endorsed by foresters who stood to benefit from
the afforestation programme and who had long stressed the importance
of expanding France's forest cover.[44] The land, they argued, could not
remain like 'abandoned islands among France's richest provinces'.[45]
Farmers, however, protested the loss of their land. Pol Robinet, in a
1927 letter to *Le Sinistré*, accused foresters of putting pressure on him to
abandon the farm which he had returned to after the war and struggled
to re-cultivate. He demanded the right to work his farm 'in peace'. *Le
Sinistré* took up the cause of this 'brave farmer', arguing that at a time
of wheat shortages and high bread prices it made no sense to transform
fields into forests.[46]

But such protests over the competing interests of forestry and agriculture did not derail the afforestation programme. The forest administration took charge of two large areas to the north of Verdun: the Masse
du Morthomme (3,103 ha) on the left bank of the Meuse River and the
Masse de Verdun (9,270 ha) on the right bank.[47] Other sites brought
the total area earmarked for afforestation to 15,672 ha. Before the war,
only approximately a third (5,700 ha) of this land had been forested.[48]
War-damaged forests that pre-existed the Western Front would simply
be subsumed within the new forest. The afforestation programme was
therefore poised to transform the region.

Planting began in 1929, with different species preferred for different
types of terrain. On land that had not been forested before the war, the
preferred species were Corsican pine mixed with alder and silver birch
on dry, sun-exposed terrain, and spruce, Douglas pine, Japanese larch
mixed with ash, sycamore, and acacia on north-facing slopes.[49] To create
a fully functioning forest infrastructure, foresters also built nine forestry
houses and introduced game.[50]

Afforestation was not a smooth process. Imported deer and hare
populations adapted so well to their new habitat that culls were deemed
necessary to protect young plantations. Other stumbling blocks included
the repeated discovery of soldiers' corpses, unexploded munitions, a
field mouse 'invasion' in 1932, and the damages reportedly caused by
the thousands of snail-hunters who came from Verdun, Metz, and the

Longwy basin.[51] The latter difficulty echoed long-term tensions between forest management and traditional uses of French forests.[52] But the corpses and munitions were obstacles specific to postwar environments.

State investment helped overcome these difficulties. Of the 14,296 ha scheduled for afforestation, 12,976 ha were planted by the end of 1933 at a cost of just over ten million francs.[53] Although traces of pre-1914 land use remained,[54] the forests planted in the 1920s and 1930s established largely homogenous pine forests, attesting to the long-term environmental impact of war and reconstruction. Yet afforestation did not remove all the traces of war quickly; it was only seventy years after the conflict that forestry production became buoyant. Even so, the impact of artillery shells on the soil is still apparent.[55]

Foresters portrayed the newly forested areas, where birds had reportedly begun to nest, as signs that nature and peace had returned to the land.[56] But not everyone was happy. Some veterans did not want the land to 'heal'. Instead, they wanted it left in its wartorn state to act as a reminder of their suffering, the deaths of their comrades, and the futility of war. Although he did not make specific reference to forestation, Pierre Dumarchey visited the former Verdun battlefields in 1933 and stated that 'this land must always remain sterile' and that life and 'outdoor *joie de vivre*' should be forever banished.[57] Another veteran believed that visitors to Verdun wanted to see traces of the 'carnage' which the new forests would hide.[58]

The tensions between foresters and veterans refused to die down. Veteran associations, along with Verdun town council, protested more formally against afforestation. During a December 1930 meeting of the Departmental Commission for Sites (a body overseeing the protection of historical and natural monuments), the deputy mayor of Verdun and president of the local Syndicat d'initiative urged that part of the red zone, and particularly Donaumont plateau, be saved from the plantations that would obscure war memorials and irredeemably alter the area. Along with the local press, they secured the postponement of planting between Vaux and Douaumont forts and Sainte-Fine chapel, a sign of the importance of veterans and local politics in war commemoration.[59]

In response to such problems, foresters challenged the view that afforestation and memorialization were incompatible. Although Forget admitted that while he understood the reasons behind the desire to preserve the 'tragic' appearance of the chaotic battlefield environment, he argued that the deputy mayor and his supporters had failed to consider time, 'the inexorable destroyer'. Without the work of foresters,

Forget argued, 'the forces of nature' would 'spontaneously' cover the hallowed sites with a 'meagre and miserable' vegetation composed of valueless trees and bushes. Rather than leaving nature to 'operate by herself haphazardly', it was better, Forget urged, for humans to decide the site's future using 'appropriately' chosen species to create 'regular and homogenous plantations' that would be a source of 'richness and beauty'.[60] Moreover, Forget argued that the trees themselves constituted a form of commemoration by ensuring the country's renewal. The colour green was itself symbolic, representing 'hope . . . fertility, [and] faith in the future'.[61] The trees were also revered because they physically embody nature's resilience. At least one observer agreed, interpreting shoots sprouting from the roots of trees flattened during the war as evidence that nature was 'stronger than the destructive madness of men!'[62] Forget was also not alone in linking forestation with memorialization; in 1927 the Société des amis des arbres and the Association nationale et industrielle du bois obtained government approval for the launch of the national Tree Day on the symbolically important date of 11 November.[63]

The conflict over the Verdun forests exposed the antagonism between state officials and local communities, as well as highlighting the importance of veterans' emotional attachments to the former militarized environments in which they lived and fought. Like wartime militarization, demilitarization was a source of social and political friction. The debate also reminds us that demilitarization through forestation existed alongside projects to memorialize former battlefields and other significant sites. This too was a 'more-than-human' process.

Transforming the red zone (II): Mobilizing nature to remember

The relationship between memory and place is complex and has a bearing on who, and what, gets remembered and how.[64] Post-1918 France was no different, as environmental considerations played a role in the construction of memory on those areas of red zone set aside for memorialization.[65]

War vestiges were meaningful sites for the veterans, pilgrims, tourists, and others who visited them in droves.[66] A key question was whether they should be actively memorialized or left alone to serve as more authentic and striking reminders of war's carnage. Atherton Fleming in his 1919 guide *How to See Battlefields* believed that they should be left alone 'untouched by aught but nature'.[67] Others recognized that nature alone could not carry out the task of commemoration. Back in 1915, during the inauguration of a memorial in Chipotte forest (Vosges), a forestry conservator predicted that 'nature will return [*la nature reprendra ses droits*], the soil will level out, vegetation will sprout again . . . and all traces of the battle will disappear'. The memorial, rather than the rejuvenated forest, would remind young male passers-by of the dead soldiers' sacrifice and inspire them to join the army to protect their country.[68] The forestry conservator recognized that without interpretation – through memorials – the environment alone could not transmit memories of the war to future generations. This was the perspective that eventually became dominant.

After 1918, memorialization intensified as governments, veterans associations, and local communities created cemeteries and memorials to bury the dead and remember the war. In doing so, they used horticulture to create an orderly memorial environment in contrast to the unruly weeds that thrived on battlefields. The use of flowers to embellish the gravestones had begun during the war. Arthur Hill, assistant director of the Botanical Gardens in Kew, visited France in 1916 to give advice on planting the temporary and *ad hoc* cemeteries that troops had erected within war-torn environment.[69] These small, isolated and fragile cemeteries were places of remembrance within the intensity of the militarized environment. After the war, the British Imperial War Graves Commission planted more formal cemeteries that stood in marked contrast to the surrounding wartorn environment. *The Times* reported in approving tones of how on travelling through the 'abomination of desolation' of the Somme, one arrives at the 'white headstones' of the cemetery at Forceville (inaugurated in 1921), which stood 'in rows linked by pathways smooth as an English lawn. Wallflowers, narcissi, forget-me-nots, pansies abound – one is dumb before the sweetness of it all'.[70] As the Commission's cemeteries became larger and more formal, their verdant lawns, hedges, and plants, created under the guidance of garden designer Gertrude Jekyll, forged a recognizably English landscape within the French countryside. Ten years after the signing of the armistice, the Commission had managed to plant over 100 km of hedgerows and over 200 ha of grass, whilst its nurseries had produced over 13 million plants.[71]

Ideas about nationality informed memorialization. The Commission's mobilization of plants tamed the disordered battlefields and gave meaning to death in a way that was congruent with notions of British national identity.[72] Its lush turfs certainly made an impression on French visitors; one marvelled at the 'bright green lawn' laid at the Thiepval memorial whose colour was a 'secret' that only the English knew.[73] Lawns, like the poppy, became associated with British memories of the war. In Germany, meanwhile, the lily-aster was mooted, unsuccessfully, as a flower of remembrance. Instead, trees, rather than flowers, became the foci for German commemoration. Drawing on long cultural traditions, the trees planted in German cemeteries were intended to root the dead soldiers' sacrifice in the soil.[74]

But the assumption that Germans remembered with trees and the British with flowers is overly simplistic. The latter also used trees to commemorate dead soldiers. One British officer in 1916 posited that a long avenue of trees should be planted along the Western Front; 'it would make a fine broad road on the no man's land between the lines, with paths for pilgrims on foot, and plant trees for shade, and fruit trees so that the soil should not be altogether waste'.[75] This vision was never realized, but trees became important elements within the design of British, and Commonwealth cemeteries, 'deepening the significances of the places concerned'.[76] At Beaumont-Hamel Newfoundland Memorial Park (opened in 1925) its creators planted 35,000 seedlings and trees to add to the Lombardy poplars that formed its perimeter. Similarly, the Canadians planted maple trees at Vimy Ridge (which, along with pine trees, now number 11,285).[77] Trees became strongly associated with national memories as seeds and saplings from the soldiers' homeland took root in French soil, linking the dead bodies, the battlefield, and the nation. Oak trees grown from South African acorns lined the avenue at Delville Wood and an avenue of trees grown in British nurseries formed part of the esplanade at Edwin Lutyens's Memorial to the Missing of the Somme at Thiepval.[78]

Different nations invested particular trees with national significance. At Beaumont-Hamel the bare skeletal remains of 'The Danger Tree' stand preserved in cement on a spot that had been particularly deadly for Newfoundland soldiers during the battle of 1 July 1916. At Delville Wood, meanwhile, the most revered tree is the 'Last Tree', the only one reputed to have survived the combats of July 1916. This resilient hornbeam was marked with its own memorial in 1988 after the visit of the South African ambassador and has become an important focal point on pilgrimages.[79] A similar story of survival is attributed to the 'Crows' Tree', near the Belvédère de Vaux (Somme), an isolated hornbeam or elm (opinion is divided) that shells and bullets miraculously left untouched. Local legend has it that crows gathered at this one remaining tree and developed a warning system to protect themselves from human hunters.

The original tree died in the 1980s and was replaced by an oak charged with 'perpetuating its history' (according to its interpretative sign).

These trees have passed into legend as hardy and lucky survivors of the Somme battles and are treated as authentic remnants of the war years. As the environment has changed around them and human survivors die, the trees' significance has increased. A recent postcard of 'The Last Tree' describes it as the 'original living witness of the Delville Wood Battle'. As is the case at other battlefield memorial sites, such as Gettysburg in the United States, the trees are called upon to bear witness to the slaughter that once unfolded around them.[80]

Trees were mobilized to support the war effort *and* commemorate the conflict. The same was true for animals. Animal imagery began to appear on memorials in the immediate postwar period to commemorate human bravery and sacrifice. This echoed Frédéric-Auguste Bartholdi's Belfort lion sculpture, which was designed to symbolize the resistance of Belfort during the Franco-Prussian War.[81] The Belfort lion represented bravery, strength, and resilience in the face of adversity. In a similar vein, veterans of the French 130th division erected a statue of a wounded lion at the former First World War site of Sainte-Fine chapel to honour their comrades slaughtered on the Verdun battlefield (see figure 5.1).

Dumarchey was deeply moved by the statue of this 'noble beast' that was now 'limp and crushed [*mou et anéantie*]'. It was, he believed, a 'beast that soldiers like, a sentimental lion made for following regiments and dying without understanding why, but with its friends'.[82] For Dumarchey, the lion represented unthinking loyalty and camaraderie. Like the human soldiers, more powerful forces overwhelmed it, but was still worthy of reverence.[83]

But although lions have strong republican connotations in France, given their appearance on statues during the revolution, surprisingly few appeared on First World War memorials.[84] Instead, stone renderings of Gallic *coqs* were far more common features of the thousands of war memorials erected across France. Like the lion, French republicanism linked these animals to France's revolutionary heritage; during the revolution they had symbolized the unity of French people and represented French pluck and aggression.[85] In a similar vein, First World War memorials featured the Gallic cock as a symbol of French courage and unity. On the war memorial at Vrigne-aux-Bois (Ardennes) a *coq* stands defiantly against the back drop of a radiant half-sun. Its raised head draws the bystanders' gaze up towards the noble profile of a moustached *poilu* (see figure 5.2). It is as if the cock, representing France, looks to the dead

5.1 French 130th division memorial, Verdun

soldier for inspiration and guidance. In comparison, at Nizy-le-Comte (Aisne), the *coq* stands alone at the top of the memorial, its head pointing boldly towards the sky.

Gallic cocks had featured regularly in French propaganda during the war, as the eagle had done on posters in the USA.[86] After the war, eagle statues came to represent American military might in the US cemeteries established on French soil. One example is the 1932 eagle statue that dominates Saint-Mihiel American Cemetery near Thiaucourt (Meurthe-et-Moselle). The close association between animals, national identity, and militarism similarly explains why a caribou statue sits atop a cairn at the Newfoundland Memorial at Beaumont-Hamel: caribou were emblems of both the island and its regiment (see figure 5.3).

5.2 First World War memorial, Vrigne-aux-Bois (Ardennes)

As well as deploying the powerful emotional and political resonances of animal statues, the designers of memorial sites exploited topography. In its introductory brochure for the Thiepval Memorial, the Imperial War Graves Commission explained how the choice of the site 'was dictated partly by the nature of the site and partly by historical associations'.[87] The

5.3 Caribou statue at Newfoundland Memorial at Beaumont-Hamel, Somme

site was one of the strongest German positions attacked by British forces on 1 July 1916, and dominated the surrounding countryside (French commentators frequently highlighted how the monument was visible from far away in all directions[88]). Like Thiepval, the American monument at the summit of Montsec was (and still is) visible for miles around. In 1931 American engineer Mr Terry claimed that it was possible to see 114 villages on a clear day from the site, which had been primarily chosen for its 'situation'.[89] A relief map in monument's interior underscores the site's topographical importance.

But cemeteries and memorials were not universally accepted. Critics, such as Vera Brittain, claimed that the combination of memorials and nature sanitized and obscured the traces of war, diluting the horror and message of the war. Veterans also complained that they changed the sites in which they fought beyond recognition.[90] Governments and private entrepreneurs responded to such concerns by buying up and maintaining certain areas within memorial sites in their supposedly war-torn state, such as Vimy Ridge and Beaumont-Hamel, where remnants of the trenches survived. But even at these sites numerous decisions were taken about what and how to remember, which undermines their authenticity. Furthermore these traces of war required protection from the onslaught of wind, rain, and vegetation if they were to be preserved at all. Indeed, by the early 1930s, grasses and plants were covering over and obscuring isolated and unmanaged war vestiges on the Verdun battlefields.[91] Nature's dynamism made 'freezing' the battlefield environments of Western Front an impossible venture.[92]

Cemeteries and memorial sites gave sections of the red zone a national purpose by turning former battlefields into sites of remembrance and commemoration. They served very human purposes – remembering the dead, perpetuating memories, transmitting lessons to future generations, and glorifying national war efforts – through the deployment of topography, vegetation, and animal imagery. Memorialization was therefore 'more-than-human', as was the continued militarization of other areas of red zone.

Transforming the red zone (III): Creating Suippes Camp[93]

In Britain and the USA, the world wars were keys episodes in the establishment of military bases and lands as the armed forces commandeered civilian land for training troops and testing weapons as part of the war effort.[94] The case of Suippes in post-1918 France differs in that the army transformed a former battlefield into an army camp.[95]

Whilst the Meuse *département* became the centre of forestation, the Marne became the focal point of postwar militarization of the red zone. The army created Suippes Camp on a site noted for its severe desolation. The Marne *département* had seen heavy fighting from September 1914 onwards and front lines had stretched across the Champagne plains from the north of Reims to the Argonne forest. Only 19,960 ha of farmland survived the war intact (out of a total agricultural area of 185,220 ha) and the war affected 50,000 ha of woodland. In all, the state placed 23,300 ha of the *département* within the red zone after the war. The most obliterated area lay to the north of the town of Suippes where combat had razed seven villages, wiped out cultivation, and strewn trenches, munitions, and corpses across the land.[96] The Bishop of Châlons visited the area in October 1918 and reported seeing 'an absolute desert, without water, people or vegetation . . . the land is colourless and is just like the corpse of a *pays*'.[97] Death stalked the region; the war had left a 'thousand wounds' and 'forests of white crosses' had replaced its pine trees.[98]

Suippes formed part of the so-called *la Champagne pouilleuse*, a region that the war had apparently further improvised. Michelin's battlefield guide asserted that whilst the *Champagne pouilleuse* had been 'poor before the war' it was now 'sterile' in places. The action of shells and other weapons had stripped away the thin vegetation to expose the layer of clay beneath. Visitors would now see only 'deserts of clay' near Suippes.[99] From the state's point of view, the extent of the destruction and the poor soils made the costs of agricultural restoration and forestation prohibitive. But the army, with its nearby camps at Châlons and Mailly, had already shown its predilection for *la Champagne pouilleuse*. Having considered the creation of a new camp near Châlons in 1911, the army secured the political decision to establish a 14,000 ha camp to the north east of Suippes on 5 March 1919, thereby creating France's largest militarized environment.[100]

In fact, only two-fifths of the camp lay within the red zone. Securing the rest of the camp's terrain required the expropriation of land from neighbouring civilians. After decrees in 1922 that declared that the camp was in the public interest, the army began the expropriation process in earnest. On 2 July 1924, for instance, decrees announced the expropriation of 306 parcels of land from Suippes commune.[101] A confidential army report of 1922 indicates that military planners attempted, to an extent, to take local agricultural interests into account when establishing the camp's boundaries, and, in March 1924, the army allowed some landowners to continue pasturing their sheep on their expropriated land.[102] Nonetheless, it faced sustained opposition from local people protesting the loss of their homes, fields, pastureland, and hunting rights. Like postwar afforestation, militarization was unpopular.

The tenacity of local protests meant that the expropriation procedure dragged on throughout the 1920s and into the 1930s. In 1927 farmers from Somme-Suippe criticized proposed changes to the camp's perimeter that would deprive them of their wheat crops.[103] Two years later, farmers at Laval-sur-Tourbe complained that the army was taking their best land.[104] Local concerns over the army's lack of consultation and unfair compensation rates were additional bones of contention. The security zones around the camp's edges were particularly controversial. The army claimed that the ever increasing power of weaponry necessitated ever larger security zones. Locals had little time for such technological determinism and believed that the apparent emptiness of security zones made them suitable pastureland.[105] Despite lines on maps and signs on the ground, the boundary between militarized and civilian environments was ambiguous and contested.

Militarization through the establishment of Suippes Camp brought a section of the red zone into France's geography of national defence. Along with Châlons and Mailly camps, it confirmed *la Champagne pouilleuse* as the army's training area of choice. But Suippes Camp was also part of a wider attempt to consolidate, improve, and expand the defence estate throughout the 1920s amid concerns that existing training facilities were insufficient.[106]

Environmental militarization in the 1920s

On 17 December 1925 the army launched a general development programme for its camps. Amongst its aims were the expansion and modernization of the camps' firing ranges and built infrastructure. The programme aimed to provide the army with 12 large camps at a cost of 60 million francs.[107]

In some cases, modernization meant expanding and rationalizing existing camps. At Caylus (Tarn-et-Garonne), General Marty, of the 17th Army Corps, recommended building a better-placed camp and extending the firing range by 4,200 ha over relatively cheap and supposedly uncultivated land characterized by 'shrivelled oak trees', abandoned villages, and 'scraggy grass' fit only for sheep.[108] The extension of Caylus Camp over a sparsely populated limestone *causse* points to the continued military desire to militarize supposedly unproductive and cheap land.[109]

In general, and mirroring Suippes Camp's establishment, the implantation of the 1925 programme was a drawn-out affair. For instance, at Garrigues Camp near Nîmes, poor planning, the wasting of resources and the cost of extending the camp over cultivated land dogged its rejuvenation.[110] And, once again, determined local opposition posed a headache for the army. At Caylus, the army had underestimated the land's value, meaning that the camp's boundaries required substantial revision. In the end, the army expropriated land in 1935 to bring the camp's size to 2,800 ha.[111]

The First World War had confirmed the aeroplane as a modern weapon. In its immediate aftermath military engineers and flight officials attempted to consolidate and expand their air base at Cazaux through the further requisitioning of civilian land.[112] The army also developed an anti-aircraft range at Biscarrosse. From the military perspective, the Landes region was ideal for high altitude bombing and training; its lagoons, sparsely populated forests, and proximity to the 'infinite' Atlantic Ocean were ideal for flying.[113] Furthermore the region did not replicate the problems caused by aerial bombing of areas of the former Western Front; bombing had to be suspended at Suippes Camp in 1927 because it churned up the land, exposing and shattering the bones of unburied soldiers.[114]

Civilians, however, were unimpressed by the militarization of the south west's lagoons, forests, and coastline, which for them were sites of work and leisure. Biscarrosse's mayor protested that the bombing ranges would ruin local tourism. The forest administration also ardently opposed the militarization of its forests, a view shared by the Minister for Agriculture. Foresters feared that forest fires would proliferate, revenue from forestry products would suffer, and the pine trees' stabilization of coastal dunes would be undermined.[115]

Military reports dismissed such fears, somewhat unconvincingly. They argued that practice bombs would cause no more damage to trees than stones falling from the same height and, in an unwitting fore-runner of atomic bomb tourism in Cold War Nevada, they claimed that bathers would enjoy the explosive spectacle provided by the planes.[116] But despite 'systematic [civilian] opposition'[117] to the modernization and expansion of the Cazaux–Biscarrosse training complex, military interests prevailed over civilian ones. The army succeeded in spite of interwar unease about rural depopulation.[118]

Interwar militarization did not mean abandoning fears over the influence of environmental factors on soldiers' health. At Suippes Camp, army officials confronted the Western Front's environmental legacies. Fertilized by the manure and waste left by soldiers, 'luxuriant vegetation' had thrived alongside the Suippe River on land abandoned between 1919 and 1924. The combination of dense vegetation and marshy land had attracted mosquitoes. The army found this marshy, insect-ridden site unacceptable and 'cleaned' and drained it, aiming to chase away the mosquitoes and supposedly harmful odours. But despite these precautions, the camp's commander and chief medical officer recommended locating a proposed officers' quarter as far away as possible from the river to mitigate the site's 'danger'. Medical General Sacquépée agreed, and recommended the complete draining of the river and the planting of trees and gardens as a further precaution, just as military hygienists had done at Châlons Camp in the mid-nineteenth century.[119] In general, maintaining soldiers' health within the militarized environment was a way of combating external criticism. In 1935, the anti-militarist Communist newspaper *L'Humanité* attacked motorized manoeuvres in Champagne during which reservists suffered from 'fatigue and exhaustion'.[120]

Despite the enlargement and modernization of bases and training grounds, military commanders complained that training facilities remained inadequate.[121] Moreover, in 1931, the Minister for War expressed alarm that some subalterns had never driven tanks 'over varied terrain' and nor had others even fired machine guns, cannons, or pistols for 'several years'.[122] These concerns point to a wider organizational and operational malaise afflicting an army that was more suited towards defensive rather than offensive operations.[123] As international tensions heightened in the 1930s after Nazi Germany begun to re-arm, France's defensive orientation became even more pronounced within the environment.

Fortifying France

The trauma and immense loss of life during the First World War made the French determined to avoid another war.[124] Informed, in part, by the successful defence of Verdun during the First World War and the declining birth rate, the belief that defence was more effective than attack held sway in political and military circles (bar the measures proposed by Charles de Gaulle in his 1934 book *Vers l'armée de metier*). France must become a fortress.[125] So alongside entering a series of international alliances, the government set about reinforcing the border with Germany. This built on General Bernesson's 1927 request to maintain the Rhine's water levels as the 'first line of resistance' against Germany and calls to preserve forest cover around Paris.[126]

The desire to turn France into a fortress militarized the environment of northern and eastern France. It culminated in the law of 14 January 1930 that financed a line of subterranean fortifications named after Minister of War André Maginot. The Maginot Line was mainly completed by 1935 and although it had some offensive capabilities, its main role was resolutely defensive. Its main section stretched from the Swiss border to Montmédy (near the Luxembourg border), protecting the newly recovered provinces of Alsace and Lorraine (a smaller, less well-known section, fortified the Alpine border with Italy). Beyond Montmédy, France's defences relied on the topography of the Ardennes and French troops moving into Belgium in the event of a German attack. Marshal Philippe Pétain, the 'victor' of Verdun and one of the main proponents of the defensive outlook, argued that the topography and forests of the Ardennes hills were 'impenetrable if one makes some special dispositions there . . . This sector is not dangerous'.[127] The German lines of invasion in 1940 would soon expose the shaky foundations of this faith in France's natural defences.

The Maginot Line added a new layer of militarized environments to the existing forts, camps, and training grounds in eastern France. It brought with it firing exercises, expropriations of land, and restricted civilian access to forests, roads, orchards, and fields.[128]

Like previous attempts to fortify the Franco-German border (see chapter 3) the Maginot Line exploited existing environmental features. The fortifications were designed to dominate, survey, and protect plains, towns, and other strategically important sites. Mountainous terrain made the construction of the 'little Maginot line' on the Italian border a tougher prospect, but once built the forts effectively exploited the Alpine topography and offered their occupants extensive views across the surrounding countryside.[129] The Maginot Line also modified terrain. Minefields, anti-tank obstacles, and flooding reinforced its fortifications. In addition, some sections of forest were levelled to improve the line of fire from the fortifications.[130]

Belief in the Maginot Line's impregnability continued once war broke out in September 1939. 'A French Officer' explained to the British public how the French army had used the 'science of camouflage' and the 'natural defences of the countryside' to conceal and strengthen the fortifications. It had taken care of the smallest details, laying turf over gun turrets and painting concrete installations the colour of the earth 'so that they would not stand out when once the ground had been ploughed up by the falling shells'. Moreover, observation points 'command[ed] the landscape in every direction'.[131] This account of the Maginot Line can either be read as an expression of pride in French military engineering or an attempt to reassure the British public of the war-readiness of its ally. In places, however, the reality of the defences fell well short of this image. One officer was 'amazed to see that nothing, absolutely nothing, has been prepared in depth' near the Gommelange-Bettange marshes. Here, the supposedly impenetrable Maginot Line consisted of a 'ridiculous network of barbed wire, together with upturned ends of some rails stuck in the earth in the foreground to stop, so it appears, tanks'.[132]

The Maginot Line, along with the creation of Suippes Camp and expansion of other military installations, meant that the militarization of the French countryside continued in the interwar period, despite the demilitarization of the Western Front. It may seem paradoxical that militarization thrived at a time when pacifism seemingly gained a stronghold with French society. The extent and meaning of pacifism are debatable (Daniel Hucker suggests 'war anxiety' as a more accurate alternative[133]). But although the majority of French policy-makers and the general public certainly wanted to avoid future wars, many were prepared, if necessary, to defend their country.[134] In this sense, militarization in interwar France was tolerated as necessary preparation for an unwanted, but possible, future conflict. But like other militarized environments established in peacetime, the Maginot Line offered no guarantee of military success in the event of war.

Militarization during the *drôle de guerre*

Environmental militarization intensified still further on 3 September 1939 as France and Britain declared war on Germany. In the subsequent period known as the phoney war (or *drôle de guerre*), France and its British ally militarized new corners of the French countryside as they prepared for what they believed would be a protracted war with Germany.

Despite the mechanized character of modern warfare and the increased importance of planes and tanks, armies still mobilized animals. In October 1939, France created a Service de chiens de guerre to train guard and sled dogs (dogs pulled sleighs in the Alps). But their numbers were small compared to those mobilized by Germany.[135] Both sides also deployed horses. Amongst its horse-borne units, France had three Spahi brigades and five light cavalry divisions, while two-thirds of its artillery units were drawn by horsepower.[136] One French cavalry lieutenant rejoiced in the continued use of horses; 'all these horses! . . . Can't you feel the romance of them? They take you back to 1914 and every war of the past . . . While our modern army with its tractors, caterpillars, and cars conjures up some horrific book of [H.G.] Wells'.[137] On the German side, the majority of infantry units still relied on horses for transportation.[138] In contrast to images of fast, efficient, and heavily mechanized Blitzkrieg tactics, animals unwittingly played a role in the Second World War, as they had during the First World War.

French military strategy during the phoney war can be caricatured as conservative, out-dated, and stuck in the defensive mindset of the First World War. But whilst the army ordered the construction of 350 new casemates and 250 km of anti-tank obstacles to bolster defences,[139] it also instigated more offensive measures, such as creating airfields. Since 1938, the French government had struggled, with some success, to boost military aircraft production. To accommodate the new planes in strategic positions the French air force hastily sought to expand its airfields and aerial training sites during the phoney war.[140] Speed was of the essence, which meant taking terrain into account. General Joseph Vuillemin, commander of the French air force, ordered that the establishment of airfields and landing grounds should involve minimal work and not require large-scale earthworks, drainage systems or grass sowing. Only the ripping up of hedges, trees, and walls should be undertaken.[141] To train its pilots, the air force turned towards sites away from the Franco-German border. Space and a benevolent climate were essential.[142] But despite the war situation, foresters protested the militarization of forests near Biscarrosse and the Société national d'acclimatation de France complained about the use of its nature reserve in the Camargue as an aerial training ground.[143]

At the same time, the British Royal Air Force (RAF) sought airfields in northern and eastern France, echoing the British Expeditionary Force militarization of the countryside during the First World War. In 1939 and 1940 the RAF sent representatives to 'prospect' for possible sites and filed numerous requisition requests. Given that planes required flat and obstacle-free terrain for take off and landing, the RAF favoured fields, placing it in direct opposition with local communities and French authorities seeking to maintain wartime food production. The RAF's coveted land in Gaye and Chichey (Marne) constituted sown fields, leading General Bouscas to ask the RAF to limit its requisition of cultivated land at a time when 'the country is preoccupied with agricultural production'.[144] Airfield requisitions contributed to wider strains within the Franco-British relationship. But cooperation did exist. RAF officers made some attempt to limit the amount of terrain requisitioned and praised the help received from their French counterparts during their 'invasion' of the French countryside.[145]

Vuillemin had instructed that air base construction should entail minimum geographical modification. However, this was difficult to implement on the ground. French proposals for new airfields recommended levelling out ground, grubbing out bushes and hedges, felling trees, and removing boundary markers.[146] Similarly, RAF plans outlined how they would adapt terrain to aviation, including filling in rabbit holes and ditches, and removing trees and roots. The proposed airfield at Pocancy (Marne), for instance, necessitated the removal of a haystack and piles of wood, and the diversion of telephone wires.[147] Once bases were established, underlying geological and geographical conditions informed the levels of maintenance required. Large stones needed removing from the ground at least every two months at Istres air base whilst some bases with poor drainage, such as Tours-Saint-Symphorien, required hard runways to make them operational in wet weather. The filling in of holes and maintenance of grass cover was needed at all bases.[148] The RAF even explored the possibility of removing potential obstacles beyond the airfield, such as telephone wires and trees, indicating how militarized environments spilled out from beyond their official boundaries.[149]

To defend their airfields from enemy aerial attack, the Allies mobilized surrounding environmental features for cover and camouflage. Like other forms of military camouflage, concealing airfields relied on mimicking the patterns, colours, and textures of the surrounding environment. Instructions recommended that paint and grass should be used to break up the airfield's monotony by mimicking nearby fields and to create the illusion of hedges, ponds, brooks, and bushes. The French air force also instructed its engineers to replicate the site's former civilian incarnation, such as fields and roads. But engineers were not to attempt the reproduction of the exact colour of beetroot or wheat crops; the overall aim was not to make the airfield invisible but to make it blend into the 'mosaic of fields' when viewed from afar by enemy pilots. And once created, the camouflaged environment required careful maintenance to prevent vegetation obscuring false roads.[150] Nonetheless, many camouflage measures floundered on the ground.[151]

The threat from the air motivated the French army to camouflage its barracks and bases to blend them into the surrounding environment.[152] Army instructions recommended building any new barracks in wooded areas or orchards as tree leaves and branches offered the most 'efficient camouflage'.[153] As had been the case on the Western Front, trees might provide life-preserving cover. But some portrayed the blending of war and nature inherent within camouflage as disturbing and disorientating. The main character in André Malraux's novel *Les noyers de l'Altenberg* (which was written in 1941 and based on Malraux's experience of war) notes that 'nothing remained of the old harmony between man and earth; these cornfields through which we were lurching in the night were no longer cornfields but camouflage; the earth no longer bred crops, but traps and mines'.[154] Once again, images of war and the sterilization of the countryside became knitted together.

Camouflage was one aspect of the countryside's militarization during the phoney war. Although little actual combat took place, army and air force engineers sought to blend military installations into the environment, making militarization a 'more-than-human' process. In addition, mobilization in 1939 brought soldiers into contact with the environment.

Experiencing nature during the *drôle de guerre*

Since at least the publication of historian Marc Bloch's classic account of the phoney war, *The Strange Defeat*, the morale of French soldiers has come under scrutiny.[155] Nature was one factor shaping soldier's morale. As during the Franco-Prussian War and First World War, meteorological conditions mattered. The hot weather of September 1939 made the countryside seem idyllic and 'full of promise', raising spirits.[156] Some soldiers made the most of the fine weather, including those who skinny-dipped in the Moselle River.[157] But like those soldiers who had found moments of peace and happiness in French countryside during the First World War, the combatants of 1939–40 soon experienced cold and mud, reminiscent, to an extent, of conditions on the Western Front.

Pierre Lesort, a reserve officer in the 120th Infantry Regiment, was disgusted by the living conditions of his men who had been left 'shivering in . . . mud' for six months.[158] Other troops soon found themselves wading through mud as the hot weather gave way to cold and rain. Gustave Fulcher, a farmer from the Gard *département*, found that the 'veritable bog' at Thiaucourt matched the stories he had heard from the First World War: 'In all my life I could never have imagined such mud'.[159] Alongside the mud, the piercing cold made life even more unbearable for soldiers during the winter of 1939–40. One recorded on 1 January 1940 that the 'cold is as harsh as ever', making it impossible to sleep.[160] Icy conditions led to accidents, frozen food and wine, and stranded horse-borne units. The alpinist soldier who missed the snow and ice of their beloved mountains were a distinct minority, as was André Maurois, who waxed lyrical about the snow-covered scene on Christmas Day 1939 that would have 'brought joy to the heart of Dickens'.[161]

But as well as experiencing the environment as harsh and hostile, soldiers also drew sustenance from it to make good deficiencies in army supply chains. The Committee of Wood and Forest Products was charged with securing military firewood and timber supplies. But despite this official structure, forest owners complained repeatedly that troops took firewood and timber without providing payment or requisition slips. It was, in the army high command's own words, 'real theft'.[162] Abandoned villages and farmland offered particularly rich pickings. After its evacuation, the Lorraine village of Holling became a 'land of milk and honey' for one officer and his men who had been instructed to live off the land:

> For immediate use we kill stray animals in the woods and in the fields. Everywhere friendly groups of men rig up their cook-houses; throughout the day the squeals of doomed pigs and poultry can be heard, whilst other men go off to thrash the walnut trees, shake down the mirabelles and the quetsches, unearth the 'spuds', uproot the salads.[163]

This level of abundance may have been rare and there is undoubtedly some degree of exaggeration. Nonetheless, the passage suggests how soldiers from rural areas used their agricultural expertise to feed themselves and their horses.[164]

Spring's arrival lifted soldiers' spirits. One combatant observed how the heat 'restored the spirit', even if it caused some discomfort.[165] With the return of leaves on the trees and birds in the air, Georges Friedman remembers the 'earth exhaling all [its] perfumes'. He drew succour from the fact that 'nature is still there . . . even this year, after this long winter when the elements seemed to want to compete with the malignant foolishness of men'.[166] For some, it was almost like being on holiday: 'beautiful weather, 95 degrees in the sun. We lunch beneath the arbour in the garden . . . we eat the first radishes from the garden . . . [and ride] through little copses of tender green foliage'.[167] But the stresses, sounds and signs of war frequently shattered the bucolic atmosphere. On 10 May 1940, sirens and planes disturbed the sense of calm Friedman had enjoyed amongst peaceful forests and fields where cows grazed happily (for Friedman, these 'wise animals' were 'living witnesses' to the 'madness of "superior" beings').[168] As had been the case during the Franco-Prussian War and the First World War, observers contrasted the calm, eternal, wisdom of nature with the madness and horror of mechanized warfare.

As well as bringing sunshine, spring brought conflict. On 10 May 1940 German troops invaded the Netherlands, Belgium, and Luxembourg, before attempting to cross the Meuse River at Sedan to enter France.

As in previous wars, environmental features had an important, but not deterministic, influence on the conflict. To reach the Meuse, German Panzer divisions had passed through the supposedly 'impenetrable' Ardennes.[169] Whilst transporting 134,000 soldiers and 1,600 vehicles through a hilly area on small roads was not easy, the Germans succeeded in their task, aided by the fact that French forces did not realize that this was the main thrust of their attack.

The Meuse River then presented a formidable obstacle. On 13 May, German troops waded through water-logged meadows before launching their dinghies, all under heavy French artillery fire. But although many died, enough troops made it to the other side to allow engineers to construct a bridge across the river for tanks. German forces had overcome a geographical obstacle, aided by the failure of the French to launch an effective counter-attack.[170] As French Prime Minister Paul Reynaud admitted, 'the Meuse – apparently a difficult river to cross – had been wrongly considered as a redoubtable obstacle for the enemy'.[171] Natural defences only worked if combined with sufficient human defences and the French had not defended the Ardennes hills or the Meuse River effectively.[172]

But environmental conditions sometimes aided French troops. Trees and undergrowth provided cover for retreating soldiers after German forces crossed the Meuse.[173] Furthermore, bad weather in the Alps sometimes thwarted Italian attacks on French positions (Italy had entered the war on 10 June 1940), and British troops retreating from Dunkirk also benefited from unfavourable flying conditions for the Luftwaffe.[174] Yet these were small crumbs of comfort. The French army never recovered from the surprise of Germany's advance through the Ardennes. Its commanders' inability to respond to the fast pace of modern warfare, combined with poor communications with Britain, and German air superiority, meant that German forces advanced quickly. Between 5–7 June they broke through the Somme/Aisne line and on 10 June 1940 the French government left Paris.[175]

The rapidly evolving militarized environments of summer 1940 caused thousands of French civilians to flee their homes as their country seemingly crumbled around them. Some saw their own fate reflected in animal suffering. Refugees on the *exode* saw 'horses lying dead beside the road, with swollen stomachs, decomposing in the hot sun, sometimes grotesquely posed with their hooves in the air; [and] unmilked cows roaming the fields, lowing in pain, their full udders trailing on the ground'. The innocent animals' sorry state mirrored the refugees' woeful situation, reminding them of their own feelings of vulnerability and dejection.[176]

Alongside human death and displacement, the invasion of France brought environmental disruption. Flooding in the Dunkirk area during the Allied evacuation caused damage, as did the flattening of trees due to military activity.[177] In the Alps, shelling and explosions pounded the mountains. One French soldier remembers how the French army's blowing up a tunnel in the Southern Alps caused an 'immense flame that lit up the whole landscape' and threw up a mass of rocks which cascaded down the mountain.[178] But the speed of the invasion meant that there was no repeat of the environmental transformations ushered in by four years of trench warfare between 1914 and 1918.

Conclusion

After 1918, the French mobilized nature to commemorate and heal the physical and mental scars of war. Whilst most of the land was restored to something resembling its prewar state, the forests of Verdun stand as living reminders of the environmental modifications ushered in by the conflict. Moreover, demilitarization was not a complete process. Unexploded ordnance and other dispersed and often hidden physical traces of the war remain embedded in the land.[179] But beyond these material remnants, the land's cultural meaning lingers on. As Bernard Giovanangeli writes, the 'soil where soldiers blood was spilt will never again be what it once was'.[180] Demilitarization was an active, contested and 'more-than-human' process. So too was the re-militarization of the red zone at Suippes Camp and the environmental militarization ushered in by expanded army camps and the Maginot Line.

During the phoney war, the militarization of the countryside intensified still further. On 14 June, German troops entered Paris and Marshal Philippe Pétain (who became premier on 16 June) sued for an armistice, which was signed on 22 June. France was divided into two. The Germans occupied the north whilst Pétain established an authoritarian and collaborationist regime in the southern zone based in the spa town of Vichy. But the militarization of the French environment did not end with the armistice.

Notes

1 Alexander B.W. Kennedy, *Ypres to Verdun: A Collection of Photographs of the War Areas in France and Flanders* (London: Country Life, 1921), captions to plates XCI and CIV.

2 Hugh, Clout, *After the Ruins: Restoring the Countryside of Northern France after the Great War* (Exeter: University of Exeter Press, 1996).

3 Albert Demangeon, *Le déclin de l'Europe* (Paris, Payot, 1920), 33.

4 J. Guicherd and C. Matrict, 'Les terres des régions dévastées', *Journal d'Agriculture pratique*, 36 (1921), 314.

5 By January 1922, the Michelin company had sold 1,430,000 guidebooks in France, Britain, and the United States. David W. Lloyd, *Battlefield Tourism: Pilgrimage and the Commemoration of the Great War in Britain, Australia and Canada, 1919–1939* (Oxford: Berg, 1998), 103.

6 Quoted in Daniel J. Sherman, *The Construction of Memory in Interwar France* (Chicago: University of Chicago Press, 1999), 37.

7 Stephen L. Harp, *Marketing Michelin: Advertising and Cultural Identity in Twentieth-Century France* (Baltimore: Johns Hopkins University Press, 2001), 89–125; Sherman, *Construction of Memory*, 35–49; Lloyd, *Battlefield Tourism*, 95–131.

8 *Les batailles de Champagne: Un guide, un panorama, une histoire* (Clermont-Ferrand: Michelin, 1921), 42.

9 *Le Chemin des Dames* (Clermont-Ferrand: Michelin, 1920), 86; *The Somme. Volume 1: The First Battle of the Somme (1916–1917): Albert, Bapaume, Péronne* (Clermont-Ferrand: Michelin, 1919); *Verdun and the Battles for its Possession* (Clermont-Ferrand: Michelin, 1919).

10 *Somme*, 10–11.

11 *Chemin des Dames*, 4.

12 *Batailles de Champagne*, 55. Harp suggests that these viewpoints mirrored the panoramic view of generals during the war. *Marketing Michelin*, 104–6. While there is much truth in this, artillery units manned by non-commissioned soldiers were also stationed on high ground.

13 Harp, *Marketing* Michelin, 90.

14 Ibid., 97, 109, 112.

15 Edmond Michel, *Les dommages de guerre de la France et leur réparation* (Paris: Editions Berger-Levrault, 1932), 207.

16 Hugh Clout 'Reconstructing the countryside of the eastern Somme after the Great War', *Erkunde*, 8 (1994), 141; ADS KZ 2759 'Situation des communes récupérées dans le departement [sic] de la Somme', 22 August 1918.

17 Hugh Clout, 'Rural reconstruction in Meuse after World War I', *Acta Geographica Lovaniensia*, 28 (1992), 600; Clout 'Reconstructing the countryside',137.

18 Demangeon, *Déclin de l'Europe*, 33–4.

19 Chris Pearson, *Scarred Landscapes: War and Nature in Vichy France* (Basingstoke: Palgrave Macmillan, 2008), 117–40; Donavan Webster, *Aftermath: The Remnants of War* (London: Constable, 1997).

20 Clout 'Reconstructing the countryside', 141; Hugh Clout, 'Rural revival in Marne, 1914–1930', *The Agricultural History Review*, 42:2 (1994), 149–50.

On wartime munitions clearance, see SHD-DAT 16 N 910 Général Malesset, Commandant d'Etapes du champ de bataille, 'Note sur le fonctionnement du Service de Ramassage du C.E.C.B', 4 August 1917.

21 Clout, 'Rural revival in Marne', 150–2.

22 Ernest Dunlop Swinton, *Twenty Years After: The Battlefields of 1914–18, Then and Now*, vol. 2 (London: Georges Newnes, 1936–38), 3.

23 Kennedy, *Ypres to Verdun*, v, 42, caption to plate LV.

24 Clinton L. Evans, *The War on Weeds in the Prairie West: An Environmental History* (Calgary: University of Calgary Press, 2002), 1–5.

25 Amat, 'Guerre et milieux naturels', 232.

26 ADME 1184 W 654 Inspecteur des Eaux et Forêts, Saint-Mihiel, 'Dégagements', 16 November 1929.

27 J. Demorlaine, 'L'importance stratégique des forêts et la guerre', *Revue des Eaux et Forêts*, 17/3, 1 February 1919, 27–9.

28 Henry S. Graves, 'Effect of the war on forests of France', *American Forestry*, 14:300 (December 1918), 710–11.

29 Quoted in *Les Eaux et Forêts du 12e au 20e siècle* (Paris: CNRS, 1987), 625–7. On the wartime destruction of architecture and cultural landmarks, see Robert Bevan, *The Destruction of Memory: Architecture at War* (London: Reaktion, 2006).

30 Michel, *Dommages de guerre*, 240–6. On the difficulties of ecological restoration more generally, see Marcus Hall, *Earth Repair: A Transatlantic History of Environmental Restoration* (Charlottesville: University of Virginia Press, 2005).

31 A. Arnould, 'Dommages aux forêts résultant de l'état de guerre', *Revue des Eaux et Forêts*, 8:42 (1 June 1915), 641–6; Charles Guyot, *La forêt et la guerre* (Nancy: Imprimerie Berger-Levrault, 1917), 17–26; Tamara Whited, *Forests and Peasant Politics in Modern France* (New Haven and London: Yale University Press, 2000), 164–5.

32 Sherman, *Construction of Memory*, 106–7.

33 Demorlaine, 'Importance stratégique', 27–9.

34 Michel, *Dommages de guerre*, 240–1.

35 Whited, *Forests and Peasant Politics*, 163; Jean-Yves Puyo, 'Les conséquences de la Première Guerre mondiale pour les forêts et les forestiers français', *Revue forestière française*, 6 (2004), 579.

36 Jules Forget, 'La reconstitution forestière et la zone rouge dans la Meuse', *Bulletin de la Société des Lettres Sciences et Arts de Bar-le-Duc et du Musée de Géographie* 3–4 (July–December 1927), 125.

37 Michel, *Dommages de Guerre*, 240–6.

38 Forget, 'La reconstitution forestière', 125.

39 Paul Arnould and Laurent Simon, 'Forêts, guerre, après-guerre autour du Chemin des Dames', in Andrée Corvol and Jean-Paul Amat (eds), *Forêt et guerre* (Paris: L'Harmattan, 1994), 257; ADME 1184 W 564 Inspecteur des

Eaux et Forêts, Saint-Mihiel, 'Restauration de peuplements dévastés par la guerre', 23 January 1930.

40 Clout, 'Reconstructing the countryside', 144.

41 Some local councils, however, succeeded in keeping their woodlands out of the red zone. ADME 1184 W 656 M. Husson, Inspecteur des Eaux et Forêts, 'Fixation des limites de la zone rouge', 25 April 1922; ADME 1184 W 656 'Extrait du procès-verbal de la réunion de la commission communale de reconstitution foncière de la commune de Fromezey', 12 October 1921; ADME 1184 W 656 Inspecteur des Eaux et Forêts, Bar-le-Duc, 'Retrait partiel des propositions du service forestier', 26 January 1923.

42 Clout, 'Rural reconstruction in Meuse', 605.

43 Joshua West, 'Forests and national security: British and American forest policy in the wake of World War I', *Environmental History*, 8:2 (2003), 270–94.

44 Forget, 'Reconstitution forestière', 131; Whited, *Forests and Peasant Politics*.

45 'Note sur le reboisement'. See also William H. Scheifley, 'The depleted forests of France', *Northern American Review*, 212:778 (1920), 386.

46 'Une injustice administrative', *Le Sinistré*, 10 July 1927, clipping in ADME 1184 W 656.

47 ADME 1184 W 654 [n.a.] 'Note sur le reboisement de la zone rouge', 1937.

48 Forget, 'Reconstitution forestière', 127.

49 'Note sur le reboisement'. See also ADME 1184 W 659 Société des amis et ancien élèves de l'École nationale des Eaux et Forêts, 'Excursion à Verdun, Journée du 4 Juin 1935'.

50 'Note sur le reboisement'.

51 Ibid.

52 Peter Sahlins, *Forest Rites: The War of the Demoiselles in Nineteenth-Century France* (Cambridge, MA: Harvard University Press, 1994); Whited, *Forests and Peasant Politics*.

53 ADME 1184 W 564 'Relève des travaux effectués sur les terrains de zone rouge (2ᵉ catégorie) remis à l'administration en vue de leur reboisement' [n.d.].

54 Jean-Paul Amat, 'L'inscription de la guerre dans les paysages ruraux du nord-est de la France', in Jean-Jacques Becker and Stéphane Audoin-Rouzeau (eds), *Les sociétés européennes et la guerre de 1914–1918* (Nanterre: Publications de l'Université de Nanterre, 1988), 422–3.

55 Jean-Paul Amat, 'Guerre et milieux naturels: Les forêts meurtries de l'est de la France 70 ans après Verdun', *L'Espace géographique*, 3 (1987), 217–33; Joseph P. Hupy and Randall J. Schaetzl, 'Soil development on the WWI battlefield of Verdun, France', *Geoderma*, 145 (2008), 37–49.

56 'Note sur le reboisement'.

57 Pierre Dumarchey [Pierre Mac Orlan, pseud.], *Verdun* (Paris: Editions Latines, 1935), 78, 94.

58 Quoted in 'En fouillant la terre de Verdun', *Verdun et la Meuse Touristique*, no. 1, March 1931, 12.

59 Jules Forget, 'Le reboisement de la zone rouge de Verdun', *Verdun et la Meuse Touristique*, no. 1, March 1931, 13; Sherman, *Construction of Memory*, 108–41. On the role of veterans in politics, see Antoine Prost, *In the Wake of War: 'Les Anciens Combattants' and French Society*, trans. Helen McPhail (Oxford: Berg, 1992), 95–115.

60 Forget, 'Le reboisement de la zone rouge', 15.

61 Forget, 'Reconstitution forestière', 131.

62 'Sur les champs de bataille de Verdun: Le circuit des forts', *Verdun et la Meuse touristique*, 7 August 1932, 32.

63 Whited, *Forests and Peasant Politics*, 187–9.

64 Kenneth Foote, *Shadowed Ground: America's Landscapes of Violence and Tragedy* (Austin: University of Texas Press, 2003 [1997]); Edward Tabor Linenthal, *Sacred Ground: Americans and their Battlefields* (Urbana and Chicago: University of Illinois Press, 1993); Simon Schama, *Landscape and Memory* (London: Fontana, 1996); James E. Young, *The Texture of Memory: Holocaust Memorials and Meaning* (New Haven and London: Yale University Press, 1993).

65 For an excellent overview and critique of theories of memory construction, see Matt Perry, *Memory of War in France, 1914–45: César Fauxbras, the Voice of the Lowly* (Basingstoke: Palgrave MacMillan, 2011), 6–11.

66 Lloyd, *Battlefield Tourism*, 112–114.

67 Quoted in ibid. 117. On the tensions between nature's regenerative powers and memorialization in a different context, see Brian Black, 'Addressing the nature of Gettysburg: "Addition and detraction" in preserving an American shrine', in Chris Pearson, Peter Coates, and Tim Cole (eds), *Militarized Landscapes: From Gettysburg to Salisbury Plain* (London: Continuum, 2010), 171–88.

68 'Inauguration d'un monument à la Chipotte', *Revue des Eaux et Forêts*, 9:1 (1 January 1916), 2–3.

69 Mandy S. Morris, 'Gardens "for ever England": Landscape, identity, and the First World War British cemeteries on the Western Front', *Ecumene*, 4:4 (1997), 413–17.

70 Quoted in ibid. 418.

71 Ibid. 412, 415, 422, 426. On planting at British war cemeteries elsewhere, see Paul Gough, 'That sacred turf: War memorial gardens as theatres of war (and peace)', (1998), www.vortex.uwe.ac.uk/places_of_peace/turf.html, accessed 2 May 2010.

72 Gough, 'That sacred turf'.

73 ADS KZ 248 Pierre Yvert, 'Le mémorial de Thiepval', 23 January 1932.

74 George L. Mosse, *Fallen Soldiers: Reshaping the Memory of the Worlds Wars* (New York: Oxford University Press, 1990), 111–12.

75 A.D. Gillespie, quoted in Paul Gough, 'Conifers and commemoration: The politics and protocol of planting', *Landscape Research*, 21:1 (1996), 86.

76 Paul Cloke and Eric Pawson, 'Memorial trees and treescape memories', *Environment and Planning D: Society and Space*, 26 (2008), 107.

77 Paul Gough, 'Sites in the imagination: The Beaumont Hamel Newfoundland Memorial on the Somme', *Cultural Geographies*, 11 (2004), 243; Gough', Conifers and commemoration', 82; Jean-Pascal Soudagne, *Chemins de mémoire 14–18* (Rennes: Editions Ouest-France, 2008), 107.

78 Soudagne, *Chémins de mémoire*, 121; 'Le voyage présidentiel à Albert et à Thiepval', *Progrès de la Somme*, 1 August 1932.

79 Gough, 'Conifers and commemoration', 83.

80 Black, 'Addressing the nature of Gettysburg', 172.

81 Stéphane Ceccaldi, *Le lion de Belfort: Un monument pour l'avenir* (Charenton-le-Pont: Citédis, 1999), 17–18. German memorials of the 1870–71 war also featured lion statues. William Kidd, 'The lion, the angel and the war memorial: Some French sites revisited', in Nicholas J. Saunders (ed.), *Matters of Conflict: Material Culture, Memory, and the First World War* (Abington: Routledge, 2004), 155. On associations between lions and bravery, see Deirdre Jackson, *Lion* (London: Reaktion, 2010).

82 Dumarchey, *Verdun*, 76–7.

83 On the sense of brotherhood amongst veterans, see Prost, *Wake of War*, 19–23.

84 Kidd estimates that only 17 French memorials featured lions. 'The lion, the angel and the war memorial', 153.

85 Michel Pastoureau, 'The Gallic Cock', in Pierre Nora (ed.), *Realms of Memory: The Construction of the French Past, Vol. 3, Symbols*, trans. Arthur Goldhammer (New York: Columbia University Press, 1998), 416; Sherman, *Construction of Memory*, 185. On French war memorials and republicanism, see Antoine Prost, *Republican Identities in War and Peace: Representations of France in the Nineteenth and Twentieth Centuries* (Oxford: Berg, 2002), 11–41.

86 Steve Baker, *Picturing the Beast: Animals, Identity, and Representation* (Urbana and Chicago: University of Illinois Press, 2001 [1993]), 37–40.

87 *Introduction to the Register of the Thiepval Memorial of France* (London: Imperial War Graves Commission, 1930), 11.

88 For instance, see Charles Quéret, 'Albert centre des champs de bataille de la Somme', [n.d.]. Brochure consulted in ADS KZ 248.

89 Quoted in M.C., 'Un beau circuit', *Verdun et la Meuse touristique*, no. 2, May 1931. Montsec was one of the German positions attacked by American forces in September 1918.

90 Lloyd, *Battlefield Tourism*, 120, 128–9. See also Mosse, *Fallen Soldiers*, 107, 112.

91 Philippe Picard, 'En parcourant les champs de bataille', *Le Meuse touristique*, no. 17, November 1933, 15.

92 On the tension between environmental conditions and memory, see Pearson, *Scarred Landscapes*, 141–74.

93 Suippes Camp was initially named Tahure Camp, but for simplicity's sake I refer to it as Suippes Camp throughout.

94 Tim Cole, 'Military presences, civilian absences: Battling nature at the Sennybridge Training Area, 1940–2008', *Journal of War and Culture Studies*, 3:2 (2010), 215–35; David Havlick, 'Militarization, conservation and US base transformations', in Pearson, Coates, and Cole, *Militarized Landscapes*, 113–33; Patrick Wright, *The Village that Died for England: The Strange Story of Tyneham* (London: Jonathan Cape, 1995).

95 This was also the case with nearby Moronvilliers Camp.

96 Clout, 'Rural revival in the Marne', 143–4.

97 Quoted in ibid. 144.

98 Geneviève Dévignes, *Le livre de Suippes* (Paris: Pierre Bossuet et Georges Leroux, 1924), postscript.

99 *Batailles de Champagne*, 2, 8.

100 SHD-DAT 3 V 30 Médecin Inspecteur Général Vaillard and Général Goetschy, 'Avis commun au sujet de la possibilité d'installer au camp de Châlons un second camp pour les troupes soit vers Suippes, soit dans l'angle sud-est du champ de manoeuvres vers Cuperly', 7 October 1911; SHD-DAT 8 N 142 Service du génie, 'Rapport particulier N° 27-R, Camp de Tahure: Acquisitions d'immeubles pour la création du camp', 25 November 1929.

101 'Rapport particulier N° 27-R'; ADMA 2 Q 424 Préfecture de la Marne, 'Arrêté', 1 July 1924; ADMA 2 Q 424 Morand, Parquet de Châlons-sur-Marne, 'Requête', 2 July 1924.

102 SHD-DAT 3 V 30 'Rapport commun du Général de Division Germain, Inspecteur technique des travaux du génie et du Médicin-Inspecteur Général Sieur, Président du Comité consultatif du Service de santé au sujet de l'organisation du Camp de Tahure', 27 October 1922; ADMA 2 Q 424 Général de Lardemelle to Préfet de la Marne, 21 March 1924.

103 ADMA 2 Q 424 Commune de Somme-Suippe, 9 April 1927.

104 'Rapport particulier N° 27-R'.

105 Ibid.

106 SHD-DAT 7 N 4014 'Avis du Général Desoings cdt la 29ᵉ D.I'., 27 September 1922.

107 SHD-DAT 8 N 141 Delande, Contrôleur général de 2° classe, 'Rapport particulier: Camp de Mailly, 9 September 1930.

108 SHD-DAT 7 N 4014 Général Marty to Ministre de la Guerre, 'Camp de Caylus', 2 November 1927.

109 SHD-DAT 8 N 141 'Rapport particulier: Camp d'instruction (acquisition de terrains)', 16 December 1929; SHD-DAT 8 N 139 'Rapport particulier: Camp des Garrigues et Camp de Carpiagne', 12 December 1928.

110 'Rapport particulier: Camp des Garrigues et Camp de Carpiagne'.

111 SHD-DAT 8 N 139 'Rapport particulier: Camp de Caylus', 12 December 1928; SHD-DAT 27 T 115 'Rapports de la Commission du Général Besson sur les camps de Caylus et du Larzac', 12 August 1963.

112 ADGI 2 R 77 Président de la République française, 5 May 1919; ADGI 2 R 78 'Extrait du registre des délibérations du conseil municipal de la Commune de la Teste-de-Buch, 'Réquisitions militaires: Offres du génie', 6 July 1922.

113 SHD-DAT 8 N 140 Cazères, Contrôleur de première classe, 'Rapport particulier: Camp d'instruction de Cazaux', 17 November 1926.

114 SHD-DAT 8 N 140 Contrôleur général Meunier, 'Rapport particulier no. 28–1 du 26 mai 1928'.

115 SHD-DAT 8 N 140 'Conférence mixte relative à l'établissement du champ de tir n°11 pour armes portative et du champ de bombardements des dunes pour le camp d'instruction de Cazaux, conférence au 2ᵉ degré, avis du conservateur des Eaux et Forêts', 30 December 1926; SHD-DAT 8 N 140 Ministre de l'Agriculture to Ministre de la Guerre et des Pensions, 14 August 1923. Recent military history gave credence to the forest fires anxieties – in 1912 fires at nearby Souge Camp had destroyed almost 2,000 ha of heathland and threatened neighbouring forests – although forest fires had struck the artificial pine forests since their planting in the mid-nineteenth century. Ministère de la Guerre, Comité consultative d'action économique de la 18ᵉ région, Section économique de la direction de l'intendance, *Enquête sur la reprise et le développement de la vie industrielle dans la région landaise* (Bordeaux: Delmas, 1917), 49; Samuel Temple, 'The natures of nation: Negotiating modernity in the *Landes de Gascogne*', *French Historical Studies*, 32:3 (2009), 438–42.

116 Cazères, 'Rapport particulier: Camp d'instruction de Cazaux'. On tourists watching atomic bombs explode in the US, see A. Costandina Titus, *Bombs in the Backyard: Atomic Testing and American Politics* (Reno: University of Nevada Press, 2001), 93.

117 SHD-DAT 8 N 140 Général de Division Fillonneau to Maréchal de France, 8 February 1928.

118 Edouard Lynch, 'Interwar France and the rural exodus: The national myth in peril', *Rural History*, 21:2 (2010), 165–76.

119 SHD-DAT 3 V 32 Général de Division Duchêne to Ministre de la Guerre, 'Camp de Tahure: Quartier des Officiers', 31 October 1929.

120 Quoted in Georges Vidal, '*L'Humanité* et la défense nationale dans les années 1930', *Cahiers d'histoire* 92 (2003), http://chrhc.revues.org/index1407.html, paragraph 15. See also, Nicholas Faucier, *Pacifisme et antimilitarisme dans l'entre-deux-guerres (1919–1939)* (Paris: Spartacus, 1983).

121 SHD-DAT 7 N 4014 Général Boquet to Ministre de la Guerre, 8 October 1929; SHD-DAT 9 N 375 Général Couraud to Ministre de la Guerre, 'Terrain de manoeuvre de circonstance', 8 May 1928.

122 SHD-DAT 9 N 154 Ministre de la Guerre to Généraux Gouverneurs militaires, 'Instruction de sous-officiers', 7 August 1931.

123 Jean Doise and Maurice Vaïse, *Diplomatie et outil militaire, 1871–1991: Politique étrangère de la France* (Paris: Editions du Seuil, 1992 [1987]), 351–2; 362.

124 Prost shows how World War I veterans embraced pacifism and were determined to prevent another war. *Wake of War*, 51–78.

125 Roxanne Panchasi, *Future Tense: The Culture of Anticipation in France between the Wars* (Ithaca and London: Cornell University Press, 2009), 78–83. It is necessary, however, to recognize that French military doctrine was not static or unified during the interwar years, even if it ultimately proved too inflexible and out-dated. Robert Allen Doughty, *The Seeds of Disaster: The Development of French Army Doctrine, 1919–1939* (Hamden: Archon Books, 1985).

126 SHD-DAT 3 V 64 Général Bernesson to Colonel Directeur du génie, 8 January 1927; CACAN 19880470/153 Commission interministérielle chargée de la révision de la législation et de la réglementation des Travaux mixtes: Exposé de M. Vel Durand, Rapporteur de la Commission', [n.d.]. See also Doughty, *The Seeds of Disaster*, 41–71.

127 Quoted in Anthony Kemp, *The Maginot Line: Myth and Reality* (London: Frederick Warne, 1981), 19.

128 ADMO 5 R 500 'Régime du champ de tir de circonstance à organiser pour les essais de tir du bloc 3 de l'ouvrage d'Anzeiling (Tourelle de 81)', 7 October 1935; ADMO 307 M 32 M. Berthon, Inspecteur adjoint des Eaux et Forêts, Thionville, 'Versement d'une indemnité d'expropriation militaire', 29 December 1937; ADME 2 R 50 Chef de bataillon, Chef du génie Mézières, 'Commune de Velosnes: Etat parcellaire no. 2 indicatif des propriétés non bâties nécessaires aux travaux d'organisation défensive de la frontière nord-est', 1 July 1937.

129 J.E. Kaufmann and H.W. Kaufmann, *The Maginot Line: None Shall Pass* (Westport: Praeger, 1997), 76–80; Philippe Lachal, *Fortifications des Alpes: Leur rôle dans les combats de 1939–1945* (L'Argentière La Bessée: Editions du Fournel, 2006).

130 Keith Mallory and Arvid Ottar, *Architecture of Aggression: A History of Military Architecture in North West Europe, 1900–1945* (London: Architectural Press, 1973), 99; Vivian Rowe, *The Great Wall of France: The Triumph of the Maginot Line* (London: Putnam, 1959), 11–12; Martin Alexander, 'In defence of the Maginot Line: Security policy, domestic politics and the economic depression in France', in Robert Boyce (ed.), *French Foreign and Defence Policy, 1918–1940* (London: Routledge, 1998), 171.

131 'A French Officer', *The Maginot Line: The Facts Revealed* (London: Duckworth, 1939), 27–9, 37.

132 D. Barlone, *A French Officer's Diary (23 August 1939–1 October 1940)*, trans. L.V. Cass (Cambridge: Cambridge University Press, 1942), 11.

133 Daniel Hucker, 'French public attitudes towards the prospect of war in 1938–1939: "Pacifism" or "war anxiety"?', *French History*, 21:4 (2007), 431–49. See also Norman Ingram, *The Politics of Dissent: Pacifism in France 1919–1930* (Oxford: Clarendon Press, 1991).

134 Mona Siegel, *The Moral Disarmament of France: Education, Pacifism, and Patriotism, 1914–1940* (Cambridge: Cambridge University Press, 2005).

135 Martin Monestier, *Les animaux-soldats: Histoire militaire des animaux des origines à nos jours* (Paris: Le Cherche Midi, 1996), 62; Etienne Plan and Eric Lefevre, *La bataille des Alpes, 10–25 juin 1940: L'armée invaincue* (Paris: Charles-Lavauzelle, 1982), 108.

136 Doise and Vaïse, *Diplomatie et outil militaire*, 723.

137 Quoted in André Maurois, *The Battle of France*, trans. F. R. Ludman (London: John Lane/The Bodley Head, 1940), 95.

138 R. L. DiNardo, *Mechanized Juggernaut or Military Anachronism? Horses and the German Army of World War II* (Mechanicsberg: Stackpole Books, 2008 [1991]), xiv.

139 SHD-DAT 27 N 144 'Compte-rendu des travaux effectués à la date du 6 octobre 1939 par la Commission d'études des zones fortifiées', 6 October 1939.

140 By the signing of the Armistice, the French air force had 96 air fields and landing strips (either already operational or in the process of becoming so). The British had 44. SHD-DAA 1 D 50 Commandant en chef des forces aériennes, Etat-major général, 'Instruction sur la recherche, l'aménagement et l'occupation des plateformes d'opérations', 25 October 1939. On the French air force before and during the phoney war, see Patrick Facon, *L'armée de l'air dans la tourmente: La bataille de France, 1939–1940* (Paris: Economica, 1997); Julian Jackson, *The Fall of France: The Nazi Invasion of 1940* (Oxford: Oxford University Press, 2003), 17–21.

141 Commandant en chef, 'Instruction sur la recherche'.

142 For instance, a report on the rocky Brittany coastline from St-Michel-en-Grève to St-Jean-du-Doigt noted how this 'little frequented' area would provide an excellent training site when the weather was fine. SHD-DAA 2 B 153 Inspecteur général technique de l'air to Etat-major de l'armée de l'air, 'Champs de tir aériens en Bretagne', 22 January 1940.

143 ADL 7 M 735 Inspecteur-adjoint des Eaux et Forêts, Mont-de-Marson, 'Atteinte porté aux droits d'usage en forêt usagère par l'affectation de terrains au Ministère de l'Air, 25 May 1940'; Pearson, *Scarred Landscapes*, 83.

144 SHD-DAA 1 D 40 A.S. Barratt, Air Marshal, Air Officer Commanding-in-Chief, British Air Forces in France to Ministre de l'Air, 4ᵉ bureau, 'Aerodromes in the Le Mans Area for the R.A.F.', 17 April 1940; SHD-DAA 1 D 140 Général de corps aérien Bouscas to Général commandant en chef les

forces aériennes, E.M.G., 4ᵉ Bureau, 'Réquisition de terrains par la R.A.F.', 16 March 1940.

145 Barratt to Ministre de l'Air, 'Aerodromes'; SHD-DAA 1 D 140 Headquarters, RAF Component, BEF, to Général Vuillemin, Commandant en chef de l'armée de l'air, 2 December 1939. On the wider tensions between French and British forces, see Facon, *Armée de l'air*, 123; John C. Cairns, 'Great Britain and the fall of France: A study in Allied disunity', *Journal of Modern History*, 27:4 (1955), 263–409.

146 SHD-DAA 2 B 154 'Ahmenancourt: Recherche d'aérodrome: Rapport preliminaire', 7 November 1939; SHD-DAA 2 B 154 Capitaine Tourret, 'Fiche de renseignements concernant le terrain d'Arcis-sur-Vaucogne', [n.d.]; SHD-DAA 2 B 154 'Notice technique d'une plate-forme étudiée en 34.N.7' [n.d.].

147 SHD-DAA 1 D 140 'Situation des terrains satellites R.A.F. à la date du 24 Octobre 1939'; SHD-DAA 1 D 140 'Terrain de Pocancy', 27 September 1939.

148 SHD-DAA 2 B 153 Ministère de l'Air, Inspection générale technique de l'air, 'Rapport d'inspection sur l'utilisation de l'état des terrains en mauvaise saison', 18 April 1940.

149 SHD-DAA 1 D 140 Air Marshal, Head of Mission, to Général commandant en chef les forces aériennes françaises, 'Removal of flying obstacles', 19 January 1940.

150 SHD-DAA 1 D 50 Vuillemin to Général commandant 1–4 régions aériennes, 7 October 1939; SHD-DAA 1 D 50 Commandant en chef des forces aériennes, Etat-major général, 4ᵉ bureau, 'Exposé sur le camouflage des bases aériennes d'opérations: Stage d'information des officiers, Coulommiers, Février 1940'. RAF camouflage instructions went into great detail because camouflage entailed taking into account and manipulating the regenerative processes of vegetation. One report recommended treating mown grass with a spray of sodium chlorate before painting because experience showed that 'the natural growth of grass had the effect of decreasing the depth of colour owing to the new green at the roots of the blades'. SHD-DAA 1 D 50 'Note on camouflage of landing grounds' [n.d.].

151 SHD-DAA 3 D 516 Commission 'G', Titre 23 infrastructure', 24 November 1941.

152 SHD-DAT 27 N 144 Direction du service du génie, Service du camouflage, 'Camouflage des camps, cantonnements, parcs et établissements divers', 27 January 1940. On the early links between nature observation and military camouflage, see Roy R. Behrens, 'Revisiting Abbott Thayer: Non-scientific reflections about camouflage in art, war and zoology', *Philosophical Transactions of the Royal Society B*, 364 (2009), 497–501.

153 SHD-DAT 27 N 144 Direction du service du génie, 'Conférence sur le camouflage', 14 February 1940; SHD-DAT 27 N 144 Direction du service du génie, 'Instruction générale pour l'aménagement des camps et cantonnements', 14 October 1939.

154 Quoted in Frederick J. Harris, *Encounters with Darkness: French and German Writers on World War II* (Oxford: Oxford University Press, 1983), 17.
155 Marc Bloch, *Strange Defeat: A Statement of Evidence Written in 1940*, trans. Gerard Hopkins (London: Oxford University Press, 1949).
156 Georges Friedman, *Journal de Guerre, 1939–1940* (Paris: Gallimard, 1987), 50.
157 René Balbaud, *Cette drôle de guerre* (Oxford: Oxford University Press, 1941), 8.
158 Quoted in Jackson, *Fall of France*, 160.
159 Gustave Fulcher, *Marching to Captivity: The War Diaries of a French Peasant, 1939–1945* (London: Brassey's, 1996 [1981]), 33, 40.
160 Balbaud, *Cette drôle de guerre*, 32.
161 Fernand Grenier, *Journal de la drôle de guerre: Septembre 1939–juillet 1940* (Paris: Editions Sociales, 1969), 103; Barlone, *French Officer's Diary*, 26; François Cochet, *Les soldats de la drôle de guerre, septembre 1939–mai 1940* (Paris: Hachette littératures, 2004), 67; Pearson, *Scarred Landscapes*, 98; Maurois, *Battle of France*, 80. In Provence, however, the winter was relatively mild, inspiring Sirius Ravel to write a poem praising 'mother nature'. *Le Petit Var*, 2 February 1940, 3.
162 SHD-DAT 27 N 144 Major général Bineau for Général commandant en chef les forces terrestres to Général commandant la IXᵉ armée, 14 January 1940; *Eaux et Forêts du 12e au 20e siècle*, 628; 'Décret relatif à la production forestière en temps de guerre', *L'Action forestière et piscicole*, no. 35, February 1940, 1.
163 Barlone, *French Officer's Diary*, 12.
164 Elsewhere, however, soldiers helped out farmers whose labourers had been mobilized. François Bédarida, 'Huit mois d'attente et d'illusion: La "drôle de guerre"', in Jean-Pierre Azéma and François Bédarida (eds), *La France des années noires, vol.1: De la défaite à Vichy* (Paris: Seuil, 1993), 56.
165 SHD-DAA 2 B 153 G701 diary [n.d.].
166 Friedman, *Journal de guerre*, 208–9.
167 Barlone, *French Officer's Diary*, 41.
168 Friedman, *Journal de guerre*, 216.
169 Jackson, *Fall of France*, 32. The French military commanders were not the only ones seduced by the hills and woods of the Ardennes. See J. F. Horrabin, *The Geography of War* (London: Victor Gollancz, 1940), 104.
170 Jackson, *Fall of France*, 39–48.
171 Quoted in Gordon Beckles, *Dunkirk and After, May 10th–June 17th 1940* (London and Melbourne: Hutchinson and Co., 1941), 80.
172 Cochet, *Soldats de la drôle de guerre*, 138–9; Alistair Horne, *To Lose a Battle: France 1940* (London: Macmillan, 1969), 167.
173 Fulcher, *Marching to Captivity*, 63, 79.

Mobilizing nature

174 Kaufmann and Kaufmann, *Maginot Line*, 134–40; Jean-Pierre Azéma, 'Le choc armée et les débandades', in Azéma and Bédarida, *France des années noires*, 100.

175 The reasons for French defeat are complex and extensively debated; there is not the space to do justice to them here. For useful introductions, see Jackson, *Fall of France*; Joel Blatt (ed.), *The French Defeat of 1940: Reassessments* (Oxford: Berghahn, 1998).

176 Andrew Shennan, *The Fall of France: 1940* (Harlow: Pearson Education, 2000), 8. On the civilian experience of defeat, see Hanna Diamond, *Fleeing Hitler: France 1940* (Oxford: Oxford University Press, 2007).

177 Commission consultative des dommages et des réparations, *Dommages subis par la France et l'Union française du fait de la guerre et de l'occupation ennemie (1939–1945)* (Paris: Imprimerie Nationale, 1951), 10 vols, vol. 1, 219; Pearson, *Scarred Landscapes*, 2; Yves Durand, *Vichy 1940–1944* (Paris: Bordas, 1972), 10.

178 Kaufmann and Kaufmann, *Maginot Line*, 133; Jean-Louis Panicacci, *Les Alpes-Maritimes de 1939 à 1945: Un département dans la tourmente* (Nice: Editions Serre, 1989), 69.

179 Stéphane Audoin-Rouzeau, Gerd Krumeich, Jean Richardot, *Cicatrices: La Grande Guerre aujourd'hui* (Paris: Editions Tallandier, 2008).

180 Bernard Giovanangeli, 'Terre sacrée', in Bernard Giovanangeli (ed.), *Hauts lieux de la Grande Guerre* (Paris: Ministère de la Défense, 2005), 8.

6

Occupied territories (1940–67)

In summer 1945, cultural theorist Paul Virilio rediscovered the Atlantic coastline after six years of war and occupation:

> I have forgotten none of the sequences of this finding in the course of a summer when recovering peace and access to the beach were one and the same event. With the barriers removed, you were henceforth free to explore the liquid continent... The waterfront villas were empty, everything within the casemates' firing range had been up, the beaches were mined, and the artificers were busy here and there rendering access to the sea.[1]

As the demilitarization process unfolded, the French were able to rediscover previously forbidden militarized zones and return land to its civilian use. Virilio's recollections indicate that this was an unforgettable experience, opening up once out-of-bounds worlds.

Virilio personally encountered a foreign instance of militarization; the remnants of German mines and casemates. His experience was both individual and typical; during the Second World War thousands, if not millions, of individuals across the globe came into contact with foreign militarized environments, from German military bases in Occupied Europe to US military installations in East Anglia and the Pacific Ocean.[2] If anything, the Cold War intensified this phenomenon, when US, NATO and Soviet bases dotted the globe, from Germany, Turkey, Panama, Spain, to Japan.[3] Militarized environments took on a cosmopolitan and transnational character as foreign military bases became key features within the environmental histories of the Second World War and the Cold War.[4]

Foreign military installations were, and are, controversial sites. They became, and remain, sources of military–civilian frictions that often unfold along class, racial, and gender lines, sparked by a range of issues including national sovereignty, pollution, prostitution, noise, and military-related accidents.[5] Foreign installation in France during the Second World War and the Cold War were no exception. This chapter considers how the French experienced and challenged the foreign militarization of their country from the German Occupation that began in 1940 to the withdrawal of NATO forces in 1967. For although historians have explored French-German and French-US relations, little attention has been paid to their environmental dimensions.[6] Furthermore, in line with other historians who argue that the Second World War needs to be set within the wider context of French history,[7] I attempt here to integrate the history of the 'dark years' with the early Cold War and link their environmental histories.[8]

The chapter also examines how Axis, Allied, and NATO forces mobilized nature during this period. However, although some similarities exist between Axis and Allied/NATO forces' mobilization of nature and occupation of French territory, the fundamental differences bound up in their aims, methods, and character must be kept in mind. Axis troops' involvement in the implementation of the Holocaust is the most obvious and important difference.[9]

The military mobilization of nature from 1940 to 1967 had a truly cosmopolitan flavour, as French, Allied, Axis, and NATO forces lived, trained, and fought on French soil. This internationalization of militarized environments made them particularly heterogeneous contact zones, as did their diffusion across France. The period's dispersed geographies of war and militarization meant that civilians throughout the countryside came into contact with militarized environments and their associated risks, restrictions, and challenges. Although they were relatively weak in comparison to foreign armed forces, particularly during the German occupation, French civilians drew some concessions from military authorities. They were certainly not reduced to the role of helpless, passive victims. Nor were environmental factors which unwittingly enabled and thwarted the varied military mobilizations of nature.

Axis militarized environments

With French armed forces defeated and reduced to 100,000 men charged with maintaining law and order under the terms of the 1940 armistice, German occupation troops were the main instigators of environmental militarization between 1940 and 1944.[10] It is hard to assess how German troops experienced the French environment but publications aimed at them offer some clues, however partial. Wartime German guidebooks on France glossed it as a seductive country that was inherently inferior to Germany, while German newspapers and organizations packaged Paris and the rustic eternal French countryside as tourist destinations for German soldiers.[11] Some soldiers did indeed treat France as a place of leisure. Hunting, for instance, offered camaraderie and entertainment. Although official German hunting parties were restricted to officers (and select members of the French elite), that did not prevent regular soldiers from allegedly hunting bulls in the Camargue wetlands.[12] But the extent of German hunting should not be overestimated: a postwar government report argued that apart from some localized 'abuses', German forces had not hunted very much.[13] François Marcot even argues that the German ban on French hunters allowed game to thrive; the war became a 'synonym of peace' for game.[14] Nonetheless, for French hunters deprived of the right to hunt, the sight of German hunting parties was galling

Although a stationing in France was certainly easier than one on the Eastern Front, it was also one of military training: a place of work, not a holiday camp. German authorities took over numerous French army camps to house and train their troops, including Auvours, La Courtine, Coëtquidan, and Sathonay.[15] They also used certain camps for specialist training, including the establishment of a parachute school at Valdahon Camp near Besançon and anti-tank commando training at Carpiagne Camp.[16] More sinisterly, German troops turned army camps into sites of persecution. At Souge Camp, German executioners shot 257 resisters and hostages between 1940 and 1944.[17] A memorial, inaugurated in October 1944, commemorates these deaths. German authorities also turned Royallieu–Compiègne Camp (Oise), a 16 ha military camp created in 1913, into an internment camp for political prisoners, resisters, and Jews. Conditions in the camp were tough. One internee, Jean-Jacques Bernard, recalls the lice, cold weather, and sense of isolation. The environment offered little comfort; even though he could observe 'beautiful skies' and 'gentle hills', his view was ruined by the barbed wire and prison walls.[18] The Vichy regime joined Germany in transforming army camps, with their barracks, fences, and relative seclusion, into internment and deportation camps as part of its reactionary programme to remake France. In doing so, it extended and expanded the Third Republic's internment of foreign nationals in military bases, including Caylus, Mourmelon (as Châlons Camp was renamed in 1935), Avord, La Braconne, Coëtquidan, and Joffre camps (the latter was better known as Rivesaltes Camp).[19] Militarized environments therefore became part of France's geographies of exclusion between 1940 and 1944.

Outside of established army camps, the German army militarized forests and fields by turning them into training grounds. As an occupying force, it was far less concerned about the disruption to civilian land uses than the British Expeditionary Force had been during the First World War. These new militarized environments became a source of danger and concern for civilians. One unlucky (and foolhardy) snail collector in the Var was thrown two metres in the air after stepping on a grenade on one firing range.[20]

French foresters became exasperated with military training because it restricted their control over the forest and increased the frequency of forest fires. Grenades, troops, and arid Mediterranean forests were a particularly hazardous combination. In the Var, manoeuvring occupation troops started a 500 ha forest fire on a firing range near Brovès in October 1942 and a 1,200 ha fire in the Estérel massif in July 1943.[21] Although occupation troops occasionally helped put out the fires they started, they had a tendency to leave once they thought the fire had been extinguished, only for the blaze to return several hours later.[22] Foresters could do little to curb this militarization of the forest other than writing critical reports, which had little influence on troops' behaviour.[23]

Civilians suffered from the militarization of the countryside. In the Calvados *département*, bullets from the firing ground at Amblie ricocheted out of the militarized environment, damaging property and putting lives at risk.[24] Even when firing ceased, unexploded bombs raised concerns. Civilian requests for their clearance, especially in fields where fast-growing crops would obscure them quickly, multiplied.[25] Live firing also restricted fishing. Target practice off the Calvados coastline meant that fisherman had to stay in port.[26]

Disruption due to military training became one of the many hardships faced by the French during the Occupation.[27] There was, however, some limited room for manoeuvre with German military authorities. Following protests from local councils, the Feldkommandant allowed farmers at Epaney (Calvados) to cultivate their land on the range outside of firing times, although he forbade the cultivation of new land and warned that damage to their property was likely.[28]

As in peacetime, the creation of firing zones involved environmental modifications. The German 725th infantry regiment on Ile Ste-Marguerite (off the Mediterranean coastline near Cannes) felled Aleppo pines to create a firing range.[29] In the Italian zone of occupation in southeast France, Italian troops damaged young plantations during target practice in the state forest at Breil-sur-Royal and in the Sociéte nationale d'Acclimatation de France (SNAF)'s Lauzanier alpine nature reserve.[30] As well as opposing the militarization of its Lauzanier reserve, the SNAF protested German bombing over its nature reserve in the Camargue wetlands (Bouches-du-Rhône), with some success.[31]

Aerial bombing elsewhere disrupted rural life. German pilots training at the airfield at Verson (Calvados) dropped practice bombs fashioned from cement on fields, making farm work all but impossible.[32] Allied bombing also brought serious disturbance. Between 1940 and 1945 British planes dropped nearly 600,000 tons of bombs over France. As well as killing an estimated 60,000 French civilians, the bombing caused serious headaches for farmers. In August 1941, British bombs flattened half-a-dozen fruit trees and wounded a cow at Saint-Désir-de-Lisieux (Calvados).[33] This was not an isolated incident.

To defend France from Allied attack and invasion, occupation authorities militarized the coastline. They laid millions of mines around the coast and at sea. Mines were a major hazard, denying civilians access to the land and sea, and claiming lives. In September 1941 winds blew a sea mine ashore at Roquebrune-Cap-Martin (Alpes-Maritimes). The mine exploded, killing a gendarme and spewing rocks 700 metres up into the air.[34]

German military authorities sought to defend the entire French Atlantic coastline with its Atlantic Wall fortification system. As Paul Virilio discovered, its casemates, observation posts, artillery batteries, and other installations removed large sections of the coastline from civilian use. Like the Maginot Line fortifications before them, these defences were often covered in earth for camouflage and protection and modified existing environmental features. For instance, trees were cut down to stumps to prevent Allied planes and parachutists from landing.[35]

With the appointment of Field Marshall Erwin Rommel as Inspector of Fortifications, the militarization of the coastline intensified with greater requisitions of labour and materials. Forests in the Pas-de-Calais, for instance, were exploited for the 'Rommel Posts' that were placed on beaches.[36] After the Allied invasion of North Africa in November 1942, the defence of the Mediterranean coastline became more urgent. On Porquerolles Island, occupation soldiers felled trees, uprooted hedges, demolished houses, and laid barbed wire and other obstacles to boost its defences.[37]

Coastal marshlands were weak points in German coastal defences because they provided potential landing sites for Allied planes and parachutists. Flooding offered a way of counteracting this threat. Following Rommel's orders of 17 July 1943, German troops successfully flooded flat, poorly drained marshland around Carentan (Manche) by opening up sea gates at La Barquette and Isigny-sur-Mer during high tide.[38] In spring 1944 they also tried to flood the Baux valley and Camargue wetlands by pumping water from the Rhône River and opening sea gates, a scheme that threatened to wipe out houses, agriculture, salt extraction industries, and the SNAF's nature reserve. But fuel shortages at the pumping stations combined with the drying influence of the *mistral* wind and hot sunny weather thwarted the flood, even after troops destroyed sections of the sea dyke.[39] German soldiers did not enjoy complete control of the environment as they sought to modify and incorporate it into their military strategies. Nonetheless, they reportedly succeeded in flooding 25,120 ha of French territory.[40]

The French case echoed the German army's flooding of the Roman coastline in Italy in 1943 to encourage malaria and thereby deter advancing Allied troops, a venture that historians describe as 'biological warfare'. Leading to a malarial epidemic in 1945 and 1946, this deliberate flooding to encourage malaria-carrying mosquitoes directly contravened the 1925 Geneva Convention banning biological and chemical warfare.[41] To the best of my knowledge, the German attempt to submerge the Camargue and other areas in France was not intended to trigger a malaria outbreak, but this instance of environmental warfare did contravene the Hague Conventions of 1899 and 1907, under which belligerent states were to protect the agricultural and forested land under their control.[42]

As well as seeking to defend France against the Allies, Axis forces extracted natural resources from French territory. Their mobilization of trees, animals, and other resources was part and parcel of their wider removal of raw materials, industrial goods, money, and labour from the French economy.[43] To construct buildings, keep warm, and cook food, German and Italian troops took vast quantities of wood from France's forests, exposing divergent military and civilian perspectives on how forests should be used and managed. For foresters trained to manage forests with long-term aims in mind, military felling seemed reckless, inconsistent, and threatening to the forests' future. For troops, forests offered an immediate way of meeting their firewood and timber needs.

In a bid to maintain what they saw as their rational management of France's forests, foresters argued that they should advise on military felling. Such lobbying led to the German army issuing a decree on 12 August 1943 ordering that 'in principle' Wehrmacht units should buy wood and charcoal from French producers. But if troops needed to fell for 'military reasons' (as opposed to securing firewood) they could by-pass all controls. Such a weak regulatory system unsurprisingly failed to prevent unauthorized felling. French postwar reports estimated that Germany misappropriated over 26,000,000 m^2 of construction and industry grade timber.[44] Italian troops similarly by passed official controls in their area of occupation, much to the exasperation of foresters. One lamented how Italian troops 'laid waste' to the communal forest of Terres Gastes.[45] For foresters and local populations alike, military felling threatened their sovereignty, livelihoods, and, it seemed, the very future of their forests.

Resistance environments

Occupation forces did not monopolize the mobilization of nature between 1940 and 1944. As the occupation continued, the hills, mountains, and forests of France became places of refuge and resistance. After the introduction of the Compulsory Labour Service (*Service du travail obligatoire* or STO) in spring 1943, more and more young men sought to evade working in German factories by joining a diverse group of foreign nationals, Jews, Communists, and rebel army officers in the remoter stretches of the countryside. These *maquisards* took their name from *maquis*, the dense, fragrant, and spiky form of vegetation that clings to Mediterranean hillsides. Basing themselves in rural camps, they ambushed occupation troops, sheltered downed Allied airmen, and conducted other clandestine activities.[46]

Maquis camps were quasi-militarized environments, especially once they became increasingly orientated towards armed struggle against the occupier. Resisters themselves invested their camps with military significance. One postwar account described woodlands on the Plateau de Malgré-Tout in the Ardennes, home of the Revin *maquis*, as a kind of 'forest barracks' ('*casernement forestier*').[47] Although the diversity of *maquis* groups does not lend itself to generalizations, *maquisards* mobilized nature in a variety of ways. As with the *francs-tireurs* during the Franco-Prussian War, *maquisards* attempted to turn the lie of the land to their advantage. If a *maquis* forest camp was betrayed and/or attacked, trees allowed for rapid dispersal and camouflage. Therefore, in an echo of soldiers' experiences of the Western Front (see chapter 4), some *maquis-ards* felt an intimate bond with the trees that sheltered them. On arriving in the forest, Etienne Renardet, of the Verneuil *maquis* near Quarré-les-Tombes (Yonne), experienced 'an indescribable sense of security. Every tree is a friend that hides me, and even if I were to meet [an enemy] patrol, I could easily slip away'.[48] From Brittany to the Cévennes, and from the Alps to the Ile de France, forests played a vital role in *maquis-ard* history and were subsequently romanticized in postwar *maquisard* literature.[49]

Mature forests were not the only arboreal ally for resisters. Sparser areas of woodland served as sites of refuge and resistance; apple trees, broom, scrubland, and copses in Brittany constituted excellent cover from which to launch ambushes on German troops.[50] In addition, *maquis* vegetation concealed the resisters to whom it gave its name. As if to reassure his American readers about the effectiveness and secu-rity of French resisters, scientist Frank Thone explained that although *maquis* might be monotonous and economically unprofitable, its sparsely populated character and vegetation made it an excellent hiding place:

> Enemy ground forces unfamiliar with the terrain will almost certainly never find their quarry, and are very likely to get lost and finally ambushed themselves. Even airplanes are of little use, for men in dust-coloured clothes crouching under dusty bushes are as invisible as quail that have taken cover against a hawk. Thus the *maquis* takes care of its own.[51]

Like regular military organisations, *maquisards* relied on their surround-ing environments for cover. But this was never an absolute guarantee of safety. As *maquisard* defeats at Mont Mouchet, Glières, and the Vercors brutally demonstrated, mountain ranges did not offer security against better equipped and more numerous German forces.[52]

Nonetheless, *maquisards* did succeed in making mountains – along with forests – unpredictable and dangerous environments for occupa-tion forces. There was some truth in resister Henri Zeller's claim that by July 1944 the German soldier was 'bewildered, demoralized, fooled . . . he looks with fear on these mountains, these forests, these crags, these narrow valleys from which at any moment a thunderbolt can crash'.[53] Mobilizing mountains and forest to harass and unsettle German forces was one of the ways in which *maquisards* contributed to the liberation of France.

The D-Day landings: Beaches and *bocage*

In his famous Paris town hall speech of 25 August 1944, Charles de Gaulle declared that Paris had 'liberated itself . . . [through] its people with the support of the armies of France'.[54] Amongst its other aims, de Gaulle's speech attempted to rebuild French pride after the humiliations and hardships of defeat and occupation.[55] But whilst Free French Forces and the resistance played important roles in the liberation of France, the contribution of Allied forces was crucial.

The Allied invasion of France in the summer of 1944 brought further layers of foreign militarized environments to the French countryside. In fact, the invasion of the Normandy coastline on 6 June 1944, otherwise known as Operation Overlord or D-Day, unfolded at German firing ranges near Gold, Utah, and Omaha beaches (to use Allied nomenclature for these sites).[56] So instead of conducting their planned training exercises, Axis troops faced an invasion force of 175,000 men bringing with them 50,000 vehicles carried on 5,333 ships and supported by 11,000 aircraft.[57]

When preparing their invasion, Allied planners had carefully observed and documented the French coastline through the maps and intelligence reports prepared by the Inter-Service Topographical Department (ISTD). The Provencal coastline was one possible invasion site. ISTD reports paid minute attention to the gradient of its beaches, prevailing wind conditions, potential obstacles, and anchorage possibilities, as well as the military potential of the terrain behind the beaches.[58] The reports' primary focus was operational, representing a militarized perspective in which environmental features are treated as either allies or enemies. But this militarized environmental perspective was never complete. Certain sections of ISTD reports read like natural histories.[59] The inclusion of postcard images of sunbathers and swimmers enjoying the Mediterranean beaches were other incongruous reminders that the coastline had other dimensions beyond its military potential. Similarly, French military planners associated these coastlines with happy memories of days spent on leave taking 'joyful picnics under the pine trees . . . and [swimming] in the clear water'.[60]

The Allied military mobilization of scientific experts and knowledge intensified once the decision was taken in August 1943 to launch the main invasion on the Normandy coastline. Major W.B.R. King, a geology professor at University College London, and his colleagues contributed to detailed invasion plans. Using maps and aerial photographs, they advised on landing beaches, beach exit points, airfield sites, water supplies, and

potential obstacles to military movement. They also made recommendations on preparing beaches for the landing of troops and vehicles, such
as laying surfacing over the shingle portion of Omaha beach. In addition,
geologists were instrumental in steering the eventual site of invasion to
the coastline north of Bayeux and Caen because the soils of the Calvados
plateau allowed for rapid airfield construction.[61]

Alongside its accommodating soils, Normandy's geography held other
advantages for the Allies. For a start, it faced the English south coast
where troops and supplies could gather before the invasion. The firm
sand of Norman beaches allowed for the unloading of heavy vehicles and
their gradual, upward slope suited invasion forces, as did the absence (in
many places) of dunes and cliffs. At the beachheads, woods and orchards
provided some cover for ammunition and petrol dumps. The built environment was similarly accommodating. Coastal tourist resorts meant the
existence of a decent road system and the Atlantic Wall was less fortified
in Normandy than the Pas-de-Calais.[62]

Weather mattered too for those Allied strategists charged with coordi-
nating air, water, and land forces.[63] Moon cycles (which controlled tides)
and weather conditions influenced the landings' eventual date. The Allies
sought good visibility for naval guns, clear skies for the effective aerial
bombing of German positions, moonlight for night-time operations,
calm seas (to counter sea-sickness and to aid landings), and light winds
to clear fog and cloud. Engineers would also need to land at low tide to
clear beach obstacles before troops and vehicles could disembark on the
rising tide.[64]

Climatic conditions seemed poised to influence the outcome of the
landings.[65] The coastal weather's unpredictability made setting a date
difficult. After an invasion in early spring 1944 was ruled out, Allied forecasters, led by Group Captain James Stagg of the RAF and Meteorological
Office, predicted that the weather was likely to be best in June, and that
the optimal moon and tide conditions would occur between 5 and 7 June.
But conditions did not bode well on 4 June, characterized as they were
by high winds, low cloud, and stormy seas. Heavy seas and skies continued on 5 June and General Dwight Eisenhower delayed the crossing on
Stagg's advice. Throughout 5 June, Allied forecasters frantically debated
the following day's weather. For his part, Stagg predicted a 36-hour
window of clear weather. Having weighed up the meteorological advice,
Eisenhower gave the order to invade on the early morning of 6 June.[66]

Luckily for the Allies, Stagg's forecast proved correct and the weather
worked in their favour. If they had waited, the invasion would have

coincided with the violent storm that lashed the Normandy coast from 19 to 20 June. The importance accorded to weather forecasting reveals that military commanders had to take into account unpredictable environmental conditions. The modern military technologies available to the Allied invasion force, such as planes, pre-fabricated floating harbours, tanks, and amphibious landing craft, could not disguise the fact that their operations took place within a dynamic and potentially risky environment which could not be predicted with complete certainty.

The Allies got the weather forecast right, but the landings did not run smoothly. At Omaha beach a lack of artillery and a determined German defence (among other factors) resulted in heavy casualties, now commemorated by memorials (see figure 6.1). The beach therefore became a disorientating and deadly militarized environment. Explosions, wrecked and burning landing craft, smoke, images of dying and wounded men, and the desperate search for shelter characterized the experience of many Allied soldiers.[67] Military misreadings of the environment contributed to casualty rates. Aquatic plants had flourished in the areas flooded by German forces (see above) and Allied strategists mistook them for marshland on aerial photographs. Consequently, many parachutists landing in the sector drowned.[68] Nonetheless, after a day of fierce fighting on the beaches, the Allies succeeded in breaking through the Atlantic Wall to land 175,000 men at the cost of approximately 4,900 lives. The front stretched over ninety kilometres, bar a few gaps, creating a semi-terrestrial, semi-aquatic militarized environment stretching between Utah and Sword beaches.

Military planners and scientific experts had documented and assessed environmental conditions from afar according to tactical and operational considerations. In the days and weeks following D-Day, Allied forces on the ground experienced them first hand. Heavy rains in June and July made negotiating and travelling through the flooded marshlands even harder. But this obstacle was not insurmountable; army engineers deployed boat bridges to traverse the flooded marshland between Longueville and Colombières that blocked the way to Saint-Lô.[69]

Normandy's *bocage* landscape was a far more serious problem. Allied intelligence had under estimated severely the difficulty of fighting in, and through, a region characterized by tall and thick hedgerows, small compartmentalized fields, ditches, clearings, orchards, and woodlands. Army geographer Second Lieutenant J. B. Jackson admitted that he only learnt about *bocage* in the library of the Norman château where he was billeted.[70] Unsurprisingly, therefore, one US soldier found that, 'our first

6.1 Memorials at Omaha beach, Normandy

encounter with the Normandy countryside was completely different to what we'd been taught to expect'.[71]

The discrepancy between military planning and conditions on the ground became all too apparent. *Bocage* – perceptively described as 'a confused mosaic'[72] – impeded easy tank movement away from the beaches. Furthermore, having failed to hold the purpose-built Atlantic Wall defences, German infantry, artillery, and anti-tank units turned *bocage* to their advantage, using it as camouflage from the air and ground. Leading a relatively inexperienced Allied attacking force through the *bocage* against experienced and determined enemy resistance was no easy task. General Bradley described it as 'the damndest country I've seen'.[73]

During the 'battle of the hedgerows' Allied units advanced field by field. The *bocage* hindered their range of vision and fighting through it was an arduous, tense, and sometime lethal operation, as German units mowed down Allied soldiers caught out in the open fields. A reconnaissance soldier with the 115th recalls the difficulties he encountered: 'Being a scout in a region of *bocage* is the worst of jobs. You advance with fear in your stomach, without ever knowing where the enemy is because of the density of the foliage. Fighting in a *bocage* region is like fighting blind against an invisible enemy'.[74] To make matters worse, German forces militarized the hedgerows with booby-traps, trip wires, mines, trenches, and snipers. Combat transformed the pastoral *bocage* countryside into a testing militarized environment laced with death; it 'swiftly lost its pleasant sylvan undertones'.[75]

The German mobilization of *bocage* slowed down the Allied advance towards Saint-Lô, turning a planned war of movement into a slow struggle through the hedgerows. It took the Eighth Army corps 12 days to cover 11 km. But like the flooded marshland, *bocage* could be overcome with perseverance, ingenuity, and heavy losses. It conditioned, but did not determine, the combat.[76] Allied tactics evolved in relationship to the *bocage*, drawing on their fraught experience of fighting within it. For instance, Allied soldiers began throwing phosphorous grenades at haystacks to smoke out hidden German snipers.[77] US troops also learnt to use the behaviour of cows to assess the dangers of particular fields. As Sergeant D. Zane Schlemmer explains:

> By watching the cows, who were by nature quite curious animals, we could tell whether there was anyone else in the field, because the cows would stand, waiting, facing anyone there in anticipation of being milked. Over all these years, I've had a place in my heart for those lovely Norman cows with their big eyes and big udders.[78]

Norman cows, normally celebrated for the quality of their milk, therefore became unwitting allies of US troops.

Tank units adapted their vehicles and tactics to the *bocage*. As too few tanks were equipped with blades to cut through hedgerows, American soldiers began to blow holes in the hedges by depositing explosive charges directly into them using pipes attached to Sherman tanks. Perhaps most ingeniously, they attached cutters and bumpers made of salvaged railway tracks to their tanks to smash their way through hedgerows (because of their shape, tanks equipped with cutters were nicknamed 'rhino' tanks) thereby opening up formerly impassable sections of the countryside.[79] *Bocage* did not determine how the battle of Normandy unfolded, but it shaped soldiers' combat experience and influenced tactics. In such a way, human ideas and action emerged and changed in relationship to the militarized environment.

The battle of Normandy was fought in, through and against the environment; soldiers, bullets, mines, shells, bombs, and tanks militarized and modified the environment. British soldiers, who compared

Normandy's countryside with their homeland, and American soldiers, who viewed it as a slightly less tidy version of Britain, realized that the combat was ruining the countryside. The frequent sight and pervasive smell of dead cows and other animals were amongst the most vivid signs of war's impact on rural Normandy, as were the green flies that gorged on rotting apples in abandoned orchards. But it was soldiers who instigated the changes: it was their bulldozers and tanks that destroyed hedgerows and their tracked vehicles that churned up fields.[80] In total, minefields, flooding, military camps, craters and other combat-related sites spread across 200,000 ha of farmland in the Manche and Calvados *départements*.[81]

Amongst the carnage, the plight of dead animals, as innocent, helpless victims of war, was one of the most painful sights. For Group-Captain Desmond Scott, 'it was the fate of the horses that upset me the most. Harnessed as they were, it had been impossible for them to escape, and they lay dead in tangled heaps, their large wide eyes crying out to me in anguish. It was a sight that pierced the soul, and I felt as if my heart would burst'.[82] Like the wounded and dying horses during the Franco-Prussian War and the First World War, the pitiful state of Normandy's animals represented the horror and futility of war.

Mobilizing nature in liberation France

With the taking of Falaise on 17 August 1944, the battle of Normandy drew to a close. Two days earlier, Operation Anvil had brought war to the Provencal coastline as Allied troops, including Free French forces from North Africa, landed on beaches between Cap Nègre and Théoule. German resistance here was far weaker than in Normandy and the Allies made rapid progress. As in Normandy, the environment did not emerge unscathed. Overall, at least 2,769 ha of Provence's forests were either partially or fully damaged.[83]

Once Allied forces broke out of Normandy and Provence, liberation unfolded across France led, in places, by *maquisards* and civilian insurrections. As General Charles de Gaulle strove to restore French republican sovereignty, and French society began to face the injustices and persecutions experienced during the 'dark years', Allied troops continued to push German forces from French soil.[84] The existence of mines and other explosives posed a major hazard; one official army instruction helpfully advised soldiers that 'when you travel through a zone infested with mines, carefully observe the ground in front of you'.[85] Following the breakout from Normandy, Allied soldiers did not face an obstacle as formidable as the *bocage*. But environmental conditions were still tough. In the Vosges mountains, they experienced navigational difficulties in the dense woodland and feared 'tree bursts', which were caused by shells hitting the top of trees and scattering trees and branches. The militarization of forests in eastern France left what we might now describe as an ecological footprint. By the end of the war, mines covered 29,000 ha of forest in the Vosges, while 258,000,000 francs worth of damage had reportedly been caused to the Moselle's forests and 50,000,000 to the Bas-Rhin's.[86]

As the war continued, Allied forces established new militarized environments, such as airfields and training grounds. The French military similarly created new airfields. Captain Liaudet, an engineer with the French air force, viewed the creation of airfields as an heroic struggle, as teams of poorly equipped and inadequately trained workers battled against the mud and cold to clear mines and construct aerodromes, thereby maintaining an 'honourable position vis-à-vis our allies'.[87] Rapid and effective militarization became a source of national pride.

As they had done during the First World War, Allied forces mobilized France's natural resources. US troops took wood for construction and firewood, placing further pressure on France's already war-depleted forests. The US army and French forest administration established a wood supply system, involving 10,000 wood cutters working in over 28 camps, the first of which was established in Cerisy forest near Bayeux. To free US troops for battle, many of the forest workers were prisoners of war, including German foresters. Perhaps reflecting the strong German influence on US 'scientific' forestry, Colonel Axel Oxholm, chief operations officer of the US Quartermaster Corps' wood-cutting project, praised them as 'being untiring in their efforts to enforce proper cutting practices'.[88]

Equipment shortages, inadequate transportation, and the previous militarization of forests hindered Allied exploitation of France's forests. Conditions were worst in Argonne forest, according to Oxholm.[89] Furthermore, although high-ranking French foresters praised Allied felling, US troops sometimes helped themselves to wood and, echoing the behaviour of German occupation troops, sometimes refused to give their identity when caught. Manoeuvring Allied troops also hampered civilian forestry production and caused forest fires. Whatever their nationality, from the foresters' perspective, military units placed a burden on the forest.[90]

As wartime press restrictions were lifted, the militarization of forests became a source of public outcry. A newspaper article in October 1945 protested the behaviour of US troops in Fontainebleau forest. Entitled 'The forest is not the Wild West', it attacked their impromptu shooting exercises that threatened the safety of walkers and lamented how, on one occasion, patrolmen had shot a 'superb stag' that wandered across their path. Hardly the kind of behaviour, the article pointed out, that would be tolerated in Yellowstone national park.[91] Such episodes reflected and contributed to the frustrations and misunderstandings that characterized the Franco-American relationship in post-liberation France. In part, this sprung from competing priorities: the US saw the liberation of France as part of the wider struggle against Nazi Germany whilst the preoccupation for many French civilians and officials was reclaiming French sovereignty over national territory after four years of occupation. In this context, criticizing the actions of US troops in Fontainebleau forest reaffirmed a sense of French national pride and identity.[92]

Although the Allied military presence stoked anti-American sentiments, key differences separated the Allied and Axis mobilizations of France's natural resources. Mindful that France was an ally and that they were guests rather than occupiers, Allied foresters urged restraint and respect for France's forests (even if their wishes were not always heeded on the ground) and worked closely with local French foresters and producers.[93] In addition, at a time of chronic food shortages, the Allies allowed hunting to recommence in certain areas. The US army did, however, advise hunters not to pursue game near front lines and to 'take particular care to look like hunters and not be mistaken for enemy agents, paratroopers or stray Allied soldiers'.[94] In such a way, the hunting season re-opened under the shadow of foreign militarization of the French countryside.

As hunters and the rest of French society adapted to the continued Allied military presence, the government began the task of demilitarization. After the First World War, France had been confronted with demilitarizing the Western Front's 'lunar' landscapes. War damage from the Second World War was less striking and less concentrated. But it was considerable, and spread across national territory, reflecting the dispersed locations of militarized environments between 1939 and 1945; only four *départements* were reported to have escaped agricultural damage.[95] Across France, seventy million cubic metres of rubble needed clearing and eighty million cubic metres of trenches and bomb craters required filling in, while one report estimated that military installations and defensive floods had rendered 304,114 ha of agricultural land unusable.[96] In addition, the forest administration estimated that damage to forests spread across 400,000 ha.[97]

Mine clearance was amongst the most-pressing tasks and mine clearance officials treated their work as way of re-establishing French control over national territory after the German occupation.[98] The Normandy beaches needed particular attention as corpses, unexploded shells, mines, wrecks, abandoned vehicles, and munitions lay scattered across them.[99] Across France, mines removed buildings, fields, forests, beaches, and other sites from civilian use. Local councils lobbied hard to have their land cleared first. But some people simply could not wait: swimmers had returned to Golfe-Juan beach (Alpes-Maritimes) before it had been cleared and, in their desperation to resume work, farmers in Normandy entered minefields on agricultural land with sometimes fatal results.[100]

Environmental conditions added to the inherent dangers of mine clearance. Areas of *maquis* and forest were harder to clear than vineyards and fields because vegetation covered up mines. Mines buried in the coastal dunes of Normandy and in quicksand near Royan (where German troops had held out until April 1945) were particularly hazardous.[101] Despite the difficulty of the task, the creation of a central mine clearance service in February 1945 speeded up operations. But there was a high human price to pay; approximately 471 French landmine clearers and 738 German prisoners of war were killed.[102] In the end, 13 million mines were found on French soil, covering 1 per cent of national territory,

Demilitarization was essential but expensive. The Consultative Commission for Damages and Reparations (CCDR) put its cost at five billion francs.[103] Only once demilitarization was completed could long-term reconstruction of urban and rural areas begin. Like the First World War, conflict between 1939 and 1945 acted as a vector of environmental change as officials and technocrats set about modernizing and rationalizing national territory, often working within institutions and methodologies established under the Vichy regime.[104] But as the French pursued reconstruction, foreign military presences lingered on.

From world war to Cold War

In 1957, the American Battle Monuments Commission published a brochure introducing the Normandy American Cemetery and memorial overlooking Omaha beach near Colleville-sur-Mer. The cemetery and memorial was intended to transform the former militarized environment into an ordered site of commemoration; the 'precise alignment' of the 9,386 headstones on 'the smooth green lawn conveys an unforgettable impression of dignity and beauty'. The frieze on the memorial's colonnade, meanwhile, asserted American values: 'This embattled shore, portal of Liberation, is forever hallowed by the ideals, the valor and the sacrifices of our fellow countrymen'. [105] The cemetery uses design and environmental features to turn the former battlefield into a place of remembrance and sacrifice. Alongside the British, Canadian, Polish, and German cemeteries that dot the Norman countryside, it reminds us of international militarization of the French countryside during the Second World War.[106] The cemetery is a distinctly American memorial site located on the French coastline.

As well as establishing the Colleville-sur-Mer and other cemeteries in the postwar period, the USA occupied other sites across France under the framework of North Atlantic Treaty Organization (NATO) agreements. These NATO installations continued the international character of militarized environments begun during the Second World War.

Why did the Fourth Republic allow this continued foreign militarization of national territory, given the strained Franco-American relationship of post-liberation France? At the end of the 1940s, France found itself in a delicate position. On the one hand, the Fourth Republic was determined to restore French independence and re-establish France on the world stage. But on the other hand, it struggled with the cost of economic and military reconstruction, war in Indochina and the need to ensure national security in the event of Germany's resurgence, all within the context of heightening international tensions between the US and USSR. So although some within French society deplored the USA's influence on France, and tensions between the French and US governments arose due to divergent views on French colonialism and German rearmament, France became increasingly drawn into US-led western defence alliances, as well as benefiting economically from the Marshall Plan.[107]

As the contours of the Cold War coalesced in the late 1940s, France, along with other Western European nations, sought to guarantee its national security against the Soviets. It therefore signed the Bidault-Caffery agreement with the USA on 16 February 1948. The agreement allowed the USA to station 1,500 military personnel in France, establish a communications line across the country, and use French air bases. In exchange, France was to receive warships and other military assistance.[108]

Military cooperation was sealed on 4 April 1949 with the establishment of NATO, with further agreements in 1949 and 1950 tightening the alliance: the USA committed military support to its European allies and an integrated command structure was established. A series of bilateral agreements between November 1950 and June 1953 cemented the US military presence in France, turning the latter into a supply and tactical support base. France had become part of the US network of military bases in Cold War-era Western Europe designed to contain Communism and ensure US security. But US forces were not simply imposed on France. Instead the Fourth Republic succeeded in obtaining the security they provided at relatively little cost.[109]

These diplomatic manoeuvres had significant environmental repercussions.[110] As US forces returned to French soil in the late 1940s and early 1950s, the militarized environments they created became politically ambiguous sites. The 4 October 1952 agreement, that enabled the construction of thirteen NATO air bases, attempted to combine operational effectiveness with French sovereignty. France maintained territorial control of the bases and their buildings and defined their territorial limits. But the USA enjoyed operational control, including security and air traffic control, and was to pay for their upkeep. As if to symbolize the bases' transnational character, the flags of both countries were to be flown from main installations.[111]

NATO militarized environments spread across rural France. Some continued the militarization of the north-east, such as the US air bases at Laon, Etain, Toul, Chambley, and Chaumont and army depots in Haye forest and Vassincourt. Canadian air force bases at Grostenquin and Marville further reinforced the region's militarization. But NATO also militarized new sites in western and central France as the US army and air force established numerous depots in places such as Chinon and Châteauroux. These were purposely located far away from Germany where military strategists assumed that any eventual confrontation with Soviet forces would take place. The militarization of secluded forests and other sites in the rear-zone echoed the Allied mobilization of natural resources away from front lines during the world wars. In fact, the US army munitions depot at Captieux was located near the site of US forestry exploitation during the First World War (see chapter 4). Regardless of their location, NATO militarized environments removed land from civilian use; by 1952, NATO forces occupied 29,178 ha, or 0.2 per cent of France's cultivatable land.[112]

Alongside bringing a taste of glamorous, North-American lifestyles to rural France, the US's military presence raised agricultural and environmental issues. The size of their installations exasperated French officials (the US air force demanded longer runways and larger air fields than its French counterpart). One official from the Ministry of Agriculture despaired that 90 m protection bands around the Loan air base (Aisne) would expropriate 4 ha of 'excellent' farmland.[113] This complaint was far from unique as officials equated militarization with sterilization: during the planning stages of Phalsbourg air base (Moselle), one Ministry of Agriculture official claimed that the base would 'sterilize the whole region' and dispossess 200 farmers.[114]

A local mayor formed a group to defend local interests, but base construction at Phalsbourg went ahead as defence considerations ultimately overrode civilian concerns.[115] But elsewhere, officials succeeded in limiting NATO militarization. In June 1953 the Somme's prefect protested against a proposed NATO aerodrome at Airaines, arguing that the *département* had already reached a level of aerodrome 'saturation'. By October 1954, the plan had been abandoned.[116] As the Phalsbourg and Airaines examples show, Fourth Republic officials were not passive when confronted with NATO environmental militarization. Instead, they actively defended French sovereignty and interests on the ground whilst geopolitical currents swirled around them.

Opposing NATO militarized environments

As with other aspects of the Franco-American relationship, the establishment of NATO air bases was marked by 'cooperation, conflict, and negotiation'.[117] Once NATO forces were settled in their air bases and other installations, tensions intensified and crystallized around environmental problems, as well as political and social ones. Drainage was the main issue at Captieux munitions depot. According to a critical French army report, the choice of this marshland of peaty sands and wetland vegetation was ill-founded. When US reconnaissance officers had hastily visited the site before rushing back to Paris it had been dry. But normally it was a 'real sponge', gathering in water from the surrounding area. To make matters worse, US modification of the site in 1952 resulted in the flooding of surrounding forestry plantations. Yet the US army refused to carry out the expensive drainage work, recommended by French engineers, to remedy the situation.[118] Despite a Franco-American conference in 1953 that aimed to reconcile the differences, recriminations and national interests overrode cooperation. One French agricultural engineer pointed out that although the US army's drainage work meant that its soldiers were no longer 'up to their stomachs' in water, the same could not be said for the surrounding area. The conference ended in disagreement, save the need for more technical reports.[119] National differences over land-management policies and finances had proved insurmountable. As in other areas, the Franco-American relationship at Captieux was intimate but strained.[120]

Tensions were also rising in Fontainebleau forest. As the site of Napoleon I's firing range (see chapter 1), the forest was hardly untouched by militarization. But for French commentators, the USA's presence seemed to jeopardize the forest's role as a picturesque site of leisure within the Paris region. Over a century after Claude François Denecourt and the Barbizon painters had transformed Fontainebleau forest into a popular tourist destination and protected site, local newspaper articles in 1951 and 1952 called on Fontainebleau forest to be spared militarization and become a national park.[121] In panicked tones, one journalist argued that the construction of US Centre-Europe headquarters there might herald the 'organized massacre of the region's forests'.[122] But whilst some called for calm, the general mood was one of apprehension. NATO militarized environments seemed poised to irreversibly transform the forest.[123]

Aesthetics considerations fed civilian worries. The president of the local nature protection group, Amis de la forêt de Fontainebleau, had initially urged the French government to repair forest roads and signs ahead of NATO forces' arrival to boost France's prestige and show that the nation could maintain its forests in a 'state of irreproachable tidiness'. But by 1951, the group had changed its tune, complaining that US felling exposed military installations to the public gaze near Rocher d'Avon.[124] This intervention demonstrates the desire to control what civilians saw of the military world, and vice versa. If properly managed, trees could act as a visually pleasing barrier between civilian and militarized environments, thereby containing the impact of militarization.

Amis de la forêt de Fontainebleau represented the voice of nature preservation in Fontainebleau forest, 1,600 ha of which had been designated an 'artistic reserve' in 1861. Since then, state foresters had sought to maintain the forest's productive functions often in conflict with the preservationists. But they united to denounce US military presence during the 1950s. In a continuation of wartime grievances, state foresters lodged numerous complaints against US troops. One recurrent bugbear was the US army's churning up of forest roads when accessing a petrol depot.[125]

Events in Fontainebleau forest were part of French foresters' wider struggle to preserve France's forests, and their control over them, from Cold War-era militarization, which they believed threatened the forests' productivity and aesthetics. Yet again, divergent civilian–military perspectives on forests' purposes came to the fore. In 1955 one forestry conservator argued that no more forested land should be given to the USA because it was not 'vacant' but in a '*state of production*'.[126]

The conservator's plea seems to have had little impact as requests to site US and NATO installations showed no sign of drying up. In response, foresters maintained their opposition. In March 1956 they opposed the creation of a US army depot in a forest near Reims, fearing it would lead to 'more or less complete deforestation'. They suggested instead that the US army should target French military land in the *Champagne pouilleuse* rather than forests where years of 'methodical care' from foresters had apparently created trees of exceptional value that helped prevent erosion.[127] Yet again, foresters confidently contrasted their rational forest management style with the carelessness and short term-ism of military forest use.

Foresters' protests sometimes met with success. Most notably, they managed to prevent the installation of a Matador nuclear missile depot in Crenay state forest (Haute-Marne). Having just invested 1.7 million francs in reforesting this former French army firing range, they argued that it would be 'incoherent' to waste this state funding of reforestation.[128] This episode underscores the diverse approaches to militarization within the forestry administration and how there was more room for manoeuvre and collaboration with American military forces than German ones.

But state foresters were empathetically not peaceniks and their quarrel was not with militarization *per se*.[129] They were willing to cooperate with the military if circumstances suited their interests. For instance, they obtained 200 ha of a disused military firing range in exchange for ceding 40 ha of state forest for the establishment of Centre-Europe HQ.[130] Nor were they oblivious to national defence imperatives. They provided terrain with little fuss if the proposed installation did not undermine the forest's future, allowing Supreme Headquarters Allied Powers Europe (SHAPE) forces to conduct an exercise in Versailles forest in February 1956, even though it would take the forest, which was heavily used by Parisian ramblers, out of civilian use for six weeks.[131]

Farmers too sought to reduce the ramifications of NATO militarized environments. In summer 1954 farmers and local authorities complained that weeds and wild grasses from Laon air base were spreading to neighbouring fields. French officials urged the US air force to keep grasses on the base under control to maintain their 'friendly neighbourly relations' with local farmers. In response the acting director of the United States Air Force (USAF) in Europe wrote to base commanders giving them instructions to 'alleviate' the situation.[132] It might seem strange that high-ranking USAF officials concerned themselves with grass-cutting on bases. But the Laon complaints took place within the context of intensive French monitoring of the USA's land management practices, and wider protests against the USA's military presence. In particular, the Communist party organized anti-US base protests, coined the slogan 'Yankee go home!' and compared the USA's presence with Nazi occupation. Such was the perceived danger from political sabotage at the Captieux depot, that the Gironde's prefect ordered the laying of an anti-personnel minefield around it.[133]

The political situation was delicate. With French memories of occupation still raw, US authorities were keen to maintain good relations with the French population and demonstrate that they were not an occupation force. In turn, French authorities wanted cordial US-Franco relations to convince public opinion of the legitimacy and necessity of the Atlantic alliance and to de-legitimize Communist protests. They had their work cut out. A 1953 opinion poll found that 46 per cent of respondents disapproved of the US military presence with only 28 per cent in favour. Further polls in the late 1950s and early 1960s showed that the level of respondents actively in favour of the US military only hovered around the 20 to 25 per cent mark.[134] Actual and anticipated anti-Americanism explains why invasive weeds, forests, and drainage became political issues, joining complaints over the behaviour of off-duty US personnel in French towns.[135]

US forces actively tried to improve their image. The air force portrayed itself as living in harmony with the local population at Phalsbourg air base. Its *Phalsbourg Falcon* publication, destined for the neighbouring French population and personnel working on 'the friendliest base in France', presented an idyllic view of the air base. Photographs published in 1962 showed a female member of staff feeding a puppy, recently delivered by the base's mascot Hexie, as well as a newly planted flower bed, a result of the base's 'recent clean up and beautification campaign'.[136] Any mention of the controversy surrounding the base's construction was banished from the pages of the *Phalsbourg Falcon*. Instead, a May 1962 article (in French) highlighted the similarities between the 'gentle and rich hills of Alsace' and New York State in an attempt to show how US personnel felt deeply attached to the French countryside.[137] In a small way, the *Phalsbourg Falcon* contributed to the transnational project of building a sense of 'Atlantic Community' that might transcend fractures in the Franco-American relationship.[138]

Despite the conciliatory tone of the *Phalsbourg Falcon*, the USA's mobilization of the French environment was fraught with the tensions arising from NATO military objectives and the French desire to safeguard sovereignty over their territory and natural resources. For although pollution and other environmental disturbances from US bases were arguably greater in West Germany, deforestation, wild grasses, and poor drainage tested Franco-US relations on the ground. So, too, did aviation noise, suspicions of fuel leaks from Etain air base, and litter from US naval ships washing up on beaches between Cannes and Saint-Raphaël in 1965.[139] The environment was therefore both a cause of disagreement and a site within which wider tensions in the US-French relationship were played out.

NATO withdraws

Charles de Gaulle's return to power in 1958 and his search for greater French autonomy heralded a shift in the relations between France and the USA. For although France accepted the arrival of eight US air squadrons, comprising 218 aircraft, 9,974 men of the Air National Guard, and 7,474 tons of *matériel* after the Berlin crisis, French hospitality had its limits; de Gaulle refused to provide land at Cherbourg and Le Harve for new US facilities and stated that the arrival of any more than 100,000 US military personnel would become an 'occupation'.[140]

By the mid-1960s the US presence in France was under immense strain. On the French side, de Gaulle opposed any further French involvement with NATO integrated command, while the USA's plans to develop communication routes through the UK and Germany rendered its French supply lines increasingly obsolete. With national interests increasingly divergent, US military planners contemplated a withdrawal from France in 1965. Then, in March 1966, de Gaulle announced that France would remain committed to NATO but withdraw from its integrated command. His decision entailed the departure of NATO troops from French soil and the repatriation of French units from

West Germany. With the withdrawal date set for 1 April 1967, the US launched Operation FRELOC to evacuate 69,576 personnel and their families, along with 813,276 tons of *matériel*, from over 437 French sites to Germany, Britain and Italy.[141]

Alongside the economic fallout in the communities that had found employment on US bases, the US evacuation modified France's Cold War militarized environments. Some sites passed into civilian use. Ponts et Chaussées engineers planned to return an abandoned NATO air base at Berry-au-Bac-Juvincourt (Aisne) to agriculture by demolishing concrete structures, levelling land and enriching soils.[142] In some cases, private companies took over the sites (for instance, turkeys were raised on the former American base at Saint-Mihiel), whilst in others, government departments took charge; the forestry administration gained control of 690 ha of La Braconne forest (Charente) which had been the site of a US army munitions depot.[143]

Demilitarization took account of the terrain's environmental attributes. At Chizé (Deux-Sèvres), American authorities had mobilized 2,600 ha of state forest as a munitions depot following a 1952 convention with the forestry administration. Wildlife had thrived alongside the military presence and had been kept within the forest by the security fence constructed by US forces. Such was the ecological vitality of the site by the time of NATO withdrawal that the Centre national de la recherche scientifique (CNRS) established a biological research station there. The facility exists today and is a reminder that although environmental disruption was a common feature at many US and NATO installations, in certain places Cold War-era militarization could co-exist with wildlife. Other sites remained militarized; the French military installed anti-aircraft regiments at Chaumont and Laon bases; a helicopter regiment at Phalsbourg; and maintained Toul as an air force base.[144]

Divergent military–civilian interests come into play over the fate of former NATO sites. With memories of the poor drainage seemingly forgotten, French army officers wanted to take over the US installation at Captieux at a time when it was proving difficult to secure other land in the south-west for training. They mooted various plans in 1966 and 1967 to use parts of its 9,342 ha for training parachute regiments or for air-ground exercises. Another possibility was making Captieux an annex of the Centre d'essais de Landes (see chapter 7).[145] Civilian authorities, however, had other ideas for the site, including afforestation and the creation of a game reserve. But military imperatives took priority over civilian interests and the army took charge of the site.[146]

Conclusion

Between 1940 and 1967 Axis, Allied, and NATO forces mobilized the French environment with divergent aims and, between 1940 and 1944, in direct opposition to each other. They treated the French environment as a site of resource extraction, combat, and war preparation. French officials and civilians did not passively accept the creation of foreign militarized environments. Instead they sought to safeguard their livelihoods and land within the limits imposed by wartime and Cold War conditions. Nor were environmental conditions necessarily compliant with military objectives. From the climatic conditions of the Camargue and Normandy coastline, to the *bocage* and unruly grasses, militarization was an unpredictable 'more-than-human' process.

Notes

1 Paul Virilio, *Bunker Archaeology*, trans. George Collins (New York: Princeton Architectural Press, 1994), 9.
2 Sam Edwards, 'Ruins, relics and restoration: The afterlife of World War Two American airfields in England, 1945–2005', in Chris Pearson, Peter Coates, and Tim Cole (eds), *Militarized Landscapes: From Gettysburg to Salisbury Plain* (London: Continuum, 2010), 209–28; Judith A. Bennett, *Natives and Exotics: World War II and Environment in the Southern Pacific* (Honolulu: University of Hawai'i Press, 2009).
3 Simon Duke, *United States Military Forces and Installations in Europe* (Oxford: Oxford University Press/SIPRI, 1989); Joseph Gerson and Bruce Birchard (eds), *The Sun Never Sets: Confronting the Network of U.S. Foreign Military Bases* (Boston: South End Press, 1991); Catherine Lutz (ed.), *The Bases of Empire: The Global Struggle against U.S. Military Posts* (New York: New York University Press, 2009); John R. McNeill and Corinna R. Unger (eds), *Environmental Histories of the Cold War* (New York: Cambridge University Press, 2010); John R. McNeill and David S. Painter, 'The global environmental footprint of the U.S. military, 1789–2003', Charles E. Closmann (ed.), *War and the Environment: Military Destruction in the Modern Age* (College Station: Texas A&M University Press, 2009), 10–31.
4 As yet, there is no global environmental history of the Second World War, but see Bennett, *Natives and Exotics*; Rauno Lahtinen and Timo Vuorisalo, '"It's war and everyone can do as they please!": An environmental history of a Finnish city in wartime', *Environmental History*, 9:4, (2004); Chris Pearson, *Scarred Landscapes: War and Nature in Vichy France* (Basingstoke:

Palgrave Macmillan, 2008); William M. Tsutsui, 'Landscapes in the dark valley: Toward an environmental history of wartime Japan', *Environmental History*, 8:2 (2003), 294–311. For the Cold War, see McNeill and Unger, *Environmental Histories of the Cold War*.

5 Kent E. Calder, *Embattled Garrisons: Comparative Base Politics and American Globalism* (Princeton: Princeton University Press, 2007); Mark E. Gillem, *American Town: Building the Outposts of Empire* (Minneapolis: University of Minnesota Press, 2007); Maria Höhn and Seungsook Moon (eds), *Over There: Living with the U.S. Military Empire from World War Two to the Present* (Durham, NC: Duke University Press, 2010); Lutz, *The Bases of Empire*.

6 French-German relations have focused on wartime collaboration and postwar reconciliation and competition. Victor Gavin, 'Power through Europe? The case of the European defence community in France (1950–1954)', *French History*, 23:1 (2009), 69–87; Bertram M. Gordon, *Collaborationism in France during the Second World War* (Ithaca: Cornell University Press, 1980); Philippe Burrin, *Living with Defeat: France under the German Occupation 1940–1944* (London: Arnold, 1996). French–US relations are tackled through the frameworks of military relations, diplomacy, and Americanization. François Cochet, Marie-Claude Genet-Delacroix, and Hélène Trocmé (eds), *Les Américains et la France, 1917–1947: Engagements et Représentations* (Paris: Maisonneuve & Larose, 1999); Hilary Footitt, *War and Liberation in France: Living with the Liberators* (Basingstoke: Palgrave Macmillan, 2004); Olivier Pottier, *Les bases américaines en France (1950–1967)* (Paris: L'Harmattan, 2003); Michel Creswell, *A Question of Balance: How France and the United States Created Cold War Europe* (Cambridge, MA: Harvard University Press, 2006); William I. Hitchcock, *France Restored: Cold War Diplomacy and the Quest for Leadership in Europe 1944–1954* (Chapel Hill: University of North Carolina Press, 1998); Christopher Endy, *Cold War Holidays: American Tourism in France* (Chapel Hill: University of North Carolina Press, 2004); Richard Kuisel, *Seducing the French: The Dilemma of Americanization* (Berkeley: University of California Press, 1997); Irwin M. Wall, *The United States and the Making of Postwar France 1945–1954* (New York: Cambridge University Press 1991).

7 Karen Adler, *Jews and Gender in Liberation France* (Cambridge: Cambridge University Press, 2003); Gérard Noiriel, *Les origines républicaines de Vichy* (Paris: Hachette Littératures, 1999); Robert O. Paxton, *Vichy France: Old Guard and New Order 1940–44* (London: Barrie and Jenkins, 2001 [1972]).

8 For an excellent introduction to the history of France during the Second World War, see Julian Jackson, *France: The Dark Years, 1940–1944* (Oxford: Oxford University Press, 2001). On the period's environmental history, see Pearson, *Scarred Landscapes*.

9 Ulrich Herbert, 'The German military command in Paris and the deportation of the French Jews', in Ulrich Herbert (ed.), *National Socialist Extermination Policies: Contemporary German Perspectives and Controversies* (Oxford: Berghahn, 2000), 128–62.

10 On the French army between 1940 and 1944, see Robert O. Paxton, *Parades and Politics at Vichy: The French Officer Corps under Marshall Pétain* (Princeton: Princeton University Press, 1966).

11 Bertram M. Gordon, 'Ist Gott Französisch? Germans, tourism, and occupied France, 1940–1944', *Modern & Contemporary France*, 4:3 (1996), 287–98.

12 Robert Gildea, *Marianne in Chains: In Search of the German Occupation of France 1940–45* (London: Macmillan, 2002), 146–8; Annelyse Chevalier, *Le Bois des Rièges: Coeur de la Camargue, entre mythe et réalité, récits de gardiens, manadiers, pêcheurs et autres camarguias* (Sommières: Editions Arnaud-Gilles, 2004), 101.

13 Commission consultative des dommages et des réparations, *Dommages subis par la France*, vol. 7, *Prélèvements allemands de produits agricoles, monographie P.A.6 oeufs, volailles, gibier* (Paris: Imprimerie nationale, 1947), 24–5.

14 François Marcot, 'La forêt sous l'occupation', in Pierre Gresser, André Robert, Claude Royer, and François Vion-Delphin (eds), *Les hommes et la forêt en Franche-Comté* (Paris: Bonneton, 1990), 138.

15 Chef de bataillon Gerrée, 'L'assainissement du camp d'Auvours, *Revue du Génie militaire* (May–June 1952), 158; Luc Dias, 'Partie D, 1939–1945', in Luc Dias (ed.), *Camp militaire national de La Courtine: 1901–2001, cent ans d'histoire* (La Courtine: Groupement de camp, 2001), 107; Edouard Maret, *Saint-Cyr Coëtquidan* (Rennes: Ouest-France, 1984), 10; M. Martin-Basse, 'Souvenirs sur le camp de Sathonay', *Revue historique de l'armée*, 2 (1958), 114.

16 Pascal Collot, *Le 5e Régiment de Dragons du Valdahon: Histoire du régiment blindé de Franche-Comté et du camp de Valdahon* (Besançon: Association Pierre Percée, 2003), 298; Capitaine Delsart, 'Construction du centre d'instruction de l'arme blindée et cavalerie (C.I.A.B.C.) au Camp de Carpiagne (Bouches-du-Rhône)', *Bulletin technique du génie militaire* (1971), 96.

17 René Terrisse, *Face aux pelotons Nazis: Souge, le Mont Valérien du Bordelais* (Bordeaux: Aubéron, 2000).

18 Jean-Jacques Bernard, *Le camp de la mort lente: Compiègne 1941–42* (Paris: Albin Michel, 1944), 62.

19 'Camp de Caylus (82)', Chemins de mémoire website, www.chemins dememoire.gouv.fr/page/affichelieu.php?idLang=fr&idLieu=3272, accessed 27 May 2010. For Vichy's exclusionary policies, see Michael R. Marrus and Robert O. Paxton, *Vichy France and the Jews* (Stanford: Stanford University Press, 1995 [1981]); Denis Peschanski, *La France des camps: L'internement, 1938–1946* (Paris: Gallimard, 2002).

20 'A Valbertrand un ramasseur d'escargots marches sur une grenade qui explose', *Le Petit Var*, 23 August 1943.

21 ADV 1790 W 130 Inspecteur des Eaux et Forêts, Draguignan, 'Rapport trimestriel', 23 October 1942; ADAM 521 W 57 Commissaire de police de Vallauris to Préfet des Alpes-Maritimes, 'Feu de forêt', 5 June 1943.

22 ADV 1790 W 130 Boutière, Inspecteur des Eaux et Forêts, Draguignan, 'Rapport trimestriel sur l'activité de l'Administration', 13 July 1943. On forests in wartime France, see Pearson, *Scarred Landscapes*, 40–67.

23 Pearson, *Scarred Landscapes*, 54.

24 ADC 5 W 8/2 minute for Öberkriegsverwaltungsrat Feldkommandantur 723, 2 June 1941.

25 ADC 5 W 8/2 Note for Feldkommandantur 723, 17 February 1941; ADC 5 W 8/2 Préfet de Calvados to Feldkommandantur 723, 'Exercices de tir sur le territoire de la commune de Villy', 10 May 1943.

26 ADC 6 W 2 Préfet du Calvados to Commandant de gendarmerie, Sous-préfet de Bayeux, Ingénieur des Ponts et Chaussées, Service de l'inscription maritime, Commissaires spécial de police, 25 July 1942.

27 On life during the Occupation, see Robert Gildea, *Marianne in Chains: In Search of the German Occupation of France 1940–45* (London: Macmillan, 2002); Dominique Veillon, *Vivre et survivre en France 1939–1947* (Paris: Editions Payot & Rivages, 1995); Richard Vinen, *The Unfree French: Life Under the Occupation* (London: Allen Lane, 2006).

28 ADC 6W1 Préfet de Calvados to Maire d'Epaney, 31 December 1940.

29 ADAM 521 W 6 'Procès-verbal', 12 October 1943.

30 ADAM 521 W 6 Inspecteur-adjoint des Eaux et Forêts, Nice, 'Rapport', 17 March 1943; 'Actes de la Réserve du Lauzanier', 5, 1940–1, in *Conférences de la Société nationale d'acclimatation de France: Actes de réserves de la Société nationale d'acclimatation de France*, 24, 1940–41, 84.

31 Pearson, *Scarred Landscapes*, 84–5.

32 ADC 5 W 8/2 Préfet du Calvados to Öberkriegsverwaltungsrat Feldkommandantur 723, 28 March 1941.

33 AMC 5 W 8/2 'Rapport du Lieutenant Lequette, Commandant provisoirement la section de Lisieux sur un bombardement aérien survenu près de Lisieux', 23 August 1941. See also Lindsey Dodd and Andrew Knapp, '"How many Frenchmen did you kill?" British bombing policy towards France (1940–1945)', *French History*, 22:4 (2008), 469.

34 ADAM 616 W 219 Captaine de vaisseau Lemaire to Préfet des Alpes-Maritimes, 16 September 1941.

35 Jean Vergeot, *Rapport sur le problème agricole français: Données et solutions* (Paris: Imprimerie de Chaix, 1944), 51; Yves Barde, *La muraille de Normandie: Le mur de l'Atlantique de Cherbourg au Havre* (Paris: Citédis, 1999).

36 Keith Mallory and Arvid Ottar, *Architecture of Aggression: A History*

of Military Architecture in North West Europe, 1900–1945 (London: Architectural Press, 1973), 175–7; CACAN 198880470/172 Conservateur des Eaux et Forêts, Lille, 'Possibilité par volume des forêts françaises', 28 June 1947.

37 Jean-Marie Guillon, 'Les îles d'Hyères aux XIXe et XXe siècles', in Jean-Pierre Brun (ed.), *Les Iles d'Hyères: Fragments d'histoire*, (Arles: Actes Sud, 1997), 112–13.

38 Madeline Hubert, *La libération d'Isigny-sur-Mer et du Col du Cotentin vue par un témoin entre Omaha et Utah Beach* (Condé-sur-Noireau: Editions Charles Corlet, 1984), 18; *Bataille de Normandie juin-août 1944* (Michelin map, 1947).

39 Pearson, *Scarred Landscapes*, 86–90.

40 Commission consultative, *Dommages subis par la France*, vol. 1, xix.

41 Frank M. Snowden, 'From triumph to disaster: Fascism and malaria in the Pontine Marshes, 1928–1946', in John Dickie, John Foot, and Frank M. Snowden (eds), *Disastro! Disasters in Italy since 1860: Culture, Politics, Society* (New York: Palgrave Macmillan, 2002), 113–40; Marcus Hall, 'World War II and the axis of disease: Battling malaria in twentieth-century Italy', in Closmann, *War and the Environment*, 112–31. On the relationship between war and insects, see Jeffrey A. Lockwood, *Six-Legged Soldiers: Using Insects as Weapons of War* (Oxford: Oxford University Press, 2009); John R, McNeill, *Mosquito Empires: Ecology and War in the Greater Caribbean* (New York: Cambridge University Press, 2010); Edmund P. Russell, *War and Nature: Fighting Humans and Insects with Chemicals from World War 1 to Silent Spring* (New York: Cambridge University Press, 2001).

42 Edmund P. Russell, '"Nicking the thin edge of the wedge": What history suggests about the environmental law of war', *Virginia Environmental Law Journal*, 24:3 (2005), 378. A further United Nations Convention in 1977 banned deliberate modification of the environment during wartime, with limited success. Jozef Goldblat, 'The Environmental Warfare Convention: How meaningful is it?', *Ambio*, 6:4 (1977), 216–21. See also Karen Hulme, *War Torn Environment: Interpreting the Legal Threshold* (Leiden: Martinus Nijhoff Publishers, 2004).

43 Alan S. Milward, *The New Order and the French Economy* (Aldershot: Gregg Revivals, 1993 [1984]); Paul Sanders, 'Economic draining: German black market operations in France, 1940–1944', *Global Crime*, 9:1–2 (2008), 136–68.

44 CACAN 19771461/41 'Ordonnance des autorités allemandes en date du 12 août 1943'; Pearson, *Scarred Landscapes*, 52–5.

45 ADAM 521 W 6 Brigadier des Eaux et Forêts, Muy, to Inspecteur des Eaux et Forêts, Draguignan, 5 July 1943.

46 Rod Kedward, *In Search of the Maquis: Rural Resistance in Southern France 1942–1944* (Oxford: Oxford University Press, 2003 [1993]).

47 G. Charot, *Le Maquis de Revin* (Mézières: Imprimerie G. Bouche, 1948), 14.

48 Quoted in Jacques Canaud, *Le temps des maquis: De la vie dans les bois à la reconquête des cités, 1943–1944* (Précy-sous-Thil: Editions de l'Armançon, 2003), 110.

49 See H. Boute-Kerollier's poem 'Le Mont Mouchet', in Christian Durandet, *Les Maquis d'Auvergne* (Paris: Editions France-Empire, 1973), 271.

50 Canaud, *Temps des maquis*, 95.

51 Frank Thone, 'Men of the maquis', *The Science News-Letter*, 46:3 (1944), 45–6.

52 Mountains were best deployed as secure sites from which to launch mobile attacks on occupation troops, rather than sites in which to engage in full-scale battles. Pearson, *Scarred Landscapes*, 107–14. See also François Boulet, 'Montagne et résistance en 1943', in Jean-Marie Guillon and Pierre Laborie (eds), *Mémoire et histoire: La Résistance* (Paris: Editions Privat, 1995), 261–9; Gilbert Garrier, 'Montagnes en résistance: Réflexions sur des exemples en Rhône-Alpes', in Jacqueline Sainclivier, and Christian Bougeard (eds), *La Résistance et les Français: Enjeux stratégiques et environnement social* (Rennes: Presses universitaires de Rennes, 1995), 207–20.

53 Quoted in Arthur Layton Funk, *Hidden Ally: The French Resistance, Special Operations, and the Landings in France, 1944* (New York: Greenwood Press, 1992), 69.

54 Quoted at La Fondation Charles de Gaulle website, www.charles-de-gaulle.org/pages/espace-pedagogique/le-point-sur/les-textes-a-connaitre/discours-de-lrsquohotel-de-ville-25-aout-1944.php, accessed 18 April 2011.

55 On the politics of liberation see Herrick Chapman, 'The liberation of France as a moment in state-making', in Kenneth Mouré and Martin S. Alexander (eds), *Crisis and Renewal in France, 1918–1962* (New York: Berghahn, 2002), 74–98.

56 ADC 6 W 4 Préfet du Calvados to Préfet de la Manche, 'Tirs de guerre', 3 June 1944.

57 Figures from Stephen E. Ambrose, *D-Day, June 6, 1944: The Climatic Battle of World War II* (New York: Touchstone, 1995), 24–5.

58 For instance, 'level cultivated land' near Beach 257 at Le Lavandou would allow for easy troop movement but vineyards, marshland, and salt pans were identified as potential obstacles. NA WO 252/198 Inter-Service Topographical Department, 'France-Mediterranean coast: Special report on coast, beaches, and exits from Toulon to the Franco-Italian border including abridged descriptions of the small ports of St. Tropez, St. Raphaël, Cannes, Antibes, Villefranche, and Monoco', 18 March 1943.

59 'The Maures mountains are notable for their dense cover of cork oak, holm oak, Spanish chestnut and pine. The steeper hill slopes are covered with bracken and stunted bushes of lavender and cytise, and the lower valley

slopes are often covered with a dense cover of Spanish chestnut'. NA WO 252/199 Inter-Service Topographical Department, 'Special Report on the Topography of the Mediterranean Coast of France (Toulon to the Italian frontier)', 19 May 1943.

60 André-Georges Lemonier, *Cap sur la Provence* (Paris: Editions France-Empire, 1955), 59–60.

61 Edward P. F. Rose, Jonathan C. Clatworthy, and C. Paul Nathanail, 'Specialist maps prepared by British military geologists for the D-Day landings and operation, Normandy, 1944', *The Cartographic Journal*, 43:2 (2006), 117–43. On military planning and preparation, see *Battle Summary No. 39: Operation 'Neptune', Landings in Normandy June, 1944* (London: HMSO, 1994), 8–75. On the Allied mobilization of geography see Trevor J. Barnes and Matthew Farish, 'Between regions: Science, militarism, and American geography from World War to Cold War', *Annals of the Association of American Geographers*, 96:4 (2006), 807–26.

62 Arthur Davis, 'Geographical factors in the invasion and battle of Normandy', *Geographical Review*, 36:4 (1946), 613–18.

63 As the head of the French meteorological service in Alger noted, weather forecasting was a major factor towards the 'successful running of combined operations'. SHD-DAA 4 D 4 Lieutenant-colonel Chabaud to Commissaire à l'air, Cabinet militaire, Alger, 3 August 1944.

64 Harold A. Winters, Gerald E. Galloway Jr., William J. Reynolds, and David W. Ryne, *Battling the Elements: Weather and Terrain in the Conduct of War* (Baltimore: Johns Hopkins University Press, 1998), 23.

65 On weather and warfare, see Patrick O'Sullivan, *Terrain and Tactics* (Westport: Greenwood Press, 1991); Winters *et al.*, *Battling the Elements*.

66 James Martin Stagg, *Forecast for Overlord, June 6, 1944* (New York: W.W. Norton, 1971); Mildred Berman, 'D-Day and geography', *Geographical Review*, 84:4 (1994), 472–4.

67 Max Hastings, *Overlord: D-Day and the Battle for Normandy* (London: Michael Joseph, 1984), 91. John Slaughter of the 1st Battalion, 116th Infantry witnessed 'dead men floating in the water . . . I was crouching down to chin-deep in the water when I saw mortar shells zeroing in at the water's edge. Sand began to kick up from the small arms fire from the bluffs'. Quoted in Footitt, *War and Liberation*, 40.

68 Ambrose, *D-Day*, 306; John Keegan, *Six Armies in Normandy: From D-Day to the Liberation of Paris, June 6th–August 25th 1944* (London: Jonathan Cape, 1982), 89.

69 Hubert, *Libération d'Isigny-sur-Mer*, 18, 55.

70 J.B. Jackson, *Discovering the Vernacular Landscape* (New Haven: Yale University Press, 1984), 134.

71 Quoted in Albert Pipet, *D'Omaha à St-Lô: La bataille des haies* (Bayeux: Heimdal, 1980), 24. Before becoming the site of the battle of Normandy, the

bocage landscape had also offered possibilities for resistance. André Debron and Louis Pinson, *La Résistance dans le bocage normand* (Paris: Editions Tirésias, 1994).

72 Davis, 'Geographical factors', 618.

73 Quoted in Michael D. Doubler, *Busting the Bocage: American Combined Arms Operations in France, 6 June–31 July 1944* (Fort Leavenworth: US Army Command and General Staff College/Combat Studies Institute, 1988), 21.

74 Quoted in Pipet, *D'Omaha à St-Lô*, 66.

75 Keegan, *Six Armies*, 153.

76 As Patrick O' Sullivan has written, 'the ability to [fight] is conditioned by the lie of the land'. *Terrain and Tactics*, 32.

77 George G. Blackburn, *The Guns of Normandy: A Soldier's Eye View, France 1944* (London: Constable Publishers, 2000), 184–5.

78 Quoted in Ambrose, *D-Day*, 296.

79 Doubler, *Busting the Bocage*, 30–52; Gerald F. Linderman, *The World within War: America's Combat Experience in World War II* (New York: Free Press, 1997), 217–18.

80 Footitt, *War and Liberation*, 42–3; Keegan, *Six Armies*, 207; Hugh Clout, 'From Utah Beach toward reconstruction: Revival in the Manche département of lower Normandy after June 1944', *Journal of Historical Geography*, 35 (2009), 163; Davis, 'Geographical factors', 623.

81 Hugh Clout, 'Beyond the landings: The reconstruction of lower Normandy after June 1944', *Journal of Historical Geography*, 32 (2006), 132.

82 Quoted in Hastings, *Overlord*, 311.

83 NA, AIR 23/4795 Mediterranean Allied Air Forces, Operational Research Section, Bombing Survey Unit, 'Report on field survey of the bombing of the coastal defence guns, St Mandrier peninsula, Toulon'; ADBDR 146 E 4 Inspecteur des Eaux et Forêts, Aix-en-Provence, 'Dommages causés par la guerre à la forêt communale', 31 October 1946; Pearson, *Scarred Landscapes*, 65–6.

84 On the French experience of liberation, see Megan Koreman, *The Expectation of Justice: France, 1944–1946* (Durham, NC: Duke University Press, 1999); Tzvetan Todorov, *A French Tragedy: Scenes of Civil War, Summer 1944* (Hanover, NH: University Press of New England, 1996); Fabrice Virgili, *La France virile: Des femmes tondues à la Libération* (Paris: Payot, 2004).

85 CHAN 307 AP 167 Allied Force HQ, Engineer Section, 'Comment enlever les mines et les pièges', January 1944.

86 Masayo Umezama Duus, *Unlikely Liberators: The Men of the 100th and 442nd*, trans. Peter Duus (Honolulu: University of Hawai'i Press, 1987), 164–7; CHAN F^{10} 7103 Ingénieur en chef du Génie rural to Inspecteur-général du Génie rural, 'Reconstitution agricole', 17 June 1946; CHAN F^{10} 7103 Inspecteur-général du Génie rural to Secrétaire-général de la Commission consultative des dommages et réparations, 23 September 1948.

87 SHD-DAA 4 D 4 Capitaine Liaudet to Général d'armée aérienne, Inspecteur-général de l'armée de l'air et commandant des force aériennes engagées, 'Rapport général sur le bataillon du génie de l'air no. 71', 28 December 1944.

88 Axel H. Oxholm, 'How French forests kept the American army warm', *Journal of Forestry*, 44:5 (1946), 328. On the influence of German forestry on American foresters see Uwe E. Schmidt, 'German impact and influences on American forestry until World War II', *Journal of Forestry*, 107:3 (2009), 139–45.

89 Oxholm, 'How French forests', 327.

90 Pearson, *Scarred Landscapes*, 119–21.

91 ADSM 3344 W 183 'La forêt n'est pas le far-West', newspaper clipping attached to Mouton, Inspecteur des Eaux et Forêt, Fontainebleau, 'Ecole d'Infanterie Américaine', 2 October 1945.

92 On the Franco-American relationship at this time, see Footitt, *War and Liberation*, 185–6.

93 Wendell R. Becton with Elwood Maunder, 'Military forestry in France after 1944', *Forest History*, 16:3 (October 1972), 39.

94 ADAM 88 W 14 Major Lincoln T. Millar to Préfet des Alpes-Maritimes, 'Thrush and wild boar hunting', 8 January 1945.

95 These were Charente-Maritime, Puy-de-Dôme, Savoie, and Vendée. Of course, the lack of damage might be attributable to missing statistics. Commission consultative, *Dommages subis par la France*, vol. 1, 234–9.

96 Commission consultative, *Dommages subis par la France*, vol. 1, xxii; Vergeot, *Rapport sur le problème*, 50.

97 Pearson, *Scarred Landscapes*, 66.

98 Danièle Voldman, *Le déminage de France après 1945* (Paris: Editions Odile Jacob, 1998), 36–46.

99 The Ministry for Reconstruction and Urbanism hired civilian contractors to clear the beaches with mixed results. Scrap merchants only took valuable metal and some contractors only cut wrecks down to beach level, meaning that they became exposed again during severe storms. Away from the coastline, unexploded munitions lay scattered across the Normandy countryside: by June 1946 858,620 shells and bombs had been dealt with. Clout, 'Beyond the Landings', 134; Clout, 'From Utah Beach toward reconstruction', 174.

100 ADAM 109 W 34 Préfet des Alpes-Maritimes to Maire de Vallauris, 8 May 1945; Clout, 'From Utah Beach toward reconstruction', 171.

101 Clout, 'Beyond the landings', 133–4; CACAN 19771615/77 Conservateur des Eaux et Forêts, Niort, 'Déminage de la forêt de la Courbe (ex-poche de Royan)', 4 February 1949.

102 Voldman, *Déminage de France*, 46; Pearson, *Scarred Landscapes*, 129.

103 Commission consultative, *Dommages subis par la France*, vol. 1, 234–9.

104 Hugh Clout, 'Ruins and revival: Paris in the aftermath of the Second

World War', *Landscape Research*, 29:2 (2004), 117–39; Pearson, *Scarred Landscapes*, 130–40; Sara B. Pritchard, 'Paris et le désert français: Urban and rural environments in post-World War II France', in Andrew C. Isenberg (ed.), *The Nature of Cities* (Rochester: University of Rochester Press, 2006), 175–91; Danièle Voldman, *La reconstruction des villes françaises de 1940 à 1954: Histoire d'une politique* (Paris: L'Harmattan, 1997).

105 The American Battle Monuments Commission, *Normandy American Cemetery and Memorial* (U.S. Government Printing Office, 1957), 5, 10, 12.

106 Normandie Mémoire website, www.normandiememoire.com, accessed 8 June 2011. See also David Livingstone, 'Remembering on foreign soil: The activities of the German War Graves Commission', in Bill Niven and Chloe Paver (eds), *Memorialization in Germany since 1945* (Basingstoke: Palgrave Macmillan, 2010), 69–77; Serge Barcellini and Annette Wieviorka, *Passant, souviens-toi! Les lieux du souvenir de la Seconde Guerre Mondiale en France* (Paris: Plon, 1995).

107 On anti-Americanism, see Richard Kuisel, *Seducing the French*.

108 Partick Facon, 'US forces in France, 1945–1958', in Simon Duke and Wolfgand Krieger (eds), *US Military Forces in Europe: The Early Years, 1945–1970* (Boulder: Westview Press, 1993), 237–8; Pottier, *Bases américaines*, 18.

109 Olivier Pottier, 'Les bases américaines en France: Un outil militaire, économique et politique (1950–1967)', *Revue historique des armées*, 215 (June 1999), 64. On the Fourth Republic as an active force in Cold War Europe, see Creswell, *Question of Balance*; Hitchcock, *France Restored*. On US bases in Europe, see Duke, *United States Military*; Diana Johnstone and Ben Cramer, 'The burdens and the glory: US bases in Europe', in Gerson and Birchard, *The Sun Never Sets*, 199–223. On France's relationship with NATO, see Frédéric Bozo, *La France et l'OTAN: De la guerre froide au nouvel ordre européen* (Paris: Masson, 1991).

110 On the links between environmental and diplomatic history, see Kurk Dorsey, 'Dealing with the dinosaur (and its swamp): Putting the environment in diplomatic history, *Diplomatic History*, 29:4 (2005), 573–87.

111 SHD-DAA 50 E 36470/1 'Accord entre la République française et les Etats-unis d'Amérique concernant certains aérodromes et installations en France métropolitaine mis à la disposition de l'armée de l'air des Etats-unis', 4 October 1952; Pottier, *Bases américaines*, 46–7; Facon, 'US Forces in France', 240.

112 By 1 February 1959 61,000 US military personnel were stationed on France soil (35,000 from the army and 26,000 from the air force) along with approximately 40,000 US civilians and 3,000 Canadian air force personnel and their families. Pottier, *Bases américaines*, 49, 52, 68–78, 86–91, 240–59. See also Philippe Mauffrey, *Phalsbourg air base: Histoire de la base de Phalsbourg période américaine 1953–1967* (Drulingen: Imprimerie Scheuer 1990), 7, 21.

113 SHD-DAA 02 E 2932 'Procès-verbal de la réunion restreinte du Conseil supérieur de l'infrastructure et de la navigation aériennes', 2 April 1954.

114 SHD-DAA 02 E 2932 'Procès-verbal de la séance restreinte du Conseil supérieur de l'infrastructure et de la Navigation Aériennes du 27 juin 1952'.

115 Mauffrey, *Phalsbourg air base*, 21.

116 SHD-DAA 02 E 2932 'Procès-verbal de la séance restreinte du Conseil supérieur de l'infrastructure et de la navigation aériennes du 26 juin 1953'; SHD-DAA 24 E 2068 Inspecteur général B. Gaspard, 'Détermination du site d'un aérodrome compris dans la 3ème tranche d'infrastructure interalliée, prévu dans la quadrilatère Lille, Boulogne, Abbeville, et Rosiers-en-Santerre', 21 October 1954. For disputes at other sites, see François Jarraud, *Les Américains à Châteauroux 1951–1967* (Le Poinçonnet: chez l'auteur, 1981), 18; and files in SHD-DAA 3 E 357.

117 Endy, *Cold War Holidays*, 12.

118 SHD-DAT 9 R 271 Corps de contrôle de l'administration de l'armée, No. 74/RN, 'Rapport particular sur la construction des routes du camp américain de Captieux', 29 November 1954.

119 SHD-DAT 9 R 271 'Compte-rendu de la réunion qui a eu lieu à Bordeaux le 5 août 1953, au sujet des inondations dues au système de drainage de Captieux'.

120 Wall, *United States*, 298.

121 Pierre D., 'Pour la préservation de nos sites forestiers', *La Libérté*, 15 January 1952. On the creation of Fontainebleau as a tourist destination in the mid-nineteenth century, see Caroline Ford, 'Nature, culture, and conservation in France and her colonies, 1840–1940', *Past and Present*, 183 (2004), 181–8; Nicholas Green, *The Spectacle of Nature: Landscape and Bourgeois Culture in Nineteenth-Century France* (Manchester: Manchester University Press, 1990), 167–81.

122 '40 hectares de la forêt de Fontainebleau seront rasés pour loger l'Etat-major "Centre-Europe,"' *La Marseillaise de Seine et Marne*, 31 August 1951.

123 Gérard Simier, 'Le déboisement prochain de 40 ha ne massacrera pas la forêt de Fontainebleau', newspaper clipping in ADSM 3344 W 187.

124 'La forêt doit être défendue contre les saccageurs', newspaper clipping from *La Marseillaise de Seine et Marne* in ADSM 3344 W 187; ADSM 3344 W 187 Secrétaire général des Amis de la forêt de Fontainebleau to Directeur général des Eaux et Forêts, 5 November 1951. On US perceptions of the French landscape, see Endy, *Cold War Holidays*, 63–4, 166.

125 SHD-DAT 13 T 103 Général de corps d'armée Morlière to Secrétaire d'état aux Forces armées terre, 21 November 1956. On the tension between the forest's preservation and productivity, see Ford, 'Nature, culture, and conservation', 181–8.

126 He also attacked 'abusive' felling that undermined the US military's claim that the camouflage offered by forests was one of the reasons that many of

their depots were situated in them. CAC 19870398/6 Conservateur des Eaux et Forêts chargé du 3ème Bureau, 'Note pour Monsieur le Directeur général', [n.d. 1955?].

127 CAC 19870398/6 Secrétaire d'état à l'Agriculture, Direction générale des Eaux et Forêts to Président du Conseil des ministres, Secrétariat général permanent de la Défense nationale, 'Projet d'implantation américaine dans des terrains boisés situés dans la région de Reims', 1 March 1956.

128 Secrétaire d'état à l'Agriculture, 'Implantation du sub-dépôt de Chaumont' [n.d.]; CACAN 19870398/6 Secrétaire d'état à l'Agriculture, Direction générale des Eaux et Forêts, to Chef de la Mission centrale de liaison pour l'assistance aux armées alliées, 'Sub-dépôt de Chaumont', 4 July 1956; Pottier, *Bases américaines*, 69.

129 The forest administration had historically maintained close relations with the French army. Tamara Whited, *Forests and Peasant Politics in Modern France* (New Haven and London: Yale University Press, 2000), 31–3.

130 Secrétaire général des Amis de la forêt de Fontainebleau to Directeur général des Eaux et Forêts.

131 CAC 19870398/5 Secrétaire d'état à l'Equipement et au Plan agricole to Secrétaire d'état aux Forces armées 'air,' Direction de l'infrastructure, Bureau de domaine, 'Implantation d'une station radiogonic dans la forêt domaniale de Pfaffenbronn (Bas-Rhin),' 28 June 1957; CACAN 19870398/6 Ingénieur principal des Eaux et Forêts, Versailles, 'Utilisation du "Plateau Saint-Martin" pour un exercise de SHAPE,' 13 January 1956; CACAN 19870398/6 Ministre de l'Agriculture to Ministre de la Défense nationale, 19 January 1956.

132 SHD-DAA 50 E 36476/1 Ponts et Chaussées Ingénieur d'arrondissement, Service des bases aériennes, Ainse, 'Aérodrome de Laon-Couvron: Entretien des installations extérieures à l'aérodrome', 19 August 1954; SHD-DAA 50 E 36476/1 Chef du Service de l'infrastructure to Directeur, Etat-major de l'USAFE, Paris, 'Entretien intérieur des aérodromes occupés par l'USAFE: Fauchage des herbes', 20 September 1954; SHD-DAA 50 E 36476/1 Donald H. King, Acting Director, USAFE, Paris, to Secrétariat d'état aux Forces armées 'air', Service de l'infrastructure, 18 October 1954.

133 SHD-DAT 13 T 150 Ministre des Armées to Général commandant la 4ème Région militaire, 'Déminage d'un champ de mines au dépôt US', 17 December 1963. On opposition to US bases, see Kuisel, *Seducing the French*, 38–40; Michel Winock, 'Les attitudes des français face à la présence américaine (1951–1967)', in Maurice Vaïsse, Pierre Mélandri, and Frédéric Bozo (eds), *La France et l'OTAN* (Brussels: Editions Complexe, 1996), 323–30.

134 Pottier, *Bases américaines*, 290–1, 309–10.

135 Kuisel, *Seducing the French*, 33.

136 *Phalsbourg Falcon*, 18 May 1962; *Phalsbourg Falcon*, 29 June 1962.

137 'Bienvenue à la Base de Phalsbourg', *Phalsbourg Falcon*, 18 May 1962.

138 Endy, *Cold War Holidays*, 100–24.

139 Pottier, *Bases américaines*, 266–7. On US base pollution in Germany, see Yarrow Cleaves, 'US military presence in Germany', in Gerson and Birchard, *Sun Never Sets*, 225–46.

140 Pottier, 'Bases américaines', 71; Facon, 'U.S. Forces in France', 246–7. On US–Franco relations in the early 1960s, see Erin R. Mahan, *Kennedy, De Gaulle and Western Europe* (Basingstoke: Palgrave Macmillan, 2002).

141 Further agreements in March 1967 and February 1968 allowed the US to continue to use its pipeline and set the amount that France was to pay for the installations the US left behind. FRELOC stood for Fast Relocation. Pottier, 'Bases américaines', 72–6. The US lost over $20 million of its investment in its French installations when it handed them over to France. Duke, *United States Military*, 154.

142 SHD-DAA 50E 36476/2 Ponts et Chaussées Ingénieur d'Arrondissement, Laon, 'Démolition des installations d'infrastructure O.T.A.N.: Aérodrome de Berry-au-Bac-Juvincourt', 19 November 1965; SHD-DAA 50E 36476/2 Ponts et Chaussées, Département de l'Aisne, Service des Base aériennes, 'Aérodrome de Juvincourt: Remise en état de culture, détail estimatif', 19 Novembre 1965.

143 Pottier, *Bases américaines*, 348–9; SHD-DAT 13 T 275 'Fiche faisant le point au 10.04.1971'.

144 Pottier, *Bases américanes*, 348.

145 SHD-DAT 13 T 150 Général de Division Multrier, 'Dévolution du camp de Captieux (Gironde)', 13 July 1967; SHD-DAT 13 T 150 'Utilisation du terrain de Captieux', 12 October 1966; SHD-DAT 13 T 150 Commandant Avalle, 'Camp de Captieux de Poteau', 27 January 1967.

146 Mission interministerielle pour l'amémagement de la côte aquitaine, 'Compte-rendu de la réunion de la mission du 28 octobre 1968 (extrait)'.

7

'A (very) large military camp':
The militarization of postwar France

Nestling amongst dusty letters and reports in a box in the French army archives lies a crudely drawn map that imagines how France will look in 1980.[1] Paris, where all the French people live, is surrounded by barbed wire. The rest of France is a '[very] large military camp', symbolized by a tank/skull-and-crossbones hybrid. The map is undated and its author unknown. Nonetheless, it expresses vividly the fear that postwar national defence imperatives would almost-totally militarize French territory.

Alongside the NATO militarized environments discussed in the last chapter, French militarized environments proliferated in the postwar period. The reasons behind this military geographical expansion were numerous. Most importantly, Cold War geopolitics and weaponry moti-vated the armed forces to seek ever larger training grounds and weapons testing sites. So although mainland France did not play host to anything as dramatic as the Agent Orange-induced defoliation of Vietnamese jungle or mushroom-shaped clouds caused by atomic weapons testing, the Cold War ushered in a new layer of militarized environments. France was therefore part of the Cold War's global environmental history and geography.[2]

Decolonization gave French Cold War-era militarized environments a particular twist. From culture to politics, decolonization informed and transformed French society in a myriad of ways.[3] Through a focus on militarized environments this chapter sketches out some of its envi-ronmental dimensions, even if the in-depth environmental histories of France's wars of decolonization lie outside this book's scope.[4] Like decol-onization, Charles de Gaulle's search for French *grandeur* and autonomy on the world had a strong bearing on the history of French militarized environments.[5] In other words, decolonization and foreign policies had environmental underpinnings and repercussions, explored here through the militarization of ever greater swathes of the French countryside.

Within the *longue durée* history of French militarized environments, the postwar period saw elements of change and continuity. The cost of land and other restraints in northern and eastern France drew military planners increasingly towards southern and western France. A further significant development was the storage, if not the testing, of nuclear weapons on French soil. But the military still continued to favour economically marginal and supposedly 'empty' land for its training grounds and testing sites. And, as it has done since at least the creation of Châlons Camp, it sought to tie its mobilization of nature to wider national concerns. In post-1945 France, military officials linked militarization with territorial balance, modernization, and rationalization. Influenced, in part, by geographer Jean-François Gravier's book *Paris et le désert français* (1947), and building on the experience gained and institutions established under the Vichy regime, state officials strove to modernize France's regions, thereby rendering them more economically productive and rational.[6] In this context, the military portrayed its geographical expansion as integral to centrally-led territorial modernization. Updating and expanding Napoleon III's rhetoric of military-led territorial improvement, they claimed that in addition to ensuring national security, army camps and other installations would act as vectors of modernization and economic progress in France's backward regions.

Whether as a genuine belief or a ploy to convince politicians and affected populations, the military bathed its mobilization of nature in the rhetorical glow of modernization. Its faith in centrally and rationally planned schemes corresponds with James C. Scott's model of high-modernist projects.[7] But throughout their expansion of militarized environments, the military's attention was repeatedly drawn to local concerns and opposition. Echoing other areas of French society, modernization was hardly a smooth process, as the postwar history of militarized environments amply demonstrates.

Thwarted militarization during the Fourth Republic

France's humiliating and rapid defeat in 1940 underscored the need for military reform in the postwar era. But throughout the Fourth Republic, endless reforms, political instability, poor morale, reduced budgets, and clashes between army, navy and air force chiefs hindered rearmament and modernization.[8] The slow pace of reform, however, did not dampen the army's expansionary ambitions as it sought to expand existing camps and create new ones.

The continued faith in training troops outdoors motivated army commanders. In April 1946 General Lattre de Tassigny requested the creation of fifty-six light training camps. A year later General Péchaud du Rieu stressed the importance of instruction camps in the formation of modern armies. According to his analysis, training in urban garrisons was obsolete. The soldier of tomorrow would fight in the vast spaces of tropical or semi-polar climes. It was impossible to train for such combat in the tight confines of urban training grounds 'far from natural sites and their obstacles'.[9] In an era of colonial conflicts and possible Cold War confrontation, army chiefs believed that the army required access to physically demanding rural environments.

The faith in outdoor training had a very recent precedent. During the Vichy years, army officers under the guidance of General de la Porte du Theil had established the Chantiers de la Jeunesse camps to physically and morally restore young men (who in normal conditions would have gone into the army) through living and working outdoors. Belief in nature's improving influence on men tainted by the vices of modern urban living lay at the core of the Chantiers' philosophy. 'Contact with nature' would provide 'virile training' and lead to the 'reconstruction of the country'.[10] Vichy-esque ruralism may have been largely discredited in postwar France but military leaders had not lost their faith in the benefits of training young recruits within, in Péchaud du Rieu's words, 'an atmosphere of fresh air and space'. Having experienced outdoor life, recruits would supposedly leave army camps 'physically and morally invigorated, transformed, and improved'.[11] Attempting to renew French masculinity through the mobilization of nature was yet another bridge between the wartime and postwar periods.[12]

Péchaud du Rieu's ideas also echoed those of Napoleon III and his supporters, who had claimed that military training at Châlons Camp would create a modern and efficient imperial army (see chapter 1). In the 1940s and 1950s, however, the training environment need not be French. Along with extracting timber from its zone of Occupation in Germany,[13] France harnessed the occupied territory for military training. In 1945, the French army moved its artillery school to Idar-Oberstein in the French zone of occupation in Germany to take advantage of the nearby Baumholder range, 'one of [Europe's] finest'. At this 'grandiose site', French soldiers would henceforth train before deployment against the

Viet Minh in Indochina.[14] As military cooperation replaced the Allied occupation of Germany, France continued to mobilize the environment of the Federal Republic of Germany for military training until its withdrawal from NATO integrated command in 1966.[15]

Nonetheless, the French environment remained the home of military training where the increased range and speed of Cold War-era weaponry pushed the military to find new sites for testing and training. In 1950 the navy turned its existing firing range on Ile du Levant (see chapter 3) into a missile testing site. Lying off the Var coastline, the island offered seclusion and water deep enough to test submarines, yet was close to the naval base at Toulon and air bases at Istres, Hyères and Saint-Raphaël. Henceforth, the majority of the island would play host to a modern weapons testing facility while a small section around Héliopolis continued to develop as a naturist holiday resort. The military and naturists both enjoyed the island's privacy. But whilst the former used the site's environment to test weapons, the latter claimed to seek physical relaxation and renewal amidst its jagged cliffs, *maquis* vegetation and inviting waters.[16]

The island's militarization did not run smoothly due to the tensions between militarization and development of mass tourism in postwar France, as increasing numbers of French workers headed south to enjoy their paid vacations on the coast.[17] Politicians in the Var, cognizant of tourism's economic importance, complained that missiles were landing near tourists and restricting access to the island. Furthermore, the mayors of coastal towns issued a statement declaring that the navy's activities threatened the 'natural beauties' of the coastline and islands, which comprised part of France's 'national heritage'. In a conciliatory gesture, the navy agreed to keep the island's camp site and some walking routes open and promised not to fire certain missiles during the peak holiday season from July to September.[18]

If anything, the co-existence of military and civilian environments was even more fraught inland. In September 1951, Secretary of State for War Georges Bidault asked the commanders of each military region to consider which camps could be extended to accommodate the increased range of modern artillery and armoured vehicles. To allow for manoeuvres of an infantry division or an armoured group, the firing of weapons up to the 76 mm tank gun, and inter-army combat training with live ammunition, he ordered that each camp have a width of 8–12 km and a length of 15–18 km. In recognition that such camps would be hard to establish, sites in mountainous areas or along coastlines were to be favoured. The relief and watery expanses of such areas as the Alps, Cévennes, and Camargue would, Bidault hoped, allow for smaller, and therefore less contentious and expensive, security zones.[19]

Bidault's recognition of the difficulties of expanding military lands was well-founded. On 15 December 1951 General Zeller, military governor of Metz, and commander of the sixth army region, ordered a 3,000 ha extension of Mailly Camp. An army engineer report claimed that 70 per cent of the proposed extension area comprised 'wastelands' (*friches*) and pine woodlands.[20] But, as the report predicted, determined local opposition greeted Zeller's decision. *L'Aube* newspaper recognized that whilst modern warfare on a continental scale required bigger training camps, local people had 'good reason' to be upset by the army's plans as they were 'strongly attached' to the land that 'nourished' them.[21] Similarly, Marcel Degois in *L'Eclair-Est* claimed that the extension threatened 'economic asphyxia' and would trigger a 'tragic and uncertain [rural] exodus'. Such an eventuality should be avoided because fertilizers and tractors had recently transformed this corner of *la Champagne pouilleuse* into a centre of agriculture.[22] Civilians once again equated militarization with the sterilization of fertile land.

As with NATO installations (see chapter 6), foresters proved uncooperative during the creation of French militarized environments. They protested a proposed firing range near Mont-de-Marsan (Landes), pointing to forest fire risks and reduced timber production.[23] To counter potential objections from foresters, military engineers made reassuring noises, suggesting, on at least one occasion, that it was in the military's interest to preserve forest cover around their installations for camouflage.[24] However, such attempts at reconciliation had little impact. In the nineteenth century, the forest administration drew retired army officers into its ranks and foresters wore military-style uniforms and adopted quasi-military training.[25] But by the mid-twentieth century its exasperation with militarization's impact on France's forests was apparent.[26]

Army officers were painfully aware of the difficultly of securing firing ranges in a heavily domesticated country, such as France, with 'few vast spaces' available.[27] To ease the army's growing pains they looked south, turning their attention to the apparently empty plan de Canjuers, an arid, karst limestone plateau covered by *maquis*, forests, and pastureland in the north of the Var *département*, where they hoped to create a 26,048 ha firing range. Their plans met with fierce local opposition. The Var's Conseil général issued a statement protesting that the army's scheme

would destroy sheep-rearing, lavender exploitation, farming and communication routes, as well as placing the nationally important Gorges de
Verdon at risk. The Var's commission on sites and natural monuments
similarly feared that the firing range would ruin Aiguines forest's 'absolutely exceptional' beech plantations.[28] Further 'expert' opposition came
from foresters who wrote to defend the area's forestry production, pasturing and picturesque qualities. Arthur Dugelay, the forestry conservator in Nice who had been horrified by the Second World War's impact on
Mediterranean forests, feared that this latest form of militarization would
upset the region's 'sylvo-pastoral balance' and destroy Châteaudouble
forest, a 'splendid . . . curiosity' of national importance'.[29]

The political pressure mounted when local councils threatened to
resign if the plans went ahead and when newspapers joined the protests.
The left-wing paper *La Marseillaise* argued that the army's proposal
heralded the area's ruin, besmirched its recent resistance history, and
brought Cold War 'politics' to the Var.[30] Cold War anxieties lent a particular flavour to the anti-Canjuers protest in other ways. Louis Gonjon,
head of the Syndicat de défense du Haut-Var, warned that the army's
plans brought the threat of nuclear attack to Provence.[31] In a *département* with a strong democratic and socialist heritage, left-wing anti-
Americanism also informed the protests: *La Marseillaise* hinted darkly
that the Americans were behind the plans.[32] The potential militarization
of culturally significant environments brought Cold War geopolitics
home and made them real. In such a way, Canjuers became part of the
Cold War's 'home front'.[33]

Differing ideas about nature infused the discussion as journalists
debated the true meaning of Canjuers, focusing on its emptiness. The left-
leaning newspaper *Provençal* highlighted, in poetic language, the camp's
threat to the area's natural beauty and 'silence'. Its emptiness should be
preserved rather than sacrificed to militarization. The newspaper evoked
the language of Provencal writer Jean Giono, who had declared that the
silence of Canjuers was such that the 'cry of larks seems monstrous', as
well as resistance publications that had celebrated regionalism in the
1940s. In contrast, an article in the right-wing paper *Nice-Matin* argued
that the deserted 'land of crows and vipers' held little interest; while its
forests might inspire poets, they could not bring prosperity to the region,
unlike a military camp.[34]

But beyond the politicized dispute over the area's supposed emptiness,
public opinion was firmly against the army's plans. In response to this
opposition, the army revised the firing range's boundaries to avoid such

sites as Aiguines forest and reduced its size.[35] The concession shows that there was some room for manoeuvre between competing military and civilian interests. The army was hardly faring better with its extension of Mailly Camp. Repeated foot-dragging and delays due to local elections meant that the army had only secured 90 ha by 1956. By November 1957 the figure had risen to 350 ha, which was still well short of the 800 ha target.[36] From the agricultural land of Champagne to the wilder Canjuers region, the army struggled to expand geographically under the Fourth Republic. Its narrative of military necessity and economic modernization had failed to win over sceptical civilians.

Militarized environments and decolonization

As it battled against civilian opposition in metropolitan France, the army engaged in bloody and morale-sapping wars against decolonization as the Fourth Republic struggled to hold onto France's colonies. In the wake of rising public hostility to the war and the army's humiliating defeat at Dien Pien Phu, Pierre Mendès-France negotiated the withdrawal of French forces from Indochina in 1954 having failed to overcome the Viet Minh. But the outbreak of war against Algerian independence in the same year meant that French officers and soldiers continued to spend the majority of their time away from France. Indeed, one of the civilian arguments against Mailly Camp's extension was that between 1954 and 1956 its military use lessened because of the Algerian war.[37] Nonetheless, metropolitan camps remained important sites of war preparation for fighting overseas. Conscript Jean-Marie Gille remembers training at Suippes Camp where he and his fellow soldiers were sent out from the poorly heated barracks into the 'surrounding nature' to run around, 'crawl like animals', and march in all weathers. Although it recalled his childhood war games, Gille felt that the training prepared troops for Algeria and portrays it as a masculine rite of passage: it 'made men out of us'.[38]

Maximizing the use of training camps was one of the ways in which the army tried to improve its performance in Algeria. In 1957 the Secretary of State for the Army asserted that life in the camps should convince the recruits of the 'value of France's objectives' in Algeria, whilst training should help them to physically withstand fatigue and imbue them with an 'aggressive [combat] spirit'. The qualities of forbearance and hardiness were to be developed 'in the great outdoors' (*au grand air*), where the recruit was also to learn how to read and use terrain to his advantage, a key concern in anti-guerrilla operations. Overall, training was intended to gradually expose recruits to Algeria-like conditions.[39] Metropolitan militarized environments, such as Suippes Camp, underpinned the army's campaign in Algeria, although we need to question whether soldiers left them convinced of the 'value of France's objectives', especially as the de-moralizing and unpopular war dragged on.[40]

The Secretary of State's instructions sought to overcome one of the main difficulties facing the French army in Algeria: terrain. French soldiers had already battled against the swamps and forests of Indochina, which guerrilla forces had turned to their advantage. The U Minh forest, for instance, had become a 'modern kind of hell' for French soldiers.[41] In Algeria, it was mountainous regions that provided sites of resistance and refuge, once *maquisards* of the Armée de libération nationale (ALN) began to exploit them. In its struggle against the ALN, the French army created new militarized environments, such as the militarization of the Moroccan and Tunisian borders with electric fences, barbed wire, armed patrols, and 3,200,000 mines.[42]

As the war intensified, distinctions between civilian and military environments became ever more blurred. Military theorist Roger Trinquier wrote that 'the battlefield today is no longer restricted. It is limitless; it can encompass entire nations. The inhabitant in his home is the center of the conflict'.[43] This militarized conception of civilian spheres came at a high human cost.[44]

The war's political repercussions in Algeria and France were far-reaching. The deployment of millions of increasingly disenchanted young conscript soldiers inclined French public opinion against the war and, as the counter-insurgency operations dragged on, its brutality deepened. Both sides committed atrocities, but the French army's systematic use of torture remains a particular source of controversy. International condemnation of French tactics, amongst other factors, caused the Fourth Republic to stutter and finally crumble as French Algerians (or *pieds-noirs*) seized government buildings in Algiers, backed by certain French generals. Charles de Gaulle emerged as the figure to resolve the situation. His plans for a new constitution were backed in the referendum of 28 September 1958: the Fifth Republic was born. With France floundering in Algeria, de Gaulle asserted, on 16 September 1959, that Algeria had the right to self-determination. The French backed de Gaulle's decision in favour of an Algerian republic in a referendum and, amidst continuing violence in France and Algeria, a ceasefire was signed on 18 March 1962, sealing Algerian independence.

The end of French colonial rule in Algeria had huge political, social, and cultural repercussions.[45] Of interest here is the impact on militarized environments in mainland France. For a start, the French state mobilized the relative seclusion and security of army camps to accommodate *harkis* (the name given to Algerians who had fought on the French side during the war) who were subjected to massacres and persecution after the declaration of Algerian independence. The 60,000 *harkis* who managed to escape to France met with indifference and humiliation as they were housed in army transit camps at Larzac and Bourg-Lastic. Military bases suited the government wish to contain *harkis*; they provided accommodation (however rudimentary), security and a degree of separation from French civilians. As the *harkis* began to arrive at Larzac, the army hastily secured tents and other supplies to accommodate them.[46]

But Larzac was only a temporary measure as the army moved the *harkis* on to Rivesaltes Camp. By December 1962, Rivesaltes housed 12,000 *harkis* in barracks and tents.[47] Army instructions charged the camp's commander with ensuring their 'physical and moral health'. But in reality, life was harsh. The conditions of the Second World War-era internment camp at Rivesaltes were not reproduced in their entirety; charitable organisations were more involved and the army provided better food. But environmental factors still combined with administrative indifference and a sense of isolation to produce harsh, and at times deadly, conditions; winter 1962 was bitterly cold and dozens of children died in snow-covered tents.[48] The sometimes tragic use of military bases as transit camps demonstrates once again their malleability and role in French history.

The internment of *harkis* on army bases was part and parcel of the wider reshaping of postcolonial France. Decolonization and the withdrawal from Algeria spurred military commanders to seek new mobilizations of the French environment. Following the abandonment of the weapons testing facility at Colomb-Béchar in Algeria, the French state established the Centre d'essais des Landes (CEL) near Biscarrosse in south-western France. The CEL extended an existing militarized environment. In the 1930s the army had militarized this stretch of forest, dune, and Atlantic coastline with its anti-aircraft range and camp at Naouas, which German forces had then modernized during the war. In the 1950s the army continued to use the site as an anti-aircraft range, while the air force installed a firing range at Biscarrosse plage despite opposition from foresters and fishermen.[49]

Researching and testing high-tech, long-range weaponry came before foresters' and fishermen's interests and even those of the army which wanted to maintain its anti-aircraft range and create a 7,500 ha training site.[50] With the situation deteriorating in Algeria, military commanders approved the recently created Délégation ministérielle pour l'Armement's (DMA) decision to establish the CEL.[51] The weight of national defence imperatives overrode any lingering opposition of the forest administration, which granted the DMA 13,000 ha of state forest. The CEL would henceforth mobilize the 'physical security' offered by the forests, dunes, and coastline to test missiles and other weapons.[52] In such a way, the decolonization of Algeria led to the army's 'internal colonization' of metropolitan France. In a similar vein, military reports repeatedly claimed that the army needed more camps in southern France because of the return of troops from Algeria.[53]

Kristen Ross has argued that during decolonization France's technocrats applied colonial techniques of spatial organisation to metropolitan France.[54] It is hard not to see the military expansion into the 'empty' and 'backward' *midi* in this light, especially as the *maghreb* environment acted as a point of reference for military personnel recently returned from North Africa. Captain Godard, for instance, compared the Cantayrac and Poux negre streams on Caylus plateau to the 'wadis' of North Africa.[55] Decolonization added a new twist to the army's longstanding view that depopulated and economically marginal land was fit only for militarization.

Gaullist foreign policy and military expansion

Decolonization spurred the expansion of French militarized environments. Other factors also came into play. Sociologists Gregory Hooks and Chad Smith highlight how US military base expansion during the Second World War and the Cold War took place within 'a distinct expansionary dynamic' sustained by geopolitics and the arms race.[56] Whilst national differences remain important, an analogous development unfolded in France. Forged within the context of Cold War geopolitics, Gaullist foreign policy and the development of ever more powerful weaponry prompted the military to seek new and larger territories.

Despite some continuity with the Fourth Republic, Charles de Gaulle's foreign policy led to reconfigurations of France's militarized environments. Gaullist foreign policy played down the importance of empire, which up until then had been treated as a guarantor of French greatness. Gaullist foreign policy placed more importance on the search for French *grandeur* and autonomy on the world stage through less dependence on the USA, and non-alignment between US and Soviet blocs. The defence of national sovereignty through conventional and nuclear weapons was deemed essential. As de Gaulle stated, 'the Government [has] as its raison d'être the defence of independence and integrity of the territory'.[57]

The Gaullist view that military modernization and strengthening were vital to France's national security and international status led to new militarized environments. A report in 1961 by General Le Puloch, the army's chief of staff, set out to identify and remedy training and weapons testing deficiencies. Adopting a form of technological determinism, the report argued that weapons' increased range and the heightened mobility of modern warfare made France's training facilities inadequate. Urban garrisons with their small training grounds held little military interest. Space was of the essence: training grounds of 2,000 ha and over were desirable. But even the army's largest camps, such as Suippes, Mourmelon, and Mailly, were found lacking: none allowed a mechanized brigade to train in a 'nuclear ambience'.[58]

Furthermore, the majority of the army's large camps were located north of the Cherbourg-Lyon line (which was marked on the map accompanying Le Puloch's report) in the most industrial and agriculturally rich part of the country. This geographical distribution was unfortunate in Le Puloch's view because the south offered better training conditions due to its light and 'gentle climate'.[59] In short, France's main training grounds were too small and in the wrong place. Le Puloch's report marked a turning point in military geographical thinking. If realized, the army's training centre of gravity would no longer be the plains of Champagne. Instead, it would mobilize heathlands and other economically marginal land in the west and the *midi*.

Like its civilian counterpart, the militarized arm of the state stressed the need for territorial balance and rationalization.[60] To make up a perceived geographical deficit of 55,000 ha, Le Puloch outlined how the army was currently searching for sites south of the Cherbourg-Lyon line to take advantage of cheaper land, better climatic conditions, and to counter the over-militarization of the north-east. The sites already under consideration were a 25,000 ha camp at Monts d'Arrée (Finistère), a 5,000 ha camp at Montagne de Berg (Ardèche), a 2,500 ha camp at Villemaury (Aude), and, in a revival of the 1950s plan, a camp at Canjuers. In addition, Le Puloch recommended extensions of Caylus and Garrigues camps.[61]

Although the army's reputation was severely tarnished after the Algerian war and the Gaullist priority was to obtain nuclear weapons (see below), the government approved many of Le Puloch's recommendations. In particular, it authorized a 50,000 ha increase of army lands through the creation of new large camps, the expansion of existing camps and a number of smaller acquisitions.[62] But significant gaps emerged between Le Puloch's aims and what could be achieved on the ground. Some of his projects, most notably the Mont d'Arrée camp, remained a glint in his eye. Others, however, saw the light of day. Most significantly, Minister for Armed Forces Pierre Messmer gave the go-ahead for the Canjuers project in October 1962. At 30,000 ha, the camp would be approximately twice the size of France's existing biggest camp at Suippes.

The army's rationale for militarizing Canjuers drew heavily on Le Puloch's report and stressed how modern forms of combat and the loss of army lands in Algeria necessitated the camp's creation. The army's language played down its own agency in selecting the plan de Canjuers for militarization. Instead, it advanced arguments resting on environmental determinism, thereby naturalizing its choice of the camp's location. More or less reproducing the military arguments used to justify the location of Châlons Camp (see chapter 1), a preliminary army report argued that the geography of Canjuers' had practically determined its militarization: it boasted a varied terrain, low population density, and excellent climatic and light conditions that allowed for year-round training. It argued how France's changing geographies had forced the army to consider southern France; Canjuers was ideal because militarization in the north east had reached a 'saturation' point and the land there was prohibitively expensive. The report also drew on technological determinism when it outlined how 30,000 ha were necessary for the training of a mechanized brigade and the firing of 155mm cannons.[63] The establishment of new militarized environments, such as Canjuers, were the environmental underpinnings of Gaullist foreign policy. But their creation was controversial. In response, the military sought to tie its expansion to wider societal concerns.

Militarized modernization

Expansion and modernization were the order of the day for the army. It launched two commissions, one headed by General Fayard to study the modernization of its camps' built environments, and one headed by General Besson to maximize the use of existing training grounds through a more efficient deployment of manoeuvring grounds and firing ranges. Besson's commission achieved some success, freeing up an additional 7,000 ha by 1969. The modernization of the built environment was far more drawn out and costly – initial estimates were put at 200 million francs – and by 1969 only a quarter of the commission's recommendations had been completed due to budget constraints.[64] Nonetheless, the reports underscore the army's desire to rationalize and maximize the use of its installations.

The language of military-led modernization emerged once more as military engineers portrayed militarization as a vector of modernization. In creating the CEL, military engineers boasted of how they constructed over 190,000 m² of buildings, 270 km of roads, and 50,000 m² of parking areas amongst the forest plantations of the Landes. Whilst taking pride in the gleaming modernity of this infrastructure, they claimed to have integrated it within the environment.[65] In their view, weapons testing could co-exist harmoniously with forest plantations. As in the civilian sphere, military engineers saw beauty and finesse as one of the hallmarks of French technological modernity.[66]

At a time when technocrat-led modernization of France's regions was centre stage (particularly after the creation of the Délégation à l'aménagement du territoire et à l'action régionale in 1963), the DMA asserted that the CEL would boost the region's economy and population. The population of nearby Biscarrosse town did indeed swell from 3,336 inhabitants in 1962 to 6,840 in 1966 as military and scientific personnel arrived in the area. But the town's rapid development brought social tensions arising from the militarized transformation of its urban and rural environment.[67] Nonetheless, the military's coupling of its own aims with those of the wider state, attests to the permeability between civilian and military spheres and the reinvention of militarized environments to fit changing national priorities.

In line with the DMA's rhetoric on the CEL, the army linked militarization with modernization. The aforementioned preliminary army on Canjuers argued that only militarization could bring prosperity to a region where 'poor and rocky soils', 'meagre' grasslands and *maquis* inhibited the development of productive agriculture. Militarization would supposedly imbue this depopulating and 'semi-desert' region with national purpose and provide an economic boost through compensation for expropriated land, and military personnel's spending power.[68] In language echoing the establishment of Châlons Camp over a hundred years earlier, Colonel Guéneau, head of the military engineering service in Nice, argued that militarization would bring 'certain progress' through its modernization of a region that had some 'beauty' but consisted essentially of a 'dry and difficult nature'.[69] From the military perspective,

Canjuers Camp was a 'win–win' situation: France would get the training camp it needed and a 'backward' region would reap the benefits of state-led modernization. But this overlooked the fact that by creating the camp the army would produce a space empty of civilians, thereby contributing to rural depopulation.[70]

Despite civilian protests – outlined in detail in the next chapter – military priorities took precedence and the Canjuers project advanced. Prime Minister Georges Pompidou declared that the camp's creation was in the public interest (*utilité publique*) on 17 September 1964. By this stage, the camp's proposed size had grown to 35,000 ha and would remove land from 14 communes. The village of Brovès was to be expropriated in its entirety.[71]

The language of military-led modernization was widespread. The army's stress on modernizing supposedly 'backward' regions infiltrated its plans to extend Garrigues Camp by 1,700 ha. Army planners stressed how the region's 'anarchic vegetation' and topography meant that it had little to contribute to the regional economy. Military training was the only way to imbue the hilly scrubland with purpose.[72] However, the army's linking of its own aims with regional development and modernization should not disguise the fact that the primary attraction of economically disadvantaged areas was cheaper land.

In the minds of army planners, the *midi* boasted vast expanses of worthless pastureland, scrub, and woodlands fit only for militarization. Like Canjuers and Garrigues, the army's proposed extension of Caylus Camp from 3,000 to 6,000 ha targeted supposedly economically marginal land to the south of Cherbourg–Lyon line. Having created Caylus Camp through expropriation orders in the interwar period, army planners believed that its extension in the 1960s would help make up for loss of military lands in Algeria. Overlooking how decades of military presence may have held back agricultural development in the region, army reports described their desired land, and its climate and vegetation, as 'favourable' for almost year-round training. The climatic attractiveness of the site seems to have overridden concerns about the area's geology which harboured '*igues*' or 'natural wells' of depths of up to 80 m that might suddenly open up if overloaded by, say, tanks and other heavy vehicles.[73] The army contrasted the area's suitability for militarization with its apparent inability to support productive civilian land use. According to Captain Godard, Caylus was a depopulating region marked by inefficient small-scale familial agriculture 'without value and lacking any appreciable economic vocation'.[74]

Civilians, however, held opposing views. One member of the Tarn-et-Garonne's Conseil général noted that Caylus Camp's extension would remove civilian access to woodlands which locals used for pasturing and truffle-hunting and so force local farmers from their properties.[75] From the civilian perspective, the land was not worthless, and militarization would force seventeen families off their land in Mouillac commune. These families constituted the community's entire agricultural population and their loss would be so significant that Mouillac's mayor requested that the army expropriate all of the commune's land and provide villagers with enough compensation to relocate elsewhere.[76] Militarization seemed poised to swamp civilian communities and their land, thereby speeding up rural depopulation.[77]

In the end, military priorities overrode fears of rural depopulation. Caylus Camp's extension through expropriation was declared of public interest on 19 September 1964.[78] By October 1969 its size had increased to 5,500 ha, by which point the army had also extended Garrigues Camp to 5,000 ha.[79] Military geographical expansion during the Fifth Republic was therefore far more successful than during the Fourth. But the army's budget was not unlimited, and the cost of the Caylus and Canjuers operations put the 7,000 ha extension of Larzac Camp on hold in 1964, at least for the time being.[80] Finances, as well as civilian protests, therefore challenged and limited the military narrative of modernization and its impact.

Nuclear militarized environments

Alongside strengthening France's conventional forces, Gaullist foreign policy placed the possession of a nuclear strike force (*force de frappe*) as a central pillar of French national security and a technological guarantee of French autonomy.[81] The pursuit of nuclear weapons had begun immediately after the Second World War as the French became captivated by the promises of the atomic age whilst they struggled with the aftermath of war and long-standing political divisions.[82] In October 1945 the National Assembly approved de Gaulle's recommendation to launch France's nuclear programme with the creation of the Commissariat à l'énergie atomique (CEA). Publicly, the CEA's aims were civilian: developing nuclear capability to ensure France's *grandeur* and survival. But the CEA's deliberate choice of reactor meant that the production of pluto-nium for nuclear bombs was always an option and one actively pursued after the arrival of its new Administrator General Pierre Guillaumat in

1951. This behind-the-scenes work meant that many steps towards the nuclear bomb had been taken by the time that the head of the government, Félix Gaillard, gave the official go-ahead for the bomb in 1958, a decision supported by de Gaulle on his return to power.[83]

Michel Martin has argued that Gaullist foreign policy tried to replace 'a landscape of marshy jungles and sunburnt *djebels*' with a 'glowing universe of electronic precision and atomic strategy'.[84] But France's nuclear weapons programme was intimately bound up in colonialism and decolonization.

Developing nuclear bombs required large-scale test sites. After geological and political factors had militated against the possibility of conducting underground tests in the Alps, Pyrenees, and Corsica, the French state chose to export the social, political and environmental risks of nuclear testing to its colonies. On 13 February 1960 General Ailleret, in the midst of the Algerian War, oversaw the first above-ground explosion at a test site near Reggane in Algeria's Saharan region, code named *Gerboise bleue* (or blue jerboa, jerboa being a type of desert rodent). Four *Gerboise* tests were completed by April 1961 with the contaminated zone stretching over 150 km and studies conducted on the effects of radiation on animals and military hardware. International outcry and protests from African countries moved the testing underground, with thirteen tests conducted near Ekker in the Hoggar massif between 7 November 1961 and 16 February 1966. But security here was far from total: on 1 May 1962 a radioactive cloud escaped from the firing gallery. It was proving hard to contain the radioactive fallout, political and actual, from these nuclear militarized environments. [85] But back in France, a largely enthusiastic press celebrated the 'part cosmic, part transcendental spectacle' of the nation's first atomic bomb tests.[86]

The mobilization of the Algerian desert echoed US nuclear weapons testing in the arid expanses of Nevada and other western states. A colonial mindset informed them both.[87] But given the political and military situation, nuclear testing in Algeria was not conceived as a long-term project; even before tests had begun, military planners were already considering possible sites in the Pacific and Indian oceans.

Motivated by the signing of the Evian accords with Algeria, in which France agreed to give up its Saharan territory by 1967, and the desire to test high yield bombs, France's defence council confirmed the choice of the Mururoa atoll in French Polynesia for nuclear bomb testing. Echoing metropolitan military arguments that militarization would bring progress and jobs to supposedly backward areas, de Gaulle presented the Pacific Test Centre (Centre d'expérimentation du Pacifique, or CEP) to Polynesians as a spur to their economic development. Despite Polynesian officials' misgivings, the Permanent Commission of Polynesia's Territorial Assembly ceded Mururoa and Fangataufa atolls to the French state on 6 February 1964. The first explosion took place on 1 July 1966 from a barge positioned on a lagoon. Testing continued from barges, planes, and balloons until, after international outcry, moving underground in 1975, where it continued until the CEP closed in 1996.[88]

Like militarized environments in metropolitan France, the nuclear ones at Mururoa and Fangataufa atolls mobilized environmental features (in this case an expanse of ocean) to further military aims. Both kinds of militarized environment were created on supposedly 'empty' and marginal sites, demarcated with barriers, signs, security posts. Yet at both sites the military actively created the 'emptiness' by displacing civilian populations.[89] But the colonial context in the Pacific meant that it paid even less attention to local concerns than it did with the expansion of militarized environments in mainland France.[90]

Although France outsourced the ecological risks and political fallout of nuclear testing to its overseas territories, nuclear weapons development created small-scale, and relatively contained, nuclear militarized environments in metropolitan France. Nuclear weapons research centres, uranium production facilities, and nuclear waste processing plants were established on existing military land or in other marginal locations. In 1957 the CEA established an annex to its Vaujours research centre facility at Moronvilliers Camp (an annex of Mourmelon Camp), much to the annoyance of army planners who resented the loss of their training ground. Since then, the CEA has used its Moronvilliers complex to store waste from nuclear weapons and as a testing facility for weapons carrying small traces of radioactive material, at least according to civilian campaigners. Whatever its exact use, this area of former red zone to the west of Reims has become part of France's nuclear-military complex and a source of anxiety for neighbouring civilians.[91] Moronvilliers was a secretive site. In contrast, the state and local politicians and journalists heralded the arrival of the CEA's Marcoule nuclear site as a beacon of progress and modernity in an economically backward area of the Gard *département*. Marcoule produced plutonium for atomic bombs but that did not prevent the mayor of nearby Bagnols declaring that his town saluted the 'promoters of this astonishing, human, and peaceful endeavour'.[92]

As with its conventional weapons sites, the French military did not deviate from its policy of targeting sparsely populated and economically marginal areas when it chose Plateau d'Albion as the location for France's nuclear missile silos. Having discounted sites in Corsica, the Vosges, and the Massif Central, General Louis Benoit, commander of the Premier groupement de missiles stratégiques, recalled his delight at seeing the plateau for the first time; it seemed 'ideal'. Once studies on the area's geology and underground water systems were complete, Messmer ordered the construction of France's first nuclear missile silos on Plateau d'Albion in April 1965.[93] Once again, and as the state did with other French nuclear power stations and facilities, the military legitimized its choice by claiming that its presence would modernize an economically marginal backwater. It would bring electricity and water to under-developed villages, whilst respecting the area's natural beauty. As with other nuclear sites, tradition and modernity would supposedly blend together in harmony.[94] Civilians, such as poet René Char, were unconvinced and deeply concerned about the risk of explosions and radioactive pollution. But their protests had little effect and the state managed to obtain 785 ha from 288 landowners with only 6 having to be dispossessed through expropriation orders.[95] National defence necessities mixed with a widely held faith that state-led technological progress would bring modernity, prosperity and prestige to France overrode the dissenting voices.[96]

In spring 1966, work therefore began on the construction of eighteen missile silos, as well as underground bunkers, communication stations, roads, and an air base at Saint-Christol. But the ground was not always compliant: when diggers unexpectedly came across huge potholes the silos had to be relocated elsewhere on the plateau. Heavy rains also hampered the construction in winter, as did dry summers, when water had to be brought up by lorries to make up concrete during the construction of satellite installations at col des Tempêtes and col de la Frache on the foothills of nearby Mont Ventoux.[97] Nonetheless, despite these unfavourable conditions, the Plateau d'Albion site became fully operational in 1971 (see figure 7.1).

The land once celebrated in the literature of Jean Giono had become a nuclear militarized environment. The charms of Provence and the plateau's poetic qualities, that had survived its militarization, were not lost on the military personnel stationed there. When seeing the region's lavender fields and farms under blue winter skies for the first time, Gérard Périnelle was reminded of the Provencal landscapes of Marcel Pagnol's films, and was similarly impressed by the plateau's oak forests

7.1 A former nuclear militarized environment, Plateau d'Albion

and surrounding mountains. He felt 'viscerally' that he would like this out-of-the-way place and admitted to finding calm and happiness during his time at Saint-Christol air base.[98] Périnelle's claims to have found solace and natural beauty within an environment transformed by high-modernist technology not only resonated with representations of US militarized nuclear environments as sites of inspirational and beautiful nature, but implied that military expansion and modernization were unproblematic processes without social and environmental costs.[99] It naturalized the postwar militarization of rural France and glossed it as respectful of the countryside's traditions. In this vein, militarization becomes part of '*la douce France*', a view of rural France as a gentle and sweet land largely free from conflict.[100]

Civilians challenged this view. Marie Mauron, an ardent supporter of Provencal traditions, lamented the plateau's militarization. Rather than fulfil its calling to be a site of 'wild nature', the plateau was now spoiled with barbed wire and nuclear rockets that evoked the 'apocalypse'. For Mauron, the silos were yet another instance of the modern, industrialized state ruining traditional Provence (other military installations, factories, and roads were also to blame).[101]

Regionalists shared the belief that militarized modernization had destroyed, rather than complemented and enhanced, rural traditions at Plateau d'Albion. One Occitan militant denounced the military's 'occupation' of Provence and the 'colonial economy' it had ushered in, arguing that one of the main reasons behind the military's selection of Plateau d'Albion was that the 'natives were brown skinned enough to help them get over their [colonial] nostalgia for Arabs'.[102] The links between militarization and colonialism were clearly evident for this commentator. Less politicized locals were, however, pleased that the military had brought running water to the region.[103]

Conclusion

Plateau d'Albion's nuclear missiles made it a new kind of militarized environment, showing the environmental changes ushered in by Cold War-era defence policies and so-called 'advances' in weapons technology. Along with decolonization they provoked and maintained the military's expansionist dynamic. With the creation of the CEL, the Plateau d'Albion complex, the extension of Caylus and other camps, and the establishment of Canjuers Camp, the mobilization of nature for war preparation reached its peak during the 1960s and early 1970s. To legitimize this extension of militarized environments, the military aligned itself with the state's wider aim of modernizing and balancing French territory. But civilians did not accept this narrative and feared that militarization would sterilize and destroy the French countryside. At Canjuers, and then Larzac, their protests reached a crescendo, as the next chapter explores.

Notes

1 SHD-DAT 27 T 116 Anonymous, undated image.
2 Matthew Farish, *The Contours of America's Cold War* (Minneapolis: University of Minnesota Press, 2010); Carole Gallagher, *American Ground Zero: The Secret Nuclear War* (Cambridge, MA: MIT Press, 1993); Valerie L. Kuletz, *The Tainted Desert: Environmental and Social Ruin in the American West* (New York: Routledge, 1998); P. Whitney Lackenbauer and Matthew Farish, 'The Cold War on Canadian soil: Militarizing a northern environment', *Environmental History*, 12:4 (2007), 920–50; John R. McNeill and Corinna R. Unger (eds), *Environmental Histories of the Cold War* (New York: Cambridge University Press, 2010).

3 Herman Lebovics, *Bringing the Empire Back Home: France in the Global Age* (Durham, NC: Duke University Press, 2004); Kristin Ross, *Fast Cars, Clean Bodies: Decolonization and the Reordering of French Culture* (Cambridge, MA: MIT Press, 1995); Todd Shepard, *The Invention of Decolonization: The Algerian War and the Remaking of France* (Ithaca: Cornell University Press, 2006).

4 To the best of my knowledge, these histories remain to be written.

5 Philip H. Gordon, *A Certain Idea of France: French Security Policy and the Gaullist Legacy* (Princeton: Princeton University Press, 1993); Maurice Vaïsse, *La grandeur: Politique étrangère du général de Gaulle, 1958–1969* (Paris: Fayard, 1998).

6 Jean-François Gravier, *Paris et le désert français: Décentralisation, équipement, population* (Paris: Le Portulan, 1947). Alain Monferrand addressed the links between defence and territorial development in his 1971 thesis 'Défense nationale et aménagement du territoire: Analyse d'une région de programme' (PhD dissertation, Université de Paris 8, 1971). See also Michael Bess, *The Light-Green Society: Ecology and Technological Modernity in France, 1960–2000* (Chicago and London: University of Chicago Press, 2003), 11–37; Sara B. Pritchard, 'Paris et le désert français: Urban and rural environments in post-World War II France', in Andrew C. Isenberg (ed.), *The Nature of Cities* (Rochester: University of Rochester Press, 2006), 175–91. It is important to recognize, however, that modernization was not a consensual or smooth process. Gabrielle Hecht, *The Radiance of France: Nuclear Power and National Identity after World War II* (Cambridge, MA: MIT Press, 1998); Sara B. Pritchard, *Confluence: The Nature of Technology and the Remaking of the Rhône* (Cambridge, MA: Harvard University Press, 2011).

7 James C. Scott, *Seeing Like a State: How Certain Schemes to Improve the Human Condition Have Failed* (New Haven and London: Yale University Press, 1998).

8 Jean Doise and Maurice Vaïse, *Diplomatie et outil militaire, 1871–1991: Politique étrangère de la France* (Paris: Editions du Seuil, 1992 [1987]), 504–5; Jean-Pierre Rioux, *The Fourth Republic, 1944–1958*, trans. Godfrey Rogers (Cambridge: Cambridge University Press, 1987), 13.

9 Général Péchaud du Rieu, 'Les camps légers d'instruction' *Revue du Génie militaire* (1947), 313–26. On climate and Cold War military training in the US, see Matthew Farish, 'Creating cold war climates: The laboratories of American globalism', in McNeill and Ungar, *Environmental Histories of the Cold War*, 51–83.

10 ADI 21 J 58 'Chantiers de Jeunesse' [n.d.]. On the links between Vichy youth movements and the environment, see Chris Pearson, *Scarred Landscapes: War and Nature in Vichy France* (Basingstoke: Palgrave Macmillan, 2008), 25, 48, 102–7.

11 Péchaud du Rieu, 'Camps légers d'instruction', 313–26.

12 On the continuities between the war and postwar periods, see chapter 6.

13 Pearson, *Scarred Landscapes*, 124–5.

14 Commandant Aublet, 'Les écoles d'artillerie: Fontainebleau-Poitiers-Châlons', *Revue historique de l'armée*, 3:4 (1954), 147, 150.

15 Claude Herbiet, *Malgré tout: Du Valdahon à Figuig, les pérégrinations d'un rappelé de 1956* (Paris: L'Harmattan, 2000), 22; 'L'école d'application de l'armée blindée et de la cavalerie', *Revue historique de l'armée*, 3:4 (1954), 205.

16 Serge Desbois and Eric Berder, 'Le centre d'essais de la méditerranée', *Nouvelle revue aéronautique et astronautique*, 2 (1995), 64–5; Pierre Audebert, *Guide illustré de l'Ile du Levant* (Paris: Editions Edicha, 1950), 3.

17 Ellen Furlough, 'Making mass vacations: Tourism and consumer culture in France, 1930s–1960s', *Comparative Studies in Society and History*, 40:2 (1998), 260–3.

18 ADV 379 W 510/1 Conseil général du Var, 'Séance plénaire du jeudi 2 juin 1955', ADV 379 W 510/2 Comité régional de tourisme de la XIᵉ région économique 'Provence-Corse', 'Procès-verbal', 2 July 1955.

19 SHD-DAT 27 T 117 Secrétaire d'état à la Guerre to Généraux commandant les régions militaires, 'Extension des camps', 28[?] September 1951.

20 SHD-DAT 27 T 117 General C.A. Zeller to Secrétaire d'état à la Guerre, 'Possibilités d'extension du champ de tir du camp de Mailly (Aube)', 15 December 1951; SHD-DAT 27 T 117 Colonel Jhean, Directeur des travaux du génie, Châlons-sur-Marne, 'Rapport relative aux possibilités d'extension du champ de tir du Camp de Mailly (Aube)', 4 December 1951.

21 SHD-DAT 27 T 117 'Extrait du journal régional 'L'Aube' septembre 1952'.

22 SHD-DAT 27 T 117 newspaper clipping, Marcel Degois, 'L'extension du camp de Mailly', *L'Est-éclair*, 11 October 1952.

23 CAC 19870398/6 Secrétariat d'état aux Forces armées 'air', 'Compte-rendu de la conférence tenue le 7 Mai 1957 à la Direction de l'infrastructure au sujet de l'installation d'un champ de tir et de bombardement expérimental dans la région de Mont-de-Marsan'.

24 CAC 19870398/5 Directeur des travaux du génie, Versailles, to Ingénieur principal des Eaux et Forêts, Saint-Germain-en-Laye, 'Implantation d'une station hertzienne dans la forêt dominale', 19 March 1959.

25 Tamara Whited, *Forests and Peasant Politics in Modern France* (New Haven and London: Yale University Press, 2000), 31–3.

26 That is not to say that foresters were anti-militarists. Important differences existed between the two groups. In the early 1970s, conscientious objectors resented having to spend a year of their national service working for the forestry administration, attacking its ecological record and commercialization of French forests. Eric Laporte, 'Le statut de Brégancon', in Jean Rabaut, *L'anti-militarisme en France 1810–1975: Faits et documents* (Paris: Hachette, 1975), 227–30.

27 Colonel P. Borie, 'Les champs de tir d'instruction', *Bulletin technique du Génie militaire*, 2 (1954), 145–66.

28 ADV 379 W 510/1 Conseil général du Var, 'Extrait du registre des délibérations', 18 November 1954; ADV 379 W 510/1 Commission départementale des sites et monuments naturels du Var, 'Séance du 24 septembre 1954; ADV 379 W 510/2 Préfet du Var to Secrétaire d'état à la Guerre', 8 December 1954.

29 ADV 379 W 510/2 Arthur Dugelay to Directeur des travaux du génie, Nice, 'Champ de tir de Plan de Canjuers (Var)', 24 August 1954; ADV 1790 W 6055 Arthur Dugelay to Directeur des travaux du génie, Nice, 'Champ de tir de Canjuers', 15 November 1954.

30 A.M., 'Haut-Var: Zone interdite', *La Marseillaise*, 22 December 1954. On resistance at Canjuers, see Pearson, *Scarred Landscapes*, 65.

31 ADV 379 W 510/2 Louis Goujon to Préfet du Var, 23 June 1955. On nuclear fears in France, see Hecht, *Radiance of France*, 227–34.

32 P.C., 'Une session extraordinaire', *La Marseillaise*, 25 July 1955. On leftwing politics in the Var, see Jacques Girault, *Le Var rouge: Les Varois et le socialisme de la fin de la Première Guerre mondiale au milieu des années 1930* (Paris: Publications de la Sorbonne, 1995).

33 Patrick Major and Rana Mitter, 'East is east and west is west?': Towards a comparative socio-cultural history of the Cold War', in Patrick Major and Rana Mitter (eds), *Across the Blocs: Cold War Cultural and Social History* (London: Frank Cass, 2004), 3.

34 L.H., 'Le Var inconnu', *Provençal*, 22 October 1954; Jean-Marie Guillon, 'L'affirmation régionale en Pays d'oc des années quarante', *Ethnologie française*, 33:3 (2003), 430–2; E.M., 'Le plan de Canjuers n'est pas un désert', *Nice Matin*, 16 October 1954. Giono quoted in Corrine Aubert, 'La politique d'installation des camps militaires: Le cas particulier du polygone de tir de Canjuers' (DESS, Université de Nice, 1983–4), 31.

35 ADV 379 W 510/1 Préfet du Var, 'Création d'un champ de tir au Plan de Canjuers', 20 May 1955; ADV 379 W 510/2 Préfet du Var to Secrétaire d'état à la Guerre, 8 December 1954.

36 SHD-DAT 27 T 117 Général Gouraud, 'Note pour le Secrétaire d'état aux Forces armées "terre"', 'Extension du camp de Mailly', 16 November 1957.

37 SHD-DAT 27 T 117 Général d'Armée Blanc to Secrétaire d'état aux Forces armées 'terres', 'Extension du camp de Mailly', 15 December 1956. Between 1946 and 1958 officers spent up to 60 per cent of their time away from France. Doise and Vaïse, *Diplomatie et outil militaire*, 544.

38 Jean-Marie Gille, *De Suippes à Bou-Saada, appelé en 1956* (Paris: Editions des Ecrivains, 2001), 26. For excellent introductions on the army's role in the Algerian war, see Martin S. Alexander, Martin Evans, and John F.V. Keiger (eds), *The Algerian War and the French Army, 1954–62: Experiences, Images, Testimonies* (Basingstoke: Palgrave MacMillan, 2002); Jacques Frémeaux,

La France et l'Algérie en guerre 1830–1870, 1954–1962 (Paris: Economica et Institut de stratégie comparée, 2002).

39 SHD-DAT 6 T 586 Secrétaire d'état aux Forces armées 'terre' to Généraux commandant les régions et territoires, 'Conduite de l'instruction en 1958', 29 November 1957.

40 Martin S. Alexander, 'Seeking France's "lost soldiers": Reflections on the French military crisis in Algeria', in Kenneth Mouré and Martin S. Alexander (eds), *Crisis and Renewal in France, 1918–1962* (New York: Berghahn, 2002), 252–7; John Steward Ambler, *The French Army in Politics, 1945–1962* (Columbus: Ohio State University Press, 1966), 101–7.

41 David Biggs, 'Managing a rebel landscape: Conservation, pioneers, and the revolutionary past in the U Minh forest, Vietnam', *Environmental History*, 10:3 (2005), 451. See also Richard L. Stevens, *The Trail: A History of the Ho Chi Minh Trail and the Role of Nature in the War in Vietnam* (New York and London: Garland Publising, 1993).

42 Martin S. Alexander, Martin Evans, and John F.V. Keiger, 'The "war without a name", the French army and the Algerians: Recovering experiences, images and testimonies', in Alexander, Evans, and Keiger (eds), *Algerian War and the French Army*, 9, 18–19. See also the testimonies of General Alain Bizard and Colonel Henri Coustaux in the same volume (225, 231) and Frémeaux, *La France et l'Algérie en guerre*, 124–7.

43 Quoted in Ross, *Fast Cars, Clean Bodies*, 110. On military attempts to break down civilian–military boundaries in the Palestine–Israeli conflict, see Eyal Weizman, *Hollow Land: Israel's Architecture of Occupation* (London: Verso, 2007).

44 Estimates on Algerian civilian deaths range from those provided by the French army (141,000) to those of the FLN (500,000). Between 4,000 and 4,500 European civilians were also killed. Rod Kedward, *La vie en bleu: France and the French since 1900* (London: Allen Lane, 2005), 346.

45 Ross, *Fast Cars, Clean Bodies*; Shepard, *Invention of Decolonization*.

46 SHD-DAT 7 T 253 Général de division de Guillibon, 'Accueil des supplétifs au camp du Larzac', 7 June 1962. Army bases, such as Larzac and Mourmelon, had already been sites of internment for FLN prisoners, much to the annoyance of army planners who resented the corresponding restrictions on training. SHD-DAT 27 T 115 Général le Puloch, Chef d'Etat-major de l'armée, 'Problèmes de l'armée de terre en matière de terrains d'entraînement et d'expérimentations', December 1961.

47 Abdel Kader Hamadi, 'La mémoire du camp de Rivesaltes', in Fatima Besnaci-Lancou and Gilles Manceron (eds), *Les harkis dans la colonisation et ses suites* (Ivry-sur-Seine: Les Editions de l'Atelier, 2008), 126–7.

48 SHD-DAT 7 T 253 'Note sur l'organisation et le fonctionnement des camps d'ex supplétifs réfugiés d'A.F.N.', 18 September 1962; Joël Mettay, *L'archipel du mépris: Histoire du camps de Rivesaltes de 1939 à nos jours* (Canet:

Trabucaire, 2001), 108; Kader Hamadi, 'Mémoire du camp de Rivesaltes', 127.

49 SHD-DAT 27 T 122 'Champ de tir de Biscarrosse', 23 January 1953; SHD-DAT 27 T 122 'Procès -verbal de conférence mixte à l'effet d'examiner un projet de révision du champ de tir de Biscarrosse en vue de la création d'un champ de tir d'expériences', 8 November 1950; 'Les pêcheurs arcachonnais déposeront-ils leur rôle d'équipage', *Sud-Ouest*, 18 May 1954, newspaper clipping in SHD-DAT 27 T 122.

50 SHD-DAT 13 T 152 Général Delteil to Ministre des Armées 'terres', 'Projet d'extension du camp de Naouas–Biscarrosse', 14 February 1962.

51 SHD-DAT 13 T 258 'Extrait du procès-verbal de la réunion du comité des chefs d'État-major du 26 décembre 1961'.

52 SHD-DAT 15 T 352 Délégation ministérielle pour l'armement, 'Instruction sur l'organisation et le fonctionnement du Centre d'essais des Landes (C.E.L.)', 30 December 1963'.

53 Le Puloch, 'Problèmes de l'Armée de terre'.

54 Ross, *Fast Cars, Clean Bodies*. See also Lebovics, *Bringing the Empire Back Home*, 58–82.

55 'SHD-DAT 27 T 115 Commission d'étude sur les projets d'acquisitions domaniales, 'Rapport du Capitaine Godard, de la Direction centrale du génie, relatif aux incidences économiques et sociales entraînées par le projet d'extension du camp de Caylus', [n.d.]. On the colonial mindsets of French army officers, see Martin Evans, 'The French army and the Algerian War: Crisis of identity', in Scriven and Wagstaff, *War and Society*, 147–62.

56 Gregory Hooks and Chad L. Smith, 'Treadmills of production and destruction: Threats to the environment posed by militarism', *Organization Environment*, 18:1 (2005), 21.

57 Quoted in Rachel Utley, *The French Defence Debate: Consensus and Continuity in The Mitterrand Era* (Basingstoke: Palgrave Macmillan, 2005), 12. These principles were reinforced two years after the General's death in the White Paper on National Defence. *Livre blanc sur la défense nationale*, vol. 1 (Paris: Centre de documentation de l'armement, 1972).

58 Le Puloch, 'Problèmes de l'Armée de terre'.

59 Ibid. Roger Chartier traces the Cherbourg–Lyon (or Saint–Malo–Geneva) Line back to the July Monarchy and its division of France into 'enlightened' and 'backward' halves. 'The Saint–Male–Geneva Line', in Pierre Nora (ed.), *Realms of Memory. Vol. 1: Conflicts and Divisions*, trans. Arthur Goldhammer (New York: Columbia University Press, 1996), 467–96.

60 Aubert, 'Politique d'installation des camps militaires', 19.

61 Le Puloch, 'Problèmes de l'Armée de terre'.

62 SHD-DAT 27 T 115 Ministre des Armées, Direction centrale du génie, 'Extension du camp militaire de Caylus: Notice explicative', 1965; SHD-DAT 13 T 258 'Point des acquisitions domaniales à la date du 1er mars 1963',

5 March 1963. On the army's reputation and morale post-Algeria, see Doise and Vaïse, *Diplomatie et outil militaire*, 619–21; Raoul Girardet (ed.), *La crise militaire française, 1945–1962* (Paris: Armand Colin, 1964).

63 ADV 1189 W 1 Direction des travaux, Nice, 'Création d'un champ de tir et de manoeuvre dans la région des plans des Canjuers', [n.d.].

64 SHD-DAT 13 T 259 'Projet d'exposé sur le problème des grands camps', 24 October 1969.

65 Colonel Briand, 'Le génie service constructeur du Centre d'essais des Landes', *Bulletin technique du génie militaire* (1971), 219–26; Colonel Pacault, 'Le service des travaux', *Revue historique des armées*, 22:1(1966), 223.

66 Hecht, *Radiance of France*, 41–2.

67 D. Chabas, *Villes et villages des Landes, vol. 2: Bénesse-lès-Dax à Capbreton* (Capbreton, D. Chabas, 1970), 73–80.

68 'Création d'un champ de tir et de manoeuvre dans la région des plans des Canjuers'.

69 ADV 1189 W 1 Colonel Guéneau, letter no. 10.616/D, 8 November 1962.

70 On the military's discourses of emptiness and its displacement of civilians, see Tim Cole, 'Military presences, civilian absences: Battling nature at the Sennybridge Training Area, 1940–2008', *Journal of War and Culture Studies*, 3:2 (2010), 215–35.

71 ADV 1189 W 1 'Décret du 17 septembre 1964'.

72 SHD-DAT 27 T 118 Commission d'étude sur les projets d'acquisitions dominales, 'Projet d'extension du Camp de Garrigues', 6 February 1963.

73 'Extension du camp militaire de Caylus: Notice explicative'; SHD-DAT 27 T 115 Commission d'étude sur les projets d'acquisitions domaniales, 'Projet d'extension du camp de Caylus', 9 October 1962, first part.

74 'Rapport du Capitaine Godard'.

75 SHD-DAT 27 T 115 'Registre des délibérations du Conseil général', 30 April 1963.

76 SHD-DAT 27 T 115 Préfet du Tarn-et-Garonne to Colonel Commandant la Subdivision du Tarn-et-Garonne, 21 September 1963.

77 From 1955 onwards 130,000 people left the countryside each year. Rioux, *The Fourth Republic*, 385. See also Gordon Wright, *Rural Revolution in France: The Peasantry in the Twentieth Century* (Stanford: Stanford University Press, 1964), 114–15.

78 'Extension du camp militaire de Caylus'.

79 These figures are taken from a map included with 'Projet d'exposé sur le problème des grands camps'.

80 SHD-DAT 27 T 116 Général d'armée Cantaral, 'Extension du camp du Larzac', 17 August 1967.

81 Jolyon Howorth, 'The defence consensus and French political culture', in Michael Scriven and Peter Wagstaff (eds), *War and Society in Twentieth*

Century France (Oxford: Berg, 1991), 166–7. For a discussion of the reception and contestation of Gaullist defence policies and their legacies, see Gordon, *Certain Idea of France*; Utley, *The French Defence Debate*.

82 David Pace, 'Old wine, new bottles: Atomic energy and the ideology of science in postwar France', *French Historical Studies*, 17:1 (1991), 36–61.

83 Hecht, *Radiance of France*, 58–78. See also Dominique Mongin, *La bombe atomique française 1945–1958* (Brussels: Bruyant, 1997).

84 Michel L. Martin, *Warriors to Managers: The French Military Establishment since 1945* (Chapel Hill: University of North Carolina Press, 1981), 66.

85 Bruno Barrillot, *Les essais nucléaires français 1960–1966: Conséquences sur l'environnement et la santé* (Lyon: Centre de Documentation et de la Recherche sur la Paix et les Conflits, 1996); Christian Bataille, *Rapport no. 179, l'évaluation de la recherche sur la gestion des déchets nucléaires à haute activité – Tome II: Les déchets militaires* (Office parlementaire d'évaluation des choix scientifiques et technologiques, 1997/1998), www.senat.fr/rap/o97-179/o97-179.html, accessed 26 November 2009; Jacques Frémeaux, 'The Sahara and the Algerian War', in Alexander, Evans, and Keiger, *Algerian War and the French Army*, 82–3; Jean-Marc Regnault, 'France's search for nuclear test sites', *Journal of Military History*, 67 (2003), 1227–32.

86 Hecht, *Radiance of France*, 209.

87 On the 'sacrifice' and 'internal colonization' of Native American lands for nuclear testing in the USA, see Gallagher, *American Ground Zero*; Gregory Hooks and Chad L. Smith, 'The treadmill of destruction: National sacrifice areas and Native Americans', *American Sociological Review*, 69:4 (2004), 558–75; Kuletz, *The Tainted Desert*.

88 Regnault, 'France's search', 1242–4; Stephen Henningham, *France and the South Pacific: A Contemporary History* (Sydney: Allen and Unwin, 1992). On the social and economic impact of the tests and their cessation, see Jean-Marc Regnault, 'Tahiti avec et sans la bombe', *Vingtième Siècle*, 53 (January–March 1997), 55–67.

89 On the creation of 'wilderness' through US nuclear testing in the Pacific Ocean, see Jeffrey Sasha Davis, 'Scales of Eden: Conservation and pristine devastation on Bikini Atoll', *Environment and Planning D: Society and Space*, 25 (2007), 213–35.

90 As with nuclear testing sites in the western United States, civilians have raised repeated concerns about the environmental and health risks inherent within French nuclear weapons development. Barrillot, *Essais nucléaires français*, 139–60, 227–332; Bataille, *Rapport no. 179*; Stephen Henningham, 'Testing times: France's underground nuclear tests and its relations with the Asia–Pacific region', *Modern and Contemporary France*, 4:1 (1996), 82–4; Moruroa e tatou association, 'Essais et environnement: Les associations exigent la vérité', 16 November 2009, www.moruroaetatou.com/index.

php/actus/1-infos-de-moruroa-e-tatou/128-essais-et-environnement-les-associations-exigent-la-verite, accessed 26 November 2009. See also the website of the Association des vétérans des essais nucléaires français et leur familles (AVEN) at www.aven.org. The French state has consistently played down the health and environmental repercussions of the tests, backed by a survey from the International Atomic Energy Agency which found that although traces of radioactive material remain in the atoll's 'terrestrial environment' the 'concentrations levels are . . . of no radiological significance'. P.R. Danesi, J. Moreno, M. Makarewicz, and Z. Radecki, 'Residual radioactivity in the terrestrial environment of the Mururoa and Fangataufa atolls nuclear weapon test sites', *Journal of Radioanalytical and Nuclear Chemistry*, 253:1 (2002), 53–65.

91 Le Puloch, 'Problèmes de l'armée de terre'; Bruno Barrillot and Mary Davis, *Les déchets nucléaires militaires français* (Lyon: Centre de Documentation et de Recherche sur la Paix et les Conflits, 1994), 14, 364; 'Le cri d'alarme des habitants de Pontfaverger-Moronvilliers', www.moruroa.org/medias/pdf/lecrid'alarmedeshabitantsdePontfaverger-Moronvilliers.pdf, accessed 8 December 2009. On the establishment of other nuclear sites in France, see Hecht, *Radiance of France*.

92 Quoted in Gabrielle Hecht, 'Peasants, engineers and atomic cathedrals: Narrating modernization in postwar provincial France', *French Historical Studies*, 20:3 (1997), 381–418.

93 Benoit quoted in Comité de rédaction de la base aérienne 200 de Saint-Christol d'Albion, *Les sentinelles de la paix* (Paris: Editions du Zéphyr, 1999), 35.

94 Hecht, *Radiance of France*; Hecht, 'Peasants, engineers and atomic cathedrals', 384.

95 Jean-Paul Bonnefoy, *Sur le plateau d'Albion: Saint-Christol d'hier et d'aujourd'hui* (Avignon: Editions A. Bathélemy, 1991); Comité de rédaction, *Sentinelles de la paix*, 43.

96 On governmental and technocratic faith in planning and technology, see Bess, *Light-Green Society*; Robert L. Frost, 'The flood of "progress": Technocrats and peasants at Tignes (Savoy), 1946–1952', *French Historical Studies*, 14:1 (1985), 117–40; Hecht, *Radiance of France*; Cecil O. Smith, 'The longest run: Public engineers and planning in France', *American Historical Review*, 95:3 (1990), 657–92.

97 Comité de rédaction, *Les sentinelles de la paix*, 40–1.

98 Ibid. 159.

99 Mark Fiege, 'The atomic scientists, the sense of wonder, and the bomb', *Environmental History*, 12:3 (2007), 578–613; Davis, 'Scales of Eden'.

100 Fernand Braudel, *The Identity of France. Volume One: History and the Environment*, trans. Siân Reynolds (London: Collins, 1988); Armand Frémont, 'The land', in Pierre Nora (ed.), *Realms of Memory: Rethinking the*

French Past. Volume 2: Traditions, trans. Arthur Goldhammer (New York: Columbia University Press, 1997), 3–35.

101 Marie Mauron, *Ombre et lumière sur la Provence* (Paris: Plon, 1974), 247.
102 J. Rd., 'Albion: "Opération réussie"', *Le Monde*, 4 May 1972, 27.
103 Ibid. 27.

~8~

Opposing militarized environments

Introduction

In 1965 the poet and former resister, René Char, published a small booklet protesting the military's proposal to establish a series of nuclear missile silos on Plateau d'Albion (see chapter 7). Dedicating *La Provence point oméga* to the region's migratory birds, Char wrote how militarization would 'wound' the soil that produced truffles, vines, wild mushrooms, apples, and peaches. Nuclear missiles – with all the social and environmental risks they entailed – would replace this natural bounty. Warning that the ground would 'collapse' rather than accept the missiles, Char organized a petition against the silos and spoke at a demonstration against them at Fontaine-de-Vaucluse in June 1967. Char's dismay at the plateau's militarization was shared by Pablo Picasso who illustrated a tract produced by Char that was then distributed in the Vaucluse.[1] High-tech weaponry, in this case nuclear missiles, seemed poised to threaten and pollute environments valued for their entwined natural and cultural significance.

Char's protest was ultimately unsuccessful. But it formed part of a wider movement of protest against the growing militarization of the countryside in the 1960s and 1970s. Civilian populations and officials had opposed the establishment of military bases since at least the creation of Châlons Camp in 1857. But from the mid-1960s onwards, environmentalists and nature protection societies played an increasingly prominent role. Before then, anti-military protests from nature conservationists had been relatively infrequent and isolated. In 1937 naturalist and speleologist Gustave Boissière had called for the creation of a North American-style national park to protect the high plateau of the Vercors mountain range (near Grenoble) from military manoeuvres and a mooted firing range.[2] The SNAF and the Amis de la forêt de Fontainebleau had also opposed firing ranges and other forms of militarization during and after the Second World War (see chapter 6). In the 1960s and 1970s these lone voices became a chorus as militarization came to be seen more widely as a threat to nature itself.

This new understanding, informed by the countercultural and militant character of environmentalist politics that emerged after the events of May 1968, existed alongside longstanding apprehensions over lost farm-land, forests, and dwellings, and the withdrawal of hunting, woodcutting, and pasturing rights. Nonetheless, alongside campaigns against tourist infrastructure and nuclear power, anti-base campaigns became testing grounds for the emerging French environmentalist movement, which, as in other countries, evolved in opposition to Cold War era-militarization.[3]

Environmentalism constituted a new development in the history of French anti-militarism. Although anti-base campaigners did not universally accept it, the equation of militarization and sterilization of land reached its peacetime peak in the 1960s and 1970s, bolstered by politically radical and grassroots environmentalism.[4] Military officials were well aware of this new challenge: in 1971 the army's general inspec-tor recognized that 'environmental policies' would increasingly limit training possibilities.[5]

A further major change in anti-base campaigns during the 1960s and 1970s was the increasing attention paid to them in France and overseas, particularly to events at Larzac. The prominence of the Larzac campaign was partly due to its ability to express and advance the anti-authoritarian and anti-militarist sentiments circulating in post-1968 France and more widely across Europe and North America.[6] Larzac therefore takes its place alongside other campaigns against Cold War-era militarization from across the globe.[7] Within French history, it needs to be treated as the militarized counterpart to other regionalist campaigns against state-led projects, such as the protest against plans to build a nuclear power station at Plogoff in Brittany (1974–81).[8]

Like Plogoff, Larzac was a rare example of a successful civil society campaign against the central state in postwar France. Its success was, in part, due to protesters' successful imaginative and physical mobilization of nature to make their case. Their environmentally informed harness-ing of nature at Larzac (and, before that, at Canjuers), challenged the army's efforts to enlist topography, vegetation, animals, and climatic conditions for its own ends. The civilian mobilization of nature, which turned militarized environments into zones of conflict between civilians and the military, forms the focus of this chapter. We begin the story at Canjuers.

Challenging Canjuers

Cries of alarm from civilian officials and local populations greeted the government's 1962 decision to create France's largest military base on Canjuers plateau in the Provencal hinterland north of Draguignan (see chapter 7). At stake, it seemed, was the Var *département*'s economic viability and its geographical survival, especially as two local villages were already due to be lost to submersion during Electricité de France's creation of Ste-Croix Lake.[9] According to the Var's prefect, locals would see the military camp as yet a further attack on the *département*'s 'integrity' and a potential threat to its tourism. Furthermore, the addition of Canjuers to existing military sites at Ile du Levant, Draguignan, Giens, Hyères and Toulon would create the impression that the Var was 'almost entirely covered by the army's installations'.[10] Similarly, the Var's director of agricultural services feared that the militarization of Canjuers would undermine local sheep-rearing, another vitally important economic activity alongside tourism.[11]

The army sought to play down worries over the camp's impact. At a meeting with local officials, Colonel Guéneau tried to soothe their fears, claiming that the churning up of land through shelling would attract game and that the army would support forest conservation (he predicted that soldiers would help put out forest fires and hinted that the camp's authorities might conduct reforestation work).[12] Given the failure to militarize Canjuers in the 1950s, Prime Minister Georges Pompidou and Minister for Armed Forces, Pierre Messmer, met local politicians to try to allay their qualms about the camp's economic impact and to confirm that no nuclear weapons would be fired at Canjuers.[13]

But local officials were far from converted to the benefits of a 35,000 ha military camp. They used the twenty-five day public inquiry into the camp to lodge their complaints. Amongst them was the president of the Chambre de métiers du Var who wanted Brovès village – a local 'gem' – to be saved and Bridges and Roads officials who feared that military firing would disturb the 'tranquillity' of the tourists who came to the region to find 'rest and silence' from the 'agitation of modern life'.[14]

At a time when rural France was experiencing profound and complex social and economic transformations,[15] the stakes felt even higher for those who stood to lose their homes and livelihoods. The Syndicat de défense des propriétaires du Haut Var (SDPHV), a grouping of landowners and local mayors formed in 1955, feared that the camp would lead to rural exodus and the region's 'ruin'. Its president, Jean-Paul Goujon, a solicitor from Vidauban, wrote to mayors and town councils asking them to formally oppose the camp.[16] Local politicians responded with a display of unity. On 15 September 1963, after a hunt and '*méchoui*' (a barbecue of a whole roast sheep) at Brovès, they passed a motion declaring that the camp would 'lead to the pure and simple ruin of this region and the people that live there'. In a defiant tone, they stated that 'we are here because of our ancestors' labour and we'll only leave through the force of bayonets'.[17] Less confrontationally, Comps-sur-Artuby town council stressed the economic and spiritual importance of the land and climate that provided grazing for sheep and a source of regeneration for tourists.[18]

Images of disaster framed the debate. The council of Bauduen, a commune which was already due to lose 700 ha of its land to the Ste-Croix Lake and stood to lose another 1,400 ha to Canjuers, raised the spectre of the collapse of the Malpasset dam in 1959 (that had caused 421 casualties), when it suggested that vibrations in the soil from military training might cause a repeat occurrence.[19]

The stakes and protests were personal as well as political. Marcel Gaimard, a farmer from Ampus, believed that the camp would ruin years of his labour and deprive him of lavender, truffles, game, and fruit. Convinced that he would be unable to find land of a similar quality elsewhere, Gaimard predicted that he and his family would be thrown out onto the street if the camp went ahead.[20] In short, militarization seemed poised to aggravate existing challenges facing rural France, such as depopulation, leading locals to take a firm stand against it.

But the state's military imperatives ultimately outweighed such concerns and the camp was declared to be in the public interest in September 1964. Nonetheless, the militarization of 35,000 ha would be a long process. It necessitated the expropriation of land, the creation of firing ranges, road-laying, and the construction of barracks and other facilities. The Groupement d'acquisition de Canjuers, a twenty-seven-person-strong group of lawyers, draftsmen, and other officials, oversaw the complicated task of acquiring land from thirteen communes and 1,045 landowners.[21] The drawn-out militarization process allowed civilians to continue their protests.

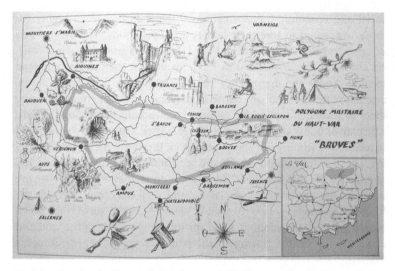

8.1 Map showing civilian activities that would be lost to militarization

The protest continues: Securing compensation and land-use rights

The decision to create Canjuers was a *fait accompli*. Protesters therefore turned their attention to securing maximum compensation rates. Throughout the expropriation process, the SDPHV continued to stress the economic and social value of the region's woods, pastures, farms, truffles, and lavender, as well as the sense of pain and 'complete disorientation' (*dépaysement*) felt by its inhabitants. To prove its point, it produced a map showing the range of human activities that took place in the Haut-Var, including bee-keeping, truffling, shooting, camping, pasturing, tourism, fishing, and caving (see figure 8.1).

The map laid bare all that would be lost to militarization and stood in stark contrast to contemporary military maps that showed how firing ranges would be laid across civilian geographies.[22] The maps were cartographic representations of the competing military and civilian environmental perspectives. They also underscore how competing civilian and military views over the land's value – was it productive land or a deserted and desolate wasteland fit only for militarization? – continued to dog the camp's creation.[23]

Self-interest informed, to an extent, the SDPHV's arguments. Its stress on the land's productivity helped justify its claims that landowners should be fully compensated for the loss of their land. Land of similar extent and quality would be hard to find for the same price elsewhere, it argued, particularly as the migration of *pieds-noirs* from Algeria to southern France had pushed up the price of land.[24] But despite their emphasis on local and traditional interests, campaigners called on outside expertise. Comps-sur-Artuby's mayor assigned an agricultural engineer to provide an independent valuation of the commune's land and natural resources.[25]

On the whole, the Canjuers Camp subsumed relatively isolated hamlets and farms and removed sections of territory from neighbouring towns and villages. But the fate of Brovès village, which was to be expropriated in its entirety, was a particular case. The villagers had until 1974 to leave their homes and territory after which date their village would be completely subsumed within the camp. They responded with symbolic protests: in 1964 they blocked the road to Brovès with trees and held a *méchoui*. The deployment of trees and ritualized eating of the sheep underscored their deep and historic attachments to the land. They also sought to achieve the best possible future for themselves. For although he was resigned to the fact that he was now mayor of a 'condemned village' (*village en sursis*), Monsieur Félix argued in October 1967 that even if the government accorded them a fair price for the land, their eviction would still mean the loss of the villagers' agricultural and practical knowledge of the land for which there would be no compensation.[26] These protests paid off, to an extent. The villagers lost their village but they extracted assurances from the government that the village would be transferred and fused with Seillans in accordance with their wish that they would be relocated together.[27]

With the weight of the state and army behind the expropriation process, the majority of landowners agreed to sell. Amongst them were the camp's most ardent opponents: by October 1967 Goujon had resigned as the SDPHV's president after selling his land. In the end, 80 per cent of the camp's surface area was ceded amicably meaning that judges only needed to issue 258 expropriation orders (the last of which on 11 August 1970).[28] Money, political will, paperwork, and the law ensured the camp's creation overrode individual and collective protests.

Once expropriation and compensation became less important issues, securing civilian access to militarized land came to the fore. Civilian sorties into the camp to gather mushrooms in 1972 provide one of the most colourful examples of this.[29] Hunting rights were a larger bone of contention. In 1969 Canjuers Camp's commander created a hunting society of 200 members comprised exclusively of military officers and former landowners prepared to pay 350 francs to join (the relatively high cost may explain why only 10 per cent of landowners took up the offer). Civilian authorities were far from impressed. Bargeme's mayor wanted hunters from neighbouring communes to hunt on the camp for free while Aiguine's mayor wanted second home owners to be allowed to hunt to encourage tourism.[30]

At the heart of the matter lay the status and meaning of hunting within French society. After the revolution, hunting had ceased to be the sole preserve of the elite. The restriction of hunting on Canjuers Camp to officers and reasonably well-off civilians was seen as an unwelcome throwback to anti-democratic times. Antoine de Bonnefoy, mayor of Tourtour, evoked hunting's revolutionary heritage to argue that the 'territory belongs to the Nation and not the army'. Any animal killed by a hunter on Canjuers would therefore constitute an attack on national property.[31] Recent French memories of German officers hunting in occupied France whilst civilian hunting was largely restricted, may well have further inflamed feelings. On a more personal level, individual hunters expressed a keen sense of loss because the camp divided up their hunting grounds into military and civilian zones. On the civilian side they could still hunt and pick mushrooms. But on the military side lurked 'death for us and our dogs, who don't know how to read the [warning] signs'.[32] Potentially lethal hazards had ruined the pleasure they once derived from hunting as their fields became the boundaries between militarized and civilian environments.

Enter environmentalism

Efforts to maintain hunting rights fitted seamlessly within long-standing concerns of civilian protests against militarization. But the campaign against Canjuers was neither static nor immune from wider political and social developments; at the start of the 1970s, environmentalist discourse began to infiltrate it. The creation of the Ministry for the Protection of Nature and Environment in 1971 buoyed protesters. Hotel owner and Comps-sur-Artuby councillor Jean-Marie Bain wrote to Robert Poujade, the newly installed Minister for the Protection of Nature and Environment, demanding that the army move warning signs and tanks from the side of the RN555 road because they gave the impression of a 'country under occupation'. At a time when environmental issues were at the fore, Bain wanted assurances that effective forest fire prevention measures were in place on the camp. Yet his tone was one of resignation. For even if his wishes were addressed, the camp would still 'clearly indicate that [France] has flouted [its] natural treasures and stupidly wasted [its] heritage'.[33] Despite the pessimistic tone, Bain's letter was a clear attempt to align the protest with emerging environmentalist concerns.

As Bain's stance indicates, the thrust of civilian protests had moved from resisting militarization to scrutinizing military management of the camp's environment and, when necessary, complaining. Locals voiced their anxieties over forest fires. Given that two fires had started in Oberhoffen Camp (Bas–Rhin) during military manoeuvres in spring 1971 and had subsequently damaged neighbouring civilian forests, their concerns about forest fires in the drier Provencal climate were not unfounded.[34] They also protested the army's deforestation of sections of the camp. One group of farmers lamented the 'massacre of very beautiful forests' to make way for training areas, roads, and fire break trenches. They also criticized alleged damage to archaeological sites, outbreaks of forest fires during manoeuvres, 'incessant noises' from weapons firing, and the pollution of water sources.[35] In short, they treated the army as an inconsiderate neighbour and land manager.

In response to these complaints, the army insisted that it was environmentally sensitive. It asserted that deforestation was necessary to create fire breaks, and that it was also planning to reforest 70,000 m² of the camp and introduce state-of-the-art fire-prevention measures. It also blamed sheep for the water pollution.[36] These claims formed part of its wider argument that it was a responsible steward of the environment of Canjuers. For instance, it argued that militarization would benefit fauna, suggesting that military game management would protect nature better than traditional Provencal hunting practices. These claims had some substance; foresters welcomed how, in the light of reports from nature protection societies, army directives had prohibited the killing of protected species.[37] The army's attempt to claim the environmentalist high ground represented an early attempt to show that military activity was compatible with responsible environmental management. In time, this seed would blossom into full-blown military environmentalism.[38] But for environmentalists, militarization equalled the sterilization and even death of nature at Canjuers. They therefore pressed for a section of the camp to become a national park.

A military base or national park for the Haut-Var?

Environmentalists drew on emerging environmentalist sentiments to contrast destructive military activity with peaceful nature. Consciously or not, this echoed narratives during the Franco-Prussian War and First World War that had equated conflict with the sterilization of bucolic fields, forests, and villages. Their position was innovative and pre-dated the interventions of US scientist Arthur Westing and the Stockholm International Peace Research Institute that highlighted the ecological damage caused by war and militarization in the mid- and late 1970s.[39]

Environmentalist anti-base sentiment crystallized at Canjuers when the Société pour la protection des paysages et de l'esthétique de la France founded the Comité des parcs naturels du Haut-Var (CPNHV or Committee for National Parks in the Haut Var) in 1967. Overseen by a collection of national and local nature protection societies, the committee's honorary president was none other than Clément Bressou who had spearheaded the Société nationale d'Acclimatation de France's national campaign to save its Camargue nature reserve against militarization during the Second World War.[40] Bressou's presence points to continuities in nature protection-inspired campaigns against militarization, even if they gained more traction in the 1960s and 1970s.

Starting with the establishment of the alpine Vanoise national park in 1963, France's national park system evolved alongside the geographic expansion of military lands in the 1960s and 1970s. Military lands and national parks share some characteristics. Both are controlled by state authorities, sometimes involve the eviction of local populations during their creation, and are policed by uniformed personnel.[41] But, as in Britain, many French environmentalists treated them as fundamentally incompatible.[42] Indeed, the CPNHV's main aim was the creation of a 150,000 ha national park in the Var stretching from the Verdon Gorges in the north to the Esterel massif on the Mediterranean coast in the south, including 5,000 ha of Canjuers Camp.

To further its objective of securing a national park, the CPNHV harnessed scientific knowledge, commissioning Professor Louis Poirion to produce a report for the Ministry of Agriculture on the environment of Canjuers. Poirion found that while the plan de Canjuers might seem semi-deserted from an agricultural point of view, it was in fact full of flora and fauna of a 'richness unknown in the rest of France and even in most of Europe'. The military base threatened this area of 'worldwide scientific renown'. A national park would be its best safeguard.[43] Poirion's heavy involvement in the national park movement and membership of the CPNHV undoubtedly influenced his findings. Nonetheless, his report shows how ecological science had began to inform anti-base campaigns alongside reports on militarization's social and economic consequences.

Although the CPNHV stressed Canjuers Camp's damaging social impact, it emphasized too the importance of protecting nature for nature's sake. According to its newsletter, the Var's politicians had ultimately given in to Paris-based planners and the military in allowing the camp to go ahead. They had led a 'policy . . . against nature' and turned the Haut-Var into a 'lost paradise'. Nature and society had lost out to militarization; 'instead of walking and horse-riding routes, we see a nature disfigured by . . . tanks and canons'.[44] The CPNHV were emphatically not deep ecologists, but they did advance a 'declensionist' or downward-spiral narrative of the impact of human activity on the environment.[45] In this case, militarization would ruin a once Edenic nature.

But in contrast to US environmentalists, who tended to favour protecting wildernesses free from human intervention, the CPNHV's Garden of Eden was peopled and productive. It supported a 1974 demonstration at Tourtour that called for 100,000 sheep to replace 10,000 soldiers on Canjuers plateau.[46] According to the CPNHV, sheep – symbols and agents of pastoralism and agriculture – were wholly compatible with nature protection. In line with other French environmentalist thinking, it was inclined to treat nature and culture has connected and reciprocal and to favour domesticated as well as wild nature.[47]

Throughout the period under study in this book, the French and other militaries mobilized trees for fuel, cover, and fortifying borders. In contrast, the CPNHV mobilized trees as symbols of life, in opposition to the death and destruction entailed by militarization. In November 1972 it organized a tree-planting ceremony on private land bordering Canjuers Camp and planned to erect a competing sign to the military ones that declared 'Forbidden Zone – Danger of Death'. The CPNHV's sign would read 'Protect the life of these trees – They ensure the survival of humanity'.[48] In April 1973 it held a similar ceremony at Tourtour, producing a poster showing a funerary wreath dedicated to nature (see figure 8.2). The equation of militarization and sterilization perhaps reached its most succinct portrayal in this poster. Sheep, like trees, represented peace, productivity, and place. The CPNHV therefore sent a letter to local politicians accompanied by a symbolic sheepskin to reiterate its demands for a national park.[49]

The fusion of traditional nature protection societies and more radical environmentalist ideas embodied in the CPNHV points to the radicalization of such groups in the 1970s.[50] The CPNHV's environmentalist stance dovetailed with the anti-authoritarian and anti-military atmosphere of post-1968 France to create a group that was unafraid to declare

8.2 Anti-Canjuers Camp poster showing the death of nature

its utopian and anti-militarist outlook. Previously, anti-base protesters tended to portray themselves as loyal patriots who broadly supported national defence objectives but thought that the proposed base would be better sited elsewhere. Although hardly free from NIMBY (not-in-my-back-yard)-ism, the CPNHV had wider aims: the partial withdrawal of the army from its bases and the replacement of military service with a national service dedicated to the environment and humanity.[51]

Environmental issues had come to the fore. But the CPNHV failed to achieve its main aim of securing a national park in the Haut-Var. The most important reason was the army's reluctance to cede any of its base for a national park. Its position was practically inevitable given the time, money, and effort it had expended on creating Canjuers Camp. But local mayors' unanimous and strident opposition to the national park was perhaps even more damaging to the CPNHV. Claiming that the proposed park would stifle tourism and economic development and represent yet another 'heavy burden' on local people, they questioned the CPNHV's very legitimacy and threatened to oppose their plans using, if necessary, the 'most extreme measures'.[52] As the mayors' stance amply demonstrates, the anti-base protesters were not a unified bloc. The mayors saw the CPNHV as yet another Paris-backed organization seeking to impose its objectives on the region. Environmentalism informed the Canjuers protest but it was not universally accepted, nor successful. Nonetheless, civilians across France were increasingly challenging the impact of militarization on the environment.

Foresters join the fray

Although the army tried to gloss its activities at Canjuers as environmentally friendly, it faced other criticisms regarding its stewardship of the French countryside. For despite some local cooperation (the army signed a convention with foresters allowing the latter to manage woodlands on Canjuers Camp[53]), foresters across France attacked the army's environmental credentials in the early 1970s. They complained about unauthorized military felling and how live ammunition was sometimes left strewn in forests after army manoeuvres. At Rouvray (near Rouen), the local forester became exasperated with soldiers repeatedly intruding into the state forest: on one occasion they were armed with bazookas and machine guns and on another they started a forest fire.[54] According to foresters, military activity menaced the serenity and safety of France's forests.

Local foresters' tough stance was encouraged by the central administration of the National Forest Office (the Office national des Forêts, or
ONF which replaced the Administration des Eaux et Forêts in 1966).
The ONF's introduction of a tougher regulatory and compensatory
framework in 1969 vis-à-vis military training in state forests was no small
financial matter for the French army, which regularly trained across
5,000 ha of state forests throughout France.[55]

As had long been the case, foresters remained concerned about the
economic value of forests and their control over them. But by the 1970s
they placed much more emphasis on the rights of an increasingly urban
population to unwind in the forest. Militarization seemingly threatened
the forest's recreational function. Foresters argued that firing at the
Mont–Merle and Glandée firing ranges in Fontainebleau forest was
'incompatible' with tourists' and Parisians' search for silence among
the trees.[56] For 'post-materialist' French society – when basic material
security was assured for the majority of the population – quality of life
issues had come to the fore and environmentalist promoted them.[57] This
helped change the way the French viewed militarized environments:
they wanted the right to roam in forests without a soundtrack of exploding shells. But if the tensions at Fontainebleau forest created a relatively
minor headache for military commanders, events on the Larzac plateau
caused them a major one.

The army targets Larzac

In Cold War France, military planners repeatedly toyed with the idea of
expanding Larzac Camp. Their Larzac schemes failed to reach fruition
in the 1950s and 1960s because of the difficulties involved in expropri-
ating the necessary land and the cost of creating Canjuers Camp.[58] But
calls for Larzac's extension refused to die down. The space needed to
manoeuvre modern mechanized units and the return of French troops
from West Germany informed the army's rational for expansion in 1967.
The favourable stance of some local politicians and inhabitants towards
the camp's extension (certain locals sent a pro-extension petition to the
Minister for Armed Forces after the abandonment of a 1964 extension
plan) had convinced some within the army that any extension of the
3,000 ha camp would run relatively smoothly.[59]

But at a time when environmentalists wanted to turn France's 'most
backward (*déshéritées*) regions' into national parks, army commanders considered their options limited, prompting them to turn towards

Larzac.[60] Unlike Canjuers, with its Mediterranean climate and varied terrain, the army did not view Larzac as an ideal training ground. Military reports depicted the plateau as tough, rocky and denuded with a challenging climate: cold in winter, stifling in summer, and battered constantly by violent winds. Furthermore, General Canonne asserted that the *causse*'s rocky terrain was unsuited to tank manoeuvres.[61]

But despite its tough climate and poor transport links, Larzac seemingly represented the only possibility to create a camp that would allow a mechanized brigade to conduct full manoeuvres.[62] From the military perspective, it also had a further major advantage: it was apparently empty, bar the sheep that supplied milk for Roquefort cheese and a few dilapidated farms. Military planners assumed that obtaining land in this *désert* would be relatively cheap and easy because the ageing population would be happy to sell up.[63] Consequently, after almost two decades of military deliberation and stalling, Minister for National Defence Michel Debré decided to extend Larzac Camp in August 1970. As a committed Gaullist and firm believer that France must be able to defend her independence and sovereignty (as outlined later in his 1972 White Paper on National Defence), Debré undoubtedly viewed the camp's extension as a key component of France's military capability.[64]

However, following the October 1970 announcement of the army's expansionary plan during a Union des Démocrates pour la République political party meeting, local officials and politicians lined up to denounce how it would ruin Larzac's past and present. Louis Balsan, the antiquities conservator of the Aveyron *département*, stated that the extension was 'madness' and would wipe out centuries of Templar history. Others were more concerned about the impact on agriculture. Roger Julien, mayor of Nant and general-secretary of the Association for the Sovereignty of the Larzac Causse, feared that the extension would turn a 'pastoral land' into a 'no man's land'. Staying with the Western Front imagery, sheep farmers and Millau's chamber of congress argued that the extension would 'sterilize' the region.[65] Other protesters pointed to the fact that the camp's climate only allowed for training in summer months (an argument which one military official privately admitted was 'exaggerated but partially true') and that increased noise would scare away tourists seeking peace and quiet.[66] Militarization seemed ready to swamp the region and campaigners once again positioned it as analogous with sterilization and destruction. At Larzac it would accelerate rural depopulation, destroy tourism, and damage Roquefort cheese production.

The complaints had some effect. The army scaled down the camp's projected size from 25,000 ha to 17,000 ha and redrew its boundary to exclude tourist sites, such as the village of La Couvertoirade and the Dourbie gorges, and to reduce the number of farms to be expropriated. To counter protests, Debré also stressed that the extension would bring an economic boost to the region and contribute to its much-needed modernization.[67] But although there was some room for civilian–military negotiations, the army was only prepared to concede limited ground. On 28 October 1971, Debré announced definitively the camp's 14,000 ha extension on national TV. Seemingly forgetting the ongoing local campaign against Canjuers Camp and the emerging one on Larzac, Debré stated that the extension would cause 'minimum inconveniences' bar the expropriation of land from 'the few peasants' who still lived there, 'more or less as they had done in the Middle Ages'.[68]

A May 1971 army report had described local opposition as 'unanimous' but not 'irreducible'.[69] However, provoked by Debré's condescending attitude, an organized anti-extension protest quickly got underway. On 6 November 1971 a 6,000-strong crowd gathered in the nearby town of Millau and four months later 103 of the farmers threatened with expropriation swore not to sell their land to the army. Although the events of 1968 cannot explain everything that subsequently followed, they undoubtedly contributed to the appeal and momentum gathered by the Larzac campaign. The area's *paysans* (peasants) were joined by a broad coalition of trade unionists, socialists, pacifists, 'neo-ruraux', Occitan regionalists, ecologists, Christians, communists, and 'young men and women of the hippy variety' (according to one gendarme report).[70] Numerous studies have analysed the politics and meaning of the non-violent Larzac campaign and its demonstrations, fasts, occupations, and study groups, a struggle which philosopher Jean-Paul Sartre described as 'one of the most beautiful of the twentieth century'.[71] Of interest here are the links between the campaign and environmentalism and the protesters' symbolic and material mobilization of the plateau's environment.

Domesticated Larzac

Protesters at Larzac advanced multiple images of the plateau and their close relationship to it in posters, newspaper articles, and at demonstrations. Amidst the diversity, two dominant representations of nature emerged. The first stressed the plateau's humanized and domesticated character whilst the second emphasized its wild and untamed qualities. The boundaries between these two images were fluid.

Individual interventions often contained depictions of the plateau's wildness and domesticity. For instance, Pierre Larret-Lagrange in *Revue de l'environnement rural* argued that the plateau should be spared 'sterilization' through militarization because it was both a 'rich agricultural land' and a 'zone of wild nature'. An image of sheep drinking at a man-made watering hole overlooked by a Christian cross on a rocky outcrop set the tone. Its caption asked if France really wanted to 'sterilize 17,000 ha of virgin nature' with tanks, shells, and helicopters.[72] Larret-Lagrange did not present the 'wild' (rocky outcrops) and 'domestic' (sheep and crosses) as binary opposites. Instead, they were overlapping and interchangeable points on a spectrum. Expressing the non-reification of 'virgin' nature within French environmentalism,[73] agriculturalist and environmentalist narratives existed in tandem throughout the Larzac campaign.

Following in the footsteps of anti-Canjuers Camp campaigners, Larzac activists attempted to persuade public opinion that militarization would ruin a historically rich region. They too produced a map showing the important historical sites that the extension would obliterate.[74] On one level, the map attests to the circulation of ideas between the campaigns (delegates from Larzac visited Canjuers and vice-versa[75]). But on another level, it shows the affective power and meaning of domesticated and peopled nature within French society.[76]

Larzac campaigners presented the plateau as agriculturally viable. Sheep rearing on the plateau's communal pastureland had traditionally ensured a degree of stability and prosperity. But since the breaking up of communal lands in the 1860s, many inhabitants had left the plateau, with some villages losing two-thirds of their population. The First World War, and the introduction of an eight-hour working day in the cities, had further drained the *causse*'s population.[77] But by the time Debré announced the camp's extension, the situation had changed. Investment and the arrival of young 'neo-ruraux' – urban outsiders attracted to the idea of farming and being close to nature – had helped restore a degree of agricultural prosperity. Innovative farming techniques, the cultivation of abandoned land, and the development of the Roquefort cheese industry all boosted agricultural production during the 1960s. According to geographers, an 'agricultural renaissance' was well underway.[78] Drawing on this agricultural renewal, protest literature explicitly contrasted military portrayals of a wild and empty *causse* with its productive and domesticated character.[79]

Campaigners argued that militarization was incompatible with farming and would crush the region's rebirth. Recent history backed up this claim. In 1963 the president of Millau's chamber of commerce bemoaned how military activity prevented a 'rational exploitation' of the land bordering the camp as farmers were unwilling to invest due to pasturing restrictions and wayward shells.[80] Farmers had particularly bitter memories of British troops manoeuvring on the plateau when tanks had flattened hedgerows and churned up fields and troops had set fire to crops, scared sheep with helicopters, and blown up trees.[81]

At times, the argument that agriculture and military activity were irreconcilable went even further, to assert that militarization equalled death and farming equalled life. According to the theme of the 1974 gathering at Rajal des Gorps, 'Wheat supports life, weapons create death' (*Le blé fait vivre, les armes font mourir*).[82] This formulation reversed the long-standing soldier-peasant myth that linked soldiers of peasant background with chauvinistic nationalism by transforming peasants into fervent anti-militarists.[83]

A further agricultural image in anti-extension literature was one of hard-working farmers successfully carving out a living through working the land. By exposing their farms to the public gaze through media outlets and the 'open farms' programme, farmers hoped to show that 'farms are active, that crops are prosperous, and that the region can survive thanks to the labour of its peasant workers'.[84] Peasants declared themselves as connected intimately to the land through their labour. At times this took precedence over other forms of connection; one protesting *paysan* argued that agricultural labour was the most important link to Larzac, rather than land ownership. In this sense, it may be better to view Larzac as a 'taskscape' than a 'landscape'.[85]

The farmers' description of themselves as '*paysans*' was as symbolic as the trees and sheepfold. *Paysan*, or peasant, has long-standing cultural connotations of rootedness, tradition, and continuity within French society. Pro-*paysan* Larzac literature appropriated tropes from the peasantry myth, such as the peasant's intimacy with the natural world. Novelist, historian, and former *maquisard* André Chamson believed that life on Larzac was lived according to tradition and the 'the rhythm of days and seasons'.[86] Similarly, a walking guide to the plateau informed readers that although the 'landscape has been deeply marked by human activity' it has not been 'destroyed' by it, because the 'peasant's work has blended naturally with the soil's model'.[87] While such language might remind us of the Vichy regime's 'back-to-the-land' rhetoric, it drew on the more rebellious history of eighteenth-century Camisard revolts and the French resistance's links with the peasantry during the Second World

War.[88] The Larzac campaign challenges the lazy assumption that rural France is necessarily politically reactionary and backward-looking. But it is necessary to emphasise that many of Larzac's paysans were in fact newly arrived city-dwellers: the politically radical 'neo-ruraux'.[89]

During the anti-base campaign, the peasants and their supporters strove to boost local agriculture and so demonstrate that the plateau was fertile. They rebuilt farm houses, sheepfolds, and roads, as well as installing telephone lines and water pipes. Their efforts sought to prove that the land was not the stony wasteland of army propaganda but 'an experimental agricultural zone' (according to campaign publication *Gardarem lo Larzac*). They achieved some success. Between 1970 and 1977 land under cultivation had increased from 3,060 to 3,950 ha.[90] If these figures are correct, the threat of the camp's extension had provided an additional spur to the agricultural renewal of the plateau. This *mise en valeur* of the agricultural environment aimed to intensify its productivity and so mobilize it as a more effective argument against militarization.

The illegal construction of La Blaquière sheepfold (which lay within the planned extension zone) is perhaps the campaigners' most famous attempt to physically demonstrate the viability of the region's agriculture and their own determination. As a symbol of resistance to militarization the large sheepfold became – according to one publication – 'the true cathedral of the Larzac movement'.[91] Symbolism was also apparent in the planting of 103 pine trees along the RN9 road to represent each of the 103 peasants who refused to sell their land to the army. According to farmer Janine Massebiau, the trees represented 'life, rootedness, and longevity', all qualities that the extension threatened.[92] Alongside their cultural resonance, the sheepfold and trees attest to the physical changes that the anti-base campaign ushered in.

Although trees and sheepfold held connotations of tradition and rootedness, farmers at Larzac claimed that they were willing to embrace progress. In a 1973 interview, local farmer and *Gardarem lo Larzac* editor Léon Maillé declared that although his family had farmed Larzac for generations, he was proud to run a profitable modern farm.[93] Whether as a political strategy or deeply held conviction, Maillé and other protesters combined the peasants' mythic qualities of tenacity and closeness to nature with a modernist and future-orientated outlook. Not only did this build on earlier attempts to unite radical politics and rural modernization but it challenged directly the army's portrayal of itself as a benevolent force bringing progress and modernity to the backward countryside.[94]

Like the vast majority of Larzac's peasants, Maillé's main source of income was sheep-rearing. Sheep quickly became a ubiquitous presence throughout the campaign. Protesters' enlistment of them further blurred the boundaries between tradition and modernity. Sheep-rearing had been intensively modernized on the plateau since the end of the Second World War, yet campaigners' representation of sheep as symbols of peace tapped into centuries old portrayals of them as peaceful and gentle creatures.

Sheep versus tanks

Sheep had long been essential to life on the plateau. Their milk and skins allowed farmers to make a living through supplying Roquefort cheese makers and Millau's glove industries.[95] Although centuries old, sheep rearing practices on the plateau had changed dramatically after the Second World War. By the 1970s, agricultural modernization had ushered in vaccination campaigns, artificial insemination, and selective breeding to boost milk and meat production. Consequently, four of the plateau's largest farms doubled milk production between 1960 and 1970.[96]

Even the army recognized that the sheep were vital to the region's economy and expressed some admiration for their ability to adapt to its tough climate and vegetation.[97] In fact, the army had first-hand knowledge of the plateau's sheep since the camp's establishment. Having ceded communal land to create the camp in 1899, La Cavalerie town council had secured pasturing rights on militarized land outside of firing times. Henceforth, local farmers vigorously defended their right to pasture sheep within the camp.[98] By the 1960s, army officials were complaining that shepherds paid little heed to firing times and grazed their sheep throughout the camp. Its sparse vegetation supposedly provided evidence of over-grazing.[99] Over-grazing or not, sheep embodied and maintained the plateau's domesticated character. They were agents in the sense that their grazing shaped its vegetation cover.[100]

During the anti-extension campaign the army tried to use the existence of 'thousands of sheep peacefully graz[ing]' on the camp's pastureland as proof that sheep and military activity could happily co-exist.[101] Protesters, however, made little mention of decades of relatively peaceful pasturing on the camp. Instead, images of defiant sheep resisting militarization abounded in campaign posters, books, and other publications. Anti-base campaigners turned them into living anti-militarist symbols, using sheep – real and imagined – to contrast their peaceful agriculture with violent militarization.

Campaigners imbued sheep with multiple meanings. A common theme was that the plateau's 'tough and obstinate' inhabitants – human and ovine – had only managed to survive in the tough environment by working together.[102] Sheep brought stability and equilibrium to the plateau. In the words of one commentator, they embodied the 'balanced relationship between man and nature, of an accord between human activities and a habitat (*milieu*) which was not a sign of desolation but one of beauty and grandeur'.[103]

Although sheep are found across France, campaigners portrayed them as representing a particular place: the Larzac plateau. In numerous cartoons, sheep are shown resisting Debré and the Paris-based French state, both represented as wolves. But perhaps the most common ovine image is that of a sheep holding a small branch in its mouth, which appeared on the first issue of the Association de sauvegarde du Larzac's newsletter *Larzac informations* (see figure 8.3). Its face looks rugged and strong but there is a hint of vulnerability in its eyes. The sheep symbolizes Larzac and its inhabitants: recalcitrant yet vulnerable to the army's whims.

Such images present sheep and militarization as binary opposites. But others are more ambiguous and blur ovine–military boundaries. One shows a semi-humanized sheep dressed as a soldier complete with helmet and gun.[104] In others, army research transforms sheep into weapons and disguises tanks as sheep.[105] Most notably, a cartoon by Jean-Marc Reiser that originally appeared in *Pilote* magazine visualized a novel way to resolve the dispute between the army and the protesters: sheep would take the place of tank tracks, providing the vehicles' propulsion whilst grazing on the plateau's grass.[106] Beyond the humorous potential of dressing sheep in uniform and imagining ovine-tank hybrids, the images' meanings remain ambiguous. Might they suggest that even innocent animals can be corrupted by militarism or that the possibilities of cohabitation between sheep and militarization are so absurd as to be against the natural order?

Either way, sheep were more than images during the anti-extension campaign as protesters mobilized actual sheep to achieve their aims. Sheep underpinned the plateau's agricultural character and farmers boosted their numbers to strengthen their claim that it was an economically viable region. Between 1970 and 1977 the total number of sheep (mainly of the Lacaune breed) had reportedly risen from 12,400 to 15,600 alongside a 42.3 per cent increase in milk production.[107]

As well as using sheep to prove that the Larzac was an agriculturally important area, protesters mobilized sheep in their 'actions' against the

8.3 Sheep's head with leaves, Association de Sauvegarde du Larzac, *Larzac informations*, 1973

army. Most famously, a group of *paysans* drove a lorry full of sheep into the centre of Paris and discharged its ovine cargo onto the grass of the champ de Mars. According to one of the peasants, the sheep were 'very cooperative' and happily began eating the grass.[108] Images of sheep grazing underneath the Eiffel Tower duly appeared in the national press and the 'action' succeeded in raising the campaign's profile. One of the *paysans*, Pierre Burguière, took much delight in the fact that when the police tried to round up the sheep they succeeded only in creating panic and scattering the flock. The sheep's alleged refusal to drink Parisian water similarly pleased him; it showed that like its *paysans*, Larzac's sheep were disdainful of Paris.

On the same day, but much closer to home, protesters released seventeen sheep in Millau to symbolize the 17,000 ha coveted by the army and the plateau's 17,000 ovine inhabitants.[109] Furthermore, in October 1977, during a trial of activists, protesters let loose a flock of sheep into Millau courthouse. As one remembers, 'about sixty sheep came in. It was spectacular! There was sheep shit everywhere'.[110] In Paris and Millau sheep brought chaos, muck, and the countryside to urban France. Whilst these 'actions' were media-savvy, they also contained elements of traditional peasant carnivals through their inversion of the established order.[111] But sheep also brought disruption to the plateau. On one occasion, protesters released sheep on country roads to impede military movement and disturb manoeuvring soldiers. And under the guidance of their shepherds, sixty sheep unwittingly joined the occupation of Cavailès farm (in which protesters had squatted after its acquisition by the army).[112]

Sheep were physical obstacles to military expansionism and reminders of the plateau's civilian and productive attributes. The Larzac militants successfully mobilized them to raise awareness of their demands. These sheep may have played an unwitting role in the campaign, but they were agents because they made a difference to the protest through their physical presence.[113] Yet important as they were, sheep were not the only animals to inhabit the campaign.

Wild Larzac

During the anti-base campaign, representations of the plateau as domestic and wild intermingled. Nonetheless, it was protesters of an environmental persuasion who mobilized most fully the plateau's fauna and flora as a counter argument to military expansion. They argued that the extension was 'incompatible with the preservation of the natural environment'.[114] For Monsieur Brosselin, scientific director of the French Federation of Nature Protection Societies, Larzac was the 'chosen land' (*aire d'élection*) for the golden eagle, eagle owl, and short-toed eagle. Yet the birds' survival was far from assured: increased troop numbers and helicopters would spell the 'end' for the rarest of them.[115] A member of Millau's Union for Nature Conservation similarly argued that the army's tanks and helicopters would disturb the Larzac's 258 species of birds and the 'rich and varied fauna' that thrived on a site thus far spared the 'errors of civilisation'.[116] Perhaps most worryingly for ecologists, long-lasting ecological degradation seemed imminent. According to one publication, militarization menaced the Larzac's 'fragile' flora and thin soils, which would not withstand the passage of tanks whose tracks remained imprinted in the land for years.[117] Such apocalyptic visions spurred campaigners to study Larzac's ecosystem so as to publicize all that would be lost if the extension went ahead. Jean-Michel Drevillaux introduced readers to the plateau's flora, including its boxwood, juniper, and amelanchier vegetation.[118]

As a wilder counterpart to the sheep, protesters mobilized the *cardabelle* (or *cardabela* in Occitan), a large thistle that grew in the plateau's least fertile soils, as a symbol of resistance. Appearing in numerous posters and other publications, the tenacious and spiky *cardabelle* represented determination and repelling enemy forces. As anthropologist Alexander Alland argues, 'it thus speaks metaphorically of the right to self-defense, a right granted by nature itself'.[119] The implication was that like those who grasped a thistle, the army would suffer on Larzac.

Like the *cardabelle*, the plateau's rocks represented rebellion. For Janine Massebiau, they symbolized the 'solidity' of the protesters' 'resistance' and 'determination'. These qualities were literally 'embedded' in the plateau's geology.[120] Campaigners also seized on General Alain de Boissieu's remarks that the plateau's rocky surface was unsuitable for tank manoeuvres as evidence that Larzac's rocks made the extension a futile project.[121]

Rocks and *cardabelle* symbolized Larzac's wild character. As with Canjuers, some protesters celebrated wildness to invert the military narrative of a rugged, silent and empty plateau fit only for militarization. The army argued that Larzac's desolation justified its militarization. In response, protesters claimed that its wild emptiness was worth saving. As Raymond Bonnefous asked, Larzac might be a 'tough land with vast horizons, a kind of 'French Wild West', but wasn't it strangely beautiful?'[122]

On the whole, however, environmentally informed protesters portrayed the plateau as humanized; they were not wilderness fetishists. In fact, one argued that the plateau's farmers were the 'guarantee' of its 'wild nature'.[123] Environmentalist narratives at Larzac stressed the importance of saving the wilder aspects of the plateau *alongside* farming. In their view, wildness and agriculture could co-exist, reflecting and reinforcing the wider character of French environmentalism, which was deeply concerned with the demise of France's peasantry and the *rural exode* as the country modernized and industrialized in the postwar period.[124]

Environmentalism on Larzac was often unashamedly anthropocentric. Like the Canjuers protesters, the Larzac campaigners were emphatically not Deep Ecologists. The majority of Larzac's environmentally informed protesters stressed the importance of preserving the plateau's environment primarily to ensure human use and enjoyment of it, rather than for nature's own sake. They argued that in an increasingly urban and industrial country the French needed outdoor spaces in which to relax and rejuvenate. Sites such as Larzac played a 'sanitary and hygienic role' in industrial civilizations. In order to 'blossom' and 'survive' the French had a 'greater need for open spaces and forests than military camps and cannons'.[125] In a similar vein, the regional delegate of the Minister for Nature Protection and the Environment wrote to military engineers asking for assurances that civilians would still have access to Larzac's 'wild grandeur'.[126] Some speleologists and walkers went further, calling for a regional park to preserve Larzac's built and natural environment for the benefit of all because 'nature's beauty is indispensable for the blooming [*épanouissement*] of modern man'.[127]

Environmentalists argued that militarized environments disrupted an otherwise peaceful countryside. Echoing previous anti-base campaigns, they contrasted militarization (noisy and destructive) with the civilian countryside (peaceful and productive). But environmentalism was not universally accepted within the campaigns. The speleologists' and walkers' preference for a regional park over a national park was meant to reassure farmers that agriculture would continue alongside conservation measures.[128] In this view, the preservation of the cultural and natural environment was not mutually exclusive. But in an echo of disputes at Canjuers, some protesters opposed the regional park proposal. One tract derided it as a form of Parisian 'colonization'. Instead, farmers wanted to be left alone to work the land in peace.[129] This intervention illustrates the anti-base campaign's diversity and the fact that environmentalism did not enjoy unanimous support in France.

Nonetheless, Larzac was a testing ground for emerging French environmentalist ideas and policies. Like the agriculture–military opposition, many came to see militarization and environmentalism as incompatible. For Friends of the Earth activist and professor Pierre Samuel, it was 'difficult to be an ecologist and not reject what we currently call [national] defence'. This was due to the pollution and energy expenditure caused by military activity, as well as the 'sterilization of good agricultural land' at Larzac.[130] Defending nature and defending nation seemed mutually exclusive.

But environmentalists and protesters at Larzac did not monopolize environmentalist rhetoric. Developing arguments previously advanced at Canjuers, the army and its supporters tried to show that militarization was a successful way of preserving the French countryside. Debré claimed that the army strove to combine military instruction with environmental preservation. His 1972 White Paper on National Defence claimed that independent research had found that military camps were 'exceptional reserves for flora and fauna' and that the military made an 'important effort', to modernize its infrastructure whilst paying attention to the 'coherent development of [French national] territory and environmental protection'.[131] De Boissieu backed Debré's contention, arguing that the army could 'participate, to an extent, in the improvement of our country's environment'. After all, it was used to operating outdoors. De Boissieu also hinted that some camps could become part of national parks and argued that soldiers could take part in forest upkeep and combat polluters and poachers in mountainous areas.[132] Colonel Devauges joined the charge, stating somewhat boldly that 'the military are the premier ecologists in France'.[133] These attempts to make bedfellows of militarization and environmentalism appear designed to counter the criticism directed at the army's environmental record at Canjuers, Larzac and elsewhere.

Claims that wildlife populations thrived on other military camps backed up the contention that Larzac's fauna had nothing to fear from the extension. A letter to *Combat Nature* alleged that military camps provided excellent protection for fauna, flora, forests, and vegetation by keeping agriculture, tourism, hunters, and fly-tipping at bay.[134] Pro-extension civilians pointed to the existence of deer, boar, wild cats, and other wildlife on other military sites as ample evidence that militarization protected valued species.[135] But such assertions held little sway against the groundswell of anti-military environmentalist rhetoric in Cold War France. As the next chapter outlines, it was not until the 1990s that they would gain greater currency. Nonetheless, the army's attempt to claim the environmentalist high ground demonstrates the malleability of its environmental perspective; it could supposedly protect France and its environment.

Ultimately, the campaign on Larzac was far more successful than the one against Canjuers Camp. The Larzac protesters kept their protest going throughout the 1970s, strengthened by national and international support. With an election approaching in 1981, socialist leader François Mitterrand sensed that votes might be won in this once conservative region and made the extension's annulment one of his manifesto policies. Soon after winning the election, he duly cancelled the extension and the army withdrew from the five farms it had occupied. The Aveyron's prefect then annulled the December 1972 decree that had declared the extension to be in the public interest.[136]

Anti-base sentiments lingered on elsewhere, however. In Brittany, Pierre Bridier railed against Coëtquidan Camp, describing it as a 'cancer' that would swallow up the region. Bridier's main worry was that any plans for an expanded weapons facility would harm what was left of the ancient and mythical Brocéliande forest and the well-being of Beignon village. Apparently influenced by the Larzac campaign, Bridier presented the army as a colonizer whose arrival spelt the destruction of local ecologies and culture. And although he did not demand that the army leave the camp, he allowed himself to wonder what might take its place; maybe a nature reserve, sporting centre, or rest place for convalescents. Militarization was once again contrasted with peaceful civilian activities unfolding within a healthy, natural environment.[137]

Bridier's intervention formed part of a series of low-key and isolated civilian attempts to limit militarized environments in the 1980s. Foresters at Fontainebleau opposed any extension and intensification of firing times at la Glandée firing range, citing restrictions on walking, hunting, and felling.[138] One forester listed numerous flaws in the army's management of the firing range: civilians entered the danger zone because of insufficient signage, troops manoeuvred outside the firing range, and army vehicles speeded on forest roads. Civilians were reportedly 'increasingly' unwilling to accept such behaviour.[139] But Larzac had halted the military's postwar expansionist drive and search for large-scale militarized environments. If military commanders had any plans to militarize other large areas of the countryside, they kept their plans to themselves.

Conclusion

The campaign against Canjuers Camp had failed but the one against Larzac Camp's extension succeeded. For the first time since the creation of Châlons Camp in 1857, civilian protesters had managed to thwart a large-scale military expansion project. Larzac campaigners raised the stakes of protest to include more than property rights or NIMBY-ism. Their protest was rooted in place but spoke to national and international concerns about militarization, the environment, and rurality.[140]

Why did Larzac succeed when other anti-base campaigns failed? Political context, such as the post-1968 atmosphere and Mitterrand's election, was undoubtedly very important. So too was the protesters' determination and ability to mobilize a wide range of supporters in France and abroad. But their mobilization of nature was essential to their success. Their articulation of the plateau as an agriculturally and ecologically rich site of national importance was formulated in response to the land itself, without which their claims would have been literally groundless. In this sense, their protest was 'more-than-human'.

How does the Larzac campaign further our understanding of

environmentalist campaigns? In her discussion of the creation of Thirlmere reservoir in Victorian Britain, Harriet Ritvo observes that 'the rhetoric of preservation and progress . . . continue to define opposed and often irreconcilable positions in environmental confrontations'.[141] The Larzac campaign was more complicated. Protesters challenged the army's narrative of progress and modernization and wanted to preserve the plateau's character and environment. But they did not reject notions of progress and modernity per se. As Herman Lebovics argues, the Larzac struggle included a passionately utopian strand.[142]

The creation and expansion of militarized environments have never been inevitable and have relied, to an extent, on civilian cooperation or indifference. These factors were lacking at Canjuers and, especially, Larzac. The Larzac campaign showed that effective civilian opposition against militarized environments was possible, despite the army's narrative of national defence imperatives.

After Larzac, major military geographical expansion was no longer a serious option. But France's military was determined to hold onto its existing bases and training grounds. To justify their control of national territory, they nurtured the seeds of military environmentalist rhetoric planted at Canjuers and Larzac, giving militarized environments an increasingly green tinge.

Notes

1 René Char, *La Provence point oméga* (Paris: Imprimerie Union, 1965).
2 Gustave Boissière, 'Un parc national dans le Vercors', *La Nature*, 3015 (15 December 1937), 583–4.
3 On the Cold War and environmentalism, see John R. McNeill and Corinna R. Unger (eds), *Environmental Histories of the Cold War* (New York: Cambridge University Press, 2010); Ralph H. Lutts, 'Chemical fallout: Rachel Carson's *Silent Spring*, radioactive fallout, and the environmental movement', *Environmental Review*, 9:3 (1985), 210–25; Thomas Robertson, '"This is the American earth": American empire, the Cold War, and American environmentalism', *Diplomatic History*, 32:4 (2008), 561–84. On French environmentalism, see Michael Bess, *The Light-Green Society: Ecology and Technological Modernity in France, 1960–2000* (Chicago and London: University of Chicago Press, 2003); Tony Chafer, 'The anti-nuclear movement and the rise of political ecology', in Philip G. Cerny (ed.), *Social Movements and Protest in France* (London: Frances Pinter, 1982), 202–20; Graeme Hayes, *Environmental Protest and the State in France* (Basingstoke: Palgrave Macmillan 2002); Brendan Prendiville, *Environmental Politics in*

France (Boulder, CO: Westview Press, 1994); Joseph Szarka, *The Shaping of Environmental Policy in France* (Oxford: Berghahn, 2002).

4 See, for instance, 'Pas une herbe, pas un caillou pour l'armée, Larzac', *Lutte antimilitariste*, no.7 [n.d.] in Jean Rabaut, *L'anti-militarisme en France 1810–1975: Faits et documents* (Paris: Hachette, 1975), 232–5. On the radical nature of post-1968 French environmentalism, see Hayes, *Environmental Protest*, 12–25; Prendiville, *Environmental Politics*, 5–18. Militant French environmentalism can be situated with the wider context of global environmental radicalism. Bron Raymond Taylor (ed.), *Ecological Resistance Movements: The Global Emergence of Radical and Popular Environmentalism* (Albany: State University of New York Press, 1995).

5 SHD-DAT 258 Général d'armée Jean Simon, to Général d'armée aérienne, Chef d'Etat-major des Armées, 'Champ de tir air-sol', 1 June 1971.

6 On the complex and contested influence of 1968, see Julian Jackson, 'The mystery of May 1968', *French Historical Studies*, 33:4 (2010), 621–53; Vincent Porhel, *Ouvriers bretons: Conflits d'usines, conflits identitaires en Bretagne dans les années 1968* (Rennes: Presses Universitaires de Rennes, 2008); Kristin Ross, *May '68 and Its Afterlifes* (Chicago: University of Chicago Press, 2002). On May 1968 and the army, including the creation of 'soldiers' committees', journals, and protests, see Oliver Pottier, *Armée-nation: Divorce ou réconciliation: De la loi Debré à la réforme du service national, 1970–2004* (Paris: L'Harmattan, 2005), 23–9. When thinking of Larzac, it is helpful to see the 'spirit' of 1968 – in France and elsewhere – stretching well into the 1970s. Gerd-Rainer Horn, *The Spirit of 1968: Rebellion in Western Europe and North America, 1956–1976* (Oxford: Oxford University Press, 2007).

7 Marianna Dudley, 'Greening the MOD: An environmental history of the UK defence estate, 1945–present' (PhD dissertation, University of Bristol, 2011); Tim Cole, 'A picturesque ruin? Landscapes of loss at Tyneham and the Epynt', in Chris Pearson, Peter Coates, and Tim Cole (eds), *Militarized Landscapes: From Gettysburg to Salisbury Plain* (London: Continuum, 2010), 95–110; Catherine Lutz (ed.), *The Bases of Empire: The Global Struggle against U.S. Military Posts* (New York: New York University Press, 2009); Holger Nehring, 'The British and West German protests against nuclear weapons and the cultures of the Cold War, 1957–64', *Contemporary British History*, 19:2 (2005), 223–41.

8 On Plogoff, see Gérard Borvon, *Plogoff: Un combat pour demain* (Saint-Thonan: Cloître, 2004); Porhel, *Ouvriers bretons*, 223–74. Larzac and Plogoff campaigners expressed their solidarity with each other in posters and during demonstrations. Borvon, *Plogoff*, 132, 144. On other campaigns against postwar state projects, see Robert L. Frost, 'The flood of "progress": Technocrats and peasants at Tignes (Savoy), 1946–1952', *French Historical Studies*, 14:1 (1985), 117–40; Gabrielle Hecht, *The Radiance of France:*

Nuclear Power and National Identity after World War II (Cambridge, MA: MIT Press, 1998). On regionalism in postwar France, see Maryon McDonald, *'We Are Not French!': Language, Culture, and Identity in Brittany* (London: Routledge, 1989); Vera Mark, 'In search of the Occitan village: Regionalist ideologies and the ethnography of Southern France', *Anthropological Quarterly*, 60:2 (1987), 64–70; Sara B. Pritchard, *Confluence: The Nature of Technology and the Remaking of the Rhône* (Cambridge, MA: Harvard University Press, 2011), 163–92.

9 On some of the ecological consequences of Lac Sainte-Croix, see Guy Brun, Réme Chappaz, Georges Olivari, 'Modification in habitat use patterns and trophic interrelationships on the fish fauna of an oligotrophic artificial lake: Sainte Croix (Provence, France), *Hydrobiologica* 207 (1990), 197–207. On the 'martyred village' of Les-Salles-sur-Verdon, see the Mémoire des Salles-sur-Verdon website, www.lessallessurverdon.com/index.html, accessed 26 April 2011.

10 ADV 1189 W 6 Préfet du Var to Général commandant la 9e Région militaire, 'Grand plan de Canjuers', 28 August 1962.

11 ADV 1189 W 1 Directeur des Services agricoles du Var, 'Observations sur conditions d'implantation d'un polygone militaire dans les plans de Canjuers', 10 July 1963.

12 ADV 1189 W 6 'Création d'un champ de manoeuvre et de tir dans la région des plan de Canjuers: Procès-verbal de la réunion du 22 avril 1963'.

13 AMC 1 W 4/2 newspaper clipping, 'Le premier ministre est formel: Pas de tirs atomiques sur le plan de Canjuers' [n.d.].

14 ADV 1189 W 1 Président de la Chambre de métiers du Var to Préfet du Var, 'Expropriations pour cause d'utilité publique des grands plans de Canjuers', 23 October 1963; ADV 1189 W 1 'Création d'un champ du tir et de manoeuvre dans le grand plan de Canjuers: Avis du service des Ponts et Chaussées du département du Var', 15 November 1963.

15 Bess, *Light-Green Society*, 38–53; *Modern and Contemporary France*, special issue on 'Tradition and Modernity in Rural France', 11:3 (2003); Susan Carol Rogers, *Shaping Modernities in Rural France: The Transformation and Reproduction of an Aveyronnais Community* (Princeton: Princeton University Press, 1991).

16 AMC 1 W 4/2 'Assemblée extraordinaire des membres du Syndicat de défense des propriétaires du Haut Var', 5 August 1962.

17 AMC 1 W 4/2 'Motion', 15 September 1963.

18 AMC 1 W 4/2 'Extrait du registre des délibérations du conseil municipal', 18 November 1963.

19 ADV 1189 W 6 Maire de Bauduen, 'Extrait du registre des délibérations du conseil municipal', 19 November 1963.

20 AMC 1 W 4/2 Marcel Gaimard to Président de la commission des enquêtes d'utilité publique, 9 November 1963.

21 Capitaine Bort, 'Une importante opération d'expropriation: Le polygone de Canjuers', *Bulletin technique du génie militaire* (1972), 63.

22 AMC 1 W 4/3 Syndicat de défense des propriétaires et habitants du Haut-Var, *Mémoire*, 3 November 1964, 25; SHD-DAT 6 T 716 'Monographie'.

23 ADV 1189 W 1 Expropriés du Haut-Var, 'Motion', 11 September 1969; ADV 1189 W 1 Préfet du Var to Chargé de mission, Présidence de la République, 28 October 1969.

24 AMC 1 W 4/3 Syndicat de défense des proprétaires et habitants du Haut-Var, 'Mémoire', 3 November 1964. By this time the Syndicat de défense des propriétaires du Haut-Var had renamed itself the Syndicat de défense des proprétaires et habitants du Haut-Var. But for the sake of simplicity, I continue to use SDPHV.

25 AMC 1 W 4/3 Henri Coutrot, 'Commune de Comps', November 1968.

26 R.B. 'Brovès'.

27 SHD-DAT 6 T 716 Etat-major de l'armée de terre, 'Dossier sur le complexe Canjuers-Draguignan', 7 December 1970. In the end, the village was transferred to new a site in Seillans's territory, becoming Brovès-en-Seillan.

28 ADV 1189 W 7 newspaper clipping, R.B. 'Brovès, le village en sursis', *Le Provençal*, 9 October 1967. Bort, 'Importante opération', 64.

29 SHD-DAT 6 T 716 'Monographie' [n.d. 1973?].

30 AMC 1 W 4/2 'Réunion de la Commission chargée d'étudier les problèmes concernant le polygone militaire de Canjuers', 7 November 1969.

31 'Dossier sur le complexe Canjuers-Draguignan'; ADV 1189 W 3 Maire de Tourtour to Directeur cabinet, Ministre des Armées, 17 August 1973; 'Réponse de M. le maire de Tourtour aux chasseurs "civils" de Canjuers', *République française*, 15 November 1973.

32 ADV 1189 W 3 'Les chasseurs des communes expropriées par le polygone de Canjuers souhaitent la création d'une zone neutre autour du camp', *Nice Matin*, 3 July 1972.

33 ADV 1189 W 3 Jean-Marie Bain to Ministre chargé de la protection de la nature et de l'environnement, 18 October 1971. In addition to Bain's intervention, one architect argued that the Canjuers Camp's proximity to outstanding natural features, such as the Gorges de Verdon, stood in stark opposition to the government's 'oft-declared desire to preserve our environment'. ADV 1189 W 3 André Chrysocheris to Préfet du Var, 'Camp militaire de Canjuers', 20 October 1972.

34 On the Oberhoffen forests fires, see the detailed correspondence in SHD-DAT 13 T 282.

35 AMC 1 W 4/2 Des paysans de Haut Var de la Bugada, 'Canjuers: Qu'est ce que c'est?' [n.d.].

36 Guy Foreau, 'Canjuers sans passion . . . ' *République-Le Provençal*, 14 October 1973. The army appears to have taken the risk of forest fires into account in its planning documents, not least because it feared how public

opinion would react if forest fires increased. 'Dossier sur le complexe Canjuers-Draguignan'.

37 Billon, 'Rapport'; 'Dossier sur le complexe Canjuers-Draguignan'; ADV 1189 W 3 Ingénieur en chef du Génie rural, des Eaux et Forêts, 'Exploitation cynégétique du camp de Canjuers', 14 February 1974.

38 Military environmentalism is the focus of the next chapter.

39 Arthur Westing, *Ecological Consequences of the Second Indochina War* (Stockholm: SIRPI, 1976); Arthur Westing, *Weapons of Mass Destruction and the Environment* (London: Taylor & Francis, 1977); Arthur Westing, *Warfare in a Fragile World: Military Impact on the Human Environment* (London: Taylor & Francis, 1980).

40 Chris Pearson, 'A "watery desert" in Vichy France: The environmental history of the Camargue wetlands, 1940–1944', *French Historical Studies*, 32:3 (2009), 479–509.

41 Edmund P. Russell, 'Afterword: Militarized landscapes', in Pearson, Coates, and Cole, *Militarized Landscapes*, 231. On the military roots of Yosemite National Park, see Harvey Meyerson, *Nature's Army: When Soldiers Fought for Yosemite* (Lawrence: University Press of Kansas, 2001).

42 Mark Blacksell and Fiona Reynolds, 'Military training in national parks: A question of land use conflict and national priorities', in Michael Bateman and Raymond Riley (eds), *The Geography of Defence* (London: Croom Helm, 1987), 215–27; Dudley, 'Greening the MOD'.

43 Louis Poirion, 'Pour la Protection de la nature dans la Haut-Var', CPNHV, Bulletin no. 6.

44 CPNHV, Bulletin no. 14, October 1974, 1.

45 On 'declensionism', see Richard White, 'Environmental history: Watching a historical field mature', *Pacific Historical Review*, 70:1(2001), 105–6.

46 CPNHV, Bulletin no. 14. On wilderness and US environmentalism, see William Cronon, 'The trouble with wilderness or, getting back to the wrong nature', *Environmental History*, 1:1 (1996), 7–28.

47 Bess, *Light-Green Society*; Kerry Whiteside, *Divided Natures: French Contributions to Political Ecology* (Cambridge, MA: MIT Press, 2002).

48 CPNHV, Bulletin no. 11, September 1972.

49 AMC 1 W 4/2 Lettre ouverte du Comité des parcs naturels du Haut-Var aux notables du Var [n.d. April 1973?].

50 Prendiville, *Environmental Politics in France*, 5–7.

51 CPNHV, Bulletin no. 14, 4.

52 AMC 1 W 4/2 'Resolution' signed by 47 mayors, 20 March 1969.

53 SHD-DAT 13 T 34 'Convention relative à la gestion forestière des forêts et terrains domaniaux du champ de tir de Canjuers (Var)', 26 January 1970.

54 SHD-DAT 13 T 33 Ingénieur du Génie rural, des Eaux et Forêts to Général commandant la 23ᵉ division militaire, 25 April 1967.

55 SHD-DAT 13 T 33 'Difficultés avec l'Office national des forêts pour

l'utilisation des forêts domaniales par le troupe en manoeuvres', 2 September 1969.

56 ADSM 3344 W 188 X. de Boyer to Directeur régional de l'Office national des Forêts, 'Terrains boisés affectés au Ministère d'Etat chargé de la Défense nationale', 23 October 1970.

57 On post-materialism, see Bess, *Light-Green Society*, 87–8.

58 SHD-DAA F 5962 Général de division Jousse to Général commandant la 4e région aérienne, 'Champ de tir aériens', 22 October 1951; SHD-DAT 27 T 116 Général Caminade, 'Extrait du rapport', 3 January 1955.

59 SHD-DAT 27 T 116 Général Offel de Villaucourt, Sous-chef d'Etat-major de l'armée de terre, 'Extension du camp du Larzac', 17 August 1967; SHD-DAT 27 T 116 Etat-major de l'armée de terre, Direction technique des armes et de l'instruction, 'Camp de Larzac', 23 September 1964.

60 SHD-DAT 27 T 116 Général de C. A. Usureau, 'Extension du camp du Larzac', 8 April 1970.

61 SHD-DAT 27 T 116 Général de division Canonne, 'Extension du camp du Larzac', 16 October 1967.

62 Usureau, 'Extension du camp du Larzac'.

63 See, for instance, SHD-DAT 27 T 116 Commission d'étude sur les projets d'acquisitions domaniales, 'Projet d'Extension du Camp du Larzac', May 1963.

64 SHD-DAT 27 T 116 Ministre d'Etat chargé de la Défense nationale to Général Commandant la 4e Région militaire, 'Camp du Larzac: Extension', 5 August 1970. For a sense of Debré's ardent Gaullism, see his memoirs. *Combattre toujours 1969–1993: Mémoires*, vol. 5 (Paris: Albin Michel, 1994).

65 Jacques Isnard, 'Les aveyronnais sont divisés sur l'opportunité de sextupler la superficie du camp de Larzac', *Le Monde*, 6 March 1971.

66 SHD-DAT 27 T 116 copy of letter from Général Boyer de la Tour to *Le Monde*, 17 March 1971 with handwritten comments; Yvon Maynadier, 'Le projet d'extension du camp du Larzac est très critiqué par les responsables locaux', *Le Monde*, 17 February 1971.

67 SHD-DAT 27 T 116 Ministre d'Etat chargé de la Défense nationale to Préfet de l'Aveyron, 'Extension du camp du Larzac', 27 October 1971.

68 Quoted in Herman Lebovics, *Bringing the Empire Back Home: France in the Global Age* (Durham, NC: Duke University Press, 2004), 32.

69 SHD-DAT 27 T 116 'Fiche concernant le projet d'extension du camp du Larzac', 25 May 1971.

70 SHD-DAT 2 T 62 Comandant la compagnie de gendarmerie du Millau, 'Actions d'opposition à l'extension du camp militaire du Larzac', 7 April 1972.

71 Sartre quoted in *Le Larzac, l'armée . . . la violence et les Chrétiens*, texte collectif, supplement au numéro 63 d'Alerte Atomique, [n.d.], 87. On the Larzac struggle, see Alexander Alland with Sonia Alland, *Crisis and*

Commitment: The Life History of a French Social Movement (Yverdon: Gordon and Breach, 1994); Yves Hardy and Emmanuel Gabey, *Dossier L . . . comme Larzac* (Paris: Editions Alain Moreau, 1974); Lebovics, *Bringing the Empire Back Home*, 13–57; Michel le Bris, *Les fous du Larzac* (Paris: Les presses d'aujourd'hui, 1975); Didier Martin, *Le Larzac: Utopies et réalités* (Paris: L'Harmattan, 1987).

72 Pierre Larret-Lagrange, 'Encore le Larzac', *Revue de l'environnement rural*, no. 5, April 1972, 16. For similar imagery, see ADA 507 W 5 *Quelques paysans du Larzac* [n.d.].

73 Bess, *Light-Green Society*, 132–4.

74 ADA 507 W 5 'Larzac en Rouergue', undated map.

75 CACAN 20050521/25 *Larzac: Un enjeu national* [n.d. 1977?], 3. In turn, Larzac protesters offered their support to the campaign against the extension of the army's Fontevrault training ground. Hardy and Gabey, *Dossier L*, 169.

76 Armand Frémont, 'The land', in Pierre Nora (ed.), *Realms of Memory: Rethinking the French Past. Volume 2: Traditions*, trans. Arthur Goldhammer (New York: Columbia University Press, 1997), 3–35.

77 Francis Laur, *Le plateau du Larzac: Contribution à l'étude de la vie économique de la région et à l'histoire des biens communaux avant et après la Révolution* (Montpellier: Imprimerie de la Charité, 1929), 145–6, 152–3.

78 J. Pilleboue, P.-Y. Péchoux, and M. Roux, 'Le nord du Causse du Larzac: Une renaissance rurale menacée', *Revue géographique des Pyrénées et du sud-ouest*, 43:4 (1972), 459.

79 SHD-DAT 2 T 62 Les jeunes agriculteurs du Larzac, 'Opération fermes ouvertes sur le plateau du Larzac', leaflet distributed on the RN9 road, 2–3 April 1972.

80 SHD-DAT 27 T 115 Président de la Chambre de commerce de Millau to Ministre de l'Agriculture, 2 May 1963. A year later one farmer complained that troops had broken into his farmhouse, leaving practice ammunition, broken tiles, and graffiti in their wake. SHD-DAT 27 T 116 Garde-champêtre de la commune de Millau, 'Plainte de M. Millet Georges, propriétaire à Combebrin', 13 August 1964. See also, Hardy and Gabey, *Dossier L*, 32–3.

81 'Nous garderons le Larzac! Des paysans parlent', supplement of *Que faire*, nos. 8–9, 1971.

82 *Larzac: Un enjeu national*, 13.

83 Gérard de Puymège, *Chauvin, le soldat-labourer: Contribution à l'étude des nationalismes* (Paris: Editions Gallimard, 1993).

84 SHD-DAT 2 T 62 'Larzac resistenso!', leaflet distributed at La Cavalerie, 2 April 1972.

85 'Un paysan raconte la véritable aventure du Larzac', *L'Express méditerranée*, no. 34, October 1973, 55. On taskscapes, see Tim Ingold, *The Perception*

of the Environment: Essays in Livelihood, Dwelling, and Skill (London: Routledge, 2000), 195.

86 André Chamson, 'Preface', in *Larzac: Terre méconnue* (Paris: Les Editions ouvrières, 1973), 7. Activists living on Larzac today still refer to themselves as 'paysans', associating it with 'a rejection of productivist agriculture and . . . resistance to hegemonic forces'. Gwyn Williams, *Struggles for an Alternative Globalization: An Ethnography of Counterpower in Southern France* (Aldershot: Ashgate, 2008), 33.

87 Larzac université, *Promenades sur le Larzac*, 4.

88 Georgette Milhau, 'L'histoire du Larzac de la fin des templiers aux maquisards', in *Larzac: Terre méconnue*, 209; Louis Balsan, 'Pour faire en exemple', *Le Monde*, 31 January 1973, 21; Larzac université, *Promenades sur le Larzac* (Millar: Imprimerie Artypo, 1979) 4. On the resistance and peasants, see H.R. Kedward, *In Search of the Maquis: Rural Resistance in Southern France 1942–1944* (Oxford: Oxford University Press, 2003 [1993]).

89 On the neo-ruraux, see Claude Mercier and Giovanni Simona, 'Le néo-ruralisme: Nouvelles approches pour un phénomène nouveau', *Revue de Géographie Alpine*, 71:3 (1983), 253–65; Daniel Leger and Bertrand Hervieu, 'La nature des néo-ruraux', in A. Cadoret (ed.), *Protection de la nature: Histoire et idéologie. De la nature à l'environnement* (Paris: L'Harmattan, 1985), 152–60.

90 *Gardons le Larzac: Dossier établi à l'occasion de la signature des arrêtés de cessibilité sur les communes de la Roque Sainte-Marguerite et de la Cavalerie* (Potensac: Gardarem lo Larzac [n.d.1978?]).

91 Larzac université, *Promenades sur le Larzac*, 18.

92 Quoted in Hardy and Gabey, *Dossier L*, 169.

93 'Un paysan raconte la véritable aventure du Larzac', 51. Regarding the construction of a hydroelectric dam at Tignes in the early 1950s, Robert L. Frost argues that 'displaced peasants could not comprehend that a price could be placed on cultural traditions, ancestral lands, and local history' by technocratic modernizers ('Flood of progress', 118). The division between tradition and modernity was less pronounced at Larzac.

94 On the Popular Front's plans to modernize rural France, see Shanny Peer, *France on Display: Peasants, Provincials and Folklore in the 1937 Paris World's Fair* (Albany: State University of New York Press, 1998).

95 This contribution had already been made clear in Millau's chamber of commerce's protests against a proposed extension to the army camp in 1926. ADA 2 Z 217 Président de la Chambre de commerce de Millau to Sous-Préfet de Millau, 30 June 1926.

96 Pilleboue et al., 'Nord du Causse du Larzac', 458–9.

97 SHD-DAT 27 T 116 Etude CEPAD, 1963.

98 ADA 31 R 2 'Extrait du registre des délibérations du conseil municipal de la commune de Millau', 24 April 1924; SHD-DAT 3 V 55 Chef de Bataillon

Borel, 'Compte-rendu sur la conférence sur les régimes des champs de tir au Larzac', 25 June 1926.

99 Commission d'Etude, 'Projet d'Extension'.

100 On animals shaping environments, see Sarah Whatmore, *Hybrid Geographies: Natures, Cultures, Spaces* (London: Sage, 2002), 52–5.

101 'Entretien avec le Général de Boissieu, Chef d'Etat-major de l'armée de terre', *Revue de la Défense nationale*, October 1974, 73.

102 Christian Rudel, 'Le causse du Larzac va-t-il vivre la guerre des moutons?' *Le pèlerin du 20e siècle*, no. 4616, 19 May 1971, 44.

103 Michel Pichol, 'Territoire à prendre, territoire à défendre: Le Larzac', *Hérodote: Stratégies, géographies, idéologies* (April–June 1978), 2. See also Comité départemental de sauvegarde du Larzac et Chambre d'agriculture Rodez, *Le Larzac* (Rodez: Association de Sauvegarde du Larzac et son environnement [n.d.]), 11.

104 Image of a protester's placard accompanying the newspaper article 'Six mille manifestants affirment leur volonté de sauvegarde du Larzac', *Midi Libre*, 7 November 1971.

105 Joëlle Ayats *et al.*, *Dessine-moi le Larzac 1971–1981: Dix ans de lutte, dix ans de dessins* (Paris: Comité Larzac de Paris, 1981), 32, 41.

106 Reproduced in *La Dépêche*, 14 November 1971, newspaper clipping in ADA 200 W 253.

107 *Gardons le Larzac*, 15.

108 'Les brébis occupant le champ de Mars', *Larzac Informations*, no. 1.

109 Hardy and Gabey, *Dossier L*, 166–7.

110 Quoted in Alland, *Crisis and Commitment*, 61. In a similar vein, sheep and Larzac protesters joined a demonstration at Plogoff in February 1980. Borvon, *Plogoff*, 114.

111 For an earlier use of carnival as a form of peasant protest, see Peter Sahlins, *Forest Rites: The War of the Demoiselles in Nineteenth-Century France* (Cambridge, MA: Harvard University Press, 1994).

112 Lebovics, *Bringing the Empire Back Home*, 46; Alland, *Crisis and Commitment*, 58; 'La guérilla écologique', *Le Monde*, 12 July 1977.

113 For discussions of nonhuman agency that moves beyond the pre-requisite of human-levels of intentionality, see Jonathan Burt, *Animals in Film* (London: Reaktion, 2002), 31–2; and Bruno Latour, *Politics of Nature: How to Bring the Sciences into Democracy* (Cambridge, MA: Harvard University Press, 2004), 76.

114 Jean-Michel Drevillaux, *A la découverte de la flore du Larzac* (Comités Larzac/Association pour la promotion de l'agriculture sur le Larzac [n.d.]).

115 M. Brosselin, 'La faune du Larzac', in *Larzac: Terre méconnue*, 67–75.

116 A. Molinier, 'Défendre le Larzac, c'est aussi protéger la Nature', *Gardarem lo Larzac*, no. 38, November 1978, 3. See also Lebovics, *Bringing the Empire*

Back Home, 43; 'Toujours à propos du camp du Larzac', *La Dépêche du midi*, 20 October, 1970.

117 Comité départemental de sauvegarde du Larzac and Chambre d'agriculture Rodez, *Le Larzac*, 11. Since at least the 1990s, a spate of scientific studies has assessed the impact of military vehicles on the soils of militarized environments. For a flavour, see Rachel A. Hirst, Richard F. Pywell, Rob H. Marrs, and Philip D. Putwain, 'The resistance of a chalk grassland to disturbance', *Journal of Applied Ecology*, 40:2 (2003), 368–79; Beatrice van Horne and Peter B. Sharpe, 'Effects of tracking by armored vehicles on Townsend's ground squirrels in the Orchard Training Area, Idaho, USA', *Environmental Management*, 22:4 (1998), 617–23.

118 Drevillaux, *A la découverte de la flore du Larzac*.

119 Alland, *Crisis and Commitment*, 106.

120 Hardy and Gabey, *Dossier L*, 169.

121 Léon Maillé raised this point in 'Pourquoi l'extension du camp du Larzac', *Le Dépêche*, 4 October 1978.

122 Raymond Bonnefous, 'En guise de conclusion', in *Larzac: Terre méconnue*, 211.

123 Molinier, 'Défendre le Larzac'.

124 Bess, *Light-Green Society*, 38–53.

125 J. Prioton, 'Les bois et forêts du Larzac et leur flore', in *Larzac: Terre méconnue*, 65. The Association de sauvegarde du Larzac et de son environnement similarly argued that city dwellers seeking peace and quiet on Larzac would not be impressed by the noise, tanks, and pollution emanating from the military base. Association de sauvegarde du Larzac et de son environnement, *Les problèmes posés par l'extension du camp militaire du Larzac*.

126 SHD-DAT13 T 275 E. Fontan to Directeur des travaux du génie, Montauban, 'Extension du camp du Larzac', 4 July 1972.

127 Pierre Goth, 'La sauvegarde du Larzac et des Causses', *Centre-Presse*, 16 December 1971.

128 Goth, 'La sauvegarde du Larzac et des Causses'.

129 SHD-DAT 2 T 62 'Larzac resistenso!' leaflet distributed at La Cavalerie, 2 April 1972.

130 CACAN 20050521/25 Pierre Samuel, 'Quelle défense?' [n.d.]

131 *Livre blanc sur la défense nationale*, vol. 1 (Paris: Centre de documentation de l'armement, 1972), 95.

132 ADA 507 W 5 Debré quoted in 'L'affaire du Larzac', *Centre-Presse* [n.d.]; 'Une interview exclusive du chef d'Etat-major de l'armée de terre', *L'Aurore-document*, 21 May 1973.

133 Quoted in Molinier, 'Défendre le Larzac'.

134 *Combat Nature*, No. 21, August 1975, 57.

135 Groupement local et régional pour le camp du Larzac, *Larzac en question*, 44–9.

136 CACAN 19950127/7 Présidence de la République, Exécution de la décision présidentielle sur le Larzac', 4 July 1981. See also Lebovics, *Bringing the Empire Back Home*, 55. It is worth noting that Mitterrand had opposed Debré's decision from at least 1972. 'M. Mitterrand demande à M. Debré de s'expliquer sur le projet d'extension du camp de Larzac', *Le Monde*, 23 January 1972. On Mitterrand's defence policies, see Rachel Utley, *The French Defence Debate: Consensus and Continuity in the Mitterrand Era* (Basingstoke: Palgrave Macmillan, 2005).

137 Pierre Bridier, *Le Camp de Coëtquidan va-t-il dévorer Brocéliande?* (Beignon: P. Bridier, 1984), 4, 15, 23. On the area's history, see Marquis de Bellevue, *Paimpont: Le Camp de Coëtquidan* (Rennes: La Découvrance Editions, 1994 [1912]).

138 ADSM 3344 W 182 'Procès-verbal de la conférence mixte relative à la révision du régime du champ de tir de la Glandée utilisé par la garnison de Melun', 7 August 1930.

139 ADSM 3344 W 182 Chef du groupe technique de Chailly-en-Bière to Ingénieur des travaux, Chef de division de Fontainebleau, 9 November 1989.

140 Harriet Ritvo argues that the 'conspicuous involvement of individuals and interests unconnected with property in the narrowest sense' is a common and necessary feature of modern environmental protests. *The Dawn of Green: Manchester, Thirlmere, and Modern Environmentalism* (Chicago: University of Chicago Press, 2009), 3–4.

141 Ritvo, *Dawn of Green*, 178.

142 Lebovics, *Bringing the Empire Back Home*, 57.

9

'Greening' militarized environments

Introduction

Within the militarized environment of Captieux firing range, plants, such as marsh clubmoss, thrive amongst the drainage lakes created by the US army during its construction of weapon storage facilities in the early 1950s.[1] The military presence at Captieux unintentionally created suitable conditions for rare species to flourish. Now, some ninety years after its militarization during the First World War, Captieux is set to be integrated into the European Union's Natura 2000 network of ecologically rare and important habitats. It is now charged with dual functions. It is simultaneously a site of war preparation *and* classified as an ecologically important habitat. Like many other militarized environments in France, it has been 'greened' in the sense that it is dubbed a site of biodiversity and managed accordingly.

Surprisingly, given the military–environmentalist conflict at Canjuers and Larzac, the Ministry of Defence now often works with, rather than against, ecologists within a shared environmentalist framework.[2] Its green credentials received a high-placed boost in 2000 when the Minister for the Environment stated that 'military activities are compatible with the maintenance of natural habitats . . . [and even] ensure the preservation of certain species of fauna and flora'.[3] The French military uses such statements to portray itself as an important environmentalist actor. By the beginning of the twenty-first century, militarized environments had therefore become thoroughly enmeshed with wider environmental policies.

The emergence of military environmentalism, or the claim that militarization and environmentalism can co-exist and flourish, is a neglected aspect of the changes undergone in the French military sphere since 1989.[4] But it is not restricted to France. Indeed, military environmentalism is a global and controversial phenomenon.[5] On the one hand, militaries across the world claim that they treat the environment responsibly and that their lands are reservoirs of biodiversity nestling among civilian environments that modern agriculture, tourism, and urbanization have ecologically depleted. Military geographers and other aligned scholars support these claims.[6] On the other hand, critical commentators attack the military appropriation of civilian environmental discourse and policies. They argue that military activity is fundamentally incompatible with environmentalism and sustainable development and that military environmentalism is no more than a cynical attempt to justify military control over vast swathes of land. In the post-Cold War era, when militaries suffer a crisis of legitimacy and purpose, military environmentalism obscures the less savoury aspects of contemporary militarization, obscures the pollution caused by military activity, and seeks to defuse civilian demands for access to military land.[7]

Much of the critique of military environmentalism holds true for France. Most notably, President Jacques Chirac relaunched France's underground Pacific Ocean nuclear testing programme in 1995, to global environmentalist dismay, in the same year as the Ministry of Defence signed an accord with the Ministry of the Environment.[8] Within France itself, the military uses the existence of rare flora and fauna on its sites to justify its ownership of land. It has frequently coopted the language of nature protection to serve its own interests (including its attempt to defuse civilian opposition during the creation of Canjuers Camp by claiming that military presence benefited wildlife[9]) whilst environmental success stories generate good PR.[10] Furthermore, the military's stress on its environmentalist activities glosses over some of its more controversial clashes with civilians. The tone of reconciliation permeates the Ministry of Defence's *Défense et protection de la nature* (2000) brochure, which reports how soldiers from the 122nd infantry regiment restored a ruined farmhouse and drinking well located within Larzac Camp with 'respect for the typical architectural style of the *causse*'. Without mentioning the decade-long Larzac campaign, the brochure describes Larzac as 'one of the rare French regions where one can observe a traditional human habitat within a preserved landscape'.[11] But the history of military environmentalism in France is more complex and profound than these cases of 'greenwashing' suggest. For however flawed, partial, and self-interested it may be, military environmentalism needs to be added to the other ways in which military personnel perceive and mobilize the environment (as a battlefield, training ground, potential obstacle, and so on).

This chapter explores the 'greening' of French militarized environments. It argues that since the 1990s the military has tried to 'green' its relationship with the environment, motivated by the desire to reduce the likelihood of civilian complaints and to align itself with an environmentally attuned age. Efforts to reduce pollution and, more recently, carbon emissions, demonstrate the flexible and varied character of military environmentalism, whilst the designation of military sites as quasi-nature reserves has opened them up to greater civilian scrutiny and management, further blurring civilian–military boundaries within militarized environments.

Although critics have portrayed France as an environmentally unfriendly country, the history of military environmentalism suggests that environmentalist ideas have spread into overlooked areas, such as national defence.[12] But like civilian environmental policies, French military environmentalism has its limits. According to Michael Bess, France has become a 'light-green society' in which environmentalist ideas are widespread but shallow: 'the result is a social order in which virtually every activity is touched by environmentalist concerns – but modestly, moderately, without upsetting the existing state of things too much'.[13] Civilian society remains, on the whole, wedded to consumerist lifestyles that are fundamentally incompatible with environmentally responsible living. Lifestyle takes priority over sustainable development. Likewise, military operational capability takes precedence over military environmentalist policies. As this chapter outlines, environmentalist ideas have pervaded the military's activities.[14] But its priority remains national defence. If its environmentalist attitudes were transposed onto a camouflaged uniform, it would be light, not dark, green.

The rise of military environmentalism

Military environmentalism in France emerged alongside its development in other Western democracies. Following civilian opposition to army training on Dartmoor and Lulworth ranges in southern England, the Defence Lands Committee commissioned a report by Lord Nugent. The most surprising aspect of Nugent's 1973 report was the finding that British nature conservationists 'tended to support the retention of land by the Services, on the general arguments that MOD land holdings are, for the most part, shielded from commercial development and public use, thus allowing the incidental protection of flora and fauna and physical features from destructive agents'.[15] Following Nugent's conclusion that military nature protection efforts were uncoordinated, the British Ministry of Defence appointed a nature protection officer, Lt Col Norman Clayden, in 1973, established military–civilian conservation groups on army bases, and began publishing a nature protection magazine entitled *Sanctuary* in 1976.[16] French military environmentalism during the 1970s and 1980s was less coordinated and extensive, but environmentalist ideas and rhetoric did begin to infiltrate military circles.

In France, military environmentalism developed, in part, as a civilian–military joint venture. For cooperation between the military and nature conservationists (as opposed to more militant environmentalists[17]) had begun to coalesce away from the flashpoints of Canjuers and Larzac camps. As discussed in the last chapter, ecologists, nature protection societies, and environmentalists had stridently opposed military expansion at Canjuers and Larzac, equating militarization with the death of domesticated and wild nature. Their narrative of militarization-as-sterilization had drowned out the army's counterclaim that militarization could co-exist with ecologically healthy environments.

Yet elsewhere the unintentional ecologies of militarized environments brought certain civilian ecologists and army officers together. In 1971 – the year the Larzac struggle began – a report by J. Ancellin of Cherbourg's Society for Natural Sciences and Mathematics highlighted the ecological importance of the army's firing range at Biville dunes in Normandy. Yellow irises and common water-crowfoot grew amongst the coastal dunes, providing habitats for little grebes, ducks, and moorhens. Significantly, Ancellin identified tourism rather than military presence as the main threat to the dunes' preservation.[18]

Ancellin's findings dovetailed with military interests. Local army commanders, worried about tourism encroaching on their artillery training ground, seized on his report as evidence that military ownership provided the dunes' ecologies with the best possible protection.[19] Army commanders had little interest in preserving the dunes' habitats and wildlife. Their main priority was preventing civilian encroachment from hindering military training. Nonetheless, by suggesting that military ownership could unintentionally help preserve ecologically significant sites, Ancellin's report showed military commanders that they shared some common ground with ecologists.

Biville was not an isolated case. On the Franco-German border, ecologists turned their attention to the ecology of Bitche Camp's impact zone.

They found that exploding shells had maintained ecologically important heathlands which supported a diverse range of flora and fauna unique to the area.[20] Once again, military presence and activity seemed to maintain ecosystems that did not exist on surrounding civilian lands. And although the army was unwilling to even entertain the idea of including Canjuers Camp within a national park (see chapter 8), it fostered closer relations with the Parc naturel régional des Vosges du Nord (PNRVN) to further nature protection at Bitche Camp. In 1975, the regional military governor signed a convention with the PNRVN that sought to reconcile military training with nature protection, authorizing Serge Müller, the PNRVN's nature protection officer, to conduct ecological surveys within the camp. In 1981 a further convention established three 'botanical reserves' in which military activities were to be banned and which park officials could access after seeking authorization from the camp commander.[21]

However, not all was plain sailing in the early days of military–civilian cooperation. Pascal Vautier, president of the Fédération des conservatoires des espaces naturels, recounts how one colonel was shocked to discover that ecologists had infiltrated an (unspecified) camp to conduct an inventory on a firing ground where live ammunition was used.[22] Military considerations trumped environmental ones. Significantly, the designation of 91,830 ha of its land as ecologically significant did not require the army to modify its training practices to protect habitats and species.[23] Furthermore, a December 1980 instruction from Minister of Defence Joël de Theule stated that although the military should 'actively participate in environmental protection policies' and support national park and nature reserve authorities, such activities should not hinder military operational readiness.[24]

The assumption that military land ownership allows ecologically important habitats and species to flourish is a central tenet of military environmentalist rhetoric.[25] In France, this claim emerged in relationship with the vitality of vegetation growth on army training grounds. From initially treating the camps' distinct ecologies as severe impediments to training, the army succeeded in reinventing militarized environments as nature reserves of national and international importance.

By the 1960s, French army officers had became acutely aware that the combination of military training, vegetation growth, and the absence of civilian land use practices on army camps created environments that differed enormously from surrounding civilian ones. Colonel Proudhom outlined how the army's camps were moving in the 'opposite direction to the current evolution of landscapes'. On civilian lands throughout western and central Europe, fields and urban areas were replacing forests and grasslands. In contrast, a 'miniature jungle of sometimes impenetrable bushes' was spreading across French military bases.[26]

The contrast was particularly striking in Champagne where, since 1945, chemical fertilizers, land clearance, and deforestation had transformed the *Champagne pouilleuse* into one of France's richest agricultural regions.[27] According to Proudhom, the camps there were like 'deserts of thickets' nestling amongst the heavily cultivated civilian fields. Encroaching undergrowth and the erosive effect of tanks had created an 'anarchic landscape' deprived of order, and impassable due to mud in winter. The camps provided a 'false' terrain unsuited to the training of troops destined to fight against Warsaw Pact forces in the countryside of central Europe. Unless military engineers uprooted and burnt the unwanted vegetation, Proudhom predicted that a 'plague of thickets and bushes' would swamp France's camps by the late 1970s thereby rendering most kinds of training impossible.[28] The Champagne camps were not alone. Erosion and invasive shrubs meant that Valdahon Camp was 'in the process of dying', according to one army report.[29]

But manpower shortages, inadequate equipment, and myxomatosis (a disease that devastated vegetation-eating rabbit populations) all hampered the army's scrub clearance efforts in the late 1960s and early 1970s.[30] Therefore, from the training point of view, the camps' environments had not improved by the mid-1970s. Tank erosion was still a serious problem and where they did not pass, trees, bushes, and undergrowth abounded. Echoing descriptions of the Western Front, General Marty lamented that some sections of the camps displayed a 'lunar appearance'.[31]

After decades broadly characterized by antagonism between foresters and the army, the perceived need to transform their camps' environments drove the latter to solicit advice from the ONF on vegetation clearance and seek financial aid for reforestation. Between 1975 and 1985 this cooperation led to the reforestation of 104 ha of Mourmelon, Mailly, and Suippes camps. The army also joined forces with state agricultural engineers and foresters to test ways of reducing soil erosion at Mourmelon Camp with fertilizer and grass-sowing.[32] The unintended and unwieldy ecologies of militarized environments posed a major headache for the army.

Certain civilian observers viewed the camps' unruly and overgrown environments as unwanted obstacles to agricultural development.[33]

Ecologists, though, took a much more favourable view. In the 1980s, the Ministry of the Environment and the National Museum of Natural History classified ecologically significant military sites amongst France's Zones naturelles d'intérêt écologique, faunistique et floristique (ZNIEFF).[34] The ZNIEFF inventory provided some evidence that militarized environments had evolved differently to civilian ones. Most notably agricultural modernization in Champagne had not impinged on the army's camps, which now reportedly contained some of the only remnants of once common habitats, such as *savart* grasslands.

According to the ZNIEFF inventory the army had unintentionally overseen the creation of an ecological treasure trove. The inventory for the 13,700 ha ZNIEFF at Suippes Camp described how the militarized environment provided habitat for regionally rare and endangered plants, such as knapweed broomrape and grass vetchling. Its woodlands, meanwhile, constituted a 'remarkable biological *milieu*' that had largely given way to fields elsewhere in the region.[35] The camp's grasslands and woodlands played host to sixty-seven species of butterflies (including the nationally protected large blue butterfly), a wide variety of insects, endangered lizards, and 114 species of birds, many of which were in decline elsewhere, such as the hoopoe and little bustard. A variety of animals, such as wild cats and otters (the latter protected in France since 1981), similarly thrived within the camp's boundaries. Overall, Suippes Camp constituted 'a very beautiful natural environment . . . in a very good state of conservation'.[36]

The ZNIEFF inventory reinvented Suippes Camp's problematic training environment into a nationally important ecological site and gave credence to those lone voices within the military establishment of the 1980s which had argued that the army's camps were 'real [animal] reserves'.[37] As the military adopted more fully environmentalist language and policies in the 1990s, the army turned Suippes Camp into a showcase of military environmentalism. Drawing on the ecologists' findings, it reinvented the camp's vibrant and unintended ecologies from a training problem into an environmental success story. It mobilized the ecological vitality of Suippes and other camps as evidence that military ownership of land could serve two apparently contradictory purposes: the defence of nature and the defence of nation.

Military environmentalism, then, emerged within the militarized environment. It was, in part, the unlikely outcome of the interrelated histories of nonhuman vibrancy, scientific knowledge, and the military's desire to reinvent its sites in line with an increasingly environmentally aware age. In such a way, the French army created its identity as an important actor in environmental politics in conjunction with nonhuman agencies.[38]

Alongside militarized environments' particular ecologies, geopolitical changes explain the surfacing of French military environmentalism in the 1990s. It is hard to pinpoint exactly why this change occurred when it did, but several reasons are suggestive. The first is that the military realized that it ignored environmentalism at its potential peril. The Larzac campaign made it acutely aware that environmental issues could trigger anti-military protests. And whilst it would be unwise to overemphasize the impact of state environmental policies and the success of the French Green Party, they undoubtedly put pressure on the Ministry of Defence to reassess and defend its environmental record.[39] It is telling that military-commissioned opinion polls between 1991 and 2001 assessed public attitudes towards the environment, alongside other topics, such as anti-militarism.[40]

Shifts in the military's sociology and politics provided a more receptive atmosphere for military environmentalism. Since 1989 the military has sought to modernize and appear more democratic through encouraging the recruitment of more women and young French citizens of Algerian and other backgrounds.[41] Furthermore, officers' training has broadened socially and intellectually, meaning that they are more attuned to the 'close integration of military with extramilitary factors' and display a greater appreciation of communication and public relations.[42] The fact that more officers have graduate degrees means that they have developed expertise in areas such as environmental management and policy.[43]

Alongside the army's changing relationship with the rest of society, the end of the Cold War was significant. The disintegration of the Soviet bloc pushed Western defence strategists to consider other sources of potential conflict, including the environment. The resultant environmental security discourse transformed natural resource scarcity, cross-border pollution, and civilian environmental expectations into defence issues. Growing awareness of the links between the environment and national defence arguably encouraged Western military establishments to consider their own roles in generating environmental tensions.[44] Moreover, military environmentalism helped to legitimize continued military control of national territory at a time when the disintegration of Cold War geopolitics, falling defence budgets, and reductions in military personnel (especially after Chirac announced the end of conscription in France in 1996) raised questions about the role of the armed forces and the amount of land they needed for training troops and testing weapons.[45] So although the influence of anti-militarism may have diminished within contemporary France,[46] the military still needs to justify its ownership of land. Having considered the multiple reasons behind the rise of French military environmentalism, the rest of the chapter will now explore different dimensions of the 'greening' of militarized environments in the 1990s and 2000s.

'Greening' the management of militarized environments

In the 1980s authorities at Mailly Camp issued the '10 Commandments' that soldiers should heed whilst living and working in the camp. The environmentally flavoured commandments stated that 'you will not degrade nature' and forbade poaching, tree felling, and littering.[47] But it was not until the 1990s that a range of supposedly environmentally sensitive policies infiltrated the management of army camps and other installations.

The Ministry of Defence now encourages the 'greening' of its personnel's interactions with militarized environments. For instance, it has introduced recycling points on air bases, army camps and naval vessels, portraying them as 'the first steps towards a more beautiful planet'.[48] Whilst there are parallels with civilian recycling programmes, some have a distinctly military flavour. At the Sedzère munitions site (near Pau) empty cartons are collected and shredded to create packaging material for storing munitions.[49]

As well as reducing waste, the military claims that recycling is a way of integrating environmental actions into everyday military life and promoting environmental values. In a similar vein, certain officers implore their colleagues to make a greater effort to inculcate *all* personnel with an internal sense of environmental awareness and values because the environment is 'everyone's business'.[50] Under the terms of a 2003 accord between the Ministry of Defence and the Ministry of the Environment, the latter was to provide help implementing environmental training programmes for military personnel. Yet such training is hardly a priority and, given that some within the military have raised doubts about its extent and effectiveness, it is highly unlikely that the military has succeeded in instilling environmental awareness into the hearts and minds of its personnel.[51] This prioritization of training needs over environmental protection is not unique to France. NATO's 'Environmental Policy Statement for the Armed Forces' (1993) called for militaries to foster environmental awareness and training 'within the constraints of military operational requirements'.[52]

Whilst some within the military are undoubtedly passionate about fighting pollution and encouraging recycling, the Ministry of Defence's main motivation behind the introduction of recycling and other measures appears to be the desire to be seen to conform to civilian environmental norms and to reduce the potential for civilian criticism.[53]

Nonetheless, encouraging recycling and environmental awareness provides a twist in long-standing attempts to police soldiers' behaviour within the militarized environment. At the beginning of the twentieth century army camp authorities sought to monitor and restrict soldiers' activities that might deplete natural resources or despoil the camps' environment. Rules at Sissonne Camp banned troops from entering civilian farms, cutting wood without permission, and poaching, while instructions issued at Mailly Camp in the 1920s forbade troops from dropping litter and disposing of rubbish outside of designated areas.[54] At that time, environmental considerations did not inform these restrictions. Instead, they were intended to promote military discipline, reduce the risk of disease, and preserve the camps' natural resources.

In addition to controlling the internal militarized environment, military regulations have long-since attempted to reduce the likelihood of the hazards of military activity spilling out onto civilian lands and straining civilian–military relations. In this vein, the Minister for War sent a mission in 1906 to investigate accusations that sewage from military buildings in Verdun was polluting a nearby river and making civilians ill.[55] Like its counterparts across the globe, the French military remains a polluter of the environment. But within the framework of military environmentalism it claims to deal conscientiously with its pollution; the Ministry of Defence now charges its inspectors with monitoring and, if need be, punishing infringements of environmental regulations.[56] Its adoption, in 1980, of the 19 July 1976 law on 'installations classified for environmental protection' (installations classées pour la protection de l'environnement, or ICPE), gives some credence to its assertions. Adopting ICPE legislation also provides a means of reducing the potential for civilian complaints – and legal action – relating to military pollution.[57]

The law on ICPE established an inspection regime designed to reduce the threat of pollution from factories, processing plants and other potentially harmful sites. It requires those responsible to declare any risk of pollution to the local prefect and, if necessary, obtain authorization for the site. But the military was not prepared to allow civilian inspectors to regulate its sites. Citing the imperatives of maintaining defence secrecy, it appointed its own inspection body to monitor and to regulate its ICPE, such as petrol depots and weapons factories.[58] The fact that its installations are not subject to independent civilian scrutiny undermines the military's claims that its ICPE are regulated as tightly as civilian ICPE. In particular, the secrecy that surrounds chemical, biological, and nuclear weapons makes it especially hard to monitor how their environmental risks are managed. Defence considerations once again trumped environmental measures: largely unaccountable self-regulation makes the ICPE policy 'light-green'. Nor have the anti-pollution measures erased moments of tension. After the discovery of two transformers (*transformateurs*) at Caylus Camp in 1998 and 2001 an association dedicated to defending the interests of the camp's civilian neighbours was alarmed to discover that a technical report found small traces of lead, arsenic, cadmium, and polychlorinated biphenyls (PCBs) in soil samples.[59]

Alongside anti-pollution measures, the military's self-proclaimed environmentalist turn has modified other long-term practices on military land, such as hunting. Hunting societies (comprised of military and civilian members) have long enjoyed pursuing game on army camps. A series of regulations governed military hunting, stipulating when and where hunting was to be allowed, who could participate, and what animals could be targeted.[60] These rules attempted to manage game populations and ensure that hunting did not interfere with manoeuvres and training. In addition to offering leisure opportunities, hunting controlled so-called 'nuisance animals', such as boar, that tended to roam out of the camps' confines to feast in neighbouring farmland, much to the chagrin of farmers.[61]

Military environmentalism now infuses the long-standing relationship between the military and game. On 7 December 2006 Minister for Defence Michèle Alliot-Marie signed a convention with the National Office for Hunting and Wild Fauna (Office national de la chasse et de la faune sauvage or ONCFS) allowing the ONCFS to access military sites of 'particularly remarkable hunting and fauna interest' to conduct inventories and advise military authorities on game and wildlife management. The convention enables the Ministry of Defence to highlight how 'the operational activities of [our] armed forces are completely compatible with the taking into account of environmental preoccupations and careful wildlife management'.[62]

No longer are boar and other animals simply symbols on regimental insignia.[63] Instead, the military mobilizes their active presence within militarized environments as evidence of the compatibility of militarization with thriving animal populations. Its collaboration with the ONCFS also enables it to portray its interactions with animals as benevolent and environmentally sensitive. However, once again, military objectives take priority. The ONCFS convention is 'light-green' in that it only functions 'within military operational restraints'.

New military companion species

Military environmentalism has modified the military's representation and mobilization of animals. Since its perusal of military environmentalist policies, the French military has enlisted charismatic animals to justify and naturalize its control over national territory.[64] Military environmentalism also transforms the types of animals that get militarized. Traditionally, the French (and other militaries) have enlisted horses, donkeys, dogs, and pigeons to wage war. Whilst dogs, and to a lesser extent horses, remain in military use, the military now associates itself with other kinds of animals in an attempt to validate its environmental credentials. In doing so, it brings to light creatures that had hitherto inhabited militarized environments in relative obscurity.

The military now foregrounds its links with creatures that previously had few military associations or uses as it repackages for public consumption its installations as sites of flourishing biodiversity rather than places of war preparation. Its glossy brochure *Defence and nature protection* (2000) presents once secretive military sites as the home of charismatic nonhumans. Glossing over the less palatable aspects of the Délégation ministérielle pour l'Armement's (DMA) Centre d'essais de la méditerranée (CEM) on Ile de Levant, the brochure highlights how the weapons testing facility is home to 1,000 tortoises, endangered orchids, and the 'extremely rare' Jupiter's beard, whilst *Argonauta argo* cephalopods inhabit its waters. Small wonder, then, that Jean Raynaud of the island's botanical club hopes that the DMA will 'remain for a long time on this site, because it is the principal guarantee of [its] nature'.[65]

Images of militarized environments are once again offered up for public consumption. But unlike the postcards of army camps that depicted soldiers' everyday lives at the beginning of the twentieth century (see chapter 3), the main focus is now on the nonhuman inhabitants of militarized environments. Whereas the postcards visually bound together the recruits, army, and nation, the main aim of the images in

Defence and nature protection is converting civilians to the idea that nature protection and militarization are inherently compatible and balanced activities, despite common associations between militarization, destruction, and death.[66]

As well as promoting the endangered species on its sites, the military claims to care for them. One example is the Alcon Blue butterfly that lives and breeds in the heathlands of the Lande d'Ouée training ground in Brittany and that is protected under the 1979 Bern Convention on the Conservation of European Wildlife and Natural Habitats. Declaring itself determined to preserve the butterfly's habitat, the 11th naval artillery regiment created a 10 ha 'natural' firebreak of grasses and shallow water pools between its training ground and the butterfly's habitat at the cost of one million francs, paid for by the Ministry of Defence under its environmental intervention fund.[67] Similarly, at Canjuers Camp, the army has joined forces with the ONF and Conservatoire d'étude des ecosystems de Provence to preserve the endangered Orsini viper.[68] These episodes illustrate how the military forms its environmental credentials in relationship to the actual presence of rare and ecologically significant animals. In other words, its ongoing environmentalist claims only make sense in relationship to the creatures that inhabit its militarized environments.

Military environmentalist has also reinvented the military's relationship with birdlife. The French air force has mobilized charismatic birds on its insignia since fighter pilots at Verdun adopted stork imagery in 1916 (storks represented the 'lost' provinces of Alsace and Lorraine).[69] Whilst certain birds continue to feature on air base insignia, the Ministry of Defence now promotes images of other birds to underscore the biodiversity of its sites. The *Defence and protection of nature* brochure alone features photos of lapwings, short-toed eagles, red-backed shrikes, turtle doves, and Bonelli's eagles.[70] Birdwatching soldiers in the First World War (chapter 4) would undoubtedly have been thrilled to see such birds in the militarized environments in which they lived and fought.

The military's avian links go beyond the symbolic. The Ministry of Defence has launched a series of bird conservation projects that are often conducted in conjunction with civilian organisations. This is the case at Montmorillon Camp where the Conservatoire des espaces naturels de Poitu-Charentes has launched a project to track the reproduction habits of short-toed eagles.[71] The Ministry of Defence has also modified some of its activities to help protect endangered avifauna. In 2009 it agreed – in a convention with the Ministry of the Environment and the League for the Protection of Birds – that military aircraft would not fly under 1,000 m over known bearded vulture nesting sites in the Pyrenees, Alps, and Corsica. The promise came after studies showed that aircraft were a major disruption for the birds during nesting season. The convention brought military activities in line with European and French legislation on the protection of bearded vultures whose numbers are declining rapidly. But it also placed limits on the Ministry of Defence's protection of the birds; the restrictions on military flying could be put aside if 'missions . . . of a priority for national defence' demand it.[72] Yet again, the military's environmental commitment was light-green.

Alongside birds, the military's light-green environmentalist turn has reconfigured its relationship with sheep. Although the Larzac campaign succeeded in reinventing sheep as fervent opponents of militarization, sheep have been pastured on military lands throughout the twentieth century. This practice continues into the twenty-first century: a 2006 survey found that 15,000 sheep graze over 91 per cent of Canjuers Camp.[73] The army draws advantages from allowing pasturing on its lands; sheep provide a cheap way of keeping down vegetation, thereby reducing the risk of fire on firing ranges.[74]

But in July 2007 the army gave pasturing a green dimension. Twenty-six years after the end of the Larzac struggle, the 503rd infantry regiment welcomed sheep from a farm in the Entre-deux-Mers region onto Souge Camp to graze the camp's vegetation, thereby bypassing the use of environmentally unfriendly tractors. According to Colonel Michel André, this way of controlling vegetation growth was a sign of the army's 'ecologically responsible management' of the camp which would ensure the survival of its heathlands for 'future generations'.[75] After a summer of grazing, the army and Conservatoire regional d'espaces naturels d'Aquitaine daubed the period of 'experimental pasturage' a success. A lamb born on the camp was even named 'Souge'.[76] It is hard to imagine shepherds naming sheep after a military camp during the Larzac campaign. But by 2007, the reconciliation between sheep and the French military seemed complete, at least according to favourable press reports.

The military mobilizes animals to justify its presence and control of national territory. Sheep, birds, snakes, and butterflies have unwittingly become militarized 'companion species' (to use Donna Haraway's term[77]). They are integral to the military's environmentalist identity, which emerged in relationship to them. Without these companion species, the military's claim to be an important environmental actor would ring hollow. Although we should not take the military's environmentalist claims at face value, the creatures' presence at least complicates and nuances the militarization-as-sterilization narrative.

Militarized environments as sites of uneasy cooperation

The presence of endangered species has, in part, drawn the military into collaboration with civilian environmental organizations. In April 1995 the Ministry of Defence signed an accord with the Ministry for the Environment that aimed to facilitate greater communication and cooperation between the two ministries through regular meetings and information exchanges. The Ministry of Defence also promised to work with environmental bodies as long as this did not undermine military training.[78] As an official affirmation that military lands played host to ecologically important habitats and wildlife, the accord publicly validated the military's environmentalist declarations. It paved the way for subsequently glowing appraisals of military nature protection, such as Espaces naturels de France president Daniel Béguin's statement that 'military lands are, without contest, exceptional sites for fauna and flora' and that scientists consider them 'unique sanctuaries of our country's natural heritage'.[79]

The accord set the stage for greater collaboration between the military and non-governmental nature protection organizations. In 1997 the Conservatoire des espaces naturels de Poitu-Charentes (CENPC) signed a convention with General Brousse, military delegate of the Vienne *département*, concerning the management of Montmorillon Camp. Following a CENPC study of the camp's woodlands, heathland, and *bocage* and the impact of military training, hunting, and farming on them, the various parties agreed on a new management plan. In exchange for civilian interference, the Ministry of Defence gets free advice on the management of its sites and a public stamp of approval of its environmental record. In addition, the convention allowed the army to trumpet the ecological importance of its land that had been spared the 'outrages of intensive agriculture, urbanisation, and industrial pollution' and enabled it to position itself as environmentally aware and responsible. Following the accord, Brousse claimed that military personnel are not 'environmental specialists, but we want to leave nature to do what it needs to do' and preserve France's natural 'heritage'.[80]

As of 2007, the army had signed conventions with a number of regional Conservatoire des espaces naturels (CEN) covering 42,000 ha of habitat spread over six camps.[81] A 2009 convention with the national federation of CEN further opened up army camps to civilian scrutiny and management. However, there are limits to this 'civilianization' of the militarized environment. A suggested model convention states that the Ministry of Defence only has to 'take into consideration' the advice of the CEN and it alone maintains control over access to the sites.[82] Civilian interventions are therefore advisory, rather than binding.

Despite their 'light-green' character, military–civilian partnerships have modified militarized environments. In 1999 Captian Montoulieu, environmental officer of Souge Camp, asked the Aquitaine Direction régionale de l'environnement (DIREN) and other nature protection bodies to conduct a study of Souge Camp's environment. Following the discovery of protected species, such as brook lamprey and European pond turtles, the army and the DIREN signed a management convention and obtained 72,000 euros of EU funding to restore the camp's wetlands. In the same year, army cooperation with the ONF resulted in the reforestation of 125 ha of the camp.[83] But overall control of Souge Camp remains firmly in military hands; foresters are not allowed to disrupt military training and must ask permission to enter the camp. Due to the existence of valuable habitats and endangered species on its land, the army once again secures good press (one local journalist has described the camp as the 'green lungs' of the Bordeaux region[84]) and receives free environmental expertise without restraining the camp's military functions. In such a way, environmentalist policies and language transform the image of militarized environments from sterile places to 'green lungs', thereby naturalizing their ongoing militarization.

International environmental obligations, in particular the European Union's (EU) Natura 2000 network, have pushed the military into further cooperation with civilian authorities. Natura 2000 sites respond to European Union directives on 'birds' (directive 79/409/CEE of 2 April 1979) and 'habitats' (directive 92/43/CEE of 21 May 1992) that aim to protect biodiversity through the creation of a coherent network of sites across the EU. The management strategies for these sites are supposed to favour the preservation of fauna and habitats of European importance, whilst taking social and economic factors into account. The fact that economic and other activities are permissible makes the Natura 2000 programme applicable to military lands, a point explicitly recognized by the EU in 1997.[85]

However this form of military–civilian cooperation has not run smoothly. In 1999, after a request by the government, the Ministry of Defence proposed 110 sites (covering 33,000 ha) suitable for inclusion within the Natura 2000 network. But the lack of an effective legal frame-work, and miscommunication between civilian and military authorities over the designation of sites, held back the process.[86] The slow progress both reflected, and contributed to, France's tardiness in designating and proposing Natura 2000 sites, for which it was criticized by the European court of justice in September 2001 and asked to remedy the situation by the end of 2006.[87]

To make up for its failings, France issued decrees in November and December 2001 which laid out the legal framework for the designation and management of Natura 2000 sites. For military sites, prefects were to consult with the relevant regional army commander and a joint deci-sion was to be made on site designation. The latter was also to appoint and chair the working group and approve the eventual site management plan.[88] The main legal obstacle preventing militarized environments from being drawn into the Natura 2000 programme had been over-come. But the military maintained control over its sites; it reserved the right to block any measures that would undermine operational readi-ness. Nonetheless, once a management plan is agreed on, the military is obliged to follow it. With EU obligations to fulfil and a legal framework in place, the designation and development of management plans for Natura 2000 sites was one of the main priorities agreed between the min-istries of defence and environment in their accord of 9 July 2003 (which superseded the 1995 accord).

The 2003 accord further blurred the distinction between militarized environments' civilian and military dimensions. So too did the October 2006 agreement between the Minister for Defence and the Minister for Environment to create a mixed defence-environment committee for each of France's five military regions. Comprised of defence infrastructure officers and regional environmental officials, and overseen by a national committee, one of the regional committees' main responsibilities was the day-to-day development and implementation of Natura 2000 man-agement plans. According to the ministers of defence and environment in their circular of 10 October 2006, the 'optimal [management plan] would lead to the least constraints on military use of the camp without undermining the aims of habitat and species conservation'.[89] The circular made clear the dual functions of military Natura 2000 sites: preservation of wildlife and habitats *and* military training.

Natura 2000 has opened up military sites to further civilian control on a local level. In particular, military commanders handed the running of some Natura 2000 sites over to civilian authorities. For instance, the

PNRVN oversees the Natura 2000 site at Bitche Camp.[90] Natura 2000 intensifies civilian scrutiny of militarized environments in other ways; the decision to produce a management plan for the Natura 2000 sites at the Captieux and Poteau firing ranges led to further detailed studies of their botany and fauna.[91] Despite the obvious dangers and restrictions of carrying out scientific surveys on an aerial bombing range, the various parties produced a 132-page inventory of the sites' habitats and fauna.[92]

Conforming to Natura 2000 regulations has at times held financial ramifications for the military. When the Ministry of Defence extended its Miramas munitions depot (Bouches-du-Rhône) into a neighbouring Natura 2000 site it agreed to finance ecological restoration, such as laying down pebbles typical of the Crau plain and studying the implementation of a pastoral regime to encourage certain plants, to the tune of 116,000 euros.[93] Placed within the overall context of military expenditure, 116,000 euros is a small sum. Nonetheless, it shows that nature protection places financial obligations on the military at a time when its budgets are under pressure.

Although Natura 2000 has increased civilian scrutiny of militarized environments and caused some inconvenience, the programme has not been without benefits for the Ministry of Defence. Its involvement in Natura 2000 allows it to promote its environmental record. Evidence of military environmental benefits is now written into publicly accessible official Natura 2000 documents. For instance, the description of the 'Complexe forestier du Chinon, Landes du Ruchard' states that the heathland has in part been maintained 'due to military activity' and that areas of ancient woodland have survived within Ruchard Camp.[94] Natura 2000 designation also cements the re-branding of Suippes Camp as a reservoir of biodiversity. The Direction régionale de l'environnement de Champagne-Ardenne describes the military camps of Champagne as the 'last vestiges of a landscape of a rare ecological quality'.[95] From 'red zone' (see chapter 5) to semi-protected militarized environment, Suippes Camp bears witness to the physical and cultural malleability of militarized environments.

Natura 2000 is arguably the Ministry of Defence's strongest commitment to nature protection. As of 2008, 189 Natura 2000 sites had been established on military lands comprising 50,000 ha (or just under one-fifth of ministry of defence lands).[96] Under Natura 2000, French militarized environments form part of a transnational environmental protection framework along with military sites in other European countries, such as Salisbury Plain in the United Kingdom and Lagland Camp in Belgium.[97] French militarized environments have long since had a transnational character in the sense that foreign troops have trained, fought, and drawn resources from them. Natura 2000 has 'greened' their transnational qualities. But the internationalization of French militarized environments has caused some unease. In 2003 one military officer admitted feeling a 'bit afraid' of the implications of exposing the management of national military sites to EU directives.[98]

It is worth underlining that although Natura 2000 sites are subject to civilian management and observation, they remain primarily militarized. The Ministry of Defence will only pursue Natura 2000 policies 'as long as they respect operational imperatives.'[99] Once again, Natura 2000 is a light-green military environmentalist policy and frictions characterize the dual functions of Natura 2000 sites. From the military perspective, militarized environments' main purpose remains training. The commander of the north-east army region rapidly refused ecologists' proposals to extend the Natura 2000 site at Bitche Camp from 191 ha to 1,900 ha (which would have taken it to over half the camp's surface area).[100] More generally, some army commanders fear that turning military camps into nature sanctuaries will inhibit possibilities for training.[101]

Natura 2000 has not been the only source of military–civilian disagreements. Fears that nature protection measures would hinder military activities and sovereignty over its training grounds led the Ministry of Defence to block a convention between Canjuers Camp and the Parc naturel régional des Gorges du Verdon. Similarly, army commanders held a 'very unfavourable opinion' of the proposal to include part of Garrigues Camp within a nature reserve.[102] Moreover, certain military modifications of their land sit at odds with nature protection objectives, generating further strains. At Canjuers Camp, military-sanctioned reforestation and restrictions on pasturing have diminished grasslands, leading to the deterioration of ecologically important habitats.[103] So although it might keep agriculture, urbanisation and tourism at bay, militarization does not freeze environmental processes and nor does it necessarily create habitats conducive to biodiversity.

But anti-military environmental protest has not extinguished itself and the military struggles to convince certain environmentalist organizations that places of war preparation are characterized by human-nonhuman harmony and mutual benefit, rather than death and destruction. In September 2008, Grenoble-based environmental group Mountain Wilderness protested a military exercise conducted in the airspace above the alpine Ecrins National Park.[104] Mountain Wilderness's 'micro-mobilization' (to use Graeme Haye's term) and anti-nuclear, pacifist protests against the Centre d'essais des Landes remind us that the harmonious image of civilian–military cooperation that dominates military environmentalist rhetoric is brittle.[105]

Sustainable militarized environments?

Whatever its flaws, the inclusion of militarized environments with the Natura 2000 network aligned military environmentalism with civilian sustainable development goals. Following the United Nations conference on sustainable development in Johannesburg (2002), and working on the principle that the state should 'lead from the front' (*l'Etat doit être exemplaire*), the French government instructed ministries to pursue their sustainable development goals with greater intensity. The Ministry of Defence was not exempt. In line with Prime Minister Jean-Pierre Raffarin's wider sustainability policies, Michèle Alliot-Marie, then Minister for Defence, declared in 2003 that she wished her ministry to be 'exemplary' in the implementation of the national sustainable development strategy from 2003 to 2008.[106] The President Chirac-initiated Charter for the Environment, which enshrined the principle that 'public authorities must promote sustainable development' into the French constitution in February 2005, made it even harder for the Ministry of Defence to ignore sustainable development.[107]

Under the banner of sustainable development the Ministry of Defence took part in the 'Grenelle Environnement' launched in 2007 by President Nicolas Sarkozy, billed as a state–society forum that would determine France's sustainability goals and enhance the nation's ability to meet them.[108] Declaring himself strongly in favour of the Grenelle's ambitions, Minister of Defence Hervé Morin launched a new environmental action plan for the military on 27 November 2007. The plan's emphasis on reducing the energy consumption of military buildings and vehicles was undoubtedly a response to the wider stress placed on energy reduction and climate change, evident in civilian environmental policies. Measures announced in the plan included investment in sustainable building practices, energy audits of military installations, and restrictions on defence officials' travel by plane within France.[109] Some progress in these areas has reportedly been made. A new building on Tours air base deploys solar panels and geothermic energy sources to reduce energy consumption by a third, building on the example set by the biomass-powered heating system at Valdahon Camp (operational since 2003).[110]

The 2007 plan and subsequent climate change mitigation measures demonstrate how far military environmentalism has moved beyond a focus on nature protection and pollution prevention. Like other militaries across the globe, France portrays itself as an actor in combating climate change, which military strategists now present as an international security issue.[111]

The 2007 plan reflects the military's attempt to ensure that its environmental policies speak to evolving civilian concerns on climate change. Military–civilian cooperation within the framework of military-environmentalism therefore needs to be set within the context of environmentalism's institutionalisation and the weakened sense of the military as a separate social sphere.[112] As Morin himself admitted, environmentalist measures are 'one of the ways of maintaining a strong link between the French and their army'.[113] In the first decade of the twenty-first century, the military mobilization of environmentalism as a source of political and social legitimacy remains as strong as ever.

Nonetheless, it is important not to overestimate the effectiveness of military efforts to combat climate change. Reducing a handful of buildings' energy consumption may be a worthwhile endeavour, but it serves to distract attention away from the far greater quantities of carbon emissions emanating from fighter jets, tanks, and other military hardware.[114] The Ministry of Defence's financial investment in its environmental measures is also relatively small. The 180 million euros dedicated to sustainable development policies in the 2008–10 period may seem substantial, but when set against the military's overall budget it is relatively insignificant.[115]

Like civilian branches of government, the Ministry of Defence has introduced a range of measures to support sustainability. But given the scale of the challenge, the military establishment, like the rest of France, is arguably falling short. Working on the assumption that sustainable development entails the 'need not to use resources more quickly than they can be replenished' and the 'need not to produce harmful effluents faster than they can be neutralized by a healthy biosphere', Bess argues that 'contemporary French society flunks both these tests'.[116] Like the rest of society, the military is light-green.

But although military environmentalist aims are diluted by operational considerations and financial constraints, environmentalist notions have spread throughout its activities, including the demilitarization of its obsolete sites.

The 'greening' of demilitarization

Neutralizing the remnants of wars and military training contained within the French soil is an extended and ongoing process. Farmers and others have unearthed the explosive debris of war from former battlefields for decades. When visiting the former Somme battlefields in the 1970s, historian John Keegan reported how as agricultural 'ploughing proceeds, little dumps of foreign objects appear along the verges of the roads. Rusty, misshapen, dirt-encrusted, these cones and globes reveal themselves, at a closer look, to be the fruit not of agriculture but of war'.[117] Such debris is an explosive problem and a source of worry, inconvenience, danger, and, at times, death for civilians. It has also become a political issue. In the late 1990s the French parliament debated the fears of residents in the Pas-de-Calais concerning the vast quantities of unexploded ordnance uncovered each year in their *département*.[118]

Removing the material traces of war and war preparation from the land is costly and time-consuming. Once uncovered, the disposal of munitions entails the risk of fire, pollution, and injury. But despite the difficulties, the Ministry of Defence is obliged to decontaminate polluted sites in line with their future use. As part of its environmental turn, it now claims to dispose of these dangerous traces of conflict in a safe and environmentally responsible way. In 1997 it decided to create an installation at Mailly Camp to destroy chemical weapons deposited on French soil during the First World War at an estimated cost of 90 million euros.[119] But local mayors are concerned about the potential risk to agriculture. Christian Lemoine, mayor of Sompuis, declared that 'agriculture is our only source of wealth. We do not want to become the region's dustbin'.[120]

Other branches of the military have introduced programmes to remove shells and other debris. Each year air base personnel participate in a 'spring cleaning' of their bases, removing metal and other debris (in 1999 they collected 30,000 tonnes of scrap metal). Furthermore, in December 2009, the navy sent divers to remove munitions exposed by shifting sands on Tamaris beach near Port-Grimaud (Var).[121] But the sheer number of sites requiring treatment (the number was 1,375 in 2008[122]), and the cost of the decontamination operations, means that it will be some time before the toxic and explosive traces of war and militarization are removed from French soil.

In some places, the sheer quantity of munitions contained in the soil means that they may never be completely demilitarized. At Verdun, the difficulties of detection means that it is 'practically impossible', in the words of one expert, to completely remove the ordnance left in the ground.[123] These explosive traces of conflict act as reminders that despite military environmentalist claims, the French and other militaries have extensively polluted the French environment.

Ministry of Defence sustainable development policies mean that its munitions *may* cause fewer environmental problems in the future. The DMA has initiated research into 'green' weapons that aims to minimize the toxic impact of munitions on training grounds and combat environments and bring them into line with environmental legislation. Studies on biodegradable anti-tank mines for use on training grounds and research into alternatives to white phosphorous point to the direction in which the research is moving, although the financial cost of creating so-called 'sustainable' weapons is likely to inhibit progress.[124]

Commentators find the idea of 'green' weapons deeply unsettling. *Le Point* journalist Frédéric Lewino dismisses 'sustainable' weaponry as a cynical attempt to 'flog' French military hardware to countries, such as Sweden, that place importance on environmental considerations.[125] Economics undoubtedly motivates the DMA. But 'green' weapons also raise deeper ethical issues that centre on the contradictions between environmentalism and weapons, whose main function is to destroy life rather than preserve it.[126] The military's efforts to portray biodegradable mines as a form of environmental progress are therefore highly problematic. Yet the very attempt to bring them into existence demonstrates the ingenious, if controversial, ways in which the French military claims to integrate sustainability into its everyday activities.

Alongside bringing an environmental dimension to its decontamination programme, the Ministry of Defence has given a green tint to its shedding of operationally obsolete land. Ceding ecologically important sites to the Conservatoire de l'espace littoral et des rivages lacustres (CELRL) allows the Ministry of Defence to portray itself as a protector of France's biodiversity and an important player in government environmental policies. Conventions in 1993 and 1994 paved the way for it to cede 28 obsolete military sites to the CELRL, and in 2005 it promised that 37 sites were to follow suit.[127] Whilst many of these maritime sites have indeed been spared the tourist infrastructure that marks much of the French coastline, the Ministry of Defence benefits from this 'greening' of demilitarization. For a start, the ceding of forts and coastal batteries provides it with good press coverage. But more importantly, it is only required to conduct decontamination and munitions clearance work to a standard that meets the site's future use. As in other countries, transforming obsolete militarized environments into wildlife refuges requires a lower standard of remedial work then if the sites were destined for housing or other uses. The Ministry of Defence's July 2008 announcement of its intention to close eighty-three military units and sites may well lead to the creation of more 'military-to-wildlife' refuges.[128]

In a parallel development, the demilitarization of former battlefields has been 'greened'. Some of the landing beaches and other D-Day sites in Normandy are now sites of commemoration and nature protection. They bear the traces of war, such as craters, decaying concrete bunkers, floating harbours, and disused batteries. But conservation bodies also protect the rare plants and birds that inhabit the beaches, dunes, and cliffs. Some birds, such as the European stonechat and the whitethroat, have even found niches in the craters and other depressions in terrain near the battery at Longues-sur-Mer created during the Allied invasion.[129] Guidebooks now describe sites, such as the US cemetery at Colleville-sur-Mer, as important historical sites and 'remarkable natural environments'.[130]

At the same time, civilians deploy 'green' ideas to physically and symbolically demilitarize former sites of war preparation. '2000 trees for the year 2000' were planted at the former bois de Bitche firing ground (Moselle) where concrete stands and disused military buildings now lie neglected among the trees.[131] Other civilian plans include establishing a nature park on the former training ground at Cuis (Marne) and solar panels on the former training ground at Savignac-les-Eglises (near Périgueux).[132] Furthermore, after the demilitarization of the Plateau d'Albion in 1996 due to changes in France's nuclear dissuasion policies, locals from Lagarde d'Apt turned one of the silos into a bistro serving locally sourced food (with help from the Parc naturel régional du Luberon). The bistro itself is environmentally friendly, boasting solar panels and hemp insulation, amongst other measures. As the bistro's owner Elisabeth Murat explains, after the military left locals wanted something 'civilian, non-polluting and useful for the population' (see figure 9.1).[133]

The placards that form the accompanying outdoor exhibition tell the story of the plateau's nuclear history, as well as discussions of wider environmental issues, such as renewable energy sources, and descriptions of the plateau's biodiversity. The placards place militarization and nature at opposite ends of the spectrum. They are a reassertion of the militarization-as-sterilization narrative and present an alternative to the military's environmentalist claims.

9.1 Bistro de Lagarde, Plateau d'Albion

Conclusion

From establishing quasi-nature reserves on its land to trying to reduce its carbon footprint, the military claims to have 'greened' its relationship with the environment. Military environmentalism has a hybrid and 'more-than-human' history. It is the ongoing outcome of militarized environments' unintentional ecologies, the rise of environmentalism, and the military's desire to demonstrate that it is attuned to wider societal aspirations in the post-Cold War era. The military has shown ingenuity in reinventing its problematic training grounds as environmental success stories and in allying itself with a range of nonhuman companion species to make the case that it is a responsible steward of national territory that might otherwise be returned to civilian use. But although the military has undertaken a *soi-disant* environmentalist turn, military planners and engineers still see themselves as technocratic controllers and managers of the ecologies of militarized environments. In this sense, there exists a striking continuity with previous military environmental perspectives.[134]

The presence of endangered habitats and species within militarized environments provides some evidence that militarization unintentionally creates particular environments within which certain kinds of species and flora can flourish. Nor is military environmentalism simply a case of the military hoodwinking civilians. Instead, civilian governmental and nongovernmental organisations are, to an extent, willing partners who mobilize the particular ecologies of militarized environments to enhance France's environmental record. As such, military environmentalism blurs further the boundaries between civilian and military environments, as well as bearing witness to the military's ability to reinvent itself to fit the concerns of wider society. It once portrayed military camps as sites of national renewal or regional modernization. It now presents them as places that contribute to the realization of France's wider sustainable development goals. Modern notions of sustainability stretch back to at least the eighteenth century.[135] The history of French military environmentalism shows that in France, as elsewhere, militarization provides a new and problematic chapter to this history.

The French military has made some progress in 'greening' its relationship with the militarized environment and some defence officials, it seems, subscribe to sustainable development aims. But this should not disguise the fact that defence secrecy makes it hard to assess accurately the military's environmental record and that it mobilizes its lands' unintentional ecologies to seek legitimacy for its control over 0.5 per cent of national territory. Nor should some environmental success stories prevent critical reflection on the military's land management practices, or blind us to the more harmful social and environmental consequences of militarization. The interventions of Mountain Wilderness and other critical groups reinforce the fact that military environmentalism has not erased civilian protest. Moreover, we need to remember that the military places operational readiness before environmental considerations. This is unlikely to change any time soon, if ever. In this sense, France has a light-green military for a light-green society.

Notes

1 *Sites Natura 2000 du champ de tir de Poteau: Etat des lieux-diagnositic*, version 4, September 2007, 24. Document supplied by Gilles Granereau of the Office national des forêts.

2 See, for instance, the 'Convention nationale de partenariat écologique entre la Fédération des conservatoires des espaces naturels (FCEN) et le Ministère de la Défense', 3 September 2009, www.defense.gouv.fr/sga/

content/download/159573/1376199/file/coventionsignéeaveclaFCENle3sep
tembre2009.pdf, accessed 24 February 2010.

3 Quoted in Direction des affaires juridiques and Délégation à l'information et à la communication de la défense, *Défense et protection de la nature* (Paris: La Documentation française, 2000), 9. The name of the Ministry of the Environment has changed repeatedly since the 1970s. It started out as Ministère de la Protection de la Nature et de l'Environnement and by 2009 had become Ministère de l'Ecologie, de l'Energie, du Développement durable et de la Mer, en charge des Technologies vertes et des négociations sur le Climat. The name changes are important because they reflect developments in environmental politics, but for simplicity's sake I refer to the department as the Ministry of the Environment throughout this chapter.

4 For instance, it is overlooked in Bernard Boëne and Michel Louis Martin, 'France: In the throes of epoch-making change', in Charles C. Moskos, John Allen Williams, and David R. Segal (eds), *The Postmodern Military: Armed Forces after the Cold War* (New York: Oxford University Press, 2000), 51–79; Oliver Pottier, *Armée-nation: Divorce ou réconciliation: De la loi Debré à la réforme du service national, 1970–2004* (Paris: L'Harmattan, 2005); Rachel Utley, *The French Defence Debate: Consensus and Continuity in the Mitterrand Era* (Basingstoke: Palgrave Macmillan, 2005).

5 Peter Coates, Tim Cole, Marianna Dudley, and Chris Pearson, 'Defending nation, defending nature? Militarized landscapes and military environmentalism in Britain, France and the US', *Environmental History*, 16:3 (2001), 456–91; Marianna Dudley, 'Greening the MOD: An environmental history of the UK defence estate, 1945–present' (PhD dissertation, University of Bristol, 2011); Robert F. Durant, *The Greening of the U.S. Military: Environmental Policy, National Security, and Organizational Change* (Washington: Georgetown University Press, 2007); Stephen Dycus, *National Defense and the Environment* (Hanover, NH, and London: University Press of New England, 1996); Rachel Woodward, 'Khaki conservation: An examination of military environmentalist discourses in the British army', *Journal of Rural Studies*, 17:2 (2001), 201–17.

6 Kent Hughes Butts, 'Why the military is good for the environment', in Jyrki Käkönen (ed.), *Green Security or Militarized Environment* (Aldershot: Dartmouth, 1994), 83–109; Michael Greenberg, Karen Lowrie, Donald Krueckeberg, Henry Mayer, and Darien Simon, 'Bombs and butterflies: A case study of the challenges of post Cold War environmental planning and management for the US nuclear weapons sites', *Journal of Environmental Planning and Management*, 40:6 (1997), 739–50; Eugene J. Palka and Francis A. Galgano (eds), *Military Geography from Peace to War* (Boston: McGraw-Hill Custom Publishing, 2005).

7 Rachel Woodward, *Military Geographies* (Oxford: Blackwell, 2004). See also Anne Ehrlich and John W. Birks (eds), *Hidden Dangers: Environmental*

Consequences of Preparing for War (San Francisco: Sierra Club Books, 1990); Tom H. Hastings, *Ecology of War and Peace: Counting the Costs of Conflict* (Lanham: University Press of America, 2000); Adrian Parr, *Hijacking Sustainability* (Cambridge, MA: MIT Press, 2009), 78–91.

8 Stephen Henningham, 'Testing times: France's underground nuclear tests and its relations with the Asia–Pacific region', *Modern and Contemporary France*, 4:1 (1996), 81–92.

9 In 1955 General Canrouzou informed the Var's Conseil général that game thrived on firing ranges because it was less bothered by hunters. ADV 379 W 510/1 Conseil général du Var, 'Séance plénière du jeudi 2 juin 1955'.

10 Olivier Bonnefon, 'La BA 118 soigne son environnement', *Sud Ouest*, 11 December 2003.

11 *Défense et protection de la nature*, 30. At least one army officer took an active interest in the camp's flora, geology, agriculture, and history before the 1970s, publishing a book on Larzac that praised the area's flora. Certain sections of the text would not have been out of place in the anti-extension literature of the 1970s. *Le Larzac: Géologie, hydrologie, flore, agriculture, histoire, sites, et monuments* (Millau: Imprimerie Artières & Maury, 1931), 35. The book can be seen as a militarized counterpart to civilian preservationist sentiments in the early twentieth century. Patrick Young, 'A tasteful patrimony? Landscape preservation and tourism in the sites and monuments campaign, 1900–1935', *French Historical Studies*, 32:3 (2009), 447–77.

12 For re-appraisals of France as a bad 'environmental citizen', see Dominique Bourg and Kerry H. Whiteside, 'France's Charter for the Environment: Of presidents, principles, and environmental protection', *Modern & Contemporary France*, 15:2 (2007), 117–18; Eloi Laurent, 'Bleu, blanc, . . . Green?: France and climate change', *French Politics, Culture*, 27:2 (2009), 142–53.

13 Michael Bess, *The Light-Green Society: Ecology and Technological Modernity in France, 1960–2000* (Chicago: University of Chicago Press, 2003), 5.

14 One defence official claimed in 2007 that 'there is no environmental area that . . . does not concern the Ministry of Defence'. 'Compte rendu de la conférence No. 1 du 10 juillet 2007 organisée par 3B Conseils, Défense et Environnement: Une nouvelle manière de penser', 17 September 2007, www.science-ethnique.org/site_ES/fichiers/docs/Conf_1_Synthese_Def_Envirt_100707_web.pdf, accessed 16 October 2008, 3.

15 Quoted in Marianna Dudley, 'A fairy (shrimp) tale of military environmentalism: The 'greening' of Salisbury Plain', in Chris Pearson, Peter Coates, and Tim Cole (eds), *Militarized Landscapes: From Gettysburg to Salisbury Plain* (London: Continuum, 2010), 140.

16 Ibid. On military environmentalism in other European countries, see 'Environment 2000', Finnish Ministry of Defence website, www.defmin.fi/index.phtml?l=en&s=231, accessed 21 February 2010; Paul J. M. Vertegaal,

'Environmental impact of Dutch military activities', *Environmental Conservation*, 16:1 (1989), 54–64.

17 Beyond metropolitan France, the French secret service's sinking of Greenpeace's boat *Rainbow Warrior* in 1985 was the most obvious flashpoint between radical environmentalists and the security establishment.

18 SHD-DAT 13 T 272 J. Ancellin, 'Note concernant la protection de la région des dunes de Vauville-Biville', 2 February 1971.

19 SHD-DAT 13 T 272 Général de corps d'armée Saint-Hillier to Ministre d'Etat chargé de la Défense nationale', 4 March 1971.

20 Christophe Kintz, 'L'évolution du domaine militaire attribué à l'Armée de terre en France métropolitaine depuis 1945 et ses implications sur l'aménagement de l'espace, l'urbanisme et l'environnement' (PhD dissertation, Université de Paris IV–Paris–Sorbonne, 2000), 209.

21 'Convention Parc-Armée', 20 October 1981. Document supplied by Jean-Claude Genot of the PNRVN; *Protocole Défense-Environnement: Dossier de presse* (Ministère de la Défense/Ministère de l'Environnement, 3 April 1995), 8. Document supplied by Claire Vignon of the Parc national de Port-Cros. Nature protection measures at Bitche Camp reached a peak in 1989 when 150 ha of military land became part of UNESCO's Réserve de la Biosphère des Vosges du Nord. *Protection de la nature et défense: Les études juridiques de la DAG*, 7 (September 1996), 61. Military collaboration with park authorities occurred elsewhere. In 1974 – as military–civilian conflicts raged on Larzac plateau – the Ministry of Defence allowed the Parc national de Port-Cros use of its Eminence and Estissac forts. The forts were definitively ceded to the national park in 1995. *Protocole Défense-Environnement*, 10.

22 Pascal Vautier, 'Expériences développées avec les camps militaires en France pour la prise en compte de la biodiversité', presentation given at Défense et environnement conference, 10 July 2007, Défense et environnement website, www.science-ethique.org/site_3bconseils/fichiers/docs/P_Vautier_Conf_100707.pdf, accessed 24 February 2010, 2. The first Conservatoires des espaces naturels were created in 1976. By 2007 there were 30 located across France.

23 *Protection de la nature et défense: Les études juridiques de la DAG*, 43–5.

24 Ministre de la Défense, 'Instruction interarmées sur la participation du Ministère de la Défense à la politique de protection de la nature', 12 December 1980, reproduced in Jacques Lafourcade, 'Défense et environnement: Aspects majeurs de la participation militaire à la protection du cadre de vie' (DESS aménagement et défense, Université de Metz, 1986), annex 6.

25 Woodward, *Military Geographies*, 92–3.

26 SHD-DAT 13 T 259 Colonel R. Proudhom, 'Grandeurs et misères des camps nationaux', [n.d. 1967?].

27 M. Bournerias and J. Timbal, 'Le hêtre et le problème du climax en

Champagne crayeuse', *Revue forestière française*, 21:3 (1979), 210; R. Leroux, 'Reboisement et défrichement de la Champagne crayeuse', *Revue forestière française*, 10 (1961), 611–15.

28 Proudhom, 'Grandeurs et misères'.

29 SHD-DAT 13 T 34 3ème Division, XIIᵉ brigade mécanisée, 26 May 1966.

30 SHD-DAT 13 T 34 Général Lagarde, Sous-chef d'Etat-major de l'Armée de terre, 'Débroussaillement des camps', 23 December 1970; SHD-DAT 13 T 34 Général de corps d'armée Saint Hillier, to Ministre d'Etat chargé de la Défense nationale, 'Débroussaillage des camps', 3 September 1970.

31 Quoted in Lafourcade, 'Défense et environnement', 76.

32 SHD-DAT 13 T 34 Ministre des Armées to Ministre de l'Agriculture, Direction générale des Eaux et Forêts, 'Destruction des épineux', 17 June 1966; Lafourcade, 'Défense et environnement', 78–9.

33 Centre d'étude et de liaison pour l'aménagement de la Marne, *Le Secteur Suippes Mourmelon joue ses atouts* (Reims: CELAM, 1973), 9.

34 *Défense et protection de la nature*, 5.

35 Ministère de l'Ecologie et du Développement durable, 'Inventaire des zones naturelles d'intérêt écologique faunistique et floristique: Pelouses et bois du camp militaire de Suippes', Nº rég: 01590000, Nº SPN: 210001121, year of description: 1984, date of public release: 31 July 2002, www.champagne-ardenne.ecologie.gouv.fr/milieux_naturels/milnat_pdf/dep51/pdf_ZNIEFF/ZNIEFF210000980.pdf, accessed 24 April 2009.

36 Ibid.

37 Christian Peyruquéou, 'Armées et environnement', *Défense Nationale* (April 1980), 115–23. See also Commissaire Lieutenant-colonel Vincent, 'Pour un prise en compte plus significative des problèmes de l'environnement sur une base aérienne' (Thèse, Centre d'enseignement supérieur aérien, Ecole supérieure de guerre aérienne, 1982–83), 4; Lafourcade, 'Défense et environnement', 93.

38 Military environmentalism is a 'relational achievement' (to use Sarah Whatmore's term) in which agencies transcend the supposed nature/culture divide. *Hybrid Geographies: Natures, Cultures, Spaces* (London: Sage, 2002), 23.

39 On environmentalism's impact on Western militaries, see Committee on the Challenges of Modern Society, *NATO-CCMS Achievements in Defence-related Environmental Studies, 1980–2001*, report no. A-2001/02 (March 2001), www.nato.int/science/publication/coul/coul-report.pdf, accessed 30 July 2010.

40 Ministère de la Défense, *10 ans de sondages: Les français et la défense, Novembre 2002* (Création DICoD, 2002), 68, 71–2.

41 Pottier, *Armée-nation*, 76–7.

42 Boëne and Martin, 'France', 51–79. Quote on page 60.

43 Phillpe Guth, 'La gestion des terrains militaires présentant un intérêt

écologique: Comment concilier les impératifs opérationnels et la préservation de la biodiversité', (DESS 'Espace et milieux', Université de Paris 7,
2004–5); Kintz, 'Evolution du domaine militaire'.

44 For a French reflection on environmental security, see Philippe Morueau
Defarges, '1989, l'année verte', *Défense nationale*, November 1989, 143–9.
On environmental security more generally, see Jon Barnett, *The Meaning
of Environmental Security: Ecological Politics and Policy in the New Security
Era* (London: Zed Books, 2001).

45 On the place of the military in the post-Cold War era, see Martin Shaw,
*Post-Military Society: Militarism, Demilitarization and War at the End of the
Twentieth Century* (Cambridge: Polity Press, 1991). On the ways in which
environmental discourse justifies military control of national territories,
see Woodward, *Military Geographies*, 89–96, 158. The number of military
personnel fell dramatically throughout the 1990s. Between 1989 and 1993
the French army alone shed 50,000 soldiers. Pottier, *Armée-nation*, 94.
On French military reform post-1989, see George A. Bloch, 'French military reform: Lessons for America's army?', *Parameters*, 3:2 (2000), 33–45;
Pottier, *Armée-nation*; Ronald Tiersky, 'French military reform and restruc-
turing', *Joint Force Quarterly* (Spring 1997), 95–102; Utley, *French Defence
Debate*, 133–58.

46 Pottier, *Armée-Nation*, 114.

47 Quoted in Lafourcade, 'Défense et environnement', 21.

48 'Tri sélectif: Un premier pas vers une planète plus belle', Armée de
terre website, www.defense.gouv.fr/terre/enjeux_defense/terre_et_societe/
developpement_durable/l_eau_et_les_dechets/tri_selectif_un_premier_pas
_vers_une_planete_plus_belle, accessed 16 October 2008.

49 'Site de Sedzère: Le développement durable à plusieurs facettes', Armée de
terre website, www.defense.gouv.fr/terre/enjeux_defense/terre_et_societe/
developpement_durable/demarches_eco_citoyennes/site_de_sedzere_le_
developpement_durable_a_plusieurs_facettes, accessed 18 May 2010.

50 Lieutenant-colonel Albert Benedetti, 'La base de l'Armée de l'air et
l'environnement', 1772/CESA/GE/CSEM, 2 November 1998. See also
'L'environnement, l'affaire de tous', *Air actualités*, 536, November 2000, 34.

51 *La culture du développement durable au ministère de la défense* (Délégation
à l'information et à la communication de la Défense, June 2005), 11;
Lieutenant-colonel Dominique Merlet, 'Planification et programmation des
opérations relevant de la protection de l'environnement au sein de l'Armée
de l'air', Mémoire, no. 11315/CESA/CEMSAIR/EMS2, 17 November 2006,
7; Guth, 'Gestion des terrains militaires', 75–7.

52 Committee on the Challenges of Modern Society, 'Pilot study on defence
environmental expectations: NATO Environmental Policy Statement for
the Armed Forces', Annex II to C-M(93)71, 13 October 1993, reproduced
in Martin Coulson (ed.), *CCMS Report No. 211: Pilot Study on Defence*

Environmental Expectations, Proceedings of the International Symposium on the Environment and Defence, 13–15 September 1995 (Swansea: University of Wales, Swansea, 1995) 419. President Nixon had overseen the creation of the CCMS in 1969 much to the annoyance of his European allies. Jacob Darwin Hamblin, 'Environmentalism for the Atlantic Alliance: NATO's experiment with the "challenges of modern society"', *Environmental History*, 15:1 (2010), 54–75.

53 'Profession: Chargé de la protection de l'environnement à l'école d'application de l'artillerie!' www.defense.gouv.fr/terre/enjeux_defense/ terre_et_societe/developpement_durable/demarches_eco_citoyennes/ profession_charge_de_la_protection_de_l_environnement_a_l_ecole_d_ application_de_l_artillerie, accessed 18 May 2010; Vincent, 'Pour un prise en compte', preface; Ingénieur principal des études et techniques d'armement Berthelier, 'Développement durable et défense: Faire et faire savoir', *La Tribune Bilingue du CID* (June 2007), www.college.interarmees. defense.gouv.fr/IMG/pdf/BERTHELIER_IPETA_C6_article_Tribune_V3 .pdf, accessed 18 May 2010.

54 2ᵉ corps d'armée, Etat-major, *Camp d'instruction de Sissonne: Consignes permanents* (Amiens: Imprimerie du Progrès de la Somme, 1912), 43–7; 8ᵉ corps d'armée, *Instruction pour le séjour des troupes au Camp de Mailly* (Bourges: 11 January 1926), 28, 53. See also *Notice sur le camp de Sissonne* (Paris: Charles-Lavauzelle, 1935); *Notice sur le camp de Mourmelon* (Paris: Charles-Lavauzelle, 1937); *Notice sur le camp de la Courtine* (Paris: Charles-Lavauzelle, 1939).

55 SHD-DAT 3 V 30 'Avis commun du Médecin inspecteur général Claudot et du Général de brigade Goetschy au sujet de l'assainissement du ruisseau "Le Biguenel" à Verdun', 12 November 1906.

56 'Le rôle des agents assermentés du SID', 2007, Ministère de la Défense website, www.defense.gouv.fr/sga/layout/set/print/content/view/full/86873, accessed 14 June 2007. On military pollution of the global environment, see Ehrlich and Birks, *Hidden Dangers*; Hastings, *Ecology of War and Peace*; Susan D. Lanier-Graham, *The Ecology of War: Environmental Impacts of Weaponry and Warfare* (New York: Walker, 1993).

57 For instance, civilian concerns that untreated sewage and petrochemical waste from Canjuers Camp were polluting water sources generated bad press for the army in the early 1970s. Félix Franceschi, 'L'affaire des eaux de Canjuers: D'où vient la pollution?' 28 June 1973, newspaper clipping in ADV 1189 W 12.

58 As of 2008 it managed 6,700 ICPE spread over 1,000 sites. *Rapport développement durable du Ministre de la Défense 2008*, Ministre de la Défense website, www.defense.gouv.fr/sga/actualité_et_dossiers/premiere_rapport_ sur_le_developpement_durable_de_la_defense, accessed 24 February 2010, 41.

59 P. Mz, 'Après la découverte de deux transformateurs sur le camp, une pollution "sans impact" sur l'environnement' [n.d.], http://membres.lycos/adricc/pages/fag.htm, accessed 16 October 2008.

60 SHD-DAT 27 T 114 Etat-major de l'Armée de terre, Direction technique des armes et de l'instruction, 'Droit de chasse dans les grands camps', 7 February 1963.

61 In Champagne, farmers whose land bordered Suippes, Mourmelon and Moronvilliers camps complained to military authorities during the 1960s that troublesome game were ruining their livelihoods. SHD-DAT 27 T 114 Préfet de la Marne to Gouverneur militaire de Metz, 'Chasse dans les camps militaires', 21 January 1963; SHD-DAT 27 T 114 Commandant le camp de Mourmelon to Ministre des Armées, 'Droits de chasse dans les camps', 10 April 1963.

62 'Mise en oeuvre de la convention de partenariat entre le Ministère de la Défense et l'Office national de la chasse et de la faune sauvage', Ministère de la défense website, www.defense.gouv.fr/defense/votre_espace/journalistes/communiques/communiques_du_ministere_de_la_defense/mise_en_aeuvre_de_la_convention_de_partenariat_entre_le_mindef_et_l_onacfs, accessed 13 June 2008.

63 See the various insignia reproduced in Jean-Yves Mary and Alain Hohnadel, *Hommes et ouvrages de la ligne Maginot*, vol. 1 (Paris: Histoire et collections, 2000).

64 On how military environmentalism naturalizes military presence, see Woodward, *Military Geographies*, 94. On how certain species are deemed charismatic, see Jamie Lorimer, 'Nonhuman charisma', *Environment and Planning D: Society and Space*, 25:5 (2007), 911–32.

65 *Défense et protection de la nature*, 12–13. Intentionally or not, Raynaud's remarks give credence to the claims of the CEM's directors that the DMA's presence on the island has 'led it to take an interest in the natural domain, therefore complementing the work of the neighbouring Port-Cros National Park'. Serge Desbois and Eric Berder, 'Le centre d'essais de la méditerranée', *Nouvelle revue aéronautique astronautique*, 2, (1995), 74.

66 On the balance metaphor in military environmentalist discourse, see Woodward, *Military Geographies*, 96.

67 Marc de Chauveron, 'En Bretagne le 11ᵉ RAM a protégé un patrimoine naturel unique', *Objectif défense*, 87, October 1999, 12–13. The Ministry of Defence established its environmental intervention fund in 1994.

68 *Défense et protection de la nature*, 20.

69 Service historique de l'Armée de l'air, *Le diable, la cigogne et le petit lapin* (Vincennes: Service historique de l'Armée de l,air, 2004), 40–1. See also Bernard Thevenet, *Les insignes des bases aériennes* (Vincennes: Service historique de l'Armée de l'air, 2000).

70 *Défense et protection de la nature*.

71 Pascal Cavallin, 'Opération de suivi par balise ARGOS/GPS d'un couple de circaètes dans la Vienne', *La plume du circaète*, No.5, September 2007, 13.

72 'Protocole d'accord relatif aux conditions de survol des aéronefs militaires pour la conservation du Gypaète barbu', 20 October 2009, www.defense. gouv.fr/sga/content/download/159577/1376344/file/plaquette_cenzub.pdf, accessed 24 February 2010.

73 Centre d'études et de réalisations pastorales Alpes Méditerranée, 'Diagnostic pastoral dans le camp militaire de Canjuers (Var)', 2 April 2006, www.loup-ours-berger.org/2006/04/camp_canjuers.html, accessed 19 March 2009.

74 Franck Dhote, 'Les interactions entre l'homme, l'animal, et l'environnement dans le camp militaire de Canjuers (Var)' (Thèse d'exercice, Université Claude-Bernard-Lyon 1, 1998), 96.

75 René Dehillotte, '1,000 moutons au camp', *Sud-ouest*, 13 July 2007.

76 René Dehillotte, 'Les moutons sont parties', *Sud-ouest*, 8 September 2007.

77 Donna Haraway, *When Species Meet* (Minneapolis: University of Minnesota Press, 2008), 134.

78 'Protocole d'accord relatif à la protection de l'environnement entre le Ministère de la Défense, d'une part, et le Ministère de l'Environnement d'autre part', 3 April 1995.

79 *Défense et protection de la nature*, 4.

80 'Les camps militaires', Armée de terre website, www.defense.gouv.fr/ terre/enjeux_defense/terre_et_societe/developpement_durable/les_camps_ militaires/les_camps_militaires, accessed 18 May 2010; 'Une gestion exem-plaire', Armée de terre website, www.defense.gouv.fr/terre/enjeux_defense/ terre_et_societe/developpement_durable/les_camps_militaires/camp_de_ montmorillon_une_gestion_exemplaire, accessed 18 May 2010. Brousse quoted in *Défense et protection de la nature*, 17.

81 The camps in question are Avon, Montmorillon, Valbonne, Sissonne, Canjuers, and Souge. Vautier, 'Expériences développées', 3.

82 Convention nationale de partenariat écologique entre la Fédération des conservatoires des espaces naturels (FCEN) et le Ministère de la défense.

83 Guth, 'Gestion des terrains militaires', 60–1. See also, 'Préserver le site est un enjeu environnemental', *20 Minutes* website, 7 March 2006, www.20minutes.fr/article/72910/Bordeaux-Preserver-le-site-est-un-enjeu-environnemental.php, accessed 13 June 2008.

84 René Dehillotte, 'Un pasturage expérimental', *Sud-ouest*, 14 July 2007.

85 Guth, 'Gestion des terrains militaires', 4.

86 Géraud Montagut, 'La défense et Natura 2000', *L'armement*, 84, December 2003, 46; Anne Nguyen, 'Aide à la rédaction du document d'objectifs (Natura 2000) sur le site Landes et tourbières du camp militaire de Bitche', (DESS aménagement et défense, Université de Metz, 2004), 25; Guth, 'Gestion des terrains militaires', 49–50.

87 Guth, 'Gestion des terrains militaires', 36. By October 2003 France had

registered 8 per cent of its territory as Natura 2000 sites. In contrast, the figure for Denmark, Holland, and Spain was 20 per cent. Sophie Moreau, 'Biodiversité et défense: Le réseau Natura 2000', *Armées d'aujourd'hui*, 289, April 2004, 45. On the controversial history of Natura 2000 in France, see Pierre Alphandéry and Agnès Fortier, 'Can a territorial policy be based on science alone? The system for creating the Natura 2000 network in France', *Sociologia Ruralis*, 41:3 (2001), 311–28.

88 Montagut, 'Défense et Natura 2000', 46.

89 'Circulaire du 10 octobre 2006 portant création de cinq commissions mixtes locales défense-environnement, pour le territoire métropolitain', Ministère de l'Ecologie et du Développement durable website, www.ecologie.gouv.fr/ IMG/bo/2006022/A0220021.htm, accessed 9 October 2007.

90 Nguyen, 'Aide à la rédaction', 20–1.

91 *Sites Natura 2000 du Champ de Tir du Poteau: Lettre d'information*, no. 1. November 2007, www.landes.pref.gouv.fr/file_pdf/Documents_brochures/ bulletin%201%20captieux.pdf, accessed 14 July 2008.

92 The attempt to deepen knowledge of the sites' heathlands, marshlands, and forests involved representatives from the League for the Protection of Birds and the Parc naturel régional des Landes de Gascogne (amongst others), under the guiding hand of the ONF. *Sites Natura 2000 du Champ de tir de Poteau.*

93 Guth, 'Gestion des terrains militaires', 62–3.

94 'Complexe forestier de Chinon, Landes du Ruchard', January 2004, http:// natura2000.environnement.gouv.fr/sites/FR2400541.html, accessed 24 October 2007; 'Présentation générale du site', *Document d'objectifs: Site Natura 2000 complexe forestier de Chinon, Landes du Ruchard*, 2003, www. centre.ecologie.gouv.fr/Natura2000/docb_FR2400541/docub_fr2400541_ presentation.pdf, accessed 24 October 2007, 14.

95 'Camp militaire de Suippes: Le comité de pilotage a validé le document d'objec-tifs', DIREN Champagne-Ardenne website, 16 June 2008, www.champagne-ardenne.ecologie.gouv.fr/spip.php?article282, accessed 21 August 2008.

96 *Rapport développement durable du Ministre de la Défense 2008*, 26.

97 *LIFE FOCUS/LIFE, Natura 2000 and the Military* (Luxembourg: Office for Official Publications of the European Communities, 2005), 18, 28–32, 37.

98 Capitaine Kintz, quoted in Guth, 'Gestion des terrains militaires', 45.

99 *Rapport développement durable du Ministre de la Défense 2008*, 26.

100 Nguyen, 'Aide à la rédaction', 32–3.

101 Guth, 'Gestion des terrains militaires', 44–5.

102 Ibid., 45; Claude Monniot, 'Enquête préalable au classement du site naturel constitué par le massif du Gardon et les Garrigues du Nîmes, du 25 septembre au 16 octobre 2006, rapport de l'adjoint au chef du service départemental de l'architecture et du patrimoine', 4 April 2007, www.gard.pref.gouv.fr/sections/relations_collectivi/environnement/sites_

et_paysages/enquete_prealable_au3683/downloadFile/file/rapport_du_chef
_de_service_charge_de_conduire_la_procedure_d_enquete_prealable_au_
classement.pdf?nocache=1177497262.83, accessed 18 May 2010.

103 Dhote, 'Interactions', 89–90.

104 Jean-Dominique Merchet, 'Jalalabad dans les Alpes: Les écologistes protes-
tant', Secret Défense blog, 29 September 2008, http://secretdefense.blogs.
liberation.fr/defense/2008/09/jalalabad-dans.html, accessed 29 September
2008.

105 Graeme Hayes, *Environmental Protest and the State in France* (Basingstoke:
Palgrave Macmillan, 2002), 22; Nicolas César, 'Centre d'essais des Landes:
Les militants anti-nucléaires, jugés coupables mais dispensés de peines',
AQUI! website, 4 November 2010, www.aqui.fr/tempsforts/centre-d-essais-
des-landes-les-militants-anti-nucleaires-juges-coupables-mais-dispenses-
de-peines,3926.html, accessed 3 June 2011.

106 Michèle Alliot-Marie, 'Préface', *L'armement*, 84, December 2003, 4;
'Protocole d'accord relatif à la protection de l'environnement entre le
Ministère de la Défense et le Ministère de l'Ecologie et du Développement
durable', 9 July 2003. On France's sustainability policies see Joesph Szarka,
'Sustainable development strategies in France: Institutional settings, policy
style and political discourse', *European Environment*, 14 (2004), 16–29.

107 'Charte de l'environnement de 2004', Conseil constitutionnel website, www.
conseil-constitutionnel.fr/conseil-constitutionnel/francais/la-constitution/
la-constitution-du-4-octobre-1958/charte-de-l-environnement-de-2004.
5078.html, accessed 26 April 2010. On the Charter's significance, see Bourg
and Whiteside, 'France's Charter for the Environment'.

108 Ministère de l'Ecologie, du Développement et de l'aménagement durables,
'Lancement du "Grenelle Environnement"', 6 July 2007, www.legrenelle-
environnement.fr/IMG/pdf/Dossier_de_presse_grenelle.pdf, accessed 18
May 2010. The 'grenelle environnement' took its name from the accords of
27 May 1968 that were agreed between the French state, trade unions and
business leaders at the Ministry of Social Affairs on rue de Grenelle, Paris.

109 Ministère de la Défense, *Le plan d'action environnement du Ministère
de la Défense*, 27 November 2007, www.defense.gouv.fr/defense/content/
download/98686/871070/file/Plan%20d'action%20environnement%20la%
20Défense.pdf, accessed 3 December 2007. On the French response to
climate change, see Joseph Szarka, 'France: The search for alternative emis-
sion reduction strategies', in Ian Bailey and Hugh Compston (eds), *Turning
Down the Heat: The Politics of Climate Policy in Affluent Democracies*
(Basingstoke: Palgrave Macmillan, 2008), 125–43.

110 'Le Ministère de la Défense inaugure son nouveau bâtiment HQE', 12
October 2009, http://defenseetenvironnement.blogspot.com/2009/10/le-
ministere-de-la-defense-inaugure-son.html, accessed 18 May 2010; 'La
chaufferie biomasse du camp du Valdahon', Armée de terre website,

www.defense.gouv.fr/terre/enjeux_defense/terre_et_societe/developpement
_durable/l_energie/la_chaufferie_biomasse_du_camp_du_valdahon, accessed
16 October 2008.

111 For the US, see Department of Defence, *Quadrennial Defence Review*,
February 2010, www.defense.gov/qdr/QDR%20as%20of%2029JAN10%20
1600.pdf, accessed 18 May 2010, 84–8.

112 Hayes, *Environmental Protest*, 13–16; Pottier, *Armée-Nation*, 72–4.

113 *Plan d'action environnement*, 2. Public opinion polls in the 2000s suggest
that the French are more concerned about climate change than other
Europeans. Laurent, 'Bleu, blanc . . . Green?', 143–4.

114 In 2008 the French military emitted 7,366,790 tons of carbon dioxide.
Rapport développement durable du Ministre de la Défense 2008, 72.

115 *Plan d'action environnement*, 3. The average yearly defence budget in
France is 32 billion euros (excluding pensions). 'French president tries
to set French defense on a new course', Defense Industry Daily Website,
3 November 2008, www.defenseindustrydaily.com/French-President-Tries-
to-Set-French-Defense-on-a-New-Course-04937/, accessed 18 May 2010.

116 Bess, *Light-Green Society*, 230.

117 John Keegan, *The Face of Battle: A Study of Agincourt, Waterloo, and the
Somme* (London: Barrie and Jenkins, 1988 [1976]), 181.

118 'Stockage et destruction des engins de guerre dans le Pas-de-Calais',
Assemblée nationale, Séance du 30 juin 1998, http//archives.assemblée-
nationale.fr/11/cri/1997-1998-ordinare1/263.pdf, accessed 12 January 2010.

119 'Un programme novateur', *Objectif Défense*, 122, April 2003, 6–8. It also
reportedly invested 50 million euros from 2003 to 2007 on decontaminating
DMA sites. *Culture du développement durable*, 22–4.

120 S.G., 'Destruction d'obus au camp de Mailly: Les élus atterrés', *L'Union*, 5
March 2008, www.lunion.presse.fr/article/faits-divers/destruction-dobus-
au-camp-de-mailly-les-elus-atterres, accessed 18 May 2010.

121 'Bases: Le cas d'Avord', *Armées d'aujourd'hui*, 251, June 2000, 38; 'Campagne
de déminage à Port Grimaud', Défense et environnement website, 8
December 2009, http://defenseetenvironnement.blogspot.com/2009/12/
campagne-de-deminage-port-grimaud.html, accessed 18 May 2010.

122 *Rapport développement durable du Ministre de la Défense 2008*, 31.

123 'Entretien avec Henry Belot, responsable du Service de déminage régional
de Lorraine', Mémorial de Verdun website, 8 June 2008, www.memorial-de-
verdun.fr/pdf/cer/zone_rouge_belot.pdf, accessed 17 March 2009.

124 Emmanuel Durliat, 'Les études amont pour munitions "vertes,"' *L'armement*,
84, December 2003, 101–4; Comité 12, Group A, Centre de hautes études
de l'armement, 41ᵉ session nationale, 2004/2005, *Armement et développement durable*, 16 May 2005, www.chear.defense.gouv.fr/fr/cahiers_chear/
session_nationale/sn41/pdef/41_sn_rap_com_12.pdf, accessed 1 March
2009, 26.

125 Frédéric Lewino, 'L'armée se met "au vert," *Le Point,* February 2004. Clipping consulted at IHEDN.

126 Parr, *Hijacking Sustainability,* 90.

127 'Un si joli cadeau', *Marine: Revue d'information maritime et de défense,* 208, July 2005, 30; 'Défense, littoral et restructurations', *La lettre de la MRAI,* 26, March 2003, 1. The Mission pour la réalisation des actifs immobiliers (or MRAI) is charged with transferring military lands to civilian use. The CELRL manages protected sites on France's coastline and freshwater lakesides and river banks. On the conversion of former military sites in urban areas, see Olivier Godet, *Patrimoine reconverti: Du militaire au civil* (Paris: Editions Scala et Ministère de la Défense, 2007).

128 'Un si joli cadeau', 30; J.B. '83 sites supprimés par la nouvelle carte militaire', *Le Figaro,* 24 July 2008, www.lefigaro.fr/actualite-france/2008/07/24/01016-20080724ARTFIG00391-sites-supprimes-par-la-nouvelle-carte-militaire-.php, accessed 18 May 2010. On the problematic aspects of 'military-to-wildlife' base transformations in the USA, see David Havlick, 'Militarization, conservation and US base transformations', in Pearson, Coates, and Cole *Militarized Landscapes,* 113–35.

129 Jean-Jacques Lerosier, *Les plages du débarquement en Normandie* (Arles: Actes Sud, 2004), 39–40. See also, M. Pasdeloup, 'Les sites du débarquement', *Service public de Basse-Normandie,* 2, 1984, 43–4; Rémy Desquennes, 'Des sites du débarquement', *Monuments historiques,* 159, October–November 1988, 87–92.

130 Fédération française de la randonnée pédestre, *18 balades sur les plages du débarquement Normandie-Calvados* (Paris: Fédération française de la randonnée pédestre, 2004), 12.

131 For a military map of the firing ground, see ADMO 5 R 500.

132 Caroline Garnier, 'Un parc nature à la place du pôle mécanique?' *L'Union,* 30 March 2009, 2; 'Un ancien terrain militaire reconvertit en parc solaire?' Défense et environnement website, 16 February 2009, http://defenseetenvironnement.blogspot.com/2009/02/un-ancien-terrain-militaire-reconvertit.html, accessed 18 May 2010.

133 'Un bistrot écolo à 1100 mètres d'altitude', newspaper clipping consulted at the Bistrot de Lagarde. On changes to France's nuclear deterrence policy, see Jean-François Bureau, 'La réforme militaire en France: Une mutation identitaire', *Politique étrangère,* 62:1 (1997), 72; Shaun Gregory, *French Defence Policy into the Twenty-First Century* (Basingstoke: Palgrave Macmillan, 2000), 94–5.

134 For a similar continuities in the USA, see William Eugene O' Brien, 'Continuity in a changing environmental discourse: Film depictions of Corps of Engineers projects in South Florida', *Geojournal,* 69 (2007), 135–49.

135 Paul Warde, 'The invention of sustainability', *Modern Intellectual History,* 8:1 (2011), 153–70.

Epilogue

From the creation of Châlons Camp to military environmentalist policies in the twenty-first century, the French and other militaries have mobilized nature within France to prepare for and wage war. Therefore, as well as being a political, social, cultural and economic process, militarization has unfolded as a 'more-than-human' process. For although war and militarization are profoundly human activities they can only take place through the active and at times difficult mobilization of nature. This has come at a huge cost. Dead animals, flattened forests, ruined fields, polluted sites, and lost homelands need to be added to war and militarization's impact on France. The existence of *some* areas of biodiversity on *some* militarized environments should not cover up the loss of life – human and nonhuman – that these processes have entailed.

Much more remains to be written about the socio-natural histories and geographies of militarized environments in France and elsewhere. If this book has succeeded in opening up secretive sites, such as army camps, as historical places worthy of critical study, then it will have achieved one of its aims. I hope that it will also generate further reflection on the links between war, militarization and the environment, as well as encourage debate on how military organizations control, manage, and modify vast areas of our planet.

This book has stressed how militarized environments have acted as contact zones between military and civilian actors and how anti-base protesters mobilized nature imaginatively and physically to challenge militarization. I want to end by exploring the military–civilian character of militarized environments at two sites in contemporary France: Suippes Camp and Larzac plateau.

At Suippes Camp, the civilian presence within the militarized environment is hidden but largely consensual. Beyond military–civilian cooperation over hunting and the management of the Natura 2000 site, Suippes Camp is a site of memorialization. The ruins of the villages of Hurlus, Mesnil-lès-Hurlus, Perthes-les-Hurlus, Ripont, and Tahure, destroyed during the First World War, lie within the camp. Based on the available evidence, the memorialization of these civilian sites has been largely consensual. In the 1970s and 1980s Abbé Kuhn, priest of Sommepy-Tahure, produced a number of publications on the ruined villages, outlining their 'calm and peaceful' pre-1914 history and subsequent destruction during the war.[1] Kuhn directed his efforts at reclaiming the villages' histories from obscurity, but he was no anti-militarist. He made no mention of the camp's contested creation (see chapter 5) and nor did he call for the villages to be demilitarized and re-integrated as sites of memory within the civilian sphere. Instead, he worked with the army to commemorate the villages (see figure E.1).[2]

Military personnel on the camp have indeed taken steps to recover the villages' past. Former camp commander Colonel Rigal published a series of articles on the villages and in 1980 soldiers removed invasive vegetation from the ruins of Tahure.[3] Civilian and military language also overlaps. For one camp commander, Suippes Camp is a 'true museum of the war'. The creators of the nearby museum agree that military ownership has kept the ruined villages as 'sanctuaries'.[4] The Suippes Camp villages are sites of post-Larzac civilian and military cooperation within a militarized environment. They fit into the memorial narrative of how once peaceful villages patriotically sacrificed themselves to defend French soil against German invaders. Like the ruined villages of the Verdun battlefield, they symbolize French heroism and the horrors of war (see figure E.2).[5]

Other civilian sites within militarized environments are far less consensual. The meaning of Brovès, subsumed within Canjuers Camp, remains more fraught and ambiguous. Some observers view it as a symbol of Provencal traditions that should be returned to civilian use. Some former residents, however, maintain a more conciliatory tone with the army, which, after all, controls their access to the site and carried out restoration work on the village in 1997.[6] Unlike the ruined villages of Suippes, Brovès does not fit within the narrative of wartime sacrifice. Attempts to reclaim and recover this once civilian site are therefore more problematic. It joins Salles-sur-Verdon (Var) and Tignes (Savoie) as villages 'lost' to Cold War-era modernization projects. But whilst the latter two are submerged under reservoirs, the ruins of Brovès are still

E.1 Ruins of Hurlus village, Suippes Camp

visible from the road that traverses Canjuers Camp. Like the ruined villages of Tyneham and Imber on army training grounds in southern England, they stand as a vivid reminder of civilian displacement during the establishment of militarized environments.[7]

But Larzac is the most prominent site of civilian opposition to

E.2 Memorial to Ripont village, Suippes Camp

militarization as the influence of the anti-base campaign lingers on. From 1981 onwards activists' attentions focused on the land spared from militarization. They aimed to turn it into an experimental zone for agricultural development, building on the period of agricultural modernization before and after the extension's announcement.[8] Mitterrand's government supported this grassroots project, yet somewhat ironically instructed officials to formulate plans to develop the plateau. These included state investment to restore farms, electrify the plateau, improve roads, build an ecomuseum, develop tourism, and boost farm revenues. The military camp, however, would remain, much to the relief of La Cavalerie's business community.[9]

The future of the land that the state had acquired through expropriation (4,876 ha) and through amiable sales (6,164 ha) during the 1970s was a major issue. After ceding land back to those owners who still wanted it, the state was left in charge of 7,736 ha. The Ministry for Agriculture took ownership of the land but handed its management to the Société d'aménagement foncier Aveyron, Lot, Tarn (SAFALT) on 27 May 1983 with the aim of bringing new farmers to the plateau and developing existing farms. In summer 1984 the Ministry of Agriculture and delegates from Larzac signed an agreement granting the Société civile des terres du Larzac (SCTL) a long-term lease on 6,300 ha, thereby enabling it to rent land to farmers.[10]

Despite recognizing that certain difficulties have marked post-extension life on the plateau, Larzac activists depict the scheme as a success. In 1991 *Gardarm lo Larzac* claimed that the SCTL had helped Larzac to continue as 'a rural zone of surprising dynamism'. The number of actual working farms may have fallen from 77 in 1971 to 61 in 1991 and ploughable land may have contracted from 4,246 ha in 1971 to 3,858 ha in 1991. But over the same period milk and meat production had increased, new jobs were created, and population levels rose. The SCTL had also helped restore and modernize farms, develop rural tourism, and create new community buildings, such as an open air theatre and a training centre in non-violence.[11] As these developments illustrate, the anti-militarization campaign physically changed Larzac and invested it with new meanings. For sympathetic observers, the plateau's agricultural renewal was 'a second victory' after the one over the army.[12]

The campaign's legacy lives on in other ways. Militarization and farming remain positioned as diametric opposites. According to a 1982 ecomuseum exhibition, the free, radical, and poetic figure of the shepherd is the 'perfect antithesis of the soldier'.[13] Sheep continue to act as symbols of protest, featuring on a sculpture outside the ecomuseum (see figure E.3).

If anything, the idea that small-scale, environmentally sensitive, and socially progressive farming is a viable and peaceful alternative to militarization has intensified. A 2007 leaflet produced by the Association pour

E.3 Sheep sculpture outside the Larzac ecomuseum

l'aménagement du Larzac informed visitors to the plateau that instead of becoming a 'training ground for death' the land was now a site of experimental and communal agriculture.[14] Larzac remains as a centre of protest of national and international renown, even if globalization has joined militarism as a one of the main enemies. As the title of one book has it, Larzac is still a 'land that says no' (see figure E.4).[15]

E.4 'The army kills': vandalized army camp sign, Larzac

Unlike the memorialization of villages at Suippes Camp, Larzac remains as a site of civilian–military confrontation, even if the intensity of the conflict has decreased markedly since 1981. As well as bearing witness to the role of militarization in transforming the meanings of particular places, the contrast between Suippes and Larzac is a reminder of the complexity of militarized environments' histories. And without wishing to glorify the Larzac campaign and its legacy, it is to be admired for its challenging of the military narrative of environmental militarization as unproblematic, necessary, and inevitable.

Notes

1 Abbé André Kuhn, *Sommepy-Tahure: Notice historique sur Tahure* (1975), 6. See also Abbé André Kuhn, *Les villages détruits en 1914–1918 du camp de Suippes* [n.d.].
2 In 1989 Kuhn contributed a foreword to the army's brochure for the 'day

of memory' (during which they allowed civilians access to the villages) in which he praised successive camp commanders' 'welcome initiatives' to commemorate the villages' 'heroism'. Abbé Kuhn in Commandement du camp de Suippes, *Journée souvenir des villages détruits 1989*; *Marne 14–18: Un centre d'interprétation de la Grande Guerre à Suippes, dossier de presse* [n.d.], www.marne14-18.fr/Presse/dos_presse_03_07.pdf, accessed 19 March 2009.

3 Jean-Pierre Husson, 'Tahure: Village détruit', www.crdp-reims.fr/memoire/lieux/1GM_CA/villages_detruits/07tahure.htm, accessed 27 September 2007. A selection of Colonel Rigal's articles from April 1979 to January 1980 were collated in *Le Heaume et l'Epée, numero spécial: Historique du camp de Suippes* [n.d.].
4 Commandement du camp de Suippes, *Journée souvenir des villages détruits 1989*. The unproblematized blending of the camp's wartime history and subsequent militarization continues in the official guide to the 2008 memorial day, which skirts over the army's decision to create the camp, instead describing in the passive tense how the red zone 'was converted into military lands'. 'Visite des villages détruits de la première guerre mondiale', November 2008, www.mourmelon.fr/villages_detruits.pdf, accessed 13 March 2009.
5 Colonel Léon Rodier, Délégué du Comité national du souvenir de Verdun', in Albert Fremont and Lionel Fremont, *L'armée à Verdun avant 1914* (Verdun: Typo-Lorraine, 1988), 115–16.
6 http://broves.blogspot.com, accessed 29 October 2007; 'Sortie à Canjuers', www.paperblog.fr/2106479/sortie-a-canjuers, 9 July 2009, accessed 19 May 2010. Former residents also strive to maintain access to Villedieu village on Valdahon Camp, which was subsumed by the camp in 1926. Pascal Collot, *Le 5ᵉ régiment de Dragons du Valdahon: Histoire de régiment blindé de Franche-Comté et du camp de Valdahon* (Besançon: Association Pierre Percée, 2003), 223, 233.
7 Tim Cole, 'A picturesque ruin? Landscapes of loss at Tyneham and the Epynt', in Chris Pearson, Peter Coates, and Tim Cole (eds), *Militarized Landscapes: From Gettysburg to Salisbury Plain* (London: Continuum, 2010), 95–110; Marianna Dudley, 'Greening the MOD: An environmental history of the UK defence estate, 1945–present' (PhD dissertation, University of Bristol, 2011).
8 CACAN 19950127/7 Paysans du Larzac, 'Charte pour les nouvelles agricoles sur le Larzac', September 1981.
9 CACAN 19950127/1 Direction départementale de l'agriculture, Aveyron, 'Plan de développement de la région du Larzac: Premières orientations et propositions', November 1981; CACAN 19950127/1 Henri Demange, 'Compte-rendu de la mission Larzac', 1 June 1982; Maire de la Cavalerie to Préfet de l'Aveyron, 'Motion sur l'arrêt de l'extension du camp du Larzac', 25 June 1981.
10 To encourage a sustainable farming population, farmers have to give up

their land on their retirement. As of 1994 there were 29 SCTL farms, eleven of which were run by new arrivals. ADA 300 W 13 'Conférence de Presse: Signature de la convention Etat-SAFALT (Larzac); Alexander Alland with Sonia Alland, *Crisis and Commitment: The Life History of a French Social Movement* (Yverdon: Gordon and Breach, 1994), 81–3. On the challenges of the *après-Larzac* period, see Henri Boyer, Philippe Gardy, and Étienne Hammel (eds), *Le Larzac revisité* (Aix-en-Provence: Édisud, 1986).

11 CACAN 19950127/7 'Larzac 1971, 1981, 1991', *Gardarem lo Larzac* supplement, August 1991.

12 Fabien Collini, Gilles Luneau, and Dominique Martin, *Chercheurs d'humanités: Larzac aujourd'hui* (Bez-et-Esparon: Etudes & Communications Editions, 2004).

13 Exhibition catalogue, *Larzac en marche: Evocation* (Ecomusée du Larzac/ Imprimerie Causses, 1997 [1982]).

14 Association pour l'aménagement du Larzac, *Le Larzac vous accueille* (2007).

15 Gérard Galtier, *Larzac: Une terre qui dit non* (Sauveterre-de-Rouergue: Editions de la Bastide, 2000). See also 'Europe écologie: L'appel au rassemblement', 20 October 2008, www.saintmaurvert.fr/spip.php?article24, accessed 14 January 2009. On contemporary political movements on Larzac, see Jean-Philippe Martin, 'José Bové un activiste sans projet?' *Modern and Contemporary France*, 11:3 (2003), 307–211; Gwyn Williams, *Struggles for an Alternative Globalization: An Ethnography of Counterpower in Southern France* (Aldershot: Ashgate, 2008).

Select bibliography

Aben, Jacques, and Jacques Rouzier (eds), *Défense et aménagement du territoire* (Montpellier: ESID, 2001).

Alexander, Martin S., Martin Evans, and J.F.V. Keiger (eds), *The Algerian War and the French Army, 1954–62: Experiences, Images, Testimonies* (Basingstoke: Palgrave Macmillan, 2002).

Alland, Alexander, with Sonia Alland, *Crisis and Commitment: The Life History of a French Social Movement* (Yverdon: Gordon and Breach, 1994).

Amat, Jean-Paul, 'Guerre et milieux naturels: Les forêts meurtries de l'est de la France 70 ans après Verdun', *L'Espace géographique*, 3 (1987), 217–33.

Amat, Jean-Paul, 'Forêt et défense du territoire: France du nord-est, 1871–1914', *Stratégique*, 56 (1992), 309–39.

Amat, Jean-Paul, 'Le rôle stratégique de la forêt, 1871–1914: Exemples dans les forêts lorraines', *Revue historique des armées*, 1 (1993), 62–9.

Audoin-Rouzeau, Stéphane, *Men at War 1914–1918: National Sentiment and Trench Journalism in France during the First World War*, trans. Helen McPhail (Oxford: Berg, 1992).

Audoin-Rouzeau, Stéphane, Gerd Krumeich, and Jean Richardot, *Cicatrices: la Grande Guerre aujourd'hui* (Paris: Éditions Tallandier, 2008).

Baguley, David, *Napoleon III and His Regime: An Extravaganza* (Baton Rouge: Louisiana State University Press, 2000).

Baldin, Damien (ed.), *La guerre des animaux, 1914–1918* (Peronne: Historial de la Grande Guerre, 2007).

Baker, Steve, *Picturing the Beast: Animals, Identity, and Representation* (Urbana and Chicago: University of Illinois Press, 2001 [1993]).

Barad, Karen, 'Posthumanist performativity: Toward an understanding of how matter comes to matter', *Signs: Journal of Women in Culture and Society*, 28:3 (2003), 801–31.

Barnes, David S., *The Great Stink of Paris and the Nineteenth-Century Struggle against Filth and Germs* (Baltimore: Johns Hopkins University Press, 2006).

Barrillot, Bruno, and Mary Davis, *Les déchets nucléaires militaires français*

(Lyon: Centre de Documentation et de Recherche sur la Paix et les Conflits, 1994).

Berman, Mildred, 'D-Day and Geography', *Geographical Review*, 84:4 (1994), 469–75.

Besnaci-Lancou, Fatima, and Gilles Manceron, *Les harkis dans la colonisation et ses suites* (Ivry-sur-Seine: Les Editions de l'Atelier, 2008).

Bess, Michael, *The Light-Green Society: Ecology and Technological Modernity in France, 1960–2000* (Chicago and London: University of Chicago Press, 2003).

Boulanger, Pierre, *La géographie militaire française, 1871–1939* (Paris: Economica, 2002).

Boulanger, Philippe, *Géographie militaire* (Paris: Ellipses, 2006).

Calder, Kent E., *Embattled Garrisons: Comparative Base Politics and American Globalism* (Princeton: Princeton University Press, 2007).

Chanet, Jean-François, *Vers l'armée nouvelle: République conservatrice et réforme militaire, 1871–1879* (Rennes: Presses Universitaires de Rennes, 2006).

Chickering, Roger, and Stig Förster (eds), *Great War, Total War: Combat and Mobilization on the Western Front, 1914–1918* (Cambridge: Cambridge University Press, 2000).

Childs, John, *The Military Use of the Land: A History of the Defence Estate* (Berne: Peter Lang, 1998).

Chossat, Nadine, *Mourmelon-le-Grand: Cité champenoise et militaire* (Mourmelon-le-Grand: Ville de Mourmelon-le-Grand, 1999).

Chrastil, Rachel, *Organizing for War: France 1870–1914* (Baton Rouge: Louisiana State University Press, 2010).

Closmann, Charles E. (ed.), *War and the Environment: Military Destruction in the Modern Age* (College Station: Texas A&M University Press, 2009).

Clout, Hugh, *The Land of France 1815–1914* (London: Allen & Unwin, 1983).

Clout, Hugh, *After the Ruins: Restoring the Countryside of Northern France after the Great War* (Exeter: University of Exeter Press, 1996).

Clout, Hugh, 'Beyond the landings: The reconstruction of lower Normandy after June 1944', *Journal of Historical Geography*, 32 (2006), 127–48.

Clout, Hugh, 'From Utah Beach toward reconstruction: Revival in the Manche département of lower Normandy after June 1944', *Journal of Historical Geography*, 35 (2009), 154–77.

Coates, Peter, *Nature: Western Attitudes since Ancient Times* (Cambridge: Polity Press, 1998).

Cole, Tim, 'Military presences, civilian absences: Battling nature at the Sennybridge Training Area, 1940–2008', *Journal of War and Culture Studies*, 3:2 (2010), 215–35.

Corvol, Andrée, and Jean-Paul Amat (eds), *Forêt et guerre* (Paris: L'Harmattan, 1994).

Dallemagne, François, *Les casernes françaises* (Paris: Editions Picard, 1990).

Dallemagne, François, and Jean Mouly, *Patrimoine militaire* (Paris: Editions Scala, 2002).

Davis, Diana K., *Resurrecting the Granary of Rome: Environmental History and French Colonial Expansion in North Africa* (Athens, OH: Ohio University Press, 2007).

Davis, Jeffrey Sasha, 'Military natures: Militarism and the environment', *Geojournal*, 69 (2007), 131–4.

de Puymège, Gérard, *Chauvin, le soldat-labourer: Contribution à l'étude des nationalismes* (Paris: Editions Gallimard, 1993).

Dhote, Franck, 'Les interactions entre l'homme, l'animal, et l'environnement dans le camp militaire de Canjuers (Var)' (Thèse d'exercice, Université Claude-Bernard-Lyon 1, 1998).

Doise, Jean, and Maurice Vaïse, *Diplomatie et outil militaire, 1871–1991: Politique étrangère de la France* (Paris: Editions du Seuil, 1992 [1987]).

Dudley, Marianna, 'Greening the MOD: An environmental history of the UK defence estate, 1945-present' (PhD dissertation, University of Bristol, 2011).

Duke, Simon, *United States Military Forces and Installations in Europe* (Oxford: Oxford University Press/SIPRI, 1989).

Duke, Simon, and Wolfgand Krieger (eds), *US Military Forces in Europe: The Early Years, 1945–1970* (Boulder: Westview Press, 1993).

Ehrlich, Anne, and John W. Birks (eds), *Hidden Dangers: Environmental Consequences of Preparing for War* (San Francisco: Sierra Club Books, 1990).

Endy, Christopher, *Cold War Holidays: American Tourism in France* (Chapel Hill: University of North Carolina Press, 2004).

Facon, Patrick, *L'armée de l'air dans la tourmente: La bataille de France, 1939–1940* (Paris: Economica, 1997).

Footitt, Hilary, *War and Liberation in France: Living with the Liberators* (Basingstoke: Palgrave Macmillan, 2004).

Ford, Caroline, 'Nature, culture, and conservation in France and her colonies, 1840–1940', *Past and Present*, 183 (2004), 173–98.

Frémeaux, Jacques, *La France et l'Algérie en guerre 1830–1870, 1954–1962* (Paris: Economica et Institut de stratégie comparée, 2002).

Gallagher, Carole, *American Ground Zero: The Secret Nuclear War* (Cambridge, MA: MIT Press, 1993).

Gibson, Craig, 'The British army, French farmers, and the war on the Western Front, 1914–1918', *Past and Present*, 180 (2003), 175–240.

Godet, Olivier, *Patrimoine reconverti: Du militaire au civil* (Paris: Editions Scala et Ministère de la Défense, 2007).

Gordon, Philip H., *A Certain Idea of France: French Security Policy and the Gaullist Legacy* (Princeton: Princeton University Press, 1993).

Gough, Paul, 'Conifers and commemoration: The politics and protocol of planting', *Landscape Research*, 21:1 (1996), 73–87.

Gough, Paul, 'Sites in the imagination: The Beaumont Hamel Newfoundland Memorial on the Somme', *Cultural Geographies*, 11 (2004), 235–58.

Green, Nicholas, *The Spectacle of Nature: Landscape and Bourgeois Culture in Nineteenth-Century France* (Manchester: Manchester University Press, 1990).

Guth, Phillpe, 'La gestion des terrains militaires présentant un intérêt écologique: Comment concilier les impératifs opérationnels et la préservation de la biodiversité' (DESS 'Espace et milieux', Université de Paris 7, 2004–5).

Haraway, Donna, *When Species Meet* (Minneapolis: University of Minnesota Press, 2008).

Hardy, Yves, and Emmanuel Gabey, *Dossier L . . . comme Larzac* (Paris: Editions Alain Moreau, 1974).

Harp, Stephen L., *Marketing Michelin: Advertising and Cultural Identity in Twentieth-Century France* (Baltimore: Johns Hopkins University Press, 2001).

Hastings, Tom H., *Ecology of War and Peace: Counting the Costs of Conflict* (Lanham: University Press of America, 2000).

Havlick, David, 'Logics of change for military-to-wildlife conversions in the United States', *Geojournal*, 69 (2007), 151–64.

Hayes, Graeme, *Environmental Protest and the State in France* (Basingstoke: Palgrave Macmillan, 2002).

Hecht, Gabrielle, *The Radiance of France: Nuclear Power and National Identity after World War II* (Cambridge, MA: MIT Press, 1998).

Helphand, Kenneth I., *Defiant Gardens: Making Gardens in Wartime* (San Antonio: Trinity University Press, 2006).

Henningham, Stephen, 'Testing times: France's underground nuclear tests and its relations with the Asia–Pacific region', *Modern and Contemporary France*, 4:1 (1996), 81–91.

Hitchcock, William I., *France Restored: Cold War Diplomacy and the Quest for Leadership in Europe 1944–1954* (Chapel Hill: University of North Carolina Press, 1998).

Holmes, Richard, *The Road to Sedan: The French Army, 1866–70* (London: Royal Historical Society, 1984).

Hooks, Gregory, and Chad L. Smith, 'The treadmill of destruction: National sacrifice areas and Native Americans', *American Sociological Review*, 69:4 (2004), 558–75.

Howard, Michael, *The Franco-Prussian War: The German Invasion of France, 1870–1871* (London: Hart-Davis, 1961).

Jackson, Julian, *The Fall of France: The Nazi Invasion of 1940* (Oxford: Oxford University Press, 2003).

Käkönen, Jyrki (ed.), *Green Security or Militarized Environment* (Aldershot: Dartmouth, 1994).

Kedward, Rod, *In Search of the Maquis: Rural Resistance in Southern France 1942–1944* (Oxford: Oxford University Press, 2003 [1993]).

Keegan, John, *Six Armies in Normandy: From D-Day to the Liberation of Paris, June 6th–August 25th 1944* (London: Jonathan Cape, 1982).

Kintz, Christophe, 'L'évolution du domaine militaire attribué à l'Armée de terre en France métropolitaine depuis 1945 et ses implications sur l'aménagement de l'espace, l'urbanisme et l'environnement' (PhD dissertation, Université de Paris IV–Paris–Sorbonne, 2000).

Kuisel, Richard, *Seducing the French: The Dilemma of Americanization* (Berkeley: University of California Press, 1997).

Kuletz, Valerie L., *The Tainted Desert: Environmental and Social Ruin in the American West* (New York: Routledge, 1998).

Lacoste, Yves, *La géographie, ça sert, d'abord, à faire la guerre* (Paris: François Maspero, 1976).

Laurent, Eloi, 'Bleu, blanc, . . . Green?: France and climate change', *French Politics, Culture*, 27:2 (2009), 142–53.

Le Bris, Michel, *Les fous du Larzac* (Paris: Les presses d'aujourd'hui, 1975).

Lebovics, Herman, *Bringing the Empire Back Home: France in the Global Age* (Durham: Duke University Press, 2004).

Lloyd, David W., *Battlefield Tourism: Pilgrimage and the Commemoration of the Great War in Britain, Australia and Canada, 1919–1939* (Oxford: Berg, 1998).

Lockwood, Jeffrey A., *Six-Legged Soldiers: Using Insects as Weapons of War* (Oxford: Oxford University Press, 2009).

Lorcin, Patricia M.E., and Daniel Brewer (eds), *France and its Spaces of War: Experience, Memory, Image* (New York: Palgrave Macmillan, 2009).

Lutz, Catherine, *Homefront: A Military City and the American Twentieth Century* (Boston: Beacon Press, 2001).

Lutz, Catherine (ed.), *The Bases of Empire: The Global Struggle against U.S. Military Posts* (New York: New York University Press, 2009).

Martin, Didier, *Le Larzac: Utopies et realités* (Paris: L'Harmattan, 1987).

McNeill, John R., and Corinna R. Unger (eds), *Environmental Histories of the Cold War* (New York: German Historical Institue/Cambridge University Press, 2010).

Mercer, Doug, 'Future-histories of Hanford: The material and semiotic production of a landscape', *Cultural Geographies*, 9 (2002), 35–67.

Meyerson, Harvey, *Nature's Army: When Soldiers Fought for Yosemite* (Lawrence: University Press of Kansas, 2001).

Miller, Paul B., *From Revolutionaries to Citizens: Antimilitarism in France, 1870–1914* (Durham: Duke University Press, 2002).

Mitchell, Allan, *Victors and Vanquished: The German Influence on Army and Church in France after 1870* (Chapel Hill: University of North Carolina Press, 1984).

Mitchell, Timothy, *Rule of Experts: Egypt, Techno-Politics, Modernity* (Berkeley: University of California Press, 2002).

Select bibliography

Monestier, Martin, *Les animaux-soldats: Histoire militaire des animaux des origines à nos jours* (Paris: Le Cherche Midi, 1996).

Monferrand, Alain, 'Défense nationale et aménagement du territoire: Analyse d'une région de programme' (PhD dissertation, Université de Paris 8, 1971).

Mongin, Dominique, *La bombe atomique française 1945–1958* (Brussels: Bruyant, 1997).

Morris, Mandy S., 'Gardens "For Ever England": Identity and the First World War British cemeteries on the Western Front', *Ecumene*, 4:4 (October 1997), 410–34.

Mosse, George L., *Fallen Soldiers: Reshaping the Memory of the Worlds Wars* (New York: Oxford University Press, 1990).

Oelschlaeger, Max, *The Idea of Wilderness: From Prehistory to the Age of Ecology* (New Haven: Yale University Press, 1991).

Paglen, Trevor, *Blank Spots on the Map: The Dark Geography of the Pentagon's Secret World* (New York: Dutton, 2009).

Palka, Eugene J., and Francis A. Galgano (eds), *Military Geography from Peace to War* (Boston: McGraw-Hill Custom Publishing, 2005).

Panchasi, Roxanne, *Future Tense: The Culture of Anticipation in France between the Wars* (Ithaca and London: Cornell University Press, 2009).

Parr, Adrian, *Hijacking Sustainability* (Cambridge, MA: MIT Press, 2009).

Pearson, Chris, *Scarred Landscapes: War and Nature in Vichy France* (Basingstoke: Palgrave Macmillan, 2008).

Pearson, Chris, 'A "watery desert" in Vichy France: The environmental history of the Camargue wetlands, 1940–1944', *French Historical Studies*, 32:3 (2009), 479–509.

Pearson, Chris, Peter Coates, and Tim Cole (eds), *Militarized Landscapes: From Gettysburg to Salisbury Plain* (London: Continuum, 2010).

Pick, Daniel, *War Machine: The Rationalization of Slaughter in the Modern Age* (New Haven: Yale University Press, 1996).

Pierrejean, Philppe, *Mailly-le-Camp* (Saint-Cyr-sur-Loire, Editions Alan Sutton, 2007).

Porch, Douglas, *The March to the Marne: The French Army, 1871–1914* (Cambridge: Cambridge University Press, 1981).

Pottier, Olivier, *Les bases américaines en France (1950–1967)* (Paris: L'Harmattan, 2003).

Pottier, Oliver, *Armée-nation: Divorce ou reconciliation: De la loi Debré à la réforme du service national, 1970–2004* (Paris: L'Harmattan, 2005).

Pritchard, Sara B., *Confluence: The Nature of Technology and the Remaking of the Rhône* (Cambridge, MA: Harvard University Press, 2011).

Ralston, David B., *The Army of the Republic: The Place of the Military in the Political Evolution of France, 1871–1914* (Cambridge, MA: MIT Press, 1967).

Regnault, Jean-Marc, 'France's search for nuclear test sites', *Journal of Military History*, 67 (October 2003), 1223–48.

Robichon, François, *L'armée française vue par les peintres, 1870–1914* (Paris: Editions Herscher/Ministère de la Défense, 1998).

Roth, François, *La guerre de 1870* (Paris: Fayard, 1990).

Ross, Kristin, *Fast Cars, Clean Bodies: Decolonization and the Reordering of French Culture* (Cambridge, MA: MIT Press, 1995).

Ross, Kristin, *May '68 and its Afterlifes* (Chicago: University of Chicago Press, 2002).

Roynette, Odile, *'Bon pour le service': L'expérience de la caserne en France à la fin du XIXe siècle* (Paris: Belin 2000).

Russell, Edmund P., *War and Nature: Fighting Humans and Insects with Chemicals from World War 1 to Silent Spring* (New York: Cambridge University Press, 2001).

Russell, Edmund P., and Richard P. Tucker (eds), *Natural Enemy, Natural Ally: Toward an Environmental History of Warfare* (Corvallis: Oregon State University Press, 2004).

Scott, James C., *Seeing Like a State: How Certain Schemes to Improve the Human Condition Have Failed* (New Haven and London: Yale University Press, 1998).

Shaw, Martin, *Post-Military Society: Militarism, Demilitarization and War at the End of the Twentieth Century* (Cambridge: Polity Press, 1991).

Sherman, Daniel J., *The Construction of Memory in Interwar France* (Chicago: University of Chicago Press, 1999).

Singleton, John, 'Britain's military use of horses, 1914–1918', *Past and Present*, 139:1 (1993), 178–203.

Smith, Leonard V., Stéphane Audoin-Rouzeau and Anette Becker, *France and the Great War, 1914–1918* (Cambridge: Cambridge University Press, 2003).

Spang, Rebecca L., '"And they ate the zoo": Relating gastronomic exoticism in the siege of Paris', *Modern Language Notes*, 107 (September 1992), 752–73.

Taithe, Bertrand, *Defeated Flesh: Welfare, Warfare, and the Making of Modern France* (Manchester: Manchester University Press, 1999).

Taithe, Bertrand, *Citizenship and Wars: France in Turmoil, 1870–1871* (London: Routledge, 2001).

Temple, Samuel, 'The natures of nation: Negotiating modernity in the *Landes de Gascogne*', *French Historical Studies*, 32:3 (2009), 419–46.

Utley, Rachel, *The French Defence Debate: Consensus and Continuity in The Mitterrand Era* (Basingstoke: Palgrave Macmillan, 2005).

Van Bergen, Leo, *Before my Helpless Sight: Suffering, Dying, and Military Medicine on the Western Front, 1914–1918* (Aldershot: Ashgate, 2009).

Varley, Karine, *Under the Shadow of Defeat: The War of 1870–71 in French Memory* (Basingstoke: Palgrave Macmillan, 2008).

Voldman, Danièle, *Le déminage de France après 1945* (Paris: Editions Odile Jacob, 1998).

Wawro, Geoffrey, *The Franco-Prussian War: The German Conquest of France in 1870–1871* (Cambridge: Cambridge University Press, 2003).

Select bibliography

Weber, Eugen, *Peasants into Frenchmen: The Modernisation of Rural France 1870–1914* (London: Chatto and Windus, 1979).

West, Joshua, 'Forests and national security: British and American forest policy in the wake of World War I', *Environmental History*, 8:2 (2003), 270–94.

Whatmore, Sarah, *Hybrid Geographies: Natures, Cultures, Spaces* (London: Sage, 2002).

Whatmore, Sarah, 'Materialist returns: Practising cultural geography in and for a more-than-human world', *Cultural Geographies*, 13 (2006), 600–9.

Whited, Tamara, *Forests and Peasant Politics in Modern France* (New Haven and London: Yale University Press, 2000).

Williams, Gwyn, *Struggles for an Alternative Globalization: An Ethnography of Counterpower in Southern France* (Aldershot: Ashgate, 2008).

Winters, Harold. A., Gerald E. Galloway Jr, William J. Reynolds, and David W. Rhyne, *Battling the Elements: Weather and Terrain in the Conduct of War* (Baltimore and London: Johns Hopkins University Press, 1998).

Woodward, Rachel, 'Khaki conservation: An examination of military environmentalist discourses in the British army', *Journal of Rural Studies*, 17 (2001), 201–17.

Woodward, Rachel, *Military Geographies* (Oxford: Blackwell, 2004).

Woodward, Rachel, 'From military geography to militarism's geographies: Disciplinary engagements with the geographies of militarism and military activities', *Progress in Human Geography*, 29:6 (2005), 718–40.

Wright, Patrick, *The Village that Died for England: The Strange Story of Tyneham* (London: Jonathan Cape, 1995).

Index

Index